SRA Imagine It!

Unit 6 · My Shadow

Level K

Program Authors

Carl Bereiter
Andrew Biemiller
Joe Campione
Iva Carruthers
Doug Fuchs

Lynn Fuchs
Steve Graham
Karen Harris
Jan Hirshberg
Anne McKeough
Peter Pannell

Marsha Roit
Marlene Scardamalia
Marcy Stein
Gerald H. Treadway Jr.
Michael Pressley

McGraw Hill SRA

Columbus, OH

21706

ACKNOWLEDGMENTS

Grateful acknowledgment is given to the following publishers and copyright owners for permissions granted to reprint selections from their publications. All possible care has been taken to trace ownership and secure permission for each selection included. In case of any errors or omissions, the Publisher will be pleased to make suitable acknowledgments in future editions.

READ ALOUD

WHAT MAKES A SHADOW?, TEXT COPYRIGHT © 1962 BY CLYDE ROBERT BULLA. © RENEWED 1994 BY CLYDE ROBERT BULLA. ILLUSTRATIONS COPYRIGHT © 1994 BY JUNE OTANI. Used by permission of HarperCollins Publishers.

BIG BOOK

"Sombra/Shadow" Reprinted with permission of the publisher, Children's Book Press, San Francisco, CA, www.childrensbookpress.org. A MOVIE IN MY PILLOW. Text copyright © 2001 by Jorge Argueta.

From BEAR SHADOW. Copyright © 1985 by Frank Asch. Reproduced by arrangement with Simon & Schuster Books For Young Readers, Simon & Schuster Children's Publishing Division. All rights reserved.

"Hide-and-Seek Shadow" Used by permission of Margaret Hillert who controls all rights.

STORY TIME COLLECTION

NOTHING STICKS LIKE A SHADOW by Ann Tompert, illustrated by Lynn Munsinger. Text copyright © 1984 by Ann Tompert. Illustrations copyright © 1984 by Lynn Munsinger. Reprinted by permission of Houghton Mifflin Co. All rights reserved.

PICKLED PEPPERS

From ONE HUNGRY MONSTER by Susan Heyboer O'Keefe. Copyright © 1989 by Susan Heyboer O'Keefe (text); copyright © 1989 by Lynn Munsinger (illustrations). By permission of Little, Brown and Company (Inc.).

"Rope Rhyme" from HONEY, I LOVE by Eloise Greenfield. Used by permission of HarperCollins Publishers.

From WHO SAID RED? By Mary Serfozo, illustrated by Keiko Narahashi. Text copyright © 1988 by Mary Serfozo, Illustrations Copyright © 1988 by Keiko Narahashi. Reprinted by arrangement with Margaret K. McElderry Books, an Imprint of Simon & Schuster Children's Publishing Division. All rights reserved.

"Rhyme," by Elizabeth Coatsworth. Reprinted with permission of Elizabeth Gartner. All rights reserved.

"Tent" from BALLOONS AND OTHER POEMS by Deborah Chandra. Reprinted by permission of Farrar, Straus & Giroux, LLC.

"Little Pine" from MAPLES IN THE MIST, Text copyright © 1996 by Minfong Ho. Reprinted with permission of McIntosh & Otis. "Little Pine" illustration: Jean & Mou-sien Tseng. Used by permission.

"Houses/Casitas" text, from MY MEXICO/MEXICO MIO by Tony Johnston, copyright © 1996 by Roger D. Johnson and Susan T. Johnson as Trustees of the Johnson Family Trust, text. Used by permission of G.P. Putnam's Sons, A Division of Penguin Young Readers Group, A Member of Penguin Group (USA) Inc., 345 Hudson Street, New York, NY 10014. All rights reserved. "Houses/Casitas," illustrations by F. John Sierra, from MY MEXICO/MEXICO MIO by Tony Johnston, Illustrated by F. John Sierra, copyright © 1996 by F. John Sierra, illustrations. Used by permission of G.P. Putnam's Sons, A Division of Penguin Young Readers Group, A Member of Penguin Group (USA) Inc., 345 Hudson Street, New York, NY 10014. All rights reserved.

"Keep a Poem in Your Pocket" From SOMETHING SPECIAL by Beatrice Schenk de Regniers. Copyright © 1958 Beatrice Schenk de Regniers. © Renewed 1986. All rights reserved. Reprinted by permission of Marian Reiner.

READ
STILLM
2008
K
tg
v. 6

National Advisory Board

Patricia Appell
Instructional
Interventionist
Annapolis, MD

Christine P. Collins
Former Assistant Superintendent
for Instruction and Curriculum
Weymouth, MA

Betsy Degen
Curriculum Director
Shawnee Mission, KS

Bryan Ertsgaard
Teacher
Dayton, OH

James T. Garvin
Assistant Principal
Charlotte, NC

Patsy M. Hall
Title I Professional Development
Coordinator
Indianapolis, IN

Michelle L. King
Reading Enhancement Coach
Indianapolis, IN

Deb Owen
Assistant Superintendent for
Curriculum and Instruction
Effingham, IL

Patricia Schmella
Curriculum Director
Toppenish, WA

JoAnn Schweda
Teacher
Worley, ID

Sylvia Teahan
Teacher
Medford Lakes, NJ

Joseph Turner
Assistant Principal
Indianapolis, IN

Sue Wennerberg
Teacher
Oak Park, IL

Contributing Author

Michael Milone
Assessment Specialist
Placitas, NM

Literature Consultant

Dr. Laura Apol
Professor, Michigan State University
East Lansing, MI

Program Reviewers

Noemi Arteaga-Gonzales
Teacher
San Antonio, TX

Susan Beede
Consulting Teacher
Nampa, ID

Lisa Beringer
Teacher
Bonita Springs, FL

Paula Bleakley
Teacher
Leesburg, FL

Lisa Bohanan
Instructional Specialist
Pflugerville, TX

Judi Braxton
Reading Coach
Marianna, FL

Benjamin Broadwater
Teacher
Fort Worth, TX

Jodie Broussard
Reading Coach
Pensacola, FL

Jennifer Brown-Mendoza
Reading First Coach
Hominy, OK

Kristine Cain
Teacher
Pensacola, FL

Kellie Campbell
Teacher
Cocoa, FL

Caroline Carithers
Reading Resource Teacher
Pensacola, FL

Jenny Cronan
Literacy Coach
Pittsburg, CA

Margo DiBasio
Reading Specialist
Chelsea, MA

Jennie Eddy
Title I Literacy Coach
Moore, OK

Bryan Ertsgaard
Teacher
Dayton, OH

Tami Ethridge
Instructional Coach
Lancaster, SC

Pamela C. Fendrick
Reading Coach
Tallahassee, FL

Melanie Flores
Teacher
Austin, TX

Tim Francisco
Teacher
Colorado Springs, CO

Kari Franklin
Reading Coach
Pensacola, FL

Rosa Elia Garcia
Reading Specialist
San Antonio, TX

Ashley Garrett
Teacher
Austin, TX

James T. Garvin
Assistant Principal
Charlotte, NC

Dr. Marsha R. Glover
Elementary Reading and
Language Arts Developer
Tallahassee, FL

Elaine M. Grohol
Elementary Instructional
Specialist
Kissimmee, FL

Patricia Ingles
Teacher
Laguna Niguel, CA

Sarah Jordan
Literacy Specialist
Longview, WA

Cindy Kearney
Teacher
Tulsa, OK

Kim Kempa
Teacher
Santa Ana, CA

Kathy Kindelan
Reading Specialist
Winter Haven, FL

Michelle L. King
Reading Enhancement
Coach
Indianapolis, IN

Linda Ann Kosinski
Reading First Coordinator
La Quinta, CA

Sheryl Kurtin
Elementary Specialist,
Curriculum and Instruction
Sarasota, FL

Teresa Lopez
Supervisor, Academic
Achievement and
Accountability
Bakersfield, CA

Jan Maglione
Teacher
Upton, MA

Barbara Maspero
Teacher
San Antonio, TX

Chaitra S. McGrew
Teacher
Austin, TX

Kathy McGuire
Instructional Coach
Roseburg, OR

Becky McPherson
Literacy Coach
Cuthbert, GA

Sheila Menning
Teacher
Largo, FL

Tamarah Michalek
Teacher
Roseburg, OR

Michele Mower
Director of Professional
Development
Fontana, CA

Pamela W. Patterson
Instructional Specialist
East Point, GA

Susan Patterson
Reading Coach
Charlotte, NC

Angela Pilcher
Teacher
Stockton, CA

Dr. Jan Rauth
Educational Consultant
Longview, WA

Carlotta Ruiz
Reading Coach
Elk Grove, CA

Dr. Lynda Samons
Curriculum Director
Magnet Cove, AR

Jake Schweikhard
Teacher
Tulsa, OK

Nancy Snyder
Reading Coach
Spring Hill, FL

Dyan Wagner
District Reading Specialist
and Intervention
Coordinator
Milwaukee, WI

Darlene Watson
Instructional Lead Teacher
Valdosta, GA

Linda Webb
LA Program Specialist
Stockton, CA

Sue Wennerberg
Teacher
Oak Park, IL

Gayle Wilson
Preprimary Department
Head
Jacksonville, FL

Linda Wiltz
Instructional Support
Teacher
Orlando, FL

Meet the Imagine It! Authors

Carl Bereiter, Ph.D.

A professor emeritus and special advisor on learning technology at the Ontario Institute for Studies in Education, University of Toronto, Dr. Bereiter also invented Computer Supported Intentional Learning Environments, the first networked system for collaborative learning, with Dr. Marlene Scardamalia.

Andrew Biemiller, Ph.D.

A coordinator of elementary teacher education programs at the University of Toronto for thirty-six years, Dr. Biemiller's research on vocabulary development and instruction has had a significant effect on the shape of vocabulary instruction for elementary education in the twenty-first century.

Joe Campione, Ph.D.

A leading researcher on cognitive development, individual differences, assessment, and the design of innovative learning environments, Dr. Campione is a professor emeritus in the School of Education at University of California, Berkeley.

Iva Carruthers, Ph.D.

Equipped with both hands-on and academic experience, Dr. Carruthers serves as a consultant and lecturer in educational technology and matters of multicultural inclusion.

Doug Fuchs Ph.D.

Dr. Fuchs, the Nicholas Hobbs Professor of Special Education and Human Development at Vanderbilt University, has conducted programmatic research on response-to-intervention as a method for preventing and identifying children with learning disabilities and on reading instructional methods for improving outcomes for students with learning disabilities.

Lynn Fuchs, Ph.D.

A co-director of the Kennedy Center Reading clinic at Vanderbilt University, Dr. Fuchs also conducted research on assessment methods for enhancing instructional planning and instructional methods for improving reading and math outcomes for students with learning disabilities.

Steve Graham, Ph.D.

A professor of literacy at Vanderbilt University, Dr. Graham's research focuses on identifying the factors that contribute to writing development and writing difficulties.

Karen Harris, Ph.D.

The Currey-Ingram Professor of Special Education and Literacy at Vanderbilt University, Dr. Harris's research focuses on theoretical and intervention issues in the development of academic and self-regulation strategies among students who are at risk.

Jan Hirshberg, Ed.D.

Focusing on how children learn to read and write and the logistics of teaching reading and writing in the early grades, Dr. Hirshberg works as a language arts resource coordinator and consultant in Alexandria, Virginia.

Anne McKeough, Ph.D.

A professor in the Division of Applied Psychology at the University of Calgary, Dr. McKeough teaches graduate courses in cognitive development and educational assessment, as well as teacher preparation courses to undergraduates.

Peter Pannell, MA

Principal of Longfellow Elementary School in Pasadena, California, Mr. Pannell has worked to develop the literacy of countless students. To help accomplish this goal, he wrote and implemented a writing project that allowed his students to make great strides in their writing performance.

Marsha Roit, Ed.D.

The Director of Professional Development for SRA/McGraw-Hill, Dr. Roit spends considerable time in classrooms developing reading curricula and working with teachers and administrators in effective instructional practices.

Marlene Scardamalia, Ph.D.

Dr. Scardamalia is the Presidents' Chair in Education and Knowledge Technologies at the University of Toronto and is also the Director of the Institute for Knowledge Innovation and Technology. She received the 2006 World Award of Education from the World Cultural Council for outstanding work in education.

Marcy Stein, Ph.D.

Professor and founding faculty member of the education program at the University of Washington, Tacoma, Dr. Stein teaches At-Risk and Special Education graduate and teacher certification programs.

Gerald H. Treadway Jr, Ph.D.

Chair of the Literacy Education Program and professor of education at San Diego State University, Dr. Treadway teaches classes on reading methods, English Language Learner methods, balanced reading programs, assessment, and reading comprehension. He is also a consultant for the California Reading and Literature Project.

In memoriam

Michael Pressley, Ph.D.
1951–2006

Dr. Pressley was a tireless supporter of education. He championed the rights of all children to a quality education, made seminal contributions in research and practice, and nurtured the development of a host of beginning teachers, young scholars, and editors. While his work and spirit lives on in those he influenced and inspired, there is no substitute for the real thing. We will all miss his wisdom and friendship every day.

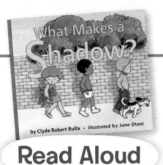

Table of Contents

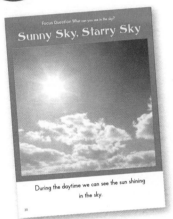
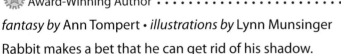

Additional Reading

You may wish to provide some of the following titles to students for additional theme-related reading.

Shadowville
by Michael Bartalos

What Makes Day and Night
by Franklyn M. Branley

Footprints and Shadows
by Anne Wescott Dodd

Me and My Shadow
by Arthur Dorros

Sun Up, Sun Down
by Gail Gibbons

I Have a Friend
by Keiko Narahashi

Shadows Are About
by Ann Whitford Paul

Guess Whose Shadow?
by Stephen R. Swinburne

Shadow Story
by Nancy Willard

My Shadow
by Susan Winter

Note: You should preview any trade books and videos for appropriateness before recommending them to students.

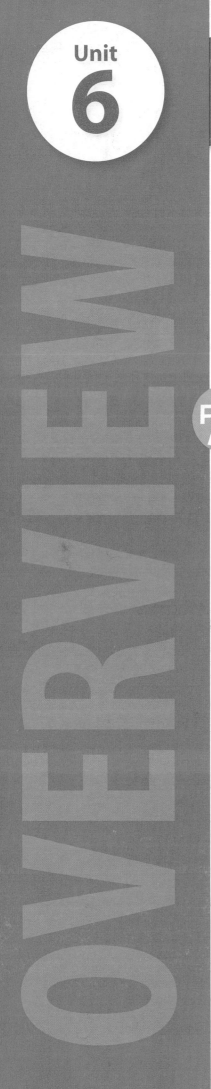

OVERVIEW

My Shadow

Have you ever noticed your shadow? It's not always around. But when it is, it follows you everywhere. Do you know what makes a shadow?

Theme Connection

Look at the painting *The First Frost* by Olga Wisinger-Florian. How many shadows do you see? What are making the shadows? Where are the shadows?

Olga Wisinger-Florian. *The First Frost*. circa 1900. Oil on canvas. 114 x 156 cm. Vienna, Austria.

BIG Idea

Why do shadows come and go?

Launching the Theme

Setting Up the Theme

Children are fascinated with shadows. Because they do not yet understand what makes shadows appear, children find them intriguing, mysterious, and even magical. The reading selections and investigations in this unit build on children's natural curiosity about shadows. As they learn more about the physical properties of shadows, children sharpen their questions and deepen their understanding of this phenomenon.

To get students excited about My Shadow, try one or more of the following ideas:

- Create several shadows on a classroom wall as a display.
- Use the Unit 6 *eBackground Builders* video to give students additional background information about the theme.

 Students will begin a unit investigation about shadows and will continue this investigation over the course of the next three weeks. They will research just as scientists do and will test their results. At the end of the unit, students will share the results of their investigation with others.

Concept/Question Board

Using the **Concept/Question Board** as a tool, students will explore concepts and develop inquiry questions. Resources from the classroom as well as from the home can be posted on the **Concept/Question Board.** Referring to the **Concept/Question Board** daily as part of your routine is a good way to emphasize to students the importance of this learning tool.

To learn more about the theme My Shadow, display a **Concept/Question Board** in your classroom. This will be a place where you and students post questions about the theme and anything related to the concept of shadows.

The following materials will encourage students to post their ideas and questions on the **Concept/Question Board:**

- Books and poems about shadows
- Assorted shapes cut out of gray and black paper

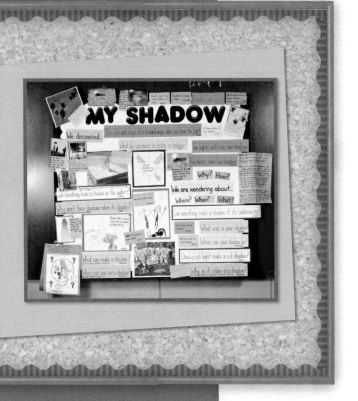

Each week students will gain a better understanding of shadows as they progress through the unit inquiry. They will begin their unit investigation by asking questions and wondering about shadows. Later on they will conduct experiments with making shadows by using flashlights and then recording their observations. Finally they will decide collectively how to share their research with others.

After discussing the Big Idea question "Why do shadows come and go?" discuss with students the following questions. These questions can be used to begin the inquiry process.

- How do shadows appear?
- Why is my shadow sometimes behind me and other times in front of me?
- Why do shadows change shape and size?

Using the Inquiry Planner

Students will research the theme My Shadow using the steps below.

	Steps	Models
Week 1	**STEP 1** Begin discussing and sharing ideas.	**MODEL 1** *Can a shadow come and go? Why do shadows disappear? How can a shadow change shape?*
	STEP 2 Think about a question for the **Concept/Question Board**.	**MODEL 2** *What makes a shadow?*
Week 2	**STEP 3** Begin investigating and collecting information.	**MODEL 3** *Make shadows grow and shrink on the wall by moving a volunteer between a light source and the wall. Trace the person's outline at different locations.*
	STEP 4 Generate a question or idea for the **Concept/Question Board**.	**MODEL 4** *Why do shadows change in size?*
Week 3	**STEP 5** Share your findings with others.	**MODEL 5** *I will show pictures of shadows I found in magazines.*
	STEP 6 Do you have more questions?	**MODEL 6** *What kinds of objects make shadows?*

About the Authors and Illustrators

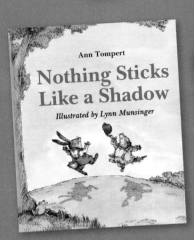

Nothing Sticks Like a Shadow

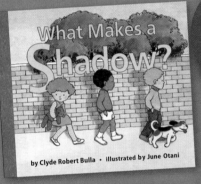

What Makes a Shadow

Author of *Shadow/Sombra*

Jorge Argueta

Argueta's family owned a small restaurant in El Salvador. Many travelers ate in the restaurant and told Argueta wonderful stories that he remembered. After moving to San Francisco, he began to write poetry. His first book won the 2001 Américas Book Award.

Author of *Bear Shadow*

Frank Asch

Asch enjoys being involved in the lives of children. He taught children in India and organized art, writing, puppetry, and dramatic workshops for children throughout the country. Asch is best known for his Moonbear picture books. He also enjoys writing a wide variety of stories, plays, and poems.

Author of *Hide-and-Seek Shadow*

Margaret Hillert

Hillert carefully selects the vocabulary in her stories and poems so children at any reading level can enjoy her books. She wants every child to feel the accomplishment of reading on his or her own. She writes books about new stories and well-loved fairy tales.

Author of *Nothing Sticks Like a Shadow*

Ann Tompert

Tompert knew she wanted to be a writer after reading the book *Little Women*. However, she taught school for twenty years before she decided to write seriously. Her first book was named the 1996 Bank Street College Book of the Year.

Illustrator of *Nothing Sticks Like a Shadow*

Lynn Munsinger

Munsinger studied art in the United States and England. She began illustrating children's books after returning to the United States. She likes to draw faces so their emotions are clearly shown. Her pictures have enriched over ninety children's books.

Author of *What Makes a Shadow?*

Clyde Robert Bulla

When Bulla was young, his father told him that he needed to experience life in order to tell good stories. Bulla continued to write, but his stories were rejected. A teacher friend gave him a story idea, which became Bulla's first children's book. His books have won several awards, including an ALA Notable Children's Book.

Unit Skills

★ Phonemic Awareness ★ Phonics
★ Fluency ★ Vocabulary ★ Comprehension

Week 1

Sounds and Letters

Phonics ★
• Initial and Final Phoneme Blending
• Initial Phoneme Segmentation
• Initial Phoneme Matching
• Initial Phoneme Manipulation
• High-Frequency Word *for*

Alphabetic Knowledge ★
• *Jj*
• *Ff*

Reading and Responding

Comprehension ★
 Strategies
 • Asking Questions
 • Clarifying
 • Predicting
 Skills
 Cause and Effect

✔ **Print and Book Awareness**

Selection Vocabulary ★

Inquiry

Language Arts

Writing
• Choosing and Sequencing Ideas
• Thank-You Cards

Grammar
• Sentence Spacing
• Sentence Variety

Week 2

Phonics ★
• Initial Phoneme Blending
• Initial Phoneme Matching
• Initial and Final Phoneme Manipulation
• Phoneme Segmentation
• High-Frequency Words *but, up*

Alphabetic Knowledge ★
• *Uu*
• *Xx*
• *Zz*

Comprehension ★
 Strategies
 • Visualizing
 • Asking Questions
 • Clarifying
 Skills
 ✔ Drawing Conclusions

Print and Book Awareness

✔ **Selection Vocabulary** ★

Inquiry

Writing
• Revising
• Illustrating Brainstorming

Grammar
Sound Patterns

Week 3

✔ **Phonics** ★
• Initial Phoneme Blending
• Phoneme Segmentation
• Word Pairs
• High-Frequency Word *all*

✔ **Alphabetic Knowledge** ★
/z/ Spelled *Ss*

Comprehension ★
 Strategies
 • Asking Questions
 • Making Connections
 • Clarifying
 Skills
 ✔ Cause and Effect
 • Reality and Fantasy

Print and Book Awareness

✔ **Selection Vocabulary** ★

Writing
• Advertisements
• Using Descriptive Words
• Problem/Resolution Plots
• Revising

Grammar
• Descriptive Words

Key: ★ = five components of Reading   ✔ = Lesson Assessment   **B** = Benchmark Assessment

Assessment Plan for Making AYP

 **is an ongoing cycle.**

1 Screen

Administer the initial **Benchmark Assessment** as a screener to target students who are at risk for failing end-of-year measures.

Diagnose students' strengths and weaknesses, and differentiate instruction according to their abilities.

2 Diagnose and Differentiate

Diagnosing, differentiating instruction, and monitoring progress is an ongoing cycle.

3 Monitor Progress

Monitor progress weekly, monthly, or anytime as needed with both formal and informal assessments.

4 Measure Outcomes

Administer summative assessments, such as lesson or state assessments, to measure student outcomes.

Screen

At the beginning of the year or for students entering class after the school year has begun, administer the initial **Benchmark Assessment**, Benchmark 1, to target students at risk for reading failure.

Diagnose and Differentiate

Use the results from the **Lesson Assessments, Benchmark Assessments,** and informal observation measures to diagnose students' strengths and weaknesses and to differentiate instructions individually and in small groups.

	Approaching Level	On Level	English Learner	Above Level
Leveled Practice	• *Reteach* • *Workshop Kit* - Activities - Games • *Intervention Guide*	• *Skills Practice* • *Workshop Kit* - Activities - Games • *Intervention Guide*	• *English Learner Support Activities* • *Workshop Kit* - Activities - Games	• *Challenge Activities* • *Workshop Kit* - Activities - Games
Technology 	• *eSkills & eGames* • *eDecodables*	• *eSkills & eGames* • *eDecodables* • *eGames*	• *eSkills & eGames* • *eDecodables*	*eSkills & eGames*

Monitor Progress

Between Benchmark Assessments, use the following to monitor student progress. Regroup students daily or as needed, based on these formative assessment results.

Monitor Progress ✓
Formal Assessment

• *Lesson Assessments*
• *Online Assessments*

• Comprehension Observation Log
• *Skills Practice 2*

Measure Outcomes

Assess student understanding and mastery of skills by using the **Lesson Assessments.**

Unit 6

Resources to Monitor Progress

	Week 1
Skills Practice 2	Letter and Sound Identification, pp. 2–3, 5–7, 9–10 Sentence Spacing, p. 4 Repeating Subjects, p. 8
Reteach	Letter and Sound Identification, pp. 103–104, 106–109 Sentence Spacing, p. 105
Challenge Activities	Letter and Sound Identification, pp. 79, 81–83 Capital Letters and Punctuation, p. 80
Decodables	*Decodable* 8: *Jam Pot*
Lesson Assessments	Lesson 5, pp. 57A–57B
Benchmark Assessments	

Technology e-Suite

e Skills	Unit 6 Phonics
e Decodables	*Decodable* 8: *Jam Pot*
e Games	
e Assess	*Lesson Assessment,* Unit 6, Lesson 5

Week 2

Letter and Sound Identification, pp. 11–16

Phoneme Matching, p. 110
Letter and Sound Identification, pp. 111–114

Letter and Sound Identification, pp. 84–86, 88
Penmanship, p. 87

Decodable 9: *Bud and Max*

Lessons 7–8, pp. 57–58

Unit 6 Phonics

Decodable 9: *Bud and Max*

Lesson Assessment, Unit 6, Lessons 7–8

Week 3

Letter and Sound Identification, pp. 17–21
Sentence Spacing, p. 22

Letter and Sound Identification, pp. 115–120, 122
Describing Words, p. 121

Letter and Sound Identification, pp. 89–92

Decodable 10: *Liz and Tad*

Lessons 11–15, pp. 59–62

Benchmark 4

Unit 6 Phonics

Decodable 10: *Liz and Tad*

Skill: Letter and sound identification

Lesson Assessment, Unit 6, Lessons 11–15

Lesson Planner

Day 1

Day 2

Sounds and Letters

MATERIALS

- ◆ Routines 1, 2, 4
- ◆ *Pocket Chart Picture Cards*
- ◆ *Alphabet Letter Cards: Jj* and *Ff*
- ◆ *Skills Practice 2,* pp. 2–3, 5–7, 9–10
- ◆ *Transparencies* 6, 10
- ◆ *Pickled Peppers Big Book,* p. 43
- ◆ *Alphabet Book Big Book,* pp. 14–15, 22–23
- ◆ *Decodable* 8

Day 1

Warming Up, pp. T24–T25
Phonemic Awareness
Phoneme Blending: Final Sounds, p. T25
Alphabetic Principle
- Introducing the Sound of *Jj*, p. T26
- Listening for Initial /j/, p. T26
- Linking the Sound to the Letter, p. T26
- Penmanship, p. T27

Day 2

Warming Up, p. T32
Phonemic Awareness
- Phoneme Segmentation: Initial Sounds, p. T33
- Phoneme Blending: Final Sounds, p. T33
Alphabetic Principle
- Reviewing the Sound of *Jj*, p. T34
- Listening for Initial /j/, p. T34
- Linking the Sound to the Letter, p. T34
- *Alphabet Book Big Book*—/j/, p. T35

Reading and Responding

MATERIALS

- ◆ *My Shadow Big Book,* pp. 4–19
- ◆ *Home Connections,* pp. 43–46
- ◆ *Read Aloud Collection: What Makes a Shadow?*
- ◆ Routines 5–7

Day 1

Preview
- Browsing the Unit, p. T28
- Setting Reading Goals, p. T28
Inquiry, p. T29

Day 2

Read Aloud Collection: What Makes a Shadow?
- Activate Prior Knowledge, p. T36
- Preview the Selection, p. T36
Vocabulary, p. T36
Discuss the Read Aloud, p. T39
Vocabulary Review, p. T39

Language Arts

MATERIALS

- ◆ *Language Arts Big Book,* pp. 15, 39, 53
- ◆ *My Shadow Big Book,* pp. 13, 35, 44
- ◆ *Skills Practice 2,* pp. 4, 8
- ◆ *Willy the Wisher,* p. 62
- ◆ *Story Lines Big Book,* pp. 10–11
- ◆ *My Neighborhood Game Mats*
- ◆ *Alphabet Letter Cards*

Day 1

Writing Process
Model: Brainstorming a List of Nouns, p. T30
Fine Art
Discussing Fine Art, p. T31

Day 2

Writing Process
Prewrite: Brainstorming List of Card Recipients, p. T40
Grammar, Usage, and Mechanics, pp. T40–T41
Willy the Wisher, p. T41

Monitor Progress

✔ = **Formal Assessment**

Ⓑ = **Benchmark Assessment**

Day 1

 Letter and Sound Identification, p. T27

Day 2

 Letter and Sound Identification, p. T34
 Sentence Spacing, p. T41

Lessons 1-5

Literature Overview

Read Aloud

What Makes a Shadow?

by Clyde Robert Bulla

illustrated by June Otani

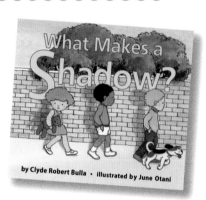

Big Book

Shadows

by Lisa Zimmerman

photographs by Bill Nieberding

Day 3

Warming Up, pp. T42–43
Phonemic Awareness
Phoneme Blending: Final Sounds, p. T43
Alphabetic Principle
• Introducing the Sound of *Ff*, p. T44
• Listening for Initial /f/, p. T44
• Linking the Sound to the Letter, p. T44
• Penmanship, p. T45

Preview and Prepare, p. T46
Vocabulary, p. T47
Read the Selection, p. T47
Comprehension Strategies, pp. T48, T50
Print and Book Awareness, pp. T49, T51
Discussing the Selection, p. T51
Vocabulary Review, p. T51

Writing Process
Prewrite: Brainstorming Ideas for a Card, p. T52
Story Crafting
Story Lines Big Book, p. T53

 Letter and Sound Identification, p. T45
 Vocabulary, p. T47

Day 4

Warming Up, p. T54
Phonemic Awareness
• Phoneme Matching: Initial Sounds, p. T55
• Phoneme Manipulation: Initial Sounds, p. T55
Alphabetic Principle
• Reviewing the Sound of *Ff*, p. T56
• Listening for Final /f/, p. T56
• Linking the Sound to the Letter, p. T56
• *Alphabet Book Big Book*—/f/, p. T57

Preview and Prepare, p. T58
Vocabulary, p. T58
Read the Selection, p. T59
Comprehension Strategies, pp. T60, T62
Comprehension Skills, p. T61
Reading with a Writer's Eye, pp. T61, T63
Discussing the Selection, p. T63
Vocabulary Review, p. T63

Writing Process
Model: Choosing and Sequencing Ideas, p. T64
Grammar, Usage, and Mechanics,
pp. T64–T65
Story Crafting
Story Lines Big Book, p. T65

 Letter and Sound Identification, p. T56
 Capital Letters and Punctuation, p. T65
 Repeating Subjects, p. T65

Day 5

Warming Up, pp. T66–T67
Phonemic Awareness
Phoneme Matching: Initial Sounds, p. T67
Alphabetic Principle
• Reviewing the Sounds of *Jj* and *Ff*, p. T68
• Listening for Initial /j/ and /f/, p. T68
• Linking the Sound to the Letter, p. T68
• Penmanship, p. T69
Reading a *Decodable*
***Decodable* 8:** *Jam Pot,* pp. T70–T71

Inquiry
• Small-Group Time, p. T72
• Whole-Group Time, p. T73
• Concept Vocabulary, p. T73

Writing Process
Draft: Collaborating to Craft Card, p. T74
Grammar, Usage, and Mechanics,
pp. T74–T75
Game Day
My Neighborhood Game, p. T75

 Lesson Assessment Annotated Teacher's Edition, pp. 57A–57B
 Comprehension Observation Log
 Letter and Sound Identification, p. T69

Student Resources

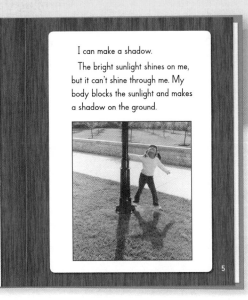

Big Books

Audio CD

Big Book Selection

My Shadow **Big Book**

Shadows by Lisa Zimmerman, pp. 4–19

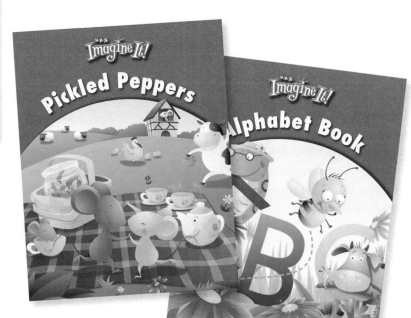

Decodable 8

Teacher Support

Language Arts Big Book

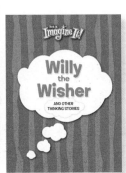

Willy the Wisher

Story Lines Big Book

Curriculum Connections

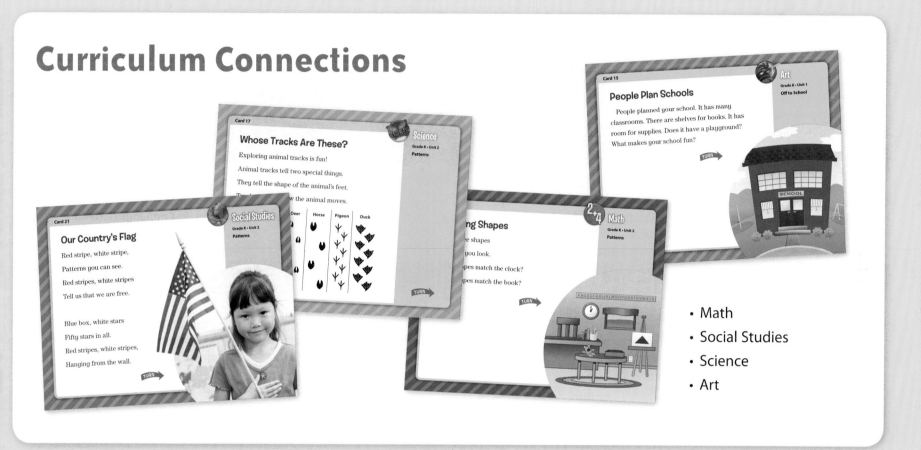

Card 17

Whose Tracks Are These?

Science
Grade K • Unit 2
Patterns

Exploring animal tracks is fun!

Animal tracks tell two special things.

They tell the shape of the animal's feet.

They tell how the animal moves.

Deer	Horse	Pigeon	Duck

Card 21

Our Country's Flag

Social Studies
Grade K • Unit 2
Patterns

Red stripe, white stripe,

Patterns you can see.

Red stripes, white stripes

Tell us that we are free.

Blue box, white stars

Fifty stars in all.

Red stripes, white stripes,

Hanging from the wall.

Card 15

People Plan Schools

Art
Grade K • Unit 1
Off to School

People planned your school. It has many classrooms. There are shelves for books. It has room for supplies. Does it have a playground? What makes your school fun?

ng Shapes

Math
Grade K • Unit 2
Patterns

e shapes

you look.

pes match the clock?

pes match the book?

- Math
- Social Studies
- Science
- Art

Additional Skills Practice

Approaching Level	On Level	English Learner	Above Level
Reteach	**Skills Practice 2**	**English Learner Support Activities**	**Challenge Activities**
• Letter and Sound Identification, pp. 103–104, 106–109	• Letter and Sound Identification, pp. 2–3, 5–7, 9–10	Lessons 1–5	• Capital Letters and Punctuation, p. 80
• Sentence Spacing, p. 105	• Repeating Subjects, p. 8		• Letter and Sound Identification, pp. 79, 81–83
	• Sentence Spacing, p. 4		

Differentiating Instruction
for Workshop

Day 1

Approaching Level	On Level	English Learner	Above Level
Sounds and Letters			
Alphabetic Principle: Students use **Alphabet Sound Card Stories CD** to listen to the story for the /j/ sound.	**Alphabetic Principle:** Have students browse the **My Shadow Little Big Book** for the letter *Jj* and make the /j/ sound each time they find the letter.	**Alphabetic Principle:** Refer to Unit 6 Lesson 1 of the **English Learner Support Guide**.	**Alphabetic Principle:** Students work independently to complete **Challenge Activities** page 79.
Reading and Responding			
Preview: Students listen to *What Makes a Shadow?* on the **Listening Library CD**.	**Preview:** Students draw any questions they have about shadows and post them on the **Concept/Question Board.**	**Preview:** Refer to Unit 6 Lesson 1 of the **English Learner Support Guide.**	**Preview:** Students draw any questions they have about shadows and post them on the **Concept/Question Board.**
Language Arts			
Writing: Students discuss farm animals.	**Writing:** Students find pictures of farm animals in magazines.	**Writing:** Refer to Unit 6 Lesson 1 of the **English Learner Support Guide.**	**Writing:** Students help you create a list of farm animals.

Day 2

Approaching Level	On Level	English Learner	Above Level

Sounds and Letters

Alphabetic Principle: Use an activity from Unit 6 Lesson 2 of the *Intervention Guide* for additional help with the /j/ sound.

Alphabetic Principle: Students use *Alphabet Sound Card Stories CD* to listen to the story for the /j/ sound.

Alphabetic Principle: Refer to Unit 6 Lesson 2 of the *English Learner Support Guide.*

Alphabetic Principle: Students listen to the rhyme for *Jj* on the *Listening Library CD* as they browse the *Alphabet Book Little Big Book.*

Reading and Responding

Vocabulary: Students browse the selection and point to any words they recognize or would like to question.

Vocabulary: Have students use the selection vocabulary words in complete sentences.

Vocabulary: Preview the selection "Shadows" with students, and have them point to any words they recognize.

Vocabulary: Students draw pictures to illustrate the selection vocabulary words.

Language Arts

Writing: With your help, students choose one animal to focus on and brainstorm words to describe their choice.

Grammar: Students look at simple sentences in "Bear Shadow."

Writing: Each student pair chooses one animal and works together to make a list of describing words.

Grammar: Students look for simple sentences in "Bear Shadow."

Writing: Have *Picture Cards* or pictures ready of a dog, a cat, and an ape. Give the name of each animal, and have students give three or four descriptive words for each animal. Write these words on the board.

Grammar: Refer to Unit 6 Lesson 2 of the *English Learner Support Guide.*

Writing: Students find farm animals in books or magazines.

Grammar: Each student creates a sentence with no spaces.

Differentiating Instruction
for Workshop

Day 3

Approaching Level	On Level	English Learner	Above Level
Sounds and Letters			
Alphabetic Principle: Students draw pictures of objects beginning with the /f/ sound.	**Alphabetic Principle:** Students match **Alphabet Letter Card** *Ff* to objects in the classroom beginning with the /f/ sound.	**Alphabetic Principle:** Refer to Unit 6 Lesson 3 of the **English Learner Support Guide.**	**Alphabetic Principle:** Browse the **My Shadow Little Big Book** for objects with the /f/ sound in their names.
Reading and Responding			
Comprehension: Browse the selection with students, and have them point out illustrations that puzzle them.	**Comprehension:** Invite students to discuss the selection and make connections to their own lives.	**Comprehension:** Refer to Unit 6 Lesson 3 of the **English Learner Support Guide.**	**Comprehension:** Help students research shadows on the Internet and post their findings and questions on the **Concept/Question Board.**
Language Arts			
Writing: With your help, students create lists of words that describe the animals they chose.	**Writing:** Students draw their animals and, with your help, write names of the animals at the tops of their pages.	**Writing:** On the board, write *cat, dog,* and *ape.* Under each word, place a **Picture Card** or a picture of each animal. Say each word, and have students repeat the word. Students then select one of the animals to draw.	**Writing:** Students draw a picture of one animal they chose.

Day 4

Approaching Level	On Level	English Learner	Above Level
Sounds and Letters			
Alphabetic Principle: Use an activity from Unit 6 Lesson 4 of the **Intervention Guide.**	**Alphabetic Principle:** Students use **eSkills** to practice phoneme manipulation.	**Alphabetic Principle:** Refer to Unit 6 Lesson 4 of the **English Learner Support Guide.**	**Phonemic Awareness:** Using the **Pocket Chart Picture Cards**, students identify and match pictures that begin with the /j/ sound.
Reading and Responding			
Comprehension: Invite students to discuss any connections they see between the selection and their own lives.	**Comprehension:** Have students try making their own shadows and observing the shadows of objects in the classroom.	**Vocabulary:** Refer to Unit 6 Lesson 4 of the **English Learner Support Guide.**	**Comprehension:** Students try making shadow puppets and discussing how the shadows are made.
Language Arts			
Writing: Students draw pictures of their animals. **Grammar:** Students place a dot above the capital letters in the selection "Bear Shadow."	**Writing:** With your help, students label parts of their animals. **Grammar:** With your help, students place a dot above the punctuation marks in the selection "Bear Shadow."	**Writing:** Help students write the first letter of the animals they drew. **Grammar:** Refer to Unit 6 Lesson 4 of the **English Learner Support Guide.**	**Writing:** With your help, students label the parts of their animal. **Grammar:** Students challenge partners with the sentences they created.

Differentiating Instruction
for Workshop

 AYP

Day 5

Approaching Level	On Level	English Learner	Above Level
Sounds and Letters			
Alphabetic Principle: Using **Alphabet Letter Cards** *Jj* and *Ff*, students walk around the room, matching the letters with environmental print.	**Alphabetic Principle:** Have students browse the **My Shadow Little Big Book** for the Letters *Jj* and *Ff* and make the sound each time they find the letter.	**Alphabetic Principle:** Refer to Unit 6 Lesson 5 of the **English Learner Support Guide.**	**Alphabetic Principle:** Students use the **eAlphabet Book** to review the /j/ and /f/ sounds.
Reading and Responding			
Inquiry: Students draw pictures of questions or wonderings about shadows and post them on the **Concept/Question Board.**	**Inquiry:** Students research shadows in the Internet with partners and generate questions or wonderings to post on the **Concept/Question Board.**	**Inquiry:** Review the selection "Shadows" with students, and have them ask any questions or share wonderings about the selection with you.	**Inquiry:** Students gather various classroom items and try to make shadows with them.
Language Arts			
Writing: Students sign their names to their drawings. **Grammar:** Students draw a line where the space is between words in the selection "Bear Shadow."	**Writing:** Students share their pictures with the group. **Grammar:** Students share what kind of sentences they see in the selection "Bear Shadow."	**Writing:** Students share their pictures with the group. **Grammar:** Refer to Unit 6 Lesson 5 of the **English Learner Support Guide.**	**Writing:** Students sign their drawings and share with the group. **Grammar:** Students switch partners and try again.

Additional Resources for
Differentiating Instruction

English Learner

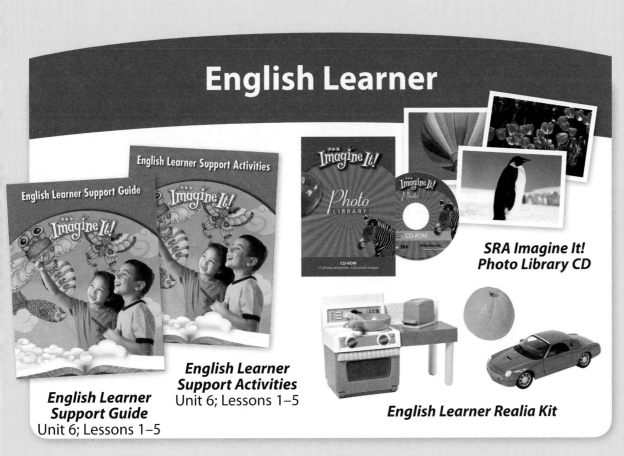

English Learner Support Activities
Unit 6; Lessons 1–5

English Learner Support Guide
Unit 6; Lessons 1–5

SRA Imagine It! Photo Library CD

English Learner Realia Kit

Approaching Level

Intervention

Intervention Guide

Intervention Workbook

Workshop Kits

- High Frequency Words
- Letter Recognition
- Phonemic Awareness
- Print and Book Awareness
- Sequencing

Technology

eAlphabet Book
eDecodables *Jam Pot*
eSkills & eGames
Listening Library CD

Listening Library Unit 6

Lessons 1-5 Overview

Lesson Assessment

Monitor Progress to Differentiate Instruction

Use these summative assessments along with your informal observations to assess student mastery.

UNIT 6 My Shadow • Lesson 5

Print and Book Awareness

Directions for Teacher

This assessment is intended to be administered to students individually. As an option, you may observe students during regular classroom activities and check the skills they demonstrate.

Duplicate page 57B for each student you choose to assess. Write the student's name and the date in the appropriate spaces. You will record the student's responses on this page. After you have completed the assessment, record the number right in the spaces below and on the STUDENT ASSESSMENT RECORD and CLASS ASSESSMENT RECORD.

Sit at a table that allows you and the student to work comfortably. You may find it easier to sit beside the student. Put the My Shadow **Big Book** on the table with the cover down. Ask the student the questions on page 57B. Check each question the student answers correctly.

Lesson Assessment Book • Print and Book Awareness   UNIT 6 • Lesson 5 **57A**

Lesson Assessment Book, p. 57A

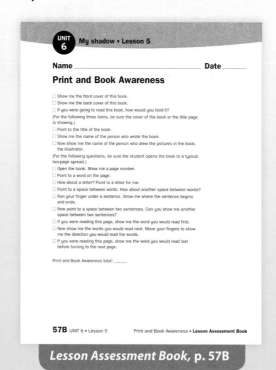

UNIT 6 My shadow • Lesson 5

Name _____   **Date** _____

Print and Book Awareness

☐ Show me the front cover of this book.
☐ Show me the back cover of this book.
☐ If you were going to read this book, how would you hold it?
(For the following three items, be sure the cover of the book or the title page is showing.)
☐ Point to the title of the book.
☐ Show me the name of the person who wrote the book.
☐ Now show me the name of the person who drew the pictures in the book, the illustrator.
(For the following questions, be sure the student opens the book to a typical two-page spread.)
☐ Open the book. Show me a page number.
☐ Point to a word on the page.
☐ How about a letter? Point to a letter for me.
☐ Point to a space between words. How about another space between words?
☐ Run your finger under a sentence. Show me where the sentence begins and ends.
☐ Now point to a space between two sentences. Can you show me another space between two sentences?
☐ If you were reading this page, show me the word you would read first.
☐ Now show me the words you would read next. Move your fingers to show me the direction you would read the words.
☐ If you were reading this page, show me the word you would read last before turning to the next page.

Print and Book Awareness total: _____

57B UNIT 6 • Lesson 5   Print and Book Awareness • **Lesson Assessment Book**

Lesson Assessment Book, p. 57B

Lesson Assessment Book

Comprehension Observation Log

Student _____ Date _____
Unit _____ Lesson _____ Selection Title _____

General Comprehension
Concepts discussed: _____

Behavior Within a Group
Articulates, expresses ideas: _____

Joins discussions: _____

Collaborates (such as works well with other students, works alone): _____

Role in Group
Role (such as leader, summarizer, questioner, critic, observer, *non-participant*): _____

Flexibility (changes roles when necessary): _____

Use of Reading Strategies
Uses strategies when needed (either those taught or student's choice of strategy)/Describes strategies used: _____

Changes strategies when appropriate: _____

Changes Since Last Observation

110 Comprehension Observation Log • **Lesson Assessment Book**

Lesson Assessment Annotated Teacher's Edition, p. 110

The Comprehension Observation Log, found in the ***Lesson Assessment Annotated Teacher's Edition,*** is a vehicle for recording anecdotal information about individual student performance on an ongoing basis. Information such as students' strengths and weaknesses can be recorded at any time the occasion warrants. It is recommended that you maintain a folder for each student where you can store the logs for purposes of comparison and analysis as the school year progresses. You will gradually build up a comprehensive file that reveals which students are progressing smoothly and which students need additional help.

Day 1 Sounds and Letters

MATERIALS
+ Weather Icons
+ Routine 1
+ *Pocket Chart Picture Cards* 91–96
+ *Alphabet Letter Card* Jj for each student
+ Supply Icons
+ *Skills Practice 2,* p. 2
+ *Transparency* 10

Point to the box that represents today. Hold up the Weather Icons, and ask students to look out the window and tell about today's weather. Have the class decide on the appropriate Weather Icon. Ask a student to place the Weather Icon next to the day of the week. Say *Today the weather is _____ .* Have students talk about what they like about today's kind of weather.

Warming Up 🕐

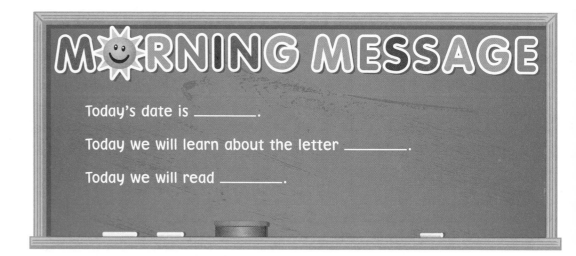

MORNING MESSAGE

Today's date is _____ .

Today we will learn about the letter _____ .

Today we will read _____ .

Kindergarten News

+ Copy the above text on the board or on chart paper. Make mistakes in the message, such as writing two words together without any space between them, writing a letter backward, or leaving a period missing at the end of a sentence.

+ Ask students to help you proofread to find the errors in the message, and have volunteers correct them. For example, they could add a slash between the two words without a space.

+ Discuss the letters and the words in the message. You might ask students to say which words appear more than once in the message or which words have letters or sounds that they recognize.

Phoneme Blending: Initial Sounds

+ Tell students the **Lion Puppet** wants to play a blending game again. Tell them you will say the beginning sound of a word and the puppet will say the rest. When the puppet asks what the word is, students should put the parts together and say the word.

◆ Practice with the following word:

Teacher:	/g/ (Emphasize the /g/ sound.)
Everyone:	/g/
Puppet:	oose. What's the word?
Everyone:	goose

◆ Continue with the following words:

/r/ . . . ock rock	/g/ . . . ame game	/f/ . . . ish fish
/m/ . . . at mat	/k/ . . . an can	/l/ . . . amp lamp
/h/ . . . ook hook	/t/ . . . ime time	/s/ . . . and sand

Phonemic Awareness

Phoneme Blending: Final Sounds

◆ Tell students the **Lion Puppet** wants to play a blending game they have played before. Tell them the puppet will say a word except for the end sound. You will say the end sound. When the puppet asks what the word is, students should put the parts together and say the word.

◆ Practice with the following word:

Puppet:	balloo . . .
Teacher:	/n/ (Emphasize the /n/ sound.)
Everyone:	/n/
Puppet:	What's the word?
Everyone:	balloon

◆ Continue with the following words:

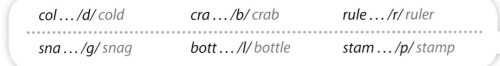

col . . . /d/ cold	cra . . . /b/ crab	rule . . . /r/ ruler
sna . . . /g/ snag	bott . . . /l/ bottle	stam . . . /p/ stamp

Teacher Tip

FINAL PHONEMES Keep in mind that working with final consonant sounds is somewhat more difficult than working with initial consonant sounds in words. Place great vocal emphasis on the final sounds in these words to draw students' attention to them.

Differentiating Instruction   **English Learners**

IF . . . students have difficulty with final phonemes, **THEN . . .** keep in mind that some languages have only one or a few consonants that appear in the final position. Provide extra practice blending final phonemes according to individual needs.

Teacher Tip

THE SOUND OF *Jj* Discuss with students that the sounds of the letters *Jj* and *Gg* are often confused. Write the words *jet* and *get* on the board. Point to and pronounce each aloud, stressing the initial consonant sound. Tell students to look closely at your mouth as you repeat the words because they can actually *see* the difference in the sounds. Exaggerate your mouth formations as you repeat the words. Then have students say each word so they can feel the difference in their own mouths.

Differentiating Instruction **English Learners**

IF ... students are native Spanish speakers, **THEN ...** they may have difficulty with the English pronunciation of the letter *j* because the /j/ sound does not exist in Spanish. In Spanish, *j* represents /h/. Demonstrate how to produce the /j/ sound, and give students many opportunities to practice it.

Technology

Use the ***Alphabet Sound Card Stories CD*** for practice with the /j/ sound.

Audio CD

Alphabetic Principle

ROUTINE **1**

Introducing the Sound of *Jj*

✦ Display **Alphabet Sound Wall Card *Jj***, and say the sound of the letter: /j/. Show the picture for the /j/ sound, and teach the short story for /j/:

Jenny and Jackson like to have fun.

They play jacks, jump rope, and juggle in the sun.

Each time they jump, their feet hit the ground.

/j/ /j/ /j/ /j/ /j/ is the jumping-rope sound.

✦ Repeat the story, emphasizing the initial /j/ sound. Invite students to join you in reciting the story and saying /j/ /j/ /j/.

Alphabet Sound Wall Card 10

Listening for Initial /j/

✦ Hold up and name each of these **Pocket Chart Picture Cards:** 91—Jack, 92—jam, 93—jars, 94—Jill, 95—jug, and 96—juice. Ask students to listen for the /j/ sound at the beginnings of the words.

✦ Give each student a *Jj* **Alphabet Letter Card,** and have them say the /j/ sound. Have students hold up their cards each time they hear the /j/ sound. Try these words:

green	**jail**	**jeans**	Gail	**Jill**
Jake	**jam**	**Jim**	gas	girl

Linking the Sound to the Letter

✦ Write the words *jacket* and *packet* on the board. Say *Which word says* jacket?

✦ Ask a student to come to the board and point to the correct word. When the student points to *jacket,* say *Correct! How did you know? The /j/ sound begins jacket.*

✦ Then point to *packet,* and ask students what they think it says. Tell students the word rhymes with *jacket* but it begins with a different letter/sound. Throughout the activity, always say the word with the initial /j/ sound first. Then ask students what they think the other word says. Try these words:

join ... coin	*Jill* ... pill	*Jake* ... cake
jam ... ham	*jingle* ... mingle	*June* ... tune

Penmanship

✦ Distribute a sheet of writing paper to each student, or use **White Boards** turned to the sides with writing lines. Place the Supply Icon for *pencil* on the board or in the **Pocket Chart.** Remind students that the pictures tell them what supplies they will need and the order in which they will use them.

✦ Demonstrate how to write capital *J.* Say *Start here, and go straight down. Then curve to the left, and go back up a little bit. Capital* J.

✦ Repeat for small *j.* Say *Start here, and go straight down. Then curve to the left, and go back up a little bit. Go back to the top, and make a dot. Small* j.

✦ Now invite students to practice writing capital *J*s across the top row of the papers or boards. Have them practice writing small *j*'s across the next row. Make sure students write from left to right and from top to bottom. When they have finished, ask them to proofread, using the established procedure.

✦ Pointing to **Alphabet Sound Wall Card** *Jj*, remind students that the letter *j* makes the /j/ sound. Have them say it aloud. /j/ /j/ /j/ /j/ /j/

Guided Practice

✦ Have students complete **Skills Practice 2** page 2 for additional practice writing the letter *Jj* and identifying the initial /j/ sound.

✦ Show students the *Jj* at the top of the page so they have a model to look at as they make their letters. Have students write the capital and small forms of the letter *Jj* on the lines at the top of the page.

✦ Explain that some of the things in the pictures begin with the /j/ sound. Review each picture, and ask students if it begins with the /j/ sound. If so, have them write a small *j* on the line below the picture.

✦ After students have finished, be sure to review their work. Remember to collect and store students' finished workbook pages; they will use the pages in later lessons to proofread their penmanship from the entire unit.

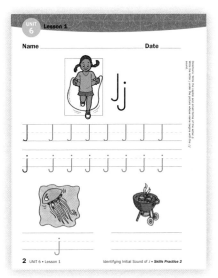

Skills Practice 2, p. 2

 Teacher Tip

USING PROGRAM MATERIALS Use *Transparency* 10 or *Alphabet Sound Wall Card Jj* to help you review the shape of *Jj.*

Monitor Progress
to Differentiate Instruction
Formal Assessment

Letter and Sound Identification Observe how well students identify the /j/ sound.

APPROACHING LEVEL

| IF ... students are having difficulty, | THEN ... guide them in completing **Reteach** pages 103 and 104. |

ON LEVEL

| IF ... students need more practice, | THEN ... continue the **Alphabet Letter Card** activity from the previous page, using the words *jet, hand, just, joke, glove, jump,* and *guess.* |

ABOVE LEVEL

| IF ... students are comfortable, | THEN ... have them work independently to complete **Challenge Activities** page 79. |

Reading and Responding

Students will

✦ locate the Table Of Contents and the title of the **Big Book.**

✦ discuss the concept of shadows.

✦ set goals for reading each selection.

✦ generate questions and statements about the theme.

✦ **My Shadow Big Book**

✦ **Home Connection,** pp. 43–44

SRA *Imagine It!*   Unit 6

My Shadow

My Shadow Big Book

From Your Teacher
Home Connection

Give each student a copy of **Home Connection** page 43. This same information is also available in Spanish on **Home Connection** page 44. Encourage students to discuss the selection "Tillie and the Wall" with their families and complete the activity provided.

Preview

Browsing the Unit

✦ Shadows fascinate children. Sometimes they are long and narrow and sometimes short and wide. Sometimes shadows disappear completely. This all depends on the light and the angle. In this unit, students' inquiry will focus on learning more about shadows as they turn wonderings into questions, develop conjectures, observe, discuss their observations, and share their new knowledge. Let the class know that their goal for this unit is to learn more about shadows.

✦ Show students the **My Shadow Big Book.** Have a volunteer come to the front of the class and identify the front and back covers. Invite students to talk about what they see on the front cover. Identify the title, read it aloud, and ask students to say it with you. Turn to the Table of Contents, and ask for a volunteer to explain the purpose of it. Discuss the contents of the **Big Book** by explaining that one of the selections is an article that gives information about shadows, one is a story about a bear's experience with his shadow, and two are poems about shadows. Browse the **Big Book** selections with students, and encourage them to make comments on the illustrations.

Setting Reading Goals

✦ Explain that the goals for reading these selections include listening for enjoyment, listening for information about how characters solve problems, and listening for ideas for answering their questions about shadows. Ask students to think of reasons for reading the first selection, "Shadows."

✦ Remind students readers are always thinking when they read. Tell them readers regularly get into the habit of setting reading goals for themselves.

Inquiry

✦ Remind students of the inquiry they did in the previous units. Ask them what they did as scientists to investigate their wonderings and questions. Just as students worked as scientists in the previous units, they will act as scientists in this unit to investigate shadows. They will learn about shadows from reading stories and poems, but they will also do activities to explore shadows: how they are made, how they change, and how to make them. Students will look for answers to their questions from books and from talking with other people as well as from making observations.

✦ Have students make a list of what they know about shadows now before they start reading. Ask the class what they want to find out or what questions they have about shadows. Responses can be in the form of statements or questions. Remind the class of the question words they have been using—how, why, when, where. Have them ask some questions about what they want to find out about shadows. List these questions under the second column of the chart. Be sure to write students' names next to the questions.

✦ Show the video clip about shadows, and take time to see if students have learned anything new about shadows or have any more questions after viewing it. Write down the new information, and post it on the **Concept/Question Board.**

Concept/Question Board

Review with students how they should use the **Concept/Question Board.** Remind students they should post their questions and wonderings about shadows on the Question side. Some students might begin by drawing pictures of their questions, while more advanced students might pose questions you could write on self-sticking notes.

Differentiating Instruction **English Learners**

IF ... students have difficulty generating questions, **THEN ...** introduce words frequently used to begin questions, such as *who, what, when, where,* and *can.* Model example questions that begin with each word, and have students echo you.

Teacher Tips

INQUIRY WORDS Write the key inquiry words on cards: *investigate, science, wonder, ask questions,* and *conjecture.* You may want to add icons to help students connect to these words. You may want to have the class make suggestions about what might be good icons for these words. The goal is to have a visual reminder of the language of inquiry so the class will begin to use these words themselves.

STUDENT WRITING At this point in the year, some children are able to write words using their developing knowledge of phonemic awareness and the alphabetic principle. You may still need to act as the transcriber for some groups. Encourage students in each group to say the words and think about each sound and what letter makes that sound. Also remind them to use the Word Bank where the high-frequency sight words are posted.

Language Arts

Students will
+ brainstorm a list of nouns.
+ view, appreciate, and react to fine art.

+ *Language Arts Big Book,* p. 53
+ *My Shadow Big Book,* p. 44

Language Arts Big Book, p. 53

 Teacher Tip

PLAN AHEAD In preparation for the following activity, have drawing paper and art supplies on hand.

Traits of Good Writing

Ideas Writers often brainstorm to develop ideas for their writing.

Writing Process

Model: Brainstorming a List of Nouns

Teach

+ Display page 53 of the *Language Arts Big Book.* Remind students that nouns are words that name something.

+ Invite volunteers to identify objects in the classroom and to say their names. Write each object identified on the board, and explain that each word is called a noun.

Apply

+ Point to the second column of items on page 53, and tell students they are all animals. Then ask students to help you brainstorm a list of animal names.

+ If time allows, point to each of the other columns, and have students brainstorm other nouns to put on lists of people (column 1), things (column 3), and places (column 4).

+ Now ask a volunteer to remind the class what brainstorming is. *working together to think of ideas*

+ Tell students they will be working together to make a thank-you card for someone who has done something nice for the class. Explain that the first step of making the card will be thinking of to whom to send it. Tell students they will work together to brainstorm ideas.

+ This writing activity will span two weeks throughout the unit. Be prepared to collect, assess, store, and reuse students' drawings and writing as you go.

Fine Art

Discussing Fine Art

✦ Turn to page 44 in the *My Shadow Big Book.* Focus students' attention on *Beach Umbrella* by David Hockney.

✦ Discuss the painting. Use questions such as the following:

- *What objects (or things) do you see in this picture?*
- *Can you tell the time of day by looking at the painting?*
- *What have you learned about shadows that can help you decide about the time of day?*

✦ Discuss the colors that Hockney uses in this painting. Ask students the following:

- *What colors do you see?*
- *Are the colors bright or dull?*
- *Are the colors like the colors that you have seen in other pictures of the beach or while you were at the beach yourselves?*

David Hockney. *Beach Umbrella.*
1971. Acrylic on canvas.
48 × 35¾ in.

 **Teacher Tip**

FOR FURTHER STUDY Students might enjoy comparing and contrasting *Beach Umbrella* with other paintings and photos of similar beach scenes.

Background Information

David Hockney (b. 1937) is a British-born painter, printmaker, photographer, and designer. He spent much of his time in California, and this beach umbrella and his colorful paintings of turquoise swimming pools reflect that state's influence. Hockney is well-known for his portraits but also for his illustrative etchings for books; notable among them is *Six Fairy Tales of the Brothers Grimm* (1969).

Differentiating Instruction | **English Learners**

IF ... your class includes English Learners from diverse cultures, **THEN ...** try to show beach or lakeside scenes from students' native cultures, and explain to the class what country each artwork shows.

Sounds and Letters

OBJECTIVES

Students will
✦ identify initial phonemes in words.
✦ blend final phonemes to make words.
✦ attach the /j/ sound to the letter *Jj*.

MATERIALS

✦ Weather Icons
✦ **Alphabet Letter Card** *Jj* for each student
✦ **Skills Practice 2**, p. 3
✦ **Alphabet Book Big Book,** pp. 22–23

Point to the box that represents today. Ask a volunteer to describe today's weather. Hold up the Weather Icons, and have the class decide on the appropriate one. Ask a student to place the Weather Icon next to the day of the week. Say *Today the weather is* _____. Have another student come up and point to the box that represents yesterday. Talk about how today's weather is similar to or different from yesterday's weather.

Warming Up

Kindergarten News

✦ Copy the text above on the board or on chart paper.

✦ Continue turning over the writing to students. Ask a student to write today's date in the blank.

✦ Ask students what letter they learned yesterday, and have someone write a *J* in the blanks of the second and third sentences. Then invite volunteers to identify and circle the capital *J* letters in the letter rows.

✦ Finish warming up by asking students what sound the letter *Jj* makes. Then practice blending initial phonemes with words such as *jug, Jill, jar, Jake,* and *jam,* using the **Lion Puppet.**

Phonemic Awareness

Phoneme Segmentation: Initial Sounds

✦ Explain to students that the **Lion Puppet** has a new game. When he hears a word, he likes to repeat only the first sound. Tell them to listen closely and, when you give the signal, to help the puppet.

Teacher:	*sailor*
Puppet:	*/s/*
Teacher:	*On the next word, help the puppet.*
Teacher:	*mister*
Everyone:	*/m/*

✦ Continue with the following words:

pail /p/	*fight* /f/	*might* /m/	*ring* /r/	*tear* /t/	*neat* /n/
beat /b/	*hole* /h/	*jail* /j/	*dart* /d/	*land* /l/	*code* /k/

Phoneme Blending: Final Sounds

✦ Tell students the **Lion Puppet** wants to play the ending-sounds blending game again. Remind them the puppet will say a word except for the end sound. You will say the final sound. Then the puppet will ask what the word is, and students should put the parts together and say the word.

✦ Practice with the following word:

Puppet:	*le …*
Teacher:	*/g/* (Emphasize the /g/ sound.)
Everyone:	*/g/*
Puppet:	*What is the word?*
Everyone:	*leg*

✦ Continue with the following words:

cro … /s/ cross	*bathtu … /b/ bathtub*	*turt … /l/ turtle*
dis … /k/ disk	*rabbi … /t/ rabbit*	*mis … /t/ mist*

Differentiating Instruction **English Learners**

IF … students have difficulty with the Phonemic Awareness activities, **THEN …** refer to Unit 6 Lesson 2 of the **English Learner Support Guide**.

 Teacher Tips

FINAL PHONEMES Remember that you, not the puppet, should say the final phoneme so students can watch your mouth as you form the sound. If students have trouble with blending, have them repeat both the beginning of the word and its final consonant individually before blending.

SUPPLEMENTAL WORDS If additional words are needed for the lesson activity, see the Appendix for a supplemental word list.

Monitor Progress

to Differentiate Instruction
Formal Assessment

Letter and Sound Identification Note how readily students identify the /j/ sound.

APPROACHING LEVEL

IF ... students are having difficulty,	THEN ... walk around the room pointing to objects—some beginning with /j/ and some not. Have them raise their hands if the objects begin with /j/.
IF ... students still have difficulty,	THEN ... refer to Unit 6 Lesson 2 of the ***Intervention Guide.***

ON LEVEL

IF ... students need more practice,	THEN ... use ***Skills Practice 2*** page 3 for additional review.

ABOVE LEVEL

IF ... students would enjoy a challenging activity,	THEN ... have them draw three pictures of objects or people whose names begin with /j/.

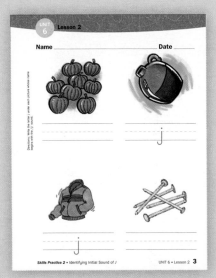

Skills Practice 2, p. 3

Alphabetic Principle

Reviewing the Sound of *Jj*

✦ Point to **Alphabet Sound Wall Card** *Jj*, and say the sound of the letter *Jj*. Once again, point out the picture for the /j/ sound, and read the short story for /j/:

Jenny and Jackson like to have fun.

They play jacks, jump rope, and juggle in the sun.

Each time they jump, their feet hit the ground.

/j/ /j/ /j/ /j/ /j/ is the jumping-rope sound.

✦ Repeat the story, emphasizing the initial /j/ sound and asking students to join you in reciting the story and saying /j/ /j/ /j/.

Listening for Initial /j/

✦ Give each student an **Alphabet Letter Card** *Jj*. Ask students to say the /j/ sound as they take their cards. Say the words *jam* and *game*. Pronounce each aloud, stressing the initial phoneme. Have students look closely at your mouth as you repeat the words to demonstrate the difference; exaggerate your mouth formations as you repeat the words. Then ask students to make the sounds by repeating the words and feeling the difference in their mouths.

✦ Have students hold up their **Alphabet Letter Cards** *Jj* and say the /j/ sound each time they hear the /j/ sound. Try these words:

jump	gap	**June**	gig	**jig**
July	Gail	go	**Joe**	**jelly**

Linking the Sound to the Letter

✦ Continue the word-pairs activity as in previous lessons. Write *Jack* and *back* on the board. Remind students the words they are looking for begin with the /j/ sound, so the correct word will begin with the /j/ sound and the letter *Jj*. Invite a volunteer to come up and point to the word that says *Jack*.

✦ Continue with the following words, and ask individual students to circle the word you say, tell how they know the correct word, and underline the letter that makes the /j/ sound.

jail ... mail	toe ... *Joe*	rim ... *Jim*
jay ... bay	*jolly* ... holly	*jumping* ... dumping

Alphabet Book Big Book—/j/

✦ Display the **Alphabet Book Big Book,** opened to pages 22–23, *Jj*. Use the rhyme to reinforce that the /j/ sound is attached to the letter *Jj*. Point to the title letters *Jj*, and have students say the name of each of the letters. *capital* J, *small* j

✦ Tell students you will read the rhyme aloud and you would like them to listen for the words that begin with the /j/ sound. Ask students to close their eyes as they listen.

✦ After reading, call on volunteers to come up to the book and to point to each word that begins with *Jj*. *Julie, jumps, just, Jaden, jokes, Janie, judges, jam, Jenna, jogs, Jordan, juggles, jacks, July, jumbo, joys* As a student points to a word, have the class say the initial /j/ sound.

✦ Ask students if they can think of another month's name—besides *July*—that begins with the /j/ sound. *January, June* Ask if they can think of any other names—besides *Julie* and the others in the rhyme—that begin with the /j/ sound. *Jamie, Joey, Jack, Jacob, Joshua, Jill*

Alphabet Book Big Book, pp. 22–23

Teacher Tip

PRINT AND BOOK AWARENESS Remember you can turn any **Big Book** activity into a teaching opportunity for print and book awareness. For this lesson on *Jj*, you might help students track print from left to right and from top to bottom, count spaces between the words in each line, or point out punctuation and capitalization.

Differentiating Instruction **English Learners**

IF ... students are native Spanish speakers, **THEN ...** they may have difficulty associating the letter *j* with the /j/ sound. In Spanish, *j* represents /h/. Provide these students with practice distinguishing between the sounds represented by English *j* and *h,* using the word pairs *jam, ham; jolly, holly; jeep, heap;* and *jail, hail.*

Technology

Each of the rhymes from the **Alphabet Book Big Book** is available on the **Listening Library CD.** Use the **eAlphabet Book** for activities that support the **Alphabet Book Big Book** lessons.

Audio CD

Reading and Responding

OBJECTIVES

Students will

✦ locate the title and the names of the author and the illustrator.

✦ connect their own life experiences to the text.

✦ develop an understanding of vocabulary words.

✦ become familiar with the unit theme My Shadow.

MATERIALS

✦ **Read Aloud Collection:** *What Makes a Shadow?*

✦ Routines 5–7

✦ **Home Connection,** pp. 45–46

Differentiating Instruction | **English Learners**

IF ... students are native speakers of Spanish, Tagalog (Filipino), Vietnamese, and some other languages, **THEN ...** they may say /s/ or /ch/ in place of /sh/ in *shadow* and *shining*. Their native languages lack the /sh/ sound. Demonstrate how to make the /sh/ sound, and provide practice saying simple words such as *shop, shape, sheep,* and *shoe*.

Vocabulary

shining	cloudy
shadow	discover

Technology

To promote independent reading, encourage students to use Workshop to listen to the recording of the selection on the **Listening Library CD.** Invite them to follow along and say the words whenever they can.

Audio CD

Read Aloud

Activate Prior Knowledge ROUTINE 5

Tell students in this unit, they will be reading and learning about shadows and how they form and change. Invite students to talk about any experiences they have had with shadows. You might prompt the discussion with questions such as *Have you ever seen your shadow get really big*? and *Have you ever seen a shadow look funny or scary?*

Preview the Selection ROUTINE 5 ROUTINE 7

✦ Display the cover of *What Makes a Shadow?* Follow Routine 5, the previewing the selection routine, as you point to and say the book title and the names of the author and the illustrator. Focus students' attention on the cover picture, and ask them to point to the shadows they see. Ask students to look at the illustrations for clues as to what the selection might tell them.

✦ Follow the reading the selection routine. Read the Focus Question printed above the **Read Aloud Collection** selection. Encourage students to listen carefully as you read to find the answer to the question. Stop to ask and answer questions about *What Makes a Shadow?*

Vocabulary ROUTINE 6

✦ Follow Routine 6, the selection vocabulary routine, as you introduce the vocabulary words for this selection.

✦ Explain that the word *shining* means "giving out bright light." Use the following sentence to illustrate: *The sun is shining very brightly today.*

✦ Tell students a *shadow* is a dark spot where light is blocked. Ask students if they can see their shadows today.

✦ Explain that the word *cloudy* means when the sky is full of clouds and you cannot see the sun. Ask students if today is sunny or cloudy.

✦ Tell students in this selection, the word *discover* means "to find out." Use the following sentence to illustrate: *Did you discover where the dog hid your shoe?*

Focus Question Where do shadows come from?

What Makes a Shadow?

by Clyde Robert Bulla

The sun is shining. It shines on the trees and the sidewalk. It shines on your house.

It shines on you, too.

When the sun is in front of you, look behind you. You can see your shadow. When you move, your shadow moves. When you run, your shadow runs. But you can never catch it.

What makes the shadow? Where does it come from?

The sun is very bright. It shines on the house. It shines on the trees. It shines on you. But the sun does not shine *through* you.

There is a dark place behind you where the sun does not shine. The darkness is your shadow.

Ask *Why does your body make a shadow behind you when the sun is in front of you?*

Look for more shadows.

A tree has a shadow. The shade of the tree is the shadow of the tree.

A house has a shadow.

The sun shines on one side of the house. There is a shadow on the other side.

Animals have shadows.

So do cars.

Airplanes have shadows. Watch as an airplane flies over your head. You may see its shadow on the ground.

A cloud has a shadow.

Sometimes the sky is dark with clouds. The sun cannot shine through them. The shadows of the clouds fall on the earth. The shadows make the day dark. We say, "This is a cloudy day."

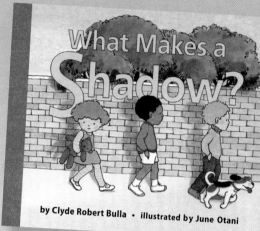

by Clyde Robert Bulla • illustrated by June Otani

What Makes a Shadow?

Some shadows are darker than others. Hold a paper towel so the sun shines on it. The paper towel makes a shadow on the ground. The shadow is not dark because some of the sunlight shines through.

Hold a book so the sun shines on it. The book makes a shadow on the ground. It makes a dark shadow because no sunlight shines through.

Ask *Why are some shadows darker than others?*

Watch the sun go down.

Watch the night come.

Night is a shadow.

The sun shines on one side of the earth. The other side is in shadow. The shadow makes the night.

Inside the house at night you can see more shadows. Hold your hand between a lamp and the wall. You will see the shadow of your hand on the wall.

Do you know how to make a big shadow?

Hold your hand close to the lamp, but not too close. The light bulb may be hot! The shadow is big because your hand shuts out so much of the light. This makes more darkness on the wall.

Move your hand away from the light. Move it farther and farther away. Now the shadow on the wall gets smaller and smaller and smaller. It is smaller because your hand does not shut out so much light. There is less darkness on the wall.

Ask *How can you make your shadow bigger or smaller?*

You can have fun with shadows. Hold your hands between the light and the wall and make shadow pictures. You can make a duck. Or a dog. Or a rabbit.

You can make shadow pictures little or big. You can move your hands to make the pictures move.

There are other shadow pictures you can make. Here are some.

Look for shadows. How many can you find?

When you find shadows, see if you can discover what makes each one.

🍎 Teacher Tip

SHADOW PLAY Because this is the introduction to the unit theme My Shadow, having students experience and observe shadows on their own is the best teaching tool.

Discuss the Read Aloud

✦ After you have finished reading *What Makes a Shadow?* invite students to ask questions about what they have heard. Turn through the pages again, and encourage students to discuss what they see in the pictures.

✦ Review the Focus Question with students: *Where do shadows come from? Shadows are made when the sun cannot shine through an object.*

✦ Lead students in a discussion of what they learned about shadows from listening to this selection. Ask them the following questions about the unit theme:

- *Why can't we see the shadow of the girl hiding behind the tree on page 8? The tree is blocking the sunlight; the girl is not.*

- *Why is a cloudy day dark? The sun cannot shine through the clouds, so the clouds make shadows on Earth.*

- *Why is it dark outside at night? The sun is shining on the other side of Earth, leaving our side of Earth in shadow.*

- *How can you tell that the sun on page 30 is behind the boy with the ball? The boy's shadow falls in front of him.*

Vocabulary Review

Review with students the selection vocabulary words *shining, shadow, cloudy,* and *discover*. Ask students the following questions:

- *When have you seen something shining?*
- *Where have you seen a shadow?*
- *What happens when the sky is cloudy?*
- *What happens when you discover something?*

Research in Action

How and *why* questions call for explanations whereas *what* and *when* questions call for descriptions. Even very young students demand explanations for *why* things happen, and teachers can play on this quality by having them explain their views on why and how shadows exist. Just as professional scientists do, they will move beyond description to explanation.

(Anne McKeough)

Differentiating Instruction **English Learners**

IF ... students need additional help with Vocabulary, **THEN ...** refer to Unit 6 Lesson 2 of the *English Learner Support Guide.*

Give each student a copy of *Home Connection* page 45. This same information is also available in Spanish on *Home Connection* page 46. Encourage students to discuss the selection "Shadows" with their families and complete the activity provided.

Language Arts

OBJECTIVES

Students will
+ brainstorm a list of possible thank-you card recipients.
+ learn about spaces between sentences.
+ participate in a Thinking Story experience.

MATERIALS

+ *Language Arts Big Book,* p. 15
+ *My Shadow Big Book,* p. 13
+ *Skills Practice 2,* p. 4
+ *Willy the Wisher,* p. 62

Writing Process

Prewrite: Brainstorming List of Card Recipients

Teach

+ Display page 15 of the **Language Arts Big Book,** and read the sentence *You've got mail.*

+ Ask students what they see on the page. Discuss each of the cards. Also discuss how the cards relate to the sentence *You've got mail.* If necessary, remind students letters and cards are quite often sent through the mail.

+ Invite students to talk about other kinds of cards with which they are familiar. *birthday cards, Mother's Day cards, Father's Day cards, wedding cards*

Guided Practice

+ Remind students they are going to write a thank-you card to someone who has done something nice for the class. Tell them to think of people whom they would like to thank for something.

+ Guide students in brainstorming a list of potential recipients for the class thank-you card. Suggest school faculty, parents who have helped with class activities, and a class visitor.

+ Write a list of at least five people on the board. Have the class vote on the choices. Tell students in the next lesson they will think of ideas to include in the card. Invite them to think about some ideas for homework.

Grammar, Usage, and Mechanics

Teach

+ Display page 13 of the **My Shadow Big Book,** and read the sentences aloud, pausing noticeably between each sentence.

+ Have students help you count the number of sentences on the page.

+ Next, point to the space between the first two sentences. Explain that spaces between sentences show readers where one sentence ends and another begins.

+ Write the following on the board: *it is lunch we eat pizza.* Do not use spaces between the words, and do not include capitalization or punctuation *(itislunchweeatpizza).*

+ Guide students in identifying where the spaces, capitalization, and punctuation should be placed.

Language Arts Big Book, p. 15

Grammar, Usage, and Mechanics continued

Guided Practice

✦ Have students open their **Skills Practice 2** to page 4.

✦ Work through the page with students, and review their answers when you finish.

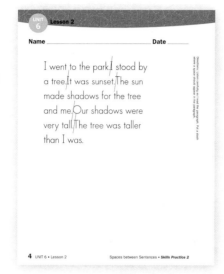

Skills Practice 2, p. 4

Monitor Progress

Formal Assessment ✓

to Differentiate Instruction

Grammar Note how easily students understand spacing.

APPROACHING LEVEL	
IF ... students are having difficulty,	**THEN ...** have students complete **Reteach** page 105.
ON LEVEL	
IF ... students need more practice,	**THEN ...** let them look through "Shadows," noting spacing.
ABOVE LEVEL	
IF ... students are comfortable,	**THEN ...** have students complete **Challenge Activities** page 80.

 ## Teacher Tip

USING THE CHARACTERS' TRAITS Try to take advantage of the particular personality traits of each character from **Willy the Wisher.** For example, Ferdie's overconfident and impulsive nature presents the opportunity for students to think about information Ferdie fails to consider.

Willy the Wisher 🕐

✦ Display the story "Ferdie and the Big Boys" on page 62 of **Willy the Wisher.**

✦ In this story, Ferdie is impulsive and overconfident. Invite students to tell what they remember about Ferdie from previous stories.

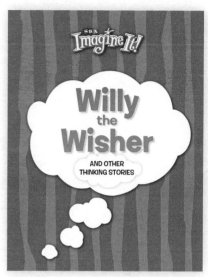

Willy the Wisher, p. 62

✦ Read the story, pausing at the red text to ask students the questions and to encourage them to share their thinking.

✦ After reading the story, have students try to explain if Ferdie's hiding places are good or not. Encourage them to think of who or what might be hiding in each place other than the big boys. Use questions such as the following:

• *What might have made the barrel move? Do you think an animal might be living in the barrel?*

• *How could Ferdie be sure of what is hiding in the barrel (standing behind the wall, living in the tree, and so on)?*

• *What lesson would you have learned from this experience if you were Ferdie? How is that lesson different from the one Ferdie learned?*

Sounds and Letters

OBJECTIVES

Students will

✦ blend final phonemes to make words.

✦ attach the /f/ sound to the letter *Ff*.

✦ practice writing the letter *Ff*.

MATERIALS

✦ ***Pickled Peppers Big Book,*** p. 43

✦ **Pocket Chart Picture Cards** 5, 58–63

✦ ***Alphabet Letter Cards*** *Ff* for each student

✦ Routine 1

✦ Supply Icons

✦ ***Skills Practice 2,*** pp. 5–6

✦ ***Transparency*** 6

Point to the box that represents today. Ask students to tell the name of the current season. Then invite students to talk about their favorite seasons and why they like those seasons the best.

Differentiating Instruction **English Learners**

IF ... students have very limited vocabulary, **THEN ...** ask them to draw pictures of their favorite seasons and something they do during those seasons that makes them their favorites.

Warming Up

MORNING MESSAGE

Today is _____.

First find Frankie the farmer and fix his finger!

Today we will learn about the letter _____.

Kindergarten News

✦ Copy the text above on the board or on chart paper. Read aloud the second sentence to students, and ask them what letter they see and what sound they hear repeated at the beginnings of words in this silly sentence. *Ff*

✦ Invite a volunteer to try to write the letter *F* in the blank of the last sentence. If the student writes the letter incorrectly, you might use hand-over-hand guidance to help him or her rewrite it correctly. Tell students they will get more practice writing the letter *Ff* today.

Focusing on Words in Print

✦ Return to the poem "Little Pine" on page 43 of the ***Pickled Peppers Big Book.*** Point to the Chinese characters that decorate the page, and explain that the poem was first written in Chinese by a poet named Wang Jian and then translated into English by someone named Minfong Ho. Explain that translating stories and poems from one language to another allows many people to learn about and share cultures and traditions from around the world.

✦ Focus attention on the first line in the poem. Call on volunteers to come to the book and to point to any words that begin with sounds and letters they have learned. Then ask them to give the sound and letter names.

✦ When a student points to a word, have him or her say the name of the initial letter then the sound the letter represents. Students should recognize most of the initial sounds and letters for the words in the first line.

Phonemic Awareness

Phoneme Blending: Final Sounds

✦ Tell students the **Lion Puppet** wants to play the ending-sounds blending game again. Remind them the puppet will say a word except for the end sound. You will say the end sound. Then the puppet will ask what the word is, and students should put the parts together and say the word.

✦ Practice with the following word:

Puppet:	*lightbul …*
Teacher:	*/b/* (Emphasize the /b/ sound.)
Everyone:	*/b/*
Puppet:	*What is the word?*
Everyone:	*lightbulb*

✦ Continue with the following words:

fin … /d/ find	*fla … /g/ flag*
bes … /t/ best	*aroun … /d/ around*
unti … /l/ until	*doorkno … /b/ doorknob*

Teacher Tip

FINAL PHONEMES Working with final consonant sounds is somewhat more difficult than working with initial sounds. You may want to provide students with more classroom support for these activities. During Workshop, work with students who need extra help.

Differentiating Instruction **English Learners**

IF … students have difficulty working with final phonemes, **THEN …** keep in mind that some languages have only one or a few consonants that appear in the final position. Provide extra practice pronouncing final consonants according to individual needs.

Alphabetic Principle

Introducing the Sound of *Ff*

✦ Refer to Routine 1 for the introducing sounds and letters procedure.

✦ Display **Alphabet Sound Wall Card** *Ff,* and say its sound. /f/ Show the picture, and recite the story for the /f/ sound:

Franny the fan spins oh, so fast.

Spreading fresh air with a regular blast.

When Franny the fan goes round and round

/f/ /f/ /f/ /f/ /f/ /f/ is her fast fan sound.

✦ Repeat the story, emphasizing the initial /f/ sound and asking students to join in on the /f/ /f/ /f/ /f/ /f/ /f/.

Alphabet Sound Wall Card 6

Listening for Initial /f/

✦ Hold up and name the following **Pocket Chart Picture Cards:** 5—four, 58—feet, 59—fish, 60—flowers, 61—footprints, 62—frog, and 63—frown. Have students repeat each word, emphasizing the /f/ sound.

✦ Give each student an **Alphabet Letter Card** *Ff.* Tell students you are going to say words and you want them to hold up the cards and say the /f/ sound when they hear a word that begins with the /f/ sound.

fame	blame	**fish**	beat	**feet**	**feel**
fit	bit	**fin**	**fist**	**fall**	ball
fat	box	**fox**	mat	bell	**fell**

Linking the Sound to the Letter

Write two words on the board, one that begins with the /f/ sound and one that does not. Say the word that begins with the /f/ sound. Ask individual students to circle the word you said and underline the letter that makes the /f/ sound, telling how they know the correct word. Try these words:

fail ... sail	past ... *fast*	sunny ... *funny*
harm ... *farm*	*found* ... sound	*fellow* ... mellow

Penmanship

✦ Distribute a sheet of writing paper to each student, or use **White Boards** turned to the sides with writing lines. Place the Supply Icon for *pencil* on the board or in the **Pocket Chart.**

✦ Use the established procedure and Routine 1 to review with students how to form a capital *F*. Say *Start at the top, and make a vertical line. Start here, and go straight out* (right). *Start here, and go straight out* (right). *Capital* F. Remind students the letter *Ff* makes the /f/ sound, and ask students to say the sound as they make the letter in the air.

✦ Review the steps for making small *f*. Say *Start here, go up a little, around, and then down. Then start here, and go straight out* (right). *Small* f.

✦ Now invite students to practice writing capital *F*s across the top row of the paper. Have them practice writing small *f*'s across the next row. Help students proofread as they have done in previous lessons.

Guided Practice

Guide students in completing **Skills Practice 2** page 5 for additional practice writing the letter *Ff* and identifying the initial /f/ sound. Have them write a row of the capital *F* letters and a row of the small *f* letters on the top two lines. Explain that some of the pictures begin with the /f/ sound. Have students write the letter *f* under each picture whose name begins with the /f/ sound.

Teacher Tip

USING PROGRAM MATERIALS Use *Transparency* 6 or *Alphabet Sound Wall Card Ff* to help you review the shape of *Ff*.

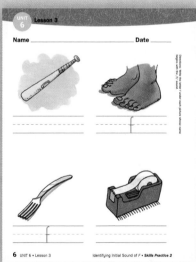

Skills Practice 2, pp. 5–6

Monitor Progress to Differentiate Instruction

Formal Assessment ✓

Letter and Sound Identification Note how readily students identify the /f/ sound.

APPROACHING LEVEL

IF ... students have difficulty, THEN ... guide them in completing **Reteach** page 106.

ON LEVEL

IF ... students need more practice, THEN ... continue the activity using **Skills Practice 2** page 6.

ABOVE LEVEL

IF ... students would enjoy a challenging activity, THEN ... have them work independently to complete **Challenge Activities** page 81.

OBJECTIVES

Students will

✦ locate the title and the name of the author.

✦ connect their own life experiences to the text.

✦ develop an understanding of vocabulary words.

✦ use the comprehension strategies Asking Questions, Clarifying, and Predicting.

✦ identify print and book features.

MATERIALS

✦ *My Shadow Big Book,* pp. 4–19

✦ Routines 5–7

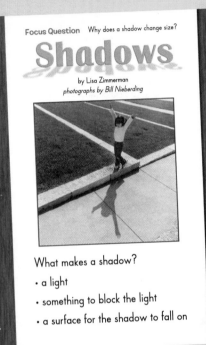

Focus Question Why does a shadow change size?

Shadows

by Lisa Zimmerman
photographs by Bill Nieberding

What makes a shadow?

• a light
• something to block the light
• a surface for the shadow to fall on

4

My Shadow Big Book, p. 4

Technology

To promote independent reading, encourage students to use Workshop to listen to the recording of the selection on the **Listening Library CD.** Invite them to follow along and to say the words whenever they can.

Audio CD

1st READ

Preview and Prepare

Activate Prior Knowledge

✦ "Shadows" is an expository, or informational, selection that introduces students to the three components necessary for shadow formation: light, something to block the light, and a surface on which the shadow falls. The text investigates how shadows are formed by common objects such as buildings, a bottle, and the human body.

✦ Ask students what they have noticed about shadows at different times of the day. Ask them to describe what shapes and sizes their shadows are in the morning, at lunchtime, and on the way home from school. Using the available light in your classroom, show students your shadow against a wall or the board. Help them notice how it moves when you move. Let them know that they will be learning many more things about shadows and light as they listen to this selection.

✦ Encourage students to discuss what they are learning about the unit theme as they listen to "Shadows." This selection provides information about what is necessary for shadow formation and photographs that show the nature of different shadows. Key concepts include the following:

• Investigation begins with questions.

• Experiments provide answers to these questions.

Preview the Selection

✦ Open the **My Shadow Big Book** to pages 4 and 5, the opening pages of "Shadows." Follow Routine 5, the previewing the selection routine, as you point to and say the title and the name of the author. Ask students why an illustrator's name does not appear. *There are photographs, not illustrations.*

✦ Turn through the pages, and focus students' attention on the photographs. Tell them to look for clues as to what the selection might tell them. Encourage students to comment on anything they find interesting or puzzling. Ask students to think of what they might learn about the unit theme My Shadow.

Vocabulary

ROUTINE **6**

✦ Follow Routine 6, the selection vocabulary routine, as you introduce the vocabulary words for this selection.

✦ Tell students the word *block* has several meanings. Explain that in this selection, it means "to keep something from passing through." Tell students people sometimes use a beach umbrella to block the sunlight.

✦ Explain that if you *climb* a mountain, you go up the mountain. Ask students what kinds of things people have to climb. *stairs, ladders, hills*

✦ Explain that when something *shines,* it gives out light. Use the following sentence to illustrate: The streetlight shines in my bedroom window.

✦ Explain that *through* means "in one side and out the other." Demonstrate by walking through the classroom door.

Read the Selection

ROUTINE **7**

✦ Before beginning the selection, read the Focus Question at the top of the first page. Tell students to keep this question in mind as they listen to the story.

✦ Follow Routine 7, the reading the selection routine, as you read the entire selection.

✦ Before, during, and after the first reading, encourage students to ask questions and to think aloud about the selection. In this way, you prepare them for the kind of thinking they will need to become independent, enthusiastic readers.

Comprehension Strategies

✦ You will introduce and model the following comprehension strategies:
  • Asking Questions
  • Clarifying
  • Predicting

✦ Think aloud through each strategy, and encourage students to share their ideas as well.

Vocabulary

block	shines
climb	through

Monitor Progress
to Differentiate Instruction
Formal Assessment

APPROACHING LEVEL

IF ... students are having difficulty with the vocabulary words,

THEN ... refer to Unit 6 Lesson 3 of the Intervention Guide.

ON LEVEL

IF ... students need to practice the vocabulary words,

THEN ... have them play Password with other students.

ABOVE LEVEL

IF ... students understand the vocabulary words,

THEN ... have them work in a small group to think of as many words as possible that are related to each vocabulary word.

Comprehension Strategies

Teacher Modeling

1 Asking Questions *Why can't the sun shine through a person? Maybe it's because a person's body is solid and doesn't let the light through the way glass does. I'll keep reading. Maybe my question will be answered later.*

2 Clarifying *In the photograph, the girl's shadow is a little crooked as it goes up the steps with her. It bends in one direction and then another. I think that zigzag means something that isn't straight, something that goes one way and then back the other way. Looking at the picture helped me clarify this.*

3 Asking Questions *I wonder why my shadow at noon is short and fat. Where is the sun at this time of day? The sun is high in the sky around noontime. Maybe this has something to do with the shape of my shadow. I'll keep reading to find out.*

4 Clarifying *The sun is always up in the sky, so I'm not quite sure what* low in the sky *means. If I picture the way the sun looks every day, I remember that in the morning and in the evening, the sun looks like it is very low. That's probably what* low in the sky *means. Thinking about what I already know helped me understand this page a little better.*

Focus Question   Why does a shadow change size?

Shadows
by Lisa Zimmerman
photographs by Bill Nieberding

What makes a shadow?
• a light
• something to block the light
• a surface for the shadow to fall on

4

I can make a shadow.

The bright sunlight shines on me, but it can't shine through me. My body blocks the sunlight and makes a shadow on the ground. **1**

5

My shadow does what I do. When I climb the wall, my shadow climbs the wall, too.

6

Sometimes my shadow does things I can't do. When I walk toward the wall, my shadow slides up the wall.

When I walk up the steps, my shadow zigzags up the steps. **2**

7

Teacher Tip

GLOSSARY The word *shines* can be found in the Glossary of the *My Shadow Big Book.*

When the sun is high in the sky, my shadow gets shorter, and it looks fat. **3**

When the sun is low in the sky, my shadow grows longer, and it looks skinny. **4**

8

9

Most things make shadows—
a tree, a fence . . .

a dog . . .   a railing . . .

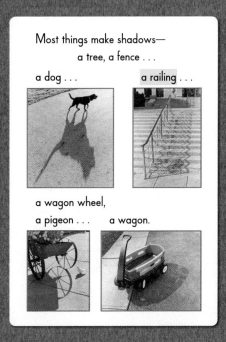

a wagon wheel,
a pigeon . . .   a wagon.

10

11

My Shadow Big Book, pp. 4–11

Print and Book Awareness

Print Directionality

Display page 5 of the *Big Book,* and have volunteers show where to start reading each sentence and where to stop. Remind students we read from left to right, that a sentence begins with a capital letter, and that some sentences end with periods. Have each volunteer run her or his hand under each line of print.

Alphabetic Knowledge

Have volunteers come to the *Big Book* to point out any letters they recognize on pages 6 and 7. Then look at page 6, and have a volunteer find and point to a word that begins with capital *M. My* Have another volunteer find a word on that page that begins with small *m. my* Say the words, then point out they are the same word. Ask if anyone knows why one begins with a capital letter and one with a small letter. If necessary, remind students capital letters are used at the beginnings of sentences.

Ellipses

Point to the first ellipsis on page 11, and explain that these three dots mean readers should pause for a moment in their reading. Demonstrate by rereading the page and pausing briefly at each ellipsis. Tell students to be on the lookout for more of these dots in the text and to let you know how to read when they see them.

Comprehension Strategies

Teacher Modeling

5 Clarifying *Most of the park in this picture is in the dark. I guess that is because the building is so big. The photograph helped me figure this out.*

6 Predicting *The picture shows that one lamp makes one shadow. What do you think would happen if there were two lamps? I predict that two lamps will make two shadows, and so on. I'll read on to see if my prediction is confirmed.*

7 Predicting *My prediction was confirmed. The picture and words tell that if there are two lamps, there are two shadows. The next picture shows three shadows. The number of lamps makes the number of shadows.*

8 Asking Questions *I can see how the shape changes the shadow. What would happen if I changed the color of the light? Does the color of the shadow change?*

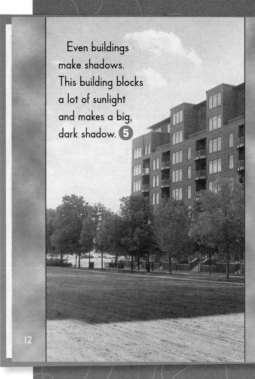

Even buildings make shadows. This building blocks a lot of sunlight and makes a big, dark shadow. **5**

12

Some things make shadows that aren't very dark at all. This bottle doesn't block much sunlight. Most of the sunlight shines right through. It makes a faint shadow.

13

Sunlight isn't the only kind of light that can make a shadow. The light from a lamp can make a shadow, too.

Two lamps make two shadows.

One lamp makes one shadow. **6**

How many lamps make three shadows? **7**

14

15

 Teacher Tip

CONFIRMING PREDICTIONS Be sure to confirm all predictions when you reach the appropriate places in the text. Also consider writing all predictions so you can refer to them throughout the selection.

I like to play with shadows. With my hands, I can make a shadow that looks like

a dog . . .

a rabbit . . .

a snail . . .

a duck . . .

a moose . . .

a bird . . .

or even the Statue of Liberty!

16   17

I can block the light with shapes cut out of cardboard and make shadow puppets.

If I hold the mouse close to the light, it blocks a lot of light. The mouse makes a big shadow.

If I move it further away from the light, it doesn't block as much light. The mouse makes a smaller shadow.

What do you need to make a shadow?
• a light
• something to block the light
• a surface for the shadow to fall on
If you change any of these three things, you can change the shadow. **8**

18   19

My Shadow Big Book, pp. 12–19

Differentiating Instruction   **English Learners**

IF . . . students have difficulty understanding the concept of prediction or stating predictions, **THEN . . .** teach them the linguistic pattern *I predict that* _____ *will* _____.

Print and Book Awareness

Picture-Text Relationship

Reread the text on pages 12–19, and have students comment about the photographs on each page. Ask *What does the photograph tell you that the story does not?*

Discussing the Selection

✦ Review the Focus Question with students: Why does a shadow change size? *The angle of the sun determines the size of the shadow.*

✦ Have students talk about the purpose of reading an infomational selection.

✦ Have students retell important facts from the selection about shadows.

Vocabulary Review

Review with students the selection vocabulary words *block, climb, shines,* and *through.* Ask students the following questions:

• *When have you tried to block something?*
• *What kinds of things can we climb?*
• *Where can we see something that shines?*
• *What kinds of things can we go through?*

Language Arts

Students will
✦ brainstorm ideas for the class thank-you card.
✦ draw and describe details missing from a story.

✦ *Language Arts Big Book,* p. 15
✦ *Story Lines Big Book,* pp. 10–11

Language Arts Big Book, p. 15

Differentiating Instruction **English Learners**

IF ... students know how to say thank you in their native languages, **THEN ...** encourage them to teach the phrase to their English-speaking classmates.

Writing Process

Prewrite: Brainstorming Ideas for a Card

Teach

✦ Display page 15 of the *Language Arts Big Book,* and ask students what they remember about the pictures on the page.

✦ Point out a get-well card that shows a picture of Doodle with chicken pox, a party invitation with a dinosaur on it, a Valentine's Day card with hearts, and a thoughtful card that wishes someone a nice day.

✦ Invite students to share anything they remember about cards they have received.

Guided Practice

✦ Remind students they are writing a thank-you card for someone who has done something nice for the class. Ask a volunteer to recall who the class chose yesterday as the recipient of the card.

✦ Tell students they must next think of what they want the card to say and what they want it to look like. Brainstorm a list of ideas for the thank-you card.

✦ When the class has generated several ideas for both pictures and words, tell them they will choose their favorite ideas in the next lesson. Record the class's ideas on paper; you will write them on the board again in the next lesson.

Story Crafting

Story Lines

✦ Display the **Story Lines Big Book,** and open it to pages 10 and 11, "Shadowland."

✦ Ask students to look at the story frames as you read the story. Tell them to listen to the story and to think about what is missing from the picture frames. As you read the captions, point to each corresponding frame.

✦ Next tell students you are going to read the story again but this time you will pause at certain frames so they can help you fill in what is missing in those frames.

✦ When you reach Frame 3, note that Jameena is missing from the frame. Draw the girl in her bed under the covers, or invite a student to come up and draw the details. Have students describe the details they are adding to the illustrations.

✦ Continue with the other frames that have blank areas.

✦ Close the activity by inviting students to talk about times they saw shadows. Begin the sharing by telling about one of your own experiences with shadows.

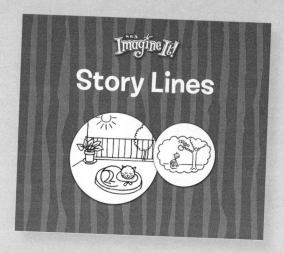

Story Lines Big Book, pp. 10–11

Teacher Tip

INTERACTIVE FRAMES Note that the illustrations for Frames 3, 4, 5, 7, 9, 10, and 11 have parts missing from the "Shadowland" story. Use these frames to help students interact with the story.

Research in Action

Support students as they begin to apply the knowledge, skills, or strategies you teach them. This can include reteaching, providing hints and reminders, giving useful feedback, and initially helping students apply what was taught.

(Steve Graham and Karen Harris)

Sounds and Letters

Students will

✦ think of words that begin with the /f/ sound.

✦ identify and match initial phonemes in words.

✦ manipulate words by deleting initial phonemes.

✦ attach the /f/ sound to the letter *Ff*.

✦ Weather Icons
✦ **Pocket Chart Picture Cards** 5, 11, 13, 49, 58–64, 66, 72, 75, 78, 86, 92, 95, 96, 102, 107, 109, 113, 117, 171, 175

✦ **Alphabet Letter Card** *Ff* for each student
✦ **Skills Practice 2,** p. 7
✦ **Alphabet Book Big Book,** pp. 14–15

Calendar

Su	M	T	W	Th	F	S
			1	2	3	4	5
6	7	8	9	10	11	12
13	14	15	16	17	18	19
20	21	22	23	24	25	26
27	28	29	30	31		

Point to the box that represents today. Have students say the name of the season again. Then ask students to tell the season that comes next. Discuss what the weather might be like in the coming months. Have the class decide on the appropriate Weather Icons for each month.

Warming Up

MORNING MESSAGE

Today's date is _____.

_____, _____, and _____ are words that begin with *Ff*.

Kindergarten News

✦ Copy the text above on the board or on chart paper. Include several errors such as missing periods, lowercase first words of sentences, and so on for students to identify. Tell students you made a few mistakes when you wrote the Morning Message, and ask them to proofread to find the errors.

✦ Use the following prompts to discuss the letters and words in the message: *How many* Ts *can you find in the message? Come circle and count them. Which word has the most letters? Come point to it. How many letters does it have? What are they?*

Oral Language

✦ Sit with students in a circle. Say *This ship is loaded with things that begin with the /f/ sound: footballs.* Then roll the ball to a student, and ask him or her to say another word that begins with the /f/ sound.

✦ Continue until students cannot think of any more /f/ words.

Phonemic Awareness

Phoneme Matching: Initial Sounds

✦ One at a time, hold up *Pocket Chart Picture Cards* 58—feet, 175—tent, and 59—fish, and have students say the name for each picture.

✦ Display the *Picture Cards* in a row, and then invite a volunteer to point to and say the names for the two pictures that begin with the same sound. Assist in identifying the picture names as necessary.

✦ Tell the volunteer to hold up one of the *Picture Cards* that she or he has named. Have the class say the name.

✦ Continue with other *Picture Card* sets and other volunteers:

11—ten, 49—dog, 171—tail *ten, tail*

109—men, 117—night, 113—moon *men, moon*

64—gate, 92—jam, 72—guitar *gate, guitar*

86—home, 75—head, 13—apple *home, head*

78—hill, 102—lamp, 107—locket *lamp, locket*

96—juice, 66—goose, 95—jug *juice, jug*

Phoneme Manipulation: Initial Sounds

✦ Continue working with initial sounds by playing the taking-away-sounds game.

Bring out the *Lion Puppet,* and tell students he wants to play the game in which he takes away sounds from words to make new words.

✦ Say a word, have students repeat it, and then have the puppet tell students to take away the beginning sound. Everyone will then say the word without the initial phoneme. For example:

Teacher: *The word is* blimp.

Students: *blimp*

Puppet: *Now take away the /b/. How do you say the word now?*

Everyone: *... limp*

✦ Continue with these words:

joker, /j/ ... oker   *stamp, /s/ ... tamp*   *jelly, /j/ ... elly*

garden, /g/ ... arden   *lost, /l/ ... ost*   *cricket, /k/ ... ricket*

Teacher Tip

FOR STRUGGLING STUDENTS For students struggling with phoneme matching, have them first identify and say aloud each word's initial sound. Then they can decide which two words begin with the same phoneme. For even more help, have them write on the board the letters that make the initial sound in each word. Then they can match the letters.

As students gain more practice with the activity, try removing one or both of these extra steps.

Technology

Have students use the *eSkills* activity for this unit for additional practice with phoneme manipulation.

Audio CD

Teacher Tip

ALPHABET REVIEW For warm-up, use the Sing Your Way to _____ game, the "Alphabet Cheer," or a quick game of Alphaball.

 Monitor Progress ✓

to Differentiate Instruction
Formal Assessment

Letter and Sound Identification Note how easily students review the /f/ sound.

APPROACHING LEVEL

IF ... students are having difficulty,

THEN ... guide them in completing **Reteach** pages 107 and 108.

ON LEVEL

IF ... students need more practice,

THEN ... have them complete **Skills Practice 2** page 7.

ABOVE LEVEL

IF ... students are comfortable,

THEN ... have them work independently to complete **Challenge Activities** page 82.

Skills Practice 2, p. 7

Alphabetic Principle 🕐

Reviewing the Sound of *Ff*

✦ Display the **Alphabet Sound Wall Card** *Ff*, and say its sound. Once again, recite the story for the /f/ sound:

Franny the fan spins oh, so fast.

Spreading fresh air with a regular blast.

When Franny the fan goes round and round

/f/ /f/ /f/ /f/ /f/ /f/ is her fast fan sound.

✦ Repeat the story, emphasizing the initial /f/ sound and asking students to join in on the /f/ /f/ /f/ /f/ /f/ /f/.

✦ Review **Pocket Chart Picture Cards** for the initial /f/ sound: 58—feet, 59—fish, 60—flowers, 61—footprints, 5—four, 62—frog, 63—frown.

Listening for Final /f/

Give each student an **Alphabet Letter Card** *Ff*. Tell students you are going to say words and you want them to hold up the cards and say /f/ when they hear a word that ends with the /f/ sound. Try these words:

off	*ant*	**half**	*hat*	*cat*	**calf**
huff	**puff**	*pet*	**leaf**	**reef**	*red*

Linking the Sound to the Letter

✦ Write the following word pairs on the board:

puff ... put   *mat ... muff*

huff ... hit   *cut ... cuff*

✦ Ask students which word in each pair ends with the /f/ sound.

✦ Point to *puff,* and explain that when they see two letter f's at the end of a word it makes one sound: */f/.* Point to *huff, muff,* and *cuff,* and say the /f/ sound as you run your finger under the *ff* spelling.

✦ Tell students the final /f/ sound can be made by just one *f* too. Write these pairs on the board, and repeat the activity having students identify the word with ending sound /f/ and tell how they knew the correct word.

if ... in   *elf ... end*

sent ... self   *beef ... bean*

Alphabet Book Big Book—/f/

✦ Display the **Alphabet Book Big Book,** and turn to pages 14–15, *Ff.* Invite a volunteer to come to the book and to point to the first word on the page. *four* Now ask the student to point to the last word on the page. *chins* Say the two words aloud, and ask the class which word begins with the /f/ sound. *Four* Ask them what letter ends the last word. *s*

✦ Then use the rhyme to reinforce how the /f/ sound is attached to the letter *Ff.* Point to the title letters *Ff,* and have students say the name of each of the letters. *capital* F, *small* f

✦ Tell students you will read the rhyme aloud and you would like them to listen for the words that begin with the /f/ sound. When finished reading, invite students to say any words beginning with /f/ they noticed while you read the rhyme aloud. *Four, funny, fishes, Fanned, fancy, fins, Feasted, fish, food, furry*

✦ Tell students you will read the rhyme once more and they should listen for words that end with the /f/ sound. Reread the rhyme, pointing to each word as you say it. Make sure students understand that no words in the rhyme end with the /f/ sound.

Four funny fishes
Fanned their fancy fins,
Feasted on some fish food,
And licked their furry chins.

Alphabet Book Big Book, pp. 14–15

Technology

Each of the rhymes from the **Alphabet Book Big Book** is available on the **Listening Library CD.** Use the **eAlphabet Book** for activities that support the **Alphabet Book Big Book** lessons.

Audio CD

Reading and Responding

Students will

✦ locate the Table of Contents, the title, and the name of the author.

✦ use the comprehension skill Cause and Effect.

✦ review the comprehension strategies Asking Questions, Clarifying, and Predicting.

✦ analyze the text structure of the selection.

✦ *My Shadow Big Book,* pp. 4–19

✦ Routines 5–7

Focus Question   Why does a shadow change size?

Shadows

by Lisa Zimmerman

photographs by Bill Nieberding

What makes a shadow?

• a light

• something to block the light

• a surface for the shadow to fall on

4

My Shadow Big Book, p. 4

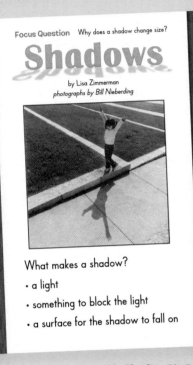

Vocabulary

slides	railing
zigzags	faint

Preview and Prepare

2nd READ

Preview the Selection   ROUTINE **5**

✦ Display the *My Shadow Big Book* opened to the Table of Contents page. Use Routine 5, the previewing the selection routine, to guide students in understanding and using the Table of Contents to locate "Shadows." Then point to and say the title and the name of the author.

✦ Prepare to reread the selection. As you turn through the pages, have students use the photographs to retell important facts from the selection.

Vocabulary   ROUTINE **6**

✦ Follow Routine 6, the selection vocabulary routine, as you introduce the vocabulary words for this selection.

✦ Explain that the word *slides* means "moves smoothly." Use the following sentence to illustrate: *She slides across the ice on one skate.* Demonstrate by sliding something across a table.

✦ Tell students the word *zigzags* means "makes short sharp turns." Ask a volunteer to zigzag across the floor. Then say _____ *zigzags across the floor.*

✦ Explain that a *railing* is a long bar on posts to hold on to when climbing stairs. Ask students if they have a railing anywhere in their homes.

✦ Tell students the word *faint* has several meanings. Explain that in this selection, it means "hard to see." Use the following sentence to illustrate: *The vase made only a faint shadow on the wall.*

Read the Selection

ROUTINE

Comprehension Strategies

✦ During the first reading of "Shadows," you introduced and modeled the following comprehension strategies:
  • Asking Questions
  • Clarifying
  • Predicting

✦ In this second reading of the selection, you will revisit each comprehension strategy model from the first reading.

Comprehension Skills

In this lesson of "Shadows," students will use the comprehension skill Cause and Effect.

Reading with a Writer's Eye

✦ In this rereading of "Shadows," you will discuss the techniques the author uses so readers better understand the information about shadows.

✦ By learning about the writing techniques the author uses, students become more aware of ways to improve their own group writing.

Concept/Question Board

Tell students readers keep thinking about any questions that are generated as they are reading. As they read, tell them to keep in mind the questions on the **Concept/Question Board.** Tell them readers are always thinking about what is important in selections and they try to remember this important information.

Technology

To promote independent reading, encourage students to use Workshop to listen to the recording of the selection on the *Listening Library CD.* Invite them to follow along and to say the words whenever they can.

Audio CD

Comprehension Strategies

Teacher Modeling

❶ Asking Questions *Let's think about some of our own questions. We wondered why light can't shine through a person. I thought we might learn more by reading on. I was right; our question was answered. A person's body blocks the light. Asking the question made us want to keep reading to find the answer.*

❷ Clarifying *Readers learn to use the words and the pictures to help them figure out things that might be confusing. When we first saw the word zigzag, we didn't know what it meant. We used the picture to help us clarify what zigzag means.*

❸ Asking Questions *When we wondered why a shadow was fat at noon, I knew we should keep reading to try to find the answer. The words on page 8 helped us understand why a shadow looks fat when the sun is high in the sky.*

❹ Clarifying *When we were confused about where the sun was and what low in the sky meant, I remembered readers use what they already know to help them clarify words and ideas. By using what we already knew about the sun, we could clarify this idea.*

Vocabulary Tip

Review the meanings of the words *slides* and *zigzags*. Then have students use the words in sentences.

Focus Question Why does a shadow change size?

Shadows
by Lisa Zimmerman
photographs by Bill Nieberding

What makes a shadow?
• a light
• something to block the light
• a surface for the shadow to fall on

4

I can make a shadow.
The bright sunlight shines on me, but it can't shine through me. My body blocks the sunlight and makes a shadow on the ground. ❶

5

My shadow does what I do. When I climb the wall, my shadow climbs the wall, too.

6

Sometimes my shadow does things I can't do. When I walk toward the wall, my shadow slides up the wall.

When I walk up the steps, my shadow zigzags up the steps. ❷

7

🍎 Teacher Tip

GLOSSARY The words *zigzags* and *railing* can be found in the Glossary of the ***My Shadow Big Book***.

When the sun is high in the sky, my shadow gets shorter, and it looks fat. **3**

8

When the sun is low in the sky, my shadow grows longer, and it looks skinny. **4**

9

Most things make shadows—
a tree, a fence . . .

a dog . . .

a railing . . .

a wagon wheel,
a pigeon . . .

a wagon.

10

11

My Shadow Big Book, pp. 4–11

Vocabulary Tip

Review the meaning of the word *railing.* Then have students use the word in a sentence.

Comprehension Skills

Cause and Effect

✦ Review *cause* and *effect* with students by explaining that certain things make other things happen.

✦ Help students use the selection to find the answers to these cause-and-effect questions:

- *What causes the girl's body to form a shadow?*
- *What causes the girl's shadow to climb the wall?*

Reading with a Writer's Eye

Text Structure: Techniques

✦ Explain to students that people write information books such as "Shadows" because people believe they have something important to say. Authors look for clear and simple ways to present information.

✦ Display page 4 of the **Big Book** as you reread the text. Ask volunteers to run their hands first under the words that ask the question and then under the words that answer the question. Point to the three bullets, and tell students these marks show the answers. Ask students how beginning the book with a question and answers helps them understand better.

✦ Point out that each photograph shows a real-life example of the information shared. Ask students how words and photos work together to make the information clear.

Reading and Responding

2nd READ

Comprehension Strategies

Teacher Modeling

5 Clarifying *Do you remember that we stopped to clarify why the park was so dark? Who can explain what we learned?*

6 Predicting *Readers try to predict, or tell what might happen next, when they read. When we read one lamp makes one shadow, we predicted two lamps would make two shadows and so on. Sometimes predictions are confirmed, and other times they are not. What did we learn that helped us make our prediction?*

7 Predicting *Reading on helped us find out that our prediction was correct. The number of lamps makes the same number of shadows. Both the words and photographs told me this.*

8 Asking Questions *This selection made me think of other questions. Because this is the end of the selection, I know we will have to look someplace else to find the answers. Readers often use other books or ask others to help them find the answers to their questions. Where else could we find information about shadows?*

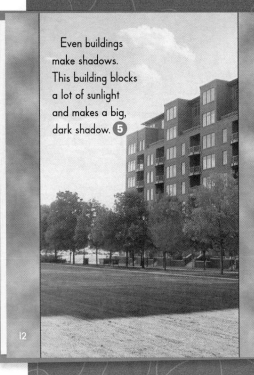

Even buildings make shadows. This building blocks a lot of sunlight and makes a big, dark shadow. **5**

12

Some things make shadows that aren't very dark at all. This bottle doesn't block much sunlight. Most of the sunlight shines right through. It makes a faint shadow.

13

Sunlight isn't the only kind of light that can make a shadow. The light from a lamp can make a shadow, too.

One lamp makes one shadow. **6**

Two lamps make two shadows.

How many lamps make three shadows? **7**

14

15

Vocabulary Tip

Review the meaning of the word *railing*. Then have students use the word in a sentence.

I like to play with shadows. With my hands, I can make a shadow that looks like

a dog . . .

a rabbit . . .

a snail . . .

16

a duck . . .   a moose . . .

a bird . . .   or even the Statue of Liberty!

17

I can block the light with shapes cut out of cardboard and make shadow puppets.

If I hold the mouse close to the light, it blocks a lot of light. The mouse makes a big shadow.

If I move it further away from the light, it doesn't block as much light. The mouse makes a smaller shadow.

18

What do you need to make a shadow?
- a light
- something to block the light
- a surface for the shadow to fall on

If you change any of these three things, you can change the shadow. ⑧

19

My Shadow Big Book, pp. 12–19

BIG Idea

Why do shadows come and go?

Write the Big Idea question on the board. Ask students what they have learned about shadows. Ask which selections added something new to their understanding about shadows.

Reading with a Writer's Eye

Text Structure: Techniques

✦ Display pages 16–17 of the **My Shadow Big Book** as you reread the text. Ask students what the three dots tell them to do. Ask how the ellipsis helps them better understand the information on these pages.

Discussing the Selection

✦ Help students identify the information they learned about shadows from this selection.

✦ Have students visit the school library and select a non-fiction text to read for pleasure.

Purposes for Reading

Remind students we read this selection to learn more about shadows. Ask students if this selection answered all their questions.

Vocabulary Review

Review with students the selection vocabulary words *slides, zigzags, railing,* and *faint.* Ask students the following questions:

- *What happens when something slides?*
- *How can we make zigzags?*
- *Where might we see a railing at school?*
- *What does it mean when something is faint?*

Language Arts

Students will

✦ sequence ideas chosen for the class thank-you card.

✦ review identifying the thoughts and feelings of a character.

✦ change and add to a story's plot.

✦ *Skills Practice 2,* p. 8

✦ *Story Lines Big Book,* pp, 10–11

✦ Thought Cloud display card

Writing Process

Model: Choosing and Sequencing Ideas

Teach

✦ Remind students that they are working as a class to write a thank-you card for someone who did something nice for the class.

✦ Display the ideas for pictures and words that the class collaborated on yesterday. Then discuss with students the person for whom they are making the card and the reason they would like to thank this person.

✦ Review the lists of ideas aloud. Guide students in choosing the ideas that best fit the tone and purpose of the card.

Guided Practice

✦ Write on the board the ideas the class has chosen to include in the card. Tell students it is time to decide where these ideas will go on the card. Explain that the class will work together to put the ideas in order.

✦ Suggest the numeral *1* will show ideas that go on the front of the card, the numeral *2* will show ideas that go on the first inside page (left), and the numeral *3* will show ideas that go on the second inside page (right).

✦ Guide students in planning the card by helping them use the numerals to sequence the ideas.

✦ Record the plan to use the following day, when the class will work together to craft the card.

Grammar, Usage, and Mechanics

Teach

✦ Remind students writers use special names (nouns), exciting action words (verbs), and words that tell how things look, taste, sound, feel, and smell. Point out that using different kinds of words helps writers make their writing interesting.

✦ Tell students another way to make writing interesting is by using sentences that do not repeat the same words. Write these sentences on the board:

I am Jared. I am five. I am a baseball player.

✦ Read the sentences to students, and point out how each one begins with the words *I am.* Tell students repeating the same words to begin sentences makes reading boring for a reader. Now write these sentences on the board:

My name is Jared. I am five. I love to play baseball.

Differentiating Instruction | **English Learners**

IF ... students need to review the names of numbers, **THEN ...** say each number's name as you write it on the board, and have students echo you.

Traits of Good Writing

Organizing Writers often use lists to help organize their ideas and notes before beginning to write.

Grammar, Usage, and Mechanics *continued*

Guided Practice

✦ Have students open their ***Skills Practice 2*** to page 8.

✦ Guide students in completing the page. When finished, review students' work carefully.

Skills Practice 2, p. 8

 Monitor Progress

Formal Assessment ✓

to Differentiate Instruction

Grammar Note how quickly students are able to use capital letters and punctuation.

APPROACHING LEVEL

IF ... students are having difficulty,

THEN ... refer to Unit 6 Lesson 4 of the ***Intervention Guide*** for additional support of the Grammar activity.

ON LEVEL

IF ... students need more practice,

THEN ... let them work with partners identifying capital letters and punctuation in *What Makes a Shadow?*

ABOVE LEVEL

IF ... students are comfortable,

THEN ... have them make a simple sentence.

Teacher Tip

SKILL REVIEW This activity reviews the skill Identifying Thoughts and Feelings to help students become more familiar with the character Jameena. In a later lesson, students will use their own creativity to continue Jameena's story. If time permits, students might benefit from also reviewing the skill Working with Problem/ Resolution Plots. To do so, help students identify the story's problem, the idea to fix it, and the resolution. *the scary shadows, calling grandmother, grandmother explaining the cause of the shadows*

Story Crafting ⏱

Story Lines

✦ Display the ***Story Lines Big Book,*** and open it to pages 10–11, "Shadowland."

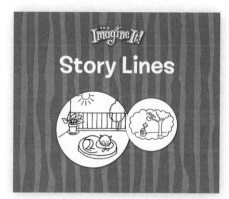

Story Lines Big Book, pp. 10–11

✦ Remind students that thought clouds are a way of showing what characters in a story think and feel.

✦ Tell students they will continue working with the story, "Shadowland." Explain that you are going to read the story again and stop at some places to hold up the Thought Cloud display card. Say *When I hold up the card, I want you to tell me what Jameena is thinking or feeling at this part of the story.* Briefly review the story drawings, stopping at a few frames to ask what Jameena might be thinking or feeling.

✦ Then ask students if they would like to add anything else to the story drawings. Work through the story frame by frame, encouraging students to provide new details to include.

✦ Ask students if they wonder what happens to Jameena and her grandmother after the story ends. Point out the extender frames, and tell students that in a later lesson they will get the chance to tell more about Jameena.

Sounds and Letters

Students will

+ identify matching initial phonemes in groups of words.
+ attach the /j/ and /f/ sounds to the letters *Jj* and *Ff*.
+ practice writing the letters *Jj* and *Ff*.
+ practice sound-by-sound blending.
+ read and respond to a **Decodable.**

+ **Alphabet Letter Cards** *Jj* and *Ff* for each student
+ Supply Icons
+ **Skills Practice 2,** pp. 9–10
+ **Decodable** 8
+ Routines 2, 4

Calendar

Su	M	T	W	Th	F	S
		1	2	3	4	5
6	7	8	9	10	11	12
13	14	15	16	17	18	19
20	21	22	23	24	25	26
27	28	29	30	31		

Point to the box that represents today. Have students say the name of the season again. Then make a simple four-column chart on the board, and write the names of the seasons as the headers of the columns. Have students tell what kinds of activities they participate in during each season, and list each activity in the appropriate column.

Differentiating Instruction | **English Learners**

IF ... students have very limited vocabulary, **THEN ...** ask them to illustrate or role-play the activities they participate in during each season. Write the names of the activities on the chart, and teach students how to say them in English.

Warming Up

M☀RNING MESSAGE

Good morning, boys and girls!

Today is _____. What color is your hair?

Let's play a game!

Kindergarten News

+ Copy the text above on the board or on chart paper. Use a self-sticking note to cover the word *game* in the fourth sentence; it can be today's Secret Word.

+ Read all four sentences, saying the word *blank* in place of the word *game* in the fourth sentence. Tell students today's Morning Message has a Secret Word. Read the fourth sentence again, and ask students to determine the Secret Word. Discuss the clues that led them to finding the correct word.

+ Then invite a student to come up to the board and to make a star next to the question, a check mark next to an exclamatory sentence, and an *X* next to the statement. Discuss with students how they can identify the three types of sentences. *end marks*

Oral Language

+ Tell students you are going to play the Catch the Letter Train game. Point to **Alphabet Sound Wall Card** *Jj*, and tell them to catch the train, they must say a word that begins with the sound for the letter *Jj*—/j/. Tell students they are allowed to say a person's name that begins with the /j/ sound.

✦ To review the /f/ sound, make silly sentences with students that involve words that start with the initial /f/ sound. Keep extending the sentences. For example:

Find the fish.

Find the funny fish.

Find and fan the funny fish.

Find and fan the four funny fish.

Phonemic Awareness

Phoneme Matching: Initial Sounds

✦ Bring out the *Lion Puppet,* and tell students he wants to play a sound-matching game again. Tell students you will say three words and they should listen closely to find the two words that begin with the same sound and then say what sound they share.

✦ Say three words, with two of the words beginning with the same phoneme. For example:

Teacher:	*jungle, garden, garage*
Puppet:	*Which words begin the same?*
Everyone:	*garden, garage* The beginning sound is /g/.

✦ Continue with these words:

horse	*goose*	*hand*	*horse, hand*	/h/
join	*gold*	*June*	*join, June*	/j/
morning	*number*	*milk*	*morning, milk*	/m/
picnic	*balloon*	*basket*	*balloon, basket*	/b/
danger	*teacher*	*ticket*	*teacher, ticket*	/t/

Teacher Tip

FOR STRUGGLING STUDENTS Some students might be confused by the sounds that begin various syllables in words. If students are having difficulty matching initial phonemes, consider using sets of one-syllable words only, such as *dip / dive / bait, sad / cart / such,* and *pay / ring / roof.*

Teacher Tip

Jj AS A FINAL CONSONANT If a curious student questions why they are not working with words that have the letter *j* at the end, explain that *j* is a special letter that does not usually appear at the ends of words.

Alphabetic Principle

Reviewing the Sounds of *Jj* and *Ff*

✦ Review the **Alphabet Sound Wall Card** for *Jj*. Read the story, and ask students to say the words along with you. Have them say /j/ /j/ /j/ to make the jumping-rope sound.

✦ Now point to the **Alphabet Sound Wall Card** for *Ff*, and have students tell what they remember about Franny the fan. Then recite the story, stressing the /f/ sound at the beginnings of words.

Listening for Initial /j/ and /f/

Give each student one *Jj* and one *Ff* **Alphabet Letter Card.** Tell them you will say a word and they should repeat it. Say that if a word starts with the /j/ sound, on your signal, they should hold up their **Alphabet Letter Cards** *Jj* and say /j/. If it starts with the /f/ sound, they should hold up their **Alphabet Letter Cards** *Ff* and say /f/. Try the following words:

just	*fox*	*jam*	*feel*
joke	*four*	*fool*	*joy*
feet	*jet*	*June*	*jack*
finger	*jelly*	*furry*	*funny*

Linking the Sound to the Letter

Write a pair of words on the board, one ending with the /f/ sound and the other ending with a different consonant sound. Say the word ending with the /f/ sound for each word pair. Have students identify the word you said by signaling thumbs-up when you point to it. For example, point to the first word pair, and ask *Which word says* leaf? Point to each word, and have students signal the correct one and then tell how they know which one you said. *Leaf ends with the /f/ sound and the letter* f.

lead ... *leaf*	*off* ... odd
wolf ... wool	*puff* ... pull
scab ... *scarf*	*cliff* ... cab

Penmanship

✦ Distribute a sheet of writing paper to each student, or use **White Boards** turned to the sides with writing lines. Place the Supply Icon for *pencil* on the board or in the **Pocket Chart.**

✦ Model how to write letter *Jj* on the board again. Then ask students to write one row of capital *J* letters and one row of small *j* letters.

✦ Then have them turn over the paper and write one row of capital *F*s and one row of small *f*'s after modeling the letter on the board.

Guided Practice

✦ Have students complete **Skills Practice 2** page 9 for additional practice writing the letters *Jj* and *Ff* and identifying the initial /j/ and /f/ sounds.

✦ Review each picture, and ask students if it begins with the /j/ sound or the /f/ sound. Have them circle the correct word and then write the letter that makes the /j/ or /f/ sound.

✦ After students have finished, tell them it is time to proofread their work. If possible, return some or all of the **Skills Practice 2** pages students have completed so far this unit.

✦ Ask students to proofread by looking for any letters they have written that they could write better. Have them use a colored pencil to rewrite one or two letters on each page. Invite volunteers to "show off" their improvements to their classmates.

Monitor Progress

Formal Assessment ✔

to Differentiate Instruction

Letter and Sound Identification Observe how easily students identify the /f/ sound.

APPROACHING LEVEL

IF . . . students are having difficulty,   THEN . . . guide them in completing **Reteach** page 109.

ON LEVEL

IF . . . students need more practice,   THEN . . . have them complete **Skills Practice 2** page 10.

ABOVE LEVEL

IF . . . students are comfortable,   THEN . . . have them work independently to complete **Challenge Activities** page 83.

Differentiating Instruction **English Learners**

IF . . . students have difficulty with penmanship, **THEN . . .** remember that some students may be more familiar with other writing systems than they are with the Roman alphabet (for example, students whose native language is Khmer). Be alert for students who need extra help with penmanship.

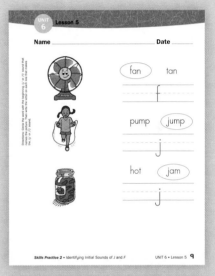

Skills Practice 2, pp. 9–10

Jam Pot

by Giulia Verzariu   illustrated by Steve Henry

Decodable 8

![apple icon] **Teacher Tips**

SOUNDS AND LETTERS Remember that each *Decodable* focuses on the sounds and letters students have learned in recent lessons. Take every opportunity to review the sounds and letters as you come across them in the *Decodables, Big Books,* and other classroom print.

STUDENT PRACTICE Before sending home the takehome versions of the *Decodables,* listen to students read a page or two during Workshop to be sure they are comfortable and confident reading their books.

Technology

Use *eDecodable Jam Pot* to reinforce high-frequency word *for* and the /j/ and /f/ sounds.

 **Audio CD**

Reading a Decodable

ROUTINE **2** ROUTINE **4**

> **Decodable 8:** *Jam Pot*

High-Frequency Word: *for*

✦ The high-frequency word introduced is *for.* Write *for* on the board, and read it aloud. Have students repeat it aloud with you. Then have students say the word on their own.

✦ Point again to *for* written on the board, and have students read the word independently.

✦ Have students work with partners to say a few sentences using the word *for.*

✦ Tell students they will often see the word *for* in books, on posters, and in other print. Ask them to find and point to examples on any classroom posters, bulletin boards, or covers of any books.

✦ Review the high-frequency words introduced in previous lessons.

Blending

Before reading **Decodable** 8, review the sound-by-sound blending procedure with students. Choose words with the /j/ and /f/ sounds and other sounds students have already learned, such as *job, flip,* and *fit.* After blending, have students make and extend sentences for each word.

Reading Recommendations

✦ Distribute copies of **Decodable** 8. Ask students to browse the books and look at the pictures, commenting on what they see and making predictions about what they think the story will be about.

✦ Point to the high-frequency word *for* in the text, and pronounce it. Then have students point to the word and read it aloud.

✦ Hold up your book, and read the title, pointing to each word. Read the names of the author and the illustrator aloud, pointing to each name as you say it. Ask students to explain the jobs of author and illustrator.

✦ Read the **Decodable,** following the established procedure. (See Routine 4 for a detailed description.) As students read independently, make sure they are reading from left to right. After you have read the story, reread the title, and have students repeat after you. Then have students read it chorally with you.

Jam Pot

by Giulia Verzariu   illustrated by Steve Henry

Jim, a big jam pot!

3

Jim, grab the jam pot!

4

Jim flips for fig jam!

5

See Fran jog in fog.

6

See the jam pot drop.

7

Fran drops jam for Jim!

8

Decodable 8
Jam Pot

High-Frequency Word
Introduced in Decodable 8
for

Previously Introduced
High-Frequency Words
a
am
and
as
at
can
did
girl
go
had
has
he
him
his
I
in
is
it
of
on
see
the
to
we
you

Sound-Spelling Correspondences in
Decodables
1. /s/, /m/, /d/, /p/, /a/
2. /h/, /t/
3. /n/, /l/
4. /i/
5. /b/, /k/ spelled c
6. /o/, /r/
7. /g/
8. /j/, /f/

Responding

◆ Display the **High-Frequency Flash Card** *for.* Have students find and point to the high-frequency word *for* in the story. Ask students to identify in the story any of the previously introduced high-frequency words.

◆ Invite students to point out any difficult words that they encountered while they read the story. Work as a class to blend the words sound by sound.

◆ Ask students to turn to page 6. Challenge students to find the words on the page that rhyme *(jog, fog).* Call on students who are reluctant to volunteer to say other words that rhyme with *jog* and *fog.*

◆ Have students work in pairs to partner-read the story. Then have them point to and count the number of times they see the jam pot in the story. After a few minutes of practice, invite a few pairs to partner-read the story aloud for the class.

◆ Make copies of the story for the students to take home. A black-and-white version of the story is available in **Pre-Decodable and Decodable Takehomes Blackline Masters.**

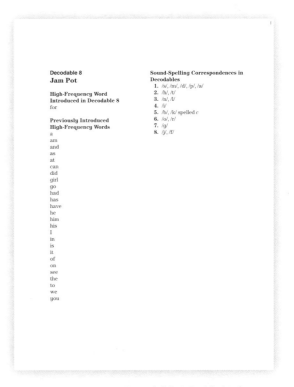

Decodable 8, inside back cover

Reading and Responding

OBJECTIVES

Students will
+ generate questions about shadows for research.
+ experiment with making shadows.
+ describe their observations orally.

MATERIALS
+ *My Shadow Big Book,* pp. 4–19

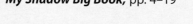

Inquiry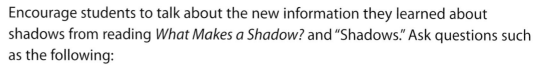

Encourage students to talk about the new information they learned about shadows from reading *What Makes a Shadow?* and "Shadows." Ask questions such as the following:

* *What did we learn about how to make a shadow?*
* *What makes shadows?*
* *Why does a shadow disappear?*
* *Why do shadows change sizes?*

Small-Group Time **Small Group**

+ Quickly review what it takes to make a shadow—a light source, an object, and a surface. Organize the class into small groups. Have each group find a place next to the wall. If you do not have enough clean wall space, hang pieces of chart paper on the walls. Give each group a flashlight, and darken the room.

+ Have students make shadows by placing various people and things between the light and the wall. Have students experiment with making shadows bigger or smaller. Have one student stand between the person holding the light and the wall. What happens as the person holding the light changes angles? What happens when the person holding the flashlight moves it up or down but still focuses on the person or object between the light and the wall? What happens when the person holding the flashlight moves closer to the object? What happens when the student moves farther away? Have two students stand in front of the light with space between them and then close together. How do the shadows change?

Inquiry Planner

WEEK 1	+ Begin discussing and sharing ideas. + Think about a question for the **Concept/ Question Board.**
WEEK 2	+ Begin investigating and collecting information. + Generate a question and/or idea for the **Concept/Question Board.**
WEEK 3	+ Share your findings with others. + Do you have more questions?

 Teacher Tips

INQUIRY A major aim of *Imagine It!* is to have students use reading as a means of knowledge building. Inquiry is at the root of knowledge building, and knowledge building is at the root of reading. Throughout each selection, have students reflect on the new knowledge they are constructing about shadows.

MATERIALS Activities for this lesson will require chart paper, markers, flashlights, and index cards.

Whole-Group Time [Whole Group]

Set up a chart with two columns: Position and What Happens. Have students discuss how the shadows change, depending on where the light is. For example, when the light source is farther away, the shadow is smaller. Do this over several days with the class, noting their observations on the chart. Let the class know they were doing an experiment—a test done by a scientist to discover why things happen. They did various things with the light source, they watched what happened, they observed, and then they charted what they saw.

Concept Vocabulary

The first concept vocabulary word for Unit 6, My Shadow, is *sunlight*. Write the word on an index card, and post it in your room. Explain to students that the word *sunlight* refers to the light that comes from the sun. Discuss what *sunlight* has to do with the formation of shadows. Use the word in a sentence, and have students practice saying it. Remind students you will use this word each day, and encourage them to use it as well. The more you use the word, the more students will feel comfortable using it too. Encourage students to bring in pictures that show *sunlight* to post on the **Concept/Question Board.**

Concept/Question Board

Read aloud any of the questions about shadows that have been added throughout the week to the **Concept/Question Board.** As you read each question, encourage students to think of possible answers. If time allows, talk about anything else students have brought in to share with the class about shadows. The more interest you show, the more interest students will have in this investigation.

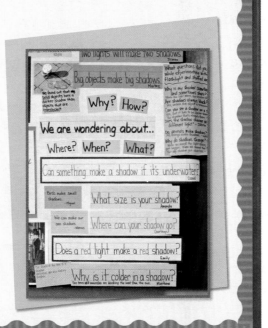

Differentiating Instruction — **English Learners**

IF ... students have difficulty understanding the meaning of *sunlight*, **THEN ...** use pictures and/or demonstrations (for example, turning classroom lights off and on) to show meanings of the two parts of the word.

 Teacher Tips

SHADOW ACTIVITY If you have a digital camera, have students take pictures of just the shadows and build a shadow book. Have students label the shadows even if the pictures do not include the actual object, only the shadow. Or, you can take pictures of the object and shadow separately, create a shadow game for Workshop, and have the students match up the shadow with the object.

SHADOW ACTIVITY During this unit, have students go on a shadow hunt when they are outside. Have them name all the different shadows they saw, what the light source was, and what they know about the light source—it was close, far away, high in the sky, and so on.

RECREATIONAL READING Because it is important to read daily to your students, choose a book from the Additional Reading listed in the Unit Overview and find a time during the day to read the book aloud to your students.

OBJECTIVES

Students will
✦ collaborate to create a thank-you card.
✦ review spacing between sentences.
✦ review varied sentence beginnings.
✦ review the letters/sounds of *Jj* and *Ff* through game play.

MATERIALS
✦ *Language Arts Big Book,* p. 39
✦ *My Shadow Big Book,* p. 35
✦ *My Neighborhood game mats*
✦ *Alphabet Letter Cards*
✦ Number cubes

Writing Process

Draft: Collaborating to Craft Card

Teach

✦ Display page 39 of the *Language Arts Big Book.* Discuss with students what is happening in each picture. Point out the words *First, Next,* and *Last.* Encourage students to talk about how the steps of making a card must be done in order.

✦ Tell students today they will make a card like students in the pictures did.

Apply

✦ Write on the board the plans for the card students made in the previous lesson. Display the ideas in the proper order: what will appear on the front page, then on the first inside page, and then on the second inside page.

✦ Review the ideas for the front page, and read aloud each idea.

✦ Take out a sheet of drawing paper, and tape it onto the board. Tell students you will draw the card based on what they tell you to do. Have students tell you where to place items for the front page of the card.

✦ Continue for the two inside pages. When finished, tell students you will keep the card until next week, when they can put their finishing touches on it.

Grammar, Usage, and Mechanics

Teach

✦ Remind students that writers put spaces between sentences to help readers know where one sentence ends and another one begins.

✦ Then write the following sentences on the board: *His shirt is too big. His shirt is inside out.* Ask students how these sentences could be better. Remind them that writers should make the beginning of a sentence different from the ones around it. Invite students to change the second sentence to make it begin differently than the first. *He wears his shirt inside out.*

Language Arts Big Book, p. 39

 **Teacher Tip**

PLAN AHEAD In preparation for the following activity, have drawing paper and art supplies on hand.

Grammar, Usage, and Mechanics continued

Guided Practice

✦ Display page 35 of the **My Shadow Big Book.** Invite students to come up to the book and point to the spaces between the sentences. Then work together as a class to count the number of sentences on the page.

✦ To review varied sentence beginnings, have students look back on their own work. For example, students might look at a letter they have written to their families. Or they might look at sentences that they have used to label their drawings. Have students work with partners to think of ways to make the sentences begin in different ways.

Differentiating Instruction   English Learners

IF ... students are native Spanish speakers, **THEN ...** they may need extra help producing the /w/ sound and associating it with the letter *w*. The letter *w* does not appear in Spanish words, although Spanish speakers use /w/ occasionally for words borrowed from other languages.

GAME Day

My Neighborhood Game

✦ Tell students they will play the My Neighborhood game. Take out the My Neighborhood game mats and the **Alphabet Letter Cards.**

✦ Separate the class into several groups, and set up game stations around the room.

✦ To play the game, a player rolls the number cube and moves a marker the correct number of spaces. When a player lands on a space, he or she must draw a card from the pack and identify the letter on the card.

✦ You can organize the game day into a tournament—the winners from each game station can play a "championship" game that the rest of the class watches.

🍎 Teacher Tip

BONUS LETTERS Again, make the letters students are learning "bonus letters." When a student chooses an *Ff* or a *Jj* card, ask them to say the letter's sound for a bonus. You can have students move forward an extra space for each correct answer.

Lesson Planner

Day 1

Day 2

Sounds and Letters

MATERIALS

- ✦ *Alphabet Letter Cards: Uu, Xx,* and *Zz*
- ✦ Routines 1, 2, 4
- ✦ *Skills Practice 2,* pp. 11–16
- ✦ Transparency 21
- ✦ *Pocket Chart Letter Cards*
- ✦ *Pocket Chart Picture Cards*
- ✦ *Alphabet Flash Cards*
- ✦ *Alphabet Book Big Book,* pp. 44–45, 50–51
- ✦ *Decodable* 9

Day 1

Warming Up, p. T88
Phonemic Awareness
- Phoneme Blending: Initial Sounds, p. T89
- Phoneme Matching: Initial Sounds, p. T89

Alphabetic Principle
- Introducing the Sound of *Uu,* p. T90
- Listening for /u/, p. T90
- Linking the Sound to the Letter, p. T90
- Penmanship, p. T91

Day 2

Warming Up, pp. T98–T99
Phonemic Awareness
- Phoneme Matching: Initial Sounds, p. T99
- Phoneme Manipulation: Initial Sounds, p. T99

Alphabetic Principle
- Reviewing the Sound of *Uu,* p. T100
- Listening for /u/, p. T100
- Linking the Sound to the Letter, p. T100
- *Alphabet Book Big Book*—/u/, p. T101

Reading and Responding

MATERIALS

- ✦ *My Shadow Big Book,* pp. 4–43
- ✦ Routines 5–7
- ✦ *Home Connection,* pp. 47–48

Day 1

Poetry
- Activate Prior Knowledge, p. T92
- Preview the Poem, p. T92

Vocabulary, p. T93
Read the Poem, p. T93
Comprehension Strategies, p. T94
Discussing the Poem, p. T95
Vocabulary Review, p. T95

Day 2

Preview and Prepare, p. T102
Vocabulary, p. T103
Read the Selection, p. T103
Comprehension Strategies, pp. T104, T106, T108
Print and Book Awareness, pp. T105, T107, T109
Discussing the Selection, p. T109
Vocabulary Review, p. T109

Language Arts

MATERIALS

- ✦ *Language Arts Big Book,* p. 9
- ✦ *My Shadow Big Book,* p. 44
- ✦ *Willy the Wisher,* p. 64
- ✦ *Story Lines Big Book,* pp. 10–11
- ✦ *Alphabet Book Big Book,* pp. 6–9
- ✦ *Pickled Peppers Big Book,* p. 15

Day 1

Writing Process
Model: Add Ideas to Writing, p. T96
Fine Art
Discussing Fine Art, p. T97

Day 2

Writing Process
Revise: Adding Ideas to Writing, p. T110
Grammar, Mechanics, and Usage, pp. T110–T111
Willy the Wisher, p. T111

Monitor Progress

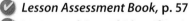

- ✅ = Formal Assessment
- Ⓑ = Benchmark Assessment

Day 1
- ✅ Phoneme Matching, p. T89
- ✅ Letter and Sound Identification, p. T91
- ✅ Visualizing, p. T95

Day 2
- ✅ *Lesson Assessment Book,* p. 57
- ✅ Letter and Sound Identification, p. T100

Literature Overview

Big Book

Shadow/Sombra
poem by Jorge Argueta
illustrated by Jamie Zollars

Poetry

Bear Shadow
written and illustrated by Frank Asch

Poetry
Hide-and-Seek Shadow
poem by Margaret Hillert
illustrated by Bob Masheris

★ Phonemic Awareness ★ Phonics
★ Fluency ★ Vocabulary ★ Comprehension

Day 3

Warming Up, pp. T112–T113
Phonemic Awareness
Phoneme Manipulation: Final Sounds, p. T113
Alphabetic Principle
- Introducing the Sound of *Xx*, p. T114
- Listening for /ks/, p. T114
- Penmanship, p. T115

Preview and Prepare, p. T116
Vocabulary, p. T116
Read the Selection, p. T117
Comprehension Strategies, pp. T118, T120, T122
Comprehension Skills, pp. T119, T121
Reading with a Writer's Eye, pp. T119, T121, T123
Discussing the Selection, p. T123
Vocabulary Review, p. T123

Writing Process
Draft: Creating Another Card, p. T124
Story Crafting
Story Lines, Big Book p. T125

✓ *Lesson Assessment Book,* pp. 57–58
✓ Letter and Sound Identification, p. T115

Day 4

Warming Up, pp. T126–T127
Phonemic Awareness
Phoneme Manipulation: Final Sounds, p. T127
Alphabetic Principle
- Reviewing the Sound of *Xx*, p. T128
- Listening for /ks/, p. T128
- Linking the Sound to the Letter, p. T128
- *Alphabet Book Big Book*—/ks/, p. T129

Poetry
- Activate Prior Knowledge, p. T130
- Preview the Poem, p. T130
Vocabulary, p. T131
Read the Poem, p. T131
Comprehension Strategies, p. T132
Discussing the Poem, p. T133
Vocabulary Review, p. T133

Writing Process
Present: Sharing Cards, p. T134
Grammar, Usage, and Mechanics, p. T134
Story Crafting
Story Lines, Big Book p. T135

✓ Visualizing, p. T132

Day 5

Warming Up, pp. T136–T137
Phonemic Awareness
Phoneme Segmentation, p. T137
Alphabetic Principle
- Introducing the Sound of *Zz*, p. T138
- Listening for Initial /z/, p. T138
- Linking the Sound to the Letter, p. T138
- Penmanship, p. T139
Reading a *Decodable*
Decodable 9: *Bud and Max,* pp. T140–T141

Inquiry
- Whole-Group Time, pp. T142–T143
- Small-Group Time, p. T143
- Concept Vocabulary, p. T143

Writing Process
Reflection: Illustrating Brainstorming, p. T144
Grammar, Usage, and Mechanics, p. T144
Game Day
Tic-Tac-Toe Tournament, p. T145

Comprehension Observation Log
✓ Penmanship, p. T139

Focus Question Why does Bear talk to his shadow?

Bear Shadow
by Frank Asch

One day Bear went down to the pond with his fishing pole and a big can of worms. While he was putting a worm on his hook, he looked down and saw a big fish. I'm going to catch that fish, thought Bear to himself.

22

But when Bear stood up to throw his line in the water, his shadow scared the big fish away.

23

Big Books

Audio CD

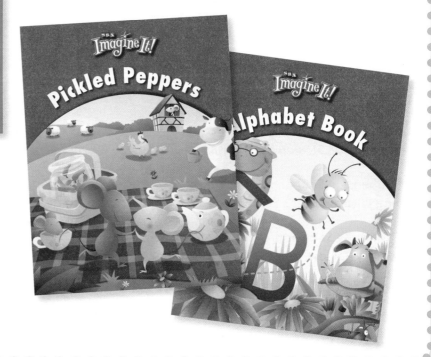

SRA Imagine It!
Pickled Peppers

SRA Imagine It!
Alphabet Book
B

Big Book Selection

My Shadow Big Book

Bear Shadow by Frank Asch, pp. 22–41

Bud and Max
by Tristan Harrom
illustrated by Laura Logan

Decodable 9: *Bud and Max*

Teacher Support

Language Arts Big Book
SRA Imagine It!

Imagine It!
Willy the Wisher
AND OTHER THINKING STORIES

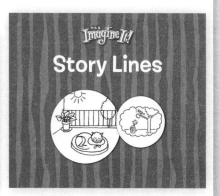

Imagine It!
Story Lines

Language Arts Big Book   **Willy the Wisher**   **Story Lines Big Book**

Curriculum Connections

Card 17

Whose Tracks Are These?

Exploring animal tracks is fun!

Animal tracks tell two special things.

They tell the shape of the animal's feet.

~~~ the animal moves.

Science
Grade K · Unit 2
Patterns

| | Deer | Horse | Pigeon | Duck |

Card 21

Our Country's Flag

Red stripe, white stripe,

Patterns you can see.

Red stripes, white stripes

Tell us that we are free.

Blue box, white stars

Fifty stars in all.

Red stripes, white stripes,

Hanging from the wall.

Social Studies
Grade K · Unit 2
Patterns

Card 15

People Plan Schools

People planned your school. It has many classrooms. There are shelves for books. It has room for supplies. Does it have a playground? What makes your school fun?

Art
Grade K · Unit 1
Off to School

~~~ing Shapes

~~~ee shapes

~~~ you look.

~~~pes match the clock?

~~~pes match the book?

Math
Grade K · Unit 2
Patterns

- Math
- Social Studies
- Science
- Art

Additional Skills Practice

Approaching Level	On Level	English Learner	Above Level
Reteach	**Skills Practice 2**	**English Learner Support Activities**	**Challenge Activities**
Letter and Sound Identification, pp. 111–114	Letter and Sound Identification, pp. 11–16	Lessons 6–10	Letter and Sound Identification, pp. 84–86, 88
Phoneme Matching, p. 110			Penmanship, p. 87

Differentiating Instruction

for Workshop

Lessons 6-10 Overview

Day 1

Approaching Level	On Level	English Learner	Above Level
Sounds and Letters			
Reading a *Decodable*: Review *Decodable* 8 with students, pointing to the high-frequency word for as you read.	**Reading a *Decodable*:** Have students partner-read ***Decodable*** 8.	**Reading a *Decodable*:** Reread ***Decodable*** 8 with students, reviewing what is happening in the illustrations and the high-frequency word for.	**Reading a *Decodable*:** Students use **eDecodable** *Jam Pot* to review the story.
Reading and Responding			
Comprehension: Have students browse the poem and point to and say the words they recognize.	**Comprehension:** Have students play the I'm Thinking of Something . . . game with partners to practice Visualizing.	**Comprehension:** Preview the selection "Bear Shadow" with students, and have them point out anything about the story that confuses or puzzles them.	**Comprehension:** Have students close their eyes as you describe a scene for them. Then have them draw what they see.
Language Arts			
Writing: Show students a revised sentence.	**Writing:** With your help, students make suggestions for rewriting sentences from the selection "Shadows."	**Writing:** Show a picture of a person riding a bike. On the board, write _____ *rides a* _____ *bike*. Read the sentence frame, pointing to each word as you read it. Then say *Let's make this sentence better.* Ask *Who is riding the bike? What color is the bike?* Point to the person and the bike as you ask the questions. Fill in the sentence frame, then read the revised sentence to the students.	**Writing:** Ask students for suggestions of simple sentences.

Day 2

Approaching Level	On Level	English Learner	Above Level
Sounds and Letters			
Alphabetic Principle: Work with students to complete the activity on **Reteach** page 112.	**Alphabetic Principle:** Students use **eAlphabet Book** to review the /u/ sound.	**Alphabetic Principle:** Refer to Unit 6 Lesson 7 of the **English Learner Support Guide.**	**Alphabetic Principle:** Students use **Alphabet Sound Card Stories CD** to listen to the story for the /u/ sound.
Reading and Responding			
Comprehension: Students browse the selection and discuss what they think they might learn about shadows based on the illustrations.	**Comprehension:** Have students retell the story "Bear's Shadow" in their own words.	**Comprehension:** Refer to Unit 6 Lesson 7 of the **English Learner Support Guide.**	**Comprehension:** Invite students to discuss Bear's problem and how he was able to solve it in the end. Make connections to problem-solving skills learned in Unit 5 Stick to It.
Language Arts			
Writing: Show students the original sentence, and discuss the differences they see. **Grammar:** With your help, students talk about patterns they see in the classroom.	**Writing:** Ask students to explain what they changed in the sentence. **Grammar:** Students make note of patterns they see in the classroom.	**Writing:** Display the picture of the person riding the bike. Write the sentence frame and the revised sentence beneath it. Help students identify the new words in the sentence. **Grammar:** Refer to Unit 6 Lesson 7 of the **English Learner Support Guide.**	**Writing:** Ask students to revise the sentences by adding details. **Grammar:** Ask students to find patterned pictures in magazines.

Day 3

Approaching Level	On Level	English Learner	Above Level
Sounds and Letters			
Alphabetic Principle: Using the *Alphabet Letter Card Xx,* students walk around the classroom, matching the letter with environmental print.	**Alphabetic Principle:** Have students look through *My Shadow Little Big Book* for the letter *Xx* and make the /ks/ sound each time they find the letter.	**Alphabetic Principle:** Refer to Unit 6 Lesson 8 of the *English Learner Support Guide.*	**Alphabetic Principle:** Students work independently to complete the activity on page 86 of *Challenge Activities.*
Reading and Responding			
Comprehension: Have students try to make their own shadows and talk about anything that puzzles them.	**Comprehension:** Students make connections between Bear's questions about shadows and their own questions.	**Comprehension:** Refer to Unit 6 Lesson 8 of the *English Learner Support Guide.*	**Comprehension:** Students review what is needed to make shadows and try to create them on their own with partners.
Language Arts			
Writing: With your help, students circle the differences in the sentence.	**Writing:** Ask students to explain why they made changes in the sentences.	**Writing:** Write the revised sentence on the board, and read the sentence. Underline the new words, and remind students that these words help make the sentence better. Have students draw a picture to illustrate the sentence.	**Writing:** Students discuss the changes they made to the sentences and why.

Day 4

Approaching Level	On Level	English Learner	Above Level

Sounds and Letters

Alphabetic Principle: Refer to Unit 6 Lesson 9 of the *Intervention Guide* for activities to help students.

Alphabetic Principle: Students use the *eAlphabet Book* to review the rhyme for the /ks/ sound.

Alphabetic Principle: Refer to Unit 6 Lesson 9 of the *English Learner Support Guide.*

Alphabetic Principle: Have students listen to the *Alphabet Book Big Book* rhyme for /ks/ on the *Listening Library CD* and raise their hands each time they hear the /ks/ sound.

Reading and Responding

Preview: Read the poem to students, and have them ask questions about anything that puzzles them or they wonder about.

Preview: Have students talk about how the poem connects with the unit theme.

Preview: Review the selection "Bear Shadow" with students, and have them share any wonderings or questions about the selection with you.

Preview: Have students dictate their own poems about shadows.

Language Arts

Writing: Discuss with students what was changed.

Grammar: Students each choose a pattern in the classroom, stand by it, and explain why they chose it and what makes it a pattern.

Writing: Ask students to write their "Shadow" sentences neatly.

Grammar: Students copy the pattern on sheets of paper.

Writing: Write the revised sentence on the board, and read the sentence. Help students compare their drawings to the sentence by asking *Who is on the bike? What color is the bike?*

Grammar: Refer to Unit 6 Lesson 9 of the *English Learner Support Guide.*

Writing: Students sign their names.

Grammar: Students try to copy the pattern on sheets of art paper.

Day 5

Approaching Level	On Level	English Learner	Above Level
Sounds and Letters			
Reading a Decodable: Review **Decodable** 9 with students, pointing to the high-frequency words *but* and *up* as you read.	**Reading a Decodable:** Review the high-frequency words *but* and *up* with students. Students reread **Decodable** 9 to partners.	**Reading a Decodable:** Use the *eDecodable Bud and Max* with students to reinforce the high-frequency words and the /u/ and /ks/ sounds.	**Reading a Decodable:** Have students partner-read **Decodables** 8 and 9.
Reading and Responding			
Inquiry: Demonstrate how to make a shadow, and have students ask questions about anything that puzzles them.	**Inquiry:** Have students experiment making shadows with various classroom items.	**Inquiry:** Refer to Unit 6 Lesson 10 of the *English Learner Support Guide.*	**Inquiry:** Have students cut out their own shapes of various sizes and use them to create shadows on the classroom wall.
Language Arts			
Writing: Discuss with students why changes were made. **Grammar:** Students draw pictures of their patterns.	**Writing:** Ask students to sign their names to their sentences. **Grammar:** Students sign their names.	**Writing:** Have students show their illustrations to the group and tell about them. **Grammar:** Refer to Unit 6 Lesson 10 of the *English Learner Support Guide.*	**Writing:** Students share their creations. **Grammar:** Students make final drawings of the copied patterns.

Resources for
Differentiating Instruction

English Learner

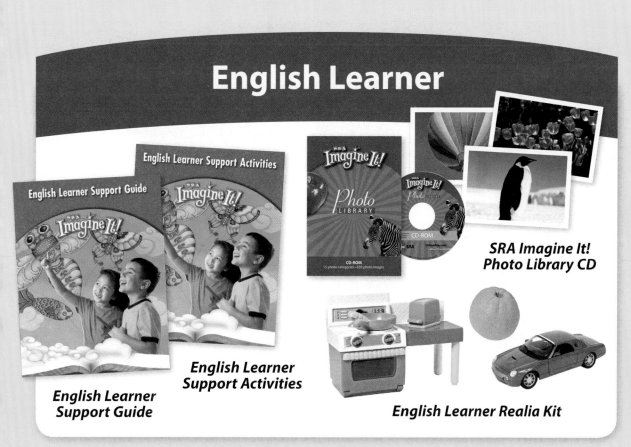

English Learner Support Guide

English Learner Support Activities

English Learner Support Guide

English Learner Support Activities

SRA Imagine It! Photo Library CD

English Learner Realia Kit

Approaching Level

Intervention

Intervention Guide

Intervention Workbook

Intervention Guide

Intervention Workbook

Workshop Kits

- High Frequency Words
- Letter Recognition
- Phonemic Awareness
- Print and Book Awareness
- Sequencing

Technology

Alphabet Sound Card Stories CD

eAlphabet Book

eDecodable Bud and Max

eSkills & eGames

Listening Library CD

Listening Library Unit 6

Monitor Progress to Differentiate Instruction

Use these summative assessments along with your informal observations to assess student mastery.

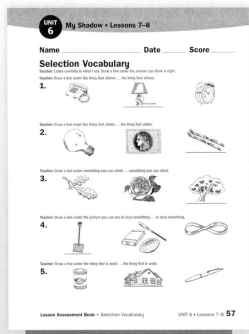

Lesson Assessment Book, p. 57

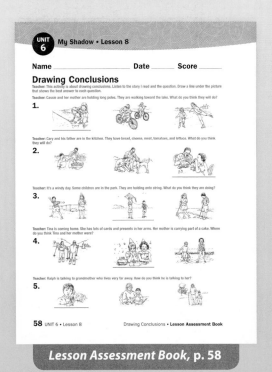

Lesson Assessment Book, p. 58

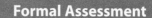

Lesson Assessment Book

Comprehension Observation Log

Student _____ Date _____

Unit _____ Lesson _____ Selection Title _____

General Comprehension
Concepts discussed: _____

Behavior Within a Group
Articulates, expresses ideas: _____

Joins discussions: _____

Collaborates (such as works well with other students, works alone): _____

Role in Group
Role (such as leader, summarizer, questioner, critic, observer, non-participant): ____

Flexibility (changes roles when necessary): _____

Use of Reading Strategies
Uses strategies when needed (either those taught or student's choice of strategy)/Describes strategies used:
_____
_____

Changes strategies when appropriate: _____

Changes Since Last Observation
_____
_____

110   Comprehension Observation Log • **Lesson Assessment Book**

Lesson Assessment Annotated Teacher's Edition, p. 110

The Comprehension Observation Log, found in the ***Lesson Assessment Annotated Teacher's Edition,*** is a vehicle for recording anecdotal information about individual student performance on an ongoing basis. Information such as students' strengths and weaknesses can be recorded at any time the occasion warrants. It is recommended that you maintain a folder for each student where you can store the logs for purposes of comparison and analysis as the school year progresses. You will gradually build up a comprehensive file that reveals which students are progressing smoothly and which students need additional help.

OBJECTIVES

Students will

✦ blend initial phonemes to make words.

✦ match initial phonemes.

✦ attach the /u/ sound to the letter *Uu*.

✦ practice writing the letter *Uu*.

MATERIALS

✦ **Alphabet Letter Card** *Uu* for each student

✦ Routine 1

✦ Supply Icons

✦ **Skills Practice 2,** pp. 11–12

✦ **Transparency** 21

Calendar

Su	M	T	W	Th	F	S
		1	2	3	4	5
6	7	8	9	10	11	12
13	14	15	16	17	18	19
20	21	22	23	24	25	26
27	28	29	30	31		

Point to the box that represents today. Say the name of a date that occurs within the current week. Invite a volunteer to point to that date on the calendar.

Warming Up 🕐

Kindergarten News

✦ Copy the text above on the board or on chart paper.

✦ Ask students if there are any words that they can read in the message today. Have students point to and say any words they can read.

✦ Invite volunteers to say words to complete the sentences. Have them write the words in the blanks. You might write the words they suggest first in dotted lines and have students trace them. Or you could help them write the words hand over hand.

✦ Discuss the other aspects of the message. For example, ask students to identify the exclamation point and the periods, or have them count the total number of sentences.

Phonemic Awareness

Phoneme Blending: Initial Sounds

✦ Tell students the **Lion Puppet** wants to play a blending game again. Tell them you will say the beginning sound of a word and they should repeat after you. The puppet will say the rest. When the puppet asks what the word is, students should put the parts together and say the word.

✦ Practice with the following word:

Teacher: /f/ (Emphasize the /f/ sound.)
Everyone: /f/
Puppet: . . . ind. What's the word?
Everyone: find

✦ Continue with the following words:

/j/ . . . ust just	/f/ . . . ire fire	/f/ . . . ish fish
/g/ . . . ave gave	/j/ . . . ail jail	/d/ . . . uck duck
/b/ . . . ank bank	/n/ . . . ose nose	/s/ . . . ong song

Phoneme Matching: Initial Sounds

✦ Tell students they are going to play another game in which they try to find two words that begin with the same sound.

✦ Explain that you want them to listen closely as you say pairs of words and to give the thumbs-up signal if a pair of words begins with the same sound and the thumbs-down signal if the words do not begin with the same sound. Then they should say the beginning sound if it is the same.

✦ Try these word pairs:

happy, hurry /h/	much, next
dress, down /d/	barn, door
color, garden	**seat, supper** /s/
nine, middle	**paper, penny** /p/
tent, tooth /t/	soft, candy
jolly, great	**happen, hunt** /h/
bigger, burn /b/	fairy, loud
rest, rabbit /r/	neat, mean

Monitor Progress
to Differentiate Instruction
Formal Assessment

Phonemic Awareness Note how easily students match phonemes.

APPROACHING LEVEL
IF . . . students are having difficulty, THEN . . . guide them in completing **Reteach** page 110.

ON LEVEL
IF . . . students need more practice, THEN . . . continue the activity using word pairs such as **big/best,** dig/great, **rack/rib, light/locker,** damp/pair, and **salt/steep.**

ABOVE LEVEL
IF . . . students would enjoy a challenging activity, THEN . . . have them cut from old magazines or catalogs pictures of objects that begin with the same sounds and lay them in pairs.

ROUTINE
1

Teacher Tip

THE SOUND OF *U* The letter *Uu* can make several different sounds, such as the /ū/ in *unit*, the /ŭ/ in *bush*, and /ü/ in *rule* in addition to the short /u/ sound presented in this lesson. If you choose additional *Uu* words to share with students, be sure these words use the short *u* sound as in *up, must, funny,* and *summer.*

Differentiating Instruction **English Learners**

IF ... students are native speakers of Spanish, Tagalog (Filipino), and some other languages, **THEN ...** they may need extra practice saying /u/ and associating it with the letter *u*. The short *u* sound found in English does not appear in their native languages.

Technology

Use the **Alphabet Sound Card Stories CD** for practice with the /u/ sound.

Audio CD

Alphabetic Principle

Introducing the Sound of *Uu*

✦ Point to the **Alphabet Sound Wall Card** Short *Uu*. Remind students sometimes a vowel makes sounds other than its name. Say that the short sound of *Uu* is /u/. Show the picture on the card, and recite the story for the /u/ sound:

Tubby the Tugboat can huff and puff

And push and pull to move big stuff.

/u/ /u/ /u/ /u/ /u/

That's the sound of Tubby the Tug

He works all day from dawn till dusk.

/u/ /u/ /u/ /u/ /u/.

✦ Tell students you will read the story again but this time you would like them to make Tubby's tugging sound. /u/ /u/ /u/ /u/ /u/

Alphabet Sound Wall Card 31

Listening for /u/

✦ Give each student an **Alphabet Letter Card** *Uu*. Tell them to hold up their cards and say /u/ when they hear the /u/ sound at the beginning of a word that you say. Say the following words:

opera	answer	**underwater**	**umpire**	**up**
igloo	**uncle**	antelope	inchworm	in

✦ Once again, explain that vowel sounds can be found in the middle of a word as well as at the beginning. Here are some words with the /u/ sound in the middle to use for students to identify: *dust, must, fun, hut, bun, lunch, bug*

Linking the Sound to the Letter

Write a pair of similar-looking words on the board, one with the /u/ sound and one without. Say the word with the short *u* for each word pair. Have students identify the word you said by using the thumbs-up signal when you point to it.

but ... bat	*run* ... ran	mist ... *must*
net ... *nut*	dock ... *duck*	sunny ... Sammy

Penmanship

✦ Distribute a sheet of writing paper to each student, or use **White Boards** turned to the sides with writing lines. Place the Supply Icon for *pencil* on the board or in the **Pocket Chart.**

✦ Using Routine 1 and the established procedure, review with students how to form a capital *U.* Say *Begin here, and draw a line straight down. Then curve up to the right, and go straight up again. Capital* U. Remind students the letter *U* makes the short /u/ sound, as in *duck.* Have them say the sound as they make the letter in the air.

✦ Review the steps for forming a small *u.* Say *Begin here, and make a short line straight down. Then curve up to the right, and go straight back up. Small* u. Then have students practice writing capital and small *Uu* on the papers or boards.

✦ Using the established procedure, have students proofread, circling one capital and one small letter they would like to make better.

Guided Practice

✦ Have students complete **Skills Practice 2** pages 11 and 12 for additional practice writing the letter *Uu* and identifying the /u/ sound in words.

✦ Have students practice writing capital *U*s and small *u*'s on the lines. Remind students some of the things in the pictures on the pages begin with the /u/ sound and others have the /u/ sound in the middle. Name each picture, and tell students to write the letter *u* under each picture whose name has the /u/ sound. After students have finished, be sure to review their work. You might save these pages for students to use during penmanship proofreading activities in later lessons.

Monitor Progress
Formal Assessment
to Differentiate Instruction

Letter and Sound Identification Note how easily students identify the /u/ sound.

APPROACHING LEVEL

IF ... students are having difficulty,	THEN ... show and read the names of **Pocket Chart Picture Cards** 28–book, 147–rug, 114–mouse, 182–tree, asking them to identify which one has the /u/ sound in its name.
IF ... students still have difficulty,	THEN ... refer to Unit 6, Lesson 6 of the **Intervention Guide.**

ON LEVEL

IF ... students need more practice,	THEN ... have them help you think of words with the sound in its name and make a list on the board.

ABOVE LEVEL

IF ... students would enjoy a challenging activity,	THEN ... have them work independently to complete **Challenge Activities** page 84.

 Teacher Tip

USING PROGRAM MATERIALS Use *Transparency* 21 or *Alphabet Sound Wall Card Uu* to help you review the shape of *Uu.* See the Appendix for step-by-step, letter-formation instruction.

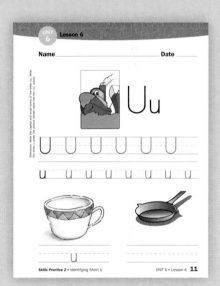

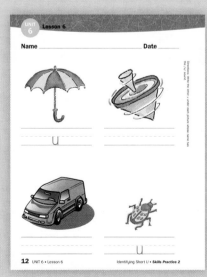

Skills Practice 2, pp. 11–12

Reading and Responding

OBJECTIVES

Students will

✦ locate the title of the poem and the names of the poet and the illustrator.

✦ connect their own life experiences to the text.

✦ develop an understanding of vocabulary words.

✦ use the comprehension strategy Visualizing.

MATERIALS

✦ *My Shadow Big Book,* pp. 20–21
✦ Routines 5–7
✦ *Home Connection,* pp. 47–48

My Shadow Big Book, p. 20–21

Technology

To promote independent reading, encourage students to use Workshop to listen to the recording of the selection on the *Listening Library CD.* Invite them to follow along and to say the words whenever they can.

Audio CD

Poetry

Activate Prior Knowledge   ROUTINE 5

✦ "Shadow/Sombra" is a simple seven-line poem in which a young child reacts to her shadow. As you read the poem, relate what you already know to what you are reading, and encourage students to do the same.

✦ Ask students if they have ever been outside when the sun was behind them and they could see their shadows in front of them. Ask them how their shadows looked—short and fat or tall and skinny. Ask students how seeing their shadows this size made them feel.

✦ Tell students you will be reading them a poem in which a child about their age gets upset with her shadow for something it does. Encourage students to make pictures in their heads of the words you read.

✦ Have students discuss the knowledge they are building about shadows as they listen to the selection. A key concept is that when the sun is behind a person, the person's shadow falls in front of the person.

Preview the Poem   ROUTINE 5

✦ Display the *My Shadow Big Book* opened to pages 20 and 21. Follow Routine 5, the previewing the selection routine, as you point to and say the poem's title and the names of the poet and the illustrator. Ask students what a poet and an illustrator do. Explain that the poem is written in both English and Spanish.

✦ Invite students to examine the picture and to share what they see. Remind students pictures can give readers clues to what a poem or a story is about.

Vocabulary

ROUTINE **6**

✦ Follow Routine 6, the selection vocabulary routine, as you introduce the vocabulary words for this selection.

✦ Explain to students that the word *sometimes* means "not all of the time." Ask students if their parents let them stay up late sometimes, like for a birthday or holiday.

✦ Tell students the word *race* means "to try to be the fastest." Ask students if they like to race with their friends.

Read the Poem

ROUTINE **7**

✦ Before reading the poem, read the Focus Question above it. Tell students to keep this question in mind as they listen to the poem.

✦ Follow Routine 7, the reading the selection routine as you read aloud "Shadow/Sombra." If you feel comfortable, read both the English and Spanish versions of the poem. Because the poem contains no punctuation, read it without stopping. Ask students if the English version of the poem has any rhyming words. Explain that some poems rhyme and that some do not.

✦ Invite students to ask questions or to think aloud about anything in the poem that interests or puzzles them.

Comprehension Strategies

For this poem, model the comprehension strategy Visualizing to help students make mental pictures of settings, characters, and actions.

Vocabulary

sometimes	race

Teacher Tip

WRITING POETRY Some students may enjoy dictating poems about shadows.

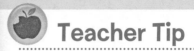

Differentiating Instruction **English Learners**

IF ... students are native Spanish speakers, **THEN ...** invite volunteers to read aloud the Spanish version of the poem.

Focus Question   How does the shadow win the race?

Shadow / Sombra

by Jorge Argueta
illustrated by Jamie Zollars

Shadow
I love you
but sometimes
you make me mad
because
every time
we race
you always win ❷

FINISH

Sombra
yo te quiero
aunque a veces
me enojas

porque siempre
llegas primero
cuando jugamos
a correr

FINAL ❶

20   21

My Shadow Big Book, pp. 20–21

 Teacher Tip

GLOSSARY The word *race* can be found in the Glossary of the *My Shadow Big Book.*

Comprehension Strategies

Teacher Modeling

❶ **Visualizing** *Close your eyes, and see whether you can make a picture in your head of the little girl's shadow crossing the finish line before she does. Can you see the girl's tall, skinny shadow reaching far out in front of her? What part of her shadow crosses the finish line first?*

❷ **Visualizing** *Now close your eyes again, and pretend to be running in a race yourself. The sun is behind you. You see the long, dark shadow of your body ahead of you. The top of your shadow, your head, reaches the finish line. Then the rest of your shadow crosses. Finally, one of your feet touches the line, and your shadow wins.*

Discussing the Poem

✦ Review the Focus Question with students: How does the shadow win the race? *The sun is behind the girl, so her shadow falls far in front of her. It reaches the finish line before she does.*

✦ Invite students to share their thoughts and ideas about the poem. Ask students if the poem has helped them think about times their shadows have fallen in front of them. Encourage them to share what that was like.

✦ Ask students where the sunlight would have to be shining for the girl to reach the finish line before her shadow. *It would have to be shining in the girl's face.*

Purposes for Reading

✦ Remind students they were listening to find out what the poem says about shadows. Invite students to share what they learned about shadows.

✦ Ask students what they liked best about the poem and why they liked it.

✦ Have students discuss the difference between reading a poem for pleasure and reading something for information.

✦ Have students identify selections in the unit that they read for pleasure and which selections provided information.

Vocabulary Review

Review with students the selection vocabulary words *sometimes* and *race.* Ask students the following questions:

• *When might you sometimes do something?*

• *Where can we see a race?*

Differentiating Instruction **English Learners**

IF ... students need additional help with Visualizing, **THEN ...** refer to Unit 6 Lesson 6 of the *English Learner Support Guide.*

Give each student a copy of *Home Connection* page 47. This same information is also available in Spanish on *Home Connection* page 48. Encourage students to discuss the selection "Bear Shadow" with their families and complete the activity provided.

Monitor Progress

to Differentiate Instruction
Formal Assessment

Visualizing Note how easily students grasp the skill visualizing.

APPROACHING LEVEL

IF ... students need help visualizing,

THEN ... refer to Unit 6 Lesson 6 of the Intervention Guide.

ON LEVEL

IF ... students need to practice visualizing,

THEN ... have them play the guessing game I'm Thinking of Something ... with partners.

ABOVE LEVEL

IF ... students understand visualizing,

THEN ... give them a scene with shadows to visualize, and have them draw what they see.

Language Arts

Students will
✦ revise writing by adding ideas.
✦ view, appreciate, and react to fine art.

✦ *Language Arts Big Book,* p. 9
✦ *My Shadow Big Book,* p. 44

Language Arts Big Book, p. 9

Research in Action

Students need to have plenty of opportunities to share their completed and in-progress work with their peers. Presenting provides another opportunity for students to receive feedback.

(Steve Graham and Karen Harris)

Teacher Tip

PLAN AHEAD In preparation for the following activity, have the classroom art supplies on hand.

Writing Process

Model: Adding Ideas to Writing

Teach

✦ Display page 9 of the **Language Arts Big Book.** Ask students to tell what they remember about making their work better, or revising.

✦ Read the items on the revising list, and use the picture on the page to give examples of each. For example:

- I can name it. *Doodle, wagon*
- I can tell what it looks like. *red*
- I can tell what it is. *Doodle, wagon*
- I can tell what it is doing. *rides*

✦ Tell students they should always look for ways to make their writing better. Invite them to think of ways to make the class thank-you card better.

Apply

✦ Display the thank-you card you created in the previous lesson. Focus students' attention on the first page, or front, of the card. Ask students if anyone has any suggestions for making the front of the card better. Say *What can we add to the card to make it better?*

✦ When students offer suggestions, ask them to also tell why they think their ideas would make the card better.

✦ Choose one or two suggestions, and add them to the card. Tell students they will revise the inside pages of the card in the next lesson.

Fine Art

Discussing Fine Art

✦ Turn to page 44 in the *My Shadow Big Book.* Focus students' attention on *Mesa de Rancagua* by Mario Carreño.

✦ Invite students to give their initial impressions of the painting. Encourage students to freely express their feelings, interpretations, and opinions about the painting. In particular, have them discuss what they think it has to do with the unit theme.

✦ Guide students in discussing what they see in the painting. Use questions such as the following:

- *What items are in the picture? Where is the fruit?*
- *What colors are used? Are they bright or dull?*
- *How would you describe the shadows? Are they long or short?*
- *From which side is the light coming? How do you know?*

✦ Invite students to show their reactions to the art by making their own drawings of their favorite fruits, using colors similar to the ones in this painting.

Mario Carreño. *Mesa de Rancagua.* 1983. Oil on canvas. 50 x 35 cm. Collection of Emilio Ellena.

Differentiating Instruction   English Learners

IF ... students are native Spanish speakers, **THEN ...** challenge them to point to a *mesa* in the classroom and to say the English word for it. *table*

Background Information

Mario Carreño (1913–1999) was a Chilean painter of Cuban origin who lived in Cuba, Spain, Mexico, France, the United States, and Chile, where he became a citizen in 1969. Although he is associated with the surrealist movement, he also did abstract painting. Several of his paintings reflect his affection for Cuba, and he was an outstanding figure in the Chilean cultural environment.

Sounds and Letters

OBJECTIVES

Students will

✦ use ending sounds and other clues to identify words.

✦ match initial phonemes in sets of words.

✦ manipulate words by deleting initial phonemes.

✦ attach the /u/ sound to the letter *Uu*.

MATERIALS

✦ *Alphabet Letter Cards*
✦ *Alphabet Book Big Book,* pp. 44–45

Calendar

Su	M	T	W	Th	F	S
		1	2	3	4	5
6	7	8	9	10	11	12
13	14	15	16	17	18	19
20	21	22	23	24	25	26
27	28	29	30	31		

Point to the box that represents today. Ask students to count aloud with you how many days are in this month. Begin with the first day of the month, and point to each day as you count aloud.

Warming Up 🕐

Kindergarten News

✦ Copy the above text on the board or on chart paper; however, make several errors in your writing. For example, you might forget to capitalize the first word of a sentence, use a period instead of a question mark, or replace the letter *T* with the letter *F* in *Today.*

✦ Ask students to help you proofread the message, and have volunteers correct them. Challenge students to identify the /u/ sound in the words in the message and to read the words where it appears. *fun, sun*

Oral Language

✦ Bring out the **Lion Puppet** to play I'm Thinking of Something That Ends with _____ game. Remind students the puppet will say the last sound of a word and then say a riddle that has clues they can use to determine what word the puppet is thinking about. Use the following procedure, pausing to allow students a chance to give the word after each clue.

Puppet: *I'm thinking of something that ends with /s/. It rhymes with us. You can ride it to school. It's usually yellow. What is it? bus*

Teacher: *What was the last sound you heard in the word? What letter makes that sound? /s/, s*

Teacher: *What was the puppet thinking of? bus*

✦ Continue, having the puppet give riddle clues for several other simple words such as *Mom, feet, lion, web,* and *dog.*

Phonemic Awareness

Phoneme Matching: Initial Sounds

✦ Holding the **Lion Puppet,** tell students he wants to play the sound-matching game again. Tell students you will say three words and they should listen closely to find the two words that begin with the same sound. Say three words, with two of the words beginning with the same phoneme. Then have students say two words whose sounds match and the matching sound. For example:

Teacher: *jolly, funny, jelly*

Puppet: *Which words begin the same?*

Everyone: *jolly, jelly The beginning sound is /j/.*

✦ Continue with these words:

mother	*ranger*	*maybe* *mother, maybe* /m/
cannot	*careful*	*tonight* *cannot, careful* /k/
light	*little*	*fence* *light, little* /l/
jungle	*greedy*	*jewel* *jungle, jewel* /j/

Phoneme Manipulation: Initial Sounds

✦ Tell students the **Lion Puppet** wants to play the game in which he takes away sounds from words to make new words.

✦ Using some of the words from the previous activity, say a word, have students repeat it, and then have the puppet tell students to take away the beginning sound. Everyone will then say the word without the initial phoneme. For example:

Teacher: *The word is* crack.

Students: *crack*

Puppet: *Now take away the /k/ at the beginning. How do you say the word now?*

Everyone: *. . . rack*

Sounds and Letters

Teacher Tip

LETTER MATCH By using index cards cut to fit together like a puzzle, this game can become self-correcting. Simply write a capital letter on the left side of an index card and its corresponding small letter on the right side, and cut each card in a slightly different pattern.

Monitor Progress
to Differentiate Instruction
Formal Assessment

Letter and Sound Identification Note how easily students identify the /u/ sound.

APPROACHING LEVEL

IF ... students are having difficulty,

THEN ... guide them in completing **Reteach** pages 111 and 112

ON LEVEL

IF ... students need more practice,

THEN ... hold up **Pocket Chart Picture Cards** bug, duck, wig, rock, jug, van, jam, rug, pin, and trunk, and have students give a thumbs-up signal for each picture whose name has the /u/ sound

ABOVE LEVEL

IF ... students are comfortable,

THEN ... have them work independently to complete **Challenge Activities** page 85.

Alphabetic Principle

Reviewing the Sound of *Uu*

✦ Arrange the class into two groups for the Letter Match game. Give each student in one group a small **Alphabet Letter Card** and each student in the other group a corresponding capital **Alphabet Letter Card.** Explain that on your signal they should find the persons with the letters that match their letters. Tell them they should hold up their hands when they have found their partners. Call on pairs, and have them say their letters—and their letters' sounds, as appropriate.

✦ Hold up **Alphabet Sound Wall Card** *Short u,* and ask the pair whose letters match the card to come up and stand or sit next to you. Review the story for the /u/ sound:

Tubby the Tugboat can huff and puff
And push and pull to move big stuff.
/u/ /u/ /u/ /u/ /u/.
That's the sound of Tubby the Tug
He works all day from dawn till dusk.
/u/ /u/ /u/ /u/ /u/.

✦ Repeat the story, this time pausing to allow the pair of students with the *Uu* cards to make Tubby's sound: */u/ /u/ /u/ /u/ /u/.*

Listening for /u/

✦ Tell students the following verse:

A bug in a rug with a mug went glug, glug, glug.

✦ Have them repeat it several times. Ask students what vowel sound they hear in *bug, rug, mug,* and *glug.* *short* u

Linking the Sound to the Letter

✦ Write *cut* and *cat* on the board. Ask students *Which word says* cut? When students give the correct answer, say *Correct! How do you know which word I said? The /u/ sound is in* cut. Point to *cat*, and ask *What does the other word say?*

✦ Continue with the following words:

nut ... net   log ... lug
rag ... rug   tug ... tag

Alphabet Book Big Book—/u/

✦ Display the **Alphabet Book Big Book,** and turn to pages 44–45, *Uu.* Point to the title letters *Uu,* and have students say the name of each of the letters. *capital U, small u*

✦ Reread the poem, asking students to listen for the /u/ sound in the words.

✦ When finished, have volunteers come to the book and point to words that begin with *U* or *u. up, umpire, ugly, underneath, upon, unlucky, upside-down* Have students say the name for the letter.

✦ Point to and say each of the following words. Ask students to give the thumbs-up signal if the word has the /u/ sound and the thumbs-down signal if it does not.

umpire	**ugly**	*pants*	**dusty**
missed	**swung**	**unlucky**	*slow*

✦ Finally, have students work in groups to find all the words in the story that begin with the /u/ sound. Have other groups find the words that have the /u/ sound in the middle. Remind students the letter *Uu* makes the /u/ sound, so the words they are looking for will have the letter *Uu* in the beginning or the middle.

Maybe I'm unlucky
Or just a little slow,
My baseball bat was upside-down
—How was I to know?

Uu

"Batter up!" called the umpire.
I took the batter's stance
And looked up at the pitcher
Who wore some ugly pants.

Underneath the hot sun
Upon the dusty field,
I swung and missed, one, two, three.
And now my luck was sealed.

44   45

Alphabet Book Big Book, pp. 44–45

Technology

Each of the rhymes from the **Alphabet Book Big Book** is available on the **Listening Library CD.** Use the **eAlphabet Book** for activities that support the **Alphabet Book Big Book** lessons.

Audio CD

Students will

✦ locate the title and the name of the author and illustrator.

✦ connect their own life experiences to the text.

✦ develop an understanding of vocabulary words.

✦ use the comprehension strategies Asking Questions and Clarifying.

✦ *My Shadow Big Book,* pp. 22–41

✦ Routines 5–7

Focus Question Why does Bear talk to his shadow?

Bear Shadow

by Frank Asch

One day Bear went down to the pond with his fishing pole and a big can of worms. While he was putting a worm on his hook, he looked down and saw a big fish. I'm going to catch that fish, thought Bear to himself.

22

My Shadow Big Book, p. 22

Technology

To promote independent reading, encourage students to use Workshop to listen to the recording of the selection on the *Listening Library CD.* Invite them to follow along and say the words whenever they can.

Audio CD

1st READ

Preview and Prepare

Activate Prior Knowledge

✦ "Bear Shadow" is a fantasy about a bear who becomes annoyed at his shadow for following him around all the time. He tries many ways to get rid of his shadow before finally getting his shadow to "cooperate." As you read, relate what you already know to what you are reading, and encourage students to do the same.

✦ Tell students "Bear Shadow" is a fantasy, or made-up story, in which animals act like people. Explain that in a fantasy, an animal might talk, wear clothes, or live in a house, just like people.

✦ Discuss with students what they have learned about shadows. Then invite students to respond to the following questions: *Have you ever tried to run away from your shadow? Is it possible to do this? Can you think of how it can be done?*

✦ Encourage students to think about the knowledge they are building about the unit theme as they listen to the selection. "Bear Shadow" is a story that illustrates how shadows change throughout the day. It also emphasizes the need for a light source to make a shadow. Key concepts include the following:

• Shadows change in size depending on the level of light.

• Shadows go where we go and do what we do.

Preview the Selection

✦ Open the **My Shadow Big Book** to pages 22 and 23, the opening pages of "Bear Shadow." Follow Routine 5, the previewing the selection routine, as you point to and say the title and the name of the author and illustrator. Ask students why only one name is given.

✦ Turn through the pages, and focus students' attention on the illustrations. Ask them if the pictures help them to predict what the story might be about. Encourage students to comment on anything they find amusing or interesting.

✦ Help students think about what they might learn from the story before they read it. Encourage students to listen also for information that will add to their understanding of shadows.

Vocabulary

ROUTINE
6

✦ Follow Routine 6, the selection vocabulary routine, as you introduce the vocabulary words for this selection.

✦ Explain that the word *brook* means "a small stream". Use the following sentence to illustrate: We like to go fishing in the brook.

✦ Tell students a *cliff* is a steep rock face. Share that climbing a cliff is a kind of sport.

✦ Ask students if they are ever *annoyed*, or bothered, by something their brother or sister does.

✦ Explain that the word *bury* means "to dig a hole and cover with dirt or sand." Tell students they must bury seeds before they will grow.

Read the Selection

ROUTINE
7

✦ Before beginning the selection, read the Focus Question at the top of the first page. Tell students to keep this question in mind as they listen to the story.

✦ Follow Routine 7, the reading the selection routine, as you read the entire selection.

✦ Before, during, and after the first reading, invite students to ask questions and to think aloud about anything in the selection. In this way, you prepare students for the kind of thinking they will use to become independent, enthusiastic readers.

Comprehension Strategies

✦ During the reading of "Bear Shadow," you will model the following comprehension strategies:

• Asking Questions

• Clarifying

✦ Think aloud through each strategy, and encourage students to share their ideas as well.

Vocabulary

brook	annoyed
cliff	bury

Concept/Question Board

Tell students readers keep thinking about any questions that are generated as they are reading. As they read, tell them to keep in mind the questions on the **Concept/Question Board.** Tell them readers are always thinking about what is important in selections and they try to remember this important information.

Comprehension Strategies

Teacher Modeling

❶ Asking Questions *Why is Bear talking to his shadow? Does he think the shadow will answer? I don't think shadows can talk, but this is a fantasy, so maybe it will.*

❷ Asking Questions *I wonder if Bear will be able to get rid of his shadow. Based on what we have learned about shadows, we might think that he couldn't. But maybe it will disappear for a little while. What do you think? Will Bear be able to get rid of his shadow? We'll read more to find out.*

❸ Clarifying *It's not clear what Bear was wrong about. Let's reread the page before this one. Bear thought his shadow was gone, but he was standing in the shade. When you are standing in the shade, there is no light to make a shadow. By rereading another page, I was able to clarify what happened.*

❹ Clarifying *Because Bear went to the cliff and climbed so high, it must be a high place. Looking at a picture will help us better understand what a cliff is.*

Focus Question Why does Bear talk to his shadow?

Bear Shadow

by Frank Asch

One day Bear went down to the pond with his fishing pole and a big can of worms. While he was putting a worm on his hook, he looked down and saw a big fish. I'm going to catch that fish, thought Bear to himself.

22

But when Bear stood up to throw his line in the water, his shadow scared the big fish away.

23

"Go away, Shadow!" cried Bear. But Bear's shadow would not go away. ❶

24

"Okay," said Bear. "If you won't go on your own, then I'll just have to get rid of you!" ❷
   And he put down his fishing pole and began to run.

25

 Teacher Tip

GLOSSARY The word *bury* can be found in the Glossary of the ***My Shadow Big Book.***

He ran around the pond. When he got to the other side he kept on running.

26

He ran through a field of flowers, jumped over the brook and hid behind a tree.

"Good!" thought Bear. "Now Shadow can't find me!"

27

But Bear was wrong. When he stepped out ❸ from behind the tree the first thing he saw was Shadow.

28

❹ Nearby was a cliff. Bear walked over to the cliff and looked up. I'll climb so high Shadow won't be able to follow me, thought Bear.

29

My Shadow Big Book, pp. 22–29

Differentiating Instruction   English Learners

IF ... students have difficulty tracking print, **THEN ...** keep in mind that their home languages may be written and read vertically or from right to left. For such students, provide explicit instruction and extra practice tracking print.

Print and Book Awareness

Sentences, Directionality

Display pages 22 and 23 of the **Big Book,** and have volunteers show where to start reading each sentence and where to stop. Remind students we read from left to right, a sentence begins with a capital letter, and some sentences end with periods. Because some sentences do not stop at the end of a line of type, you might have to help students track from one line to the next.

Alphabetic Knowledge

Display pages 26 and 27 of the **Big Book,** and have volunteers point to and say any letters they recognize. Then have a volunteer find and point to a word on one of the pages that begins with a capital letter. Say the word, and then ask if anyone knows why some words begin with capital letters. If necessary, remind students capital letters are used at the beginnings of names and sentences. Have the volunteer count the number of words in that sentence.

Exclamation Points

Display page 27, and have a volunteer point to the two exclamation points. Remind students this sign shows the speaker is saying something with strong feeling. Then read the sentences with strong feeling, and have students do the same.

Differentiating Instruction   English Learners

IF ... students are native speakers of Spanish, **THEN ...** remind them that the English exclamation point appears only at the end of a sentence, never at the beginning.

Comprehension Strategies

Teacher Modeling

5 **Asking Questions** *I wonder why Bear was huffing and puffing. Oh, I know—he was out of breath from climbing up the cliff.*

6 **Asking Questions** *I wonder if Bear will be able to nail his shadow to the ground. I don't think so, but in a fantasy, or make-believe story, you never know. Let's read on and see what happens.*

7 **Asking Questions** *I wonder why Shadow was nowhere to be seen. Oh, I know. It was noon, and the sun was high in the sky. When the sun is straight above, there aren't any shadows. By thinking about what I already know about shadows, I was able to answer my question.*

Differentiating Instruction **English Learners**

IF ... students need help with multiple-meaning words, **THEN ...** point out that *nail* on page 32 is used as both a noun and a verb. Explain that the same word can mean more than one thing. In this case, *nail* is a noun meaning "a piece of metal used to hold things together" and a verb meaning "to hammer onto something."

Bear climbed higher and higher until at last he pulled himself up to the top. Huffing and **5** puffing, he smiled with pride.

30

Then he looked down and saw Shadow.

31

Now Bear was very annoyed, so he went home and got a hammer and some nails to nail his shadow to the ground. **6**

32

He hammered and hammered and hammered, but no matter how many nails he hammered, he couldn't nail his shadow down.

33

 Teacher Tip

ASKING QUESTIONS Inform students that they should keep asking questions and trying to answer them as they read.

If I can't nail him down, thought Bear, maybe I can bury him. So he got his shovel and dug a hole. When the hole was deep and wide, he let his shadow fall in the hole.

34

Then Bear filled in the hole with dirt. When he was finished it was almost noon. The sun was high in the sky and Shadow was nowhere to be seen. **7**

"At last!" sighed Bear. "No more shadow!"

35

But now Bear was very tired. So he went inside and took a little nap.

36

While he slept, time passed and the sun once again cast shadows everywhere.

37

My Shadow Big Book, pp. 30–37

Print and Book Awareness

Picture-Text Relationship

✦ Have students look closely at the picture on page 31. Invite them to talk about what they see. Ask *What is Bear doing? looking at his shadow How does he seem to feel? puzzled, confused How do you know? the expression on his face Why is he puzzled? He thought he had lost his shadow by climbing the cliff.*

✦ Have students look at the picture on page 36. Then ask *What is Bear doing? yawning Can you tell just by looking at the picture?* Reread the text, and ask students how the words help them understand the picture better. *Bear is tired, so he is yawning.*

✦ Have students look at the picture on page 37 and tell what it shows. Then ask *How does this picture let you know that the story is made-up and not real? Bear is sleeping in a bed in a house, and real bears do not do that.*

Alphabetic Knowledge, Word Recognition

Have volunteers come to the **Big Book** and point to and say the names of any letters or words they recognize.

Comprehension Strategies

Teacher Modeling

8 Clarifying *What does the author mean by saying Shadow was too quick? We can reread the sentence before this one to see if it helps us understand. Bear slammed the door, hoping Shadow would be locked inside. I get it. Bear doesn't realize that you can't stop your shadow by closing a door behind you. Shadow stayed with Bear because the sunlight didn't change.*

9 Asking Questions *How can Shadow let Bear catch a fish? Shadow scared the fish away before. Can he do something so they won't be scared? Let's read on to see if we can figure this out.*

10 Clarifying *Let's think about what just happened. If Shadow kept his part of the deal, then he let Bear catch a fish. The sun was in a different part of the sky, so Shadow must be behind Bear now. That means he wouldn't have scared away the fish, so Bear would have been able to catch one. By thinking about what we already know about shadows, we can figure this out.*

When Bear got up and opened his door, he saw his shadow on the floor. "Not you again!" exclaimed Bear. And he slammed the door, hoping to lock Shadow inside. But Shadow was too quick. **8**

38

"Mmm," sighed Bear. "How about this . . . If you let me catch a fish, I'll let you catch one, too. Nod your head like this if it's a deal." When Bear nodded his head, Shadow nodded too. **9**

39

So Bear went back to the pond and once again threw his line in the water. By this time the sun was in a different part of the sky, which made it easy for Shadow to keep his part of the deal. **10**

40

And when Bear caught that big fish, Shadow caught one too.

41

My Shadow Big Book, pp. 38–41

Print and Book Awareness

Ellipses

Show students page 39, and have a volunteer point to the three dots they have learned about.

Quotation Marks

Point out the quotation marks on page 39, and explain that quotation marks show the words a person or a story character is saying.

Discussing the Selection

✦ Review the Focus Question with students: Why does Bear talk to his shadow? *This is a fantasy, and in a fantasy, animals can act like humans, and shadows can talk.*

✦ Visit the school library, and choose selections from several genres such as fairy tales, tall tales, nursery rhymes, and fables. Have students discuss the differences between each and identify each genre. Have students discuss characters, setting, sequence of events, and any connections they can make among themselves, the text, and their world.

✦ Have students retell the main events of "Bear Shadow" and describe the characters and setting.

✦ Have students select fiction selections to read for pleasure.

Vocabulary Review

Review with students the selection vocabulary words *rid, cliff, annoyed,* and *bury.* Ask students the following questions:

• *What are some things we get rid of?*
• *Where might we see a cliff?*
• *When have you felt annoyed?*
• *What kinds of things can we bury?*

 Teacher Tip

DISCUSSING THE SELECTION Tell students after reading, they should always ask, *What did I find interesting? What is important here? What did I learn?* Later, remind students again that whenever they conclude a reading, they should ask themselves questions about what was in the text.

Language Arts

Students will
- ✦ revise writing by adding ideas.
- ✦ listen to sentences and edit them to make improvements.
- ✦ participate in a Thinking Story experience.

- ✦ *Language Arts Big Book,* p. 9
- ✦ *Willy the Wisher,* p. 64

Writing Process

Revise: Adding Ideas to Writing

Teach

- ✦ Display page 9 of the *Language Arts Big Book.* Remind students of what they added to the class thank-you card to make it better. If you feel it would benefit students, discuss the items on the revising list once more.

- ✦ Tell students today they will add ideas to the inside pages of the class thank-you card to make it better.

Apply

- ✦ Display the class thank-you card again. Focus students' attention on the first inside page (left-hand side) of the card. Ask students if anyone has any suggestions for making this page of the card better. Say *What can we add to this page to make it better?* When students offer suggestions, ask them to also tell why they think their ideas would make the card better.

- ✦ Choose one or two suggestions, and add them to the card.

- ✦ Repeat the process for the right-hand inside page of the card.

- ✦ When the card is finished, allow students to sign their names. Then send the card to the intended recipient, either through the mail or by hand delivery if the recipient is in the school.

Grammar, Usage, and Mechanics

Teach

Display the *Language Arts Big Book,* and turn to page 9. Remind students that when writers revise something, they make it better. Explain that the way to make writing better is to change something about it.

Language Arts Big Book, p. 9

Differentiating Instruction **English Learners**

IF ... students need additional help with revising, **THEN ...** refer to Unit 6 Lesson 7 of the *English-Learner Support Guide.*

Grammar, Usage, and Mechanics continued

Guided Practice

✦ Write the following sentence on the board: *Mom said, Don't forget your coat!* Read the sentence aloud, pointing to each word as you say it. Have students repeat after you.

✦ Ask students *How can we make this sentence better?* If they offer no suggestions, tell them you can change the word *said* to *yelled* to make the action word better. Tell them you can also add the word *brown* before *coat* to tell more about the coat.

✦ Write the new sentence on the board: *Mom yelled, Don't forget your brown coat!* Have students read the sentence aloud with you.

Teacher Tip

NEW SKILLS The story questions for "I Forgot What You Needed" challenges students to make some predictions about the items that Phil fetches for his grandfather. These questions elicit answers that build upon Phil's actions earlier in the story. If students are having difficulty making predictions, have them reflect on Phil's earlier choices. For example, say *Last time, Grandfather asked for a box of tacks, and Phil brought him an empty box. Now Grandfather has asked for a brush. What do you think Phil might come back with?*

Differentiating Instruction **English Learners**

IF ... students lack vocabulary to suggest words to replace *said*, **THEN ...** teach words such as *yelled, shouted, whispered, mumbled,* and *pleaded*. Demonstrate their meanings by using each one in place of *said* in the example sentence.

Willy the Wisher ⏱

✦ Display the book *Willy the Wisher.* Ask a volunteer to come to the book and to identify its Table of Contents. Together, find the story "I Forgot What You Needed" on page 64 of the book.

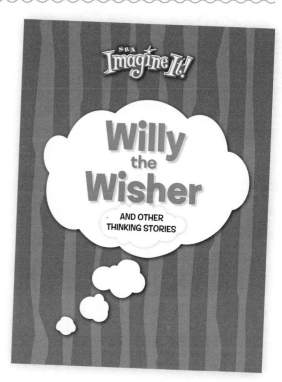

Willy the Wisher, p. 64

✦ Before reading the story to students, invite them to discuss what they know about Phil. Phil likes to help people but has trouble remembering exactly what he is supposed to do and easily forgets details. In this story, Phil is helping his grandfather complete some chores on the farm.

✦ Read the story, pausing at the red text to ask students the questions. If necessary, model the thinking process, and ask specific students to share their thinking.

✦ After reading the story, discuss Phil's experience helping his grandfather build a rabbit pen. Use questions such as the following:

- *Why does Phil keep returning with the wrong items?*
- *What would you do if you were Phil? How would that help?*
- *What should Grandfather do to help Phil remember the right things?*

✦ To ensure that students get the point of Phil's misunderstandings of what his grandfather wants, have several individuals retell the episodes in the story in which Grandfather asks Phil to get paper, a brush, and so on.

Sounds and Letters

Students will

✦ use letters in different combinations to form words.

✦ change the sounds in words by deleting final phonemes.

✦ attach the /ks/ sound to the letter *Xx*.

✦ practice writing the letter *Xx*.

MATERIALS

✦ *Pocket Chart Letter Cards* a, d, f, g, h, i, j, m, n, o, p, s, t

✦ *Routine* 1

✦ *Pocket Chart Picture Cards* 7, 31

✦ Supply Icons

✦ *Skills Practice 2,* pp. 13–14

Calendar

Su	M	T	W	Th	F	S
		1	2	3	4	5
6	7	8	9	10	11	12
13	14	15	16	17	18	19
20	21	22	23	24	25	26
27	28	29	30	31		

Point to the box that represents today. Then ask a volunteer to come up to the calendar and to point to the day that will happen one week from today.

Warming Up

MORNING MESSAGE

Today is _____.

We use the letters _____ and _____ to play tic-tac-toe.

Let's play tic-tac-toe!

Kindergarten News

✦ Copy the text above on the board or on chart paper.

✦ Ask students to identify the letters used for tic-tac-toe. *X and O* Have volunteers write the letters in the blanks. If possible, draw a tic-tac-toe board, and have a pair of students play the game. Tell students they will learn more about the letter *Xx* in today's class.

✦ Use prompts such as the following to discuss the letters and the words in the message: *What is the name of the mark at the end of the last sentence? exclamation point Come draw a box around it. How many times does the letter Tt appear in the message? Let's circle and count them.*

Phoneme Manipulation

✦ Using a paper bag and the **Pocket Chart Letter Cards** listed with the materials, place two copies each of the *p, d, n,* and *g* **Letter Cards** in the bag.

✦ Put the letters *o* and *t* in the chart. Say *The sounds are /o/ /t/. Blend them together: /ot/.* Call on a student to reach into the bag for a letter and to place it before *ot.* Say *Can you say the new word?*

✦ Continue by changing the letters in the **Pocket Chart** and the **Letter Cards** in the bag to make new words. Some word sets you might use include the following:

m … at *mat*	p … at *pat*	f … ast *fast*
p … it *pit*	s … it *sit*	f … it *fit*
d … ip *dip*	s … ip *sip*	t … ip *tip*
t … op *top*	p … op *pop*	m … op *mop*
j … am *jam*	d … ot *dot*	h … am *ham*

Phonemic Awareness

Phoneme Manipulation: Final Sounds

✦ Bring out the **Lion Puppet,** and tell students he wants to play the game in which he takes away sounds from words to make new words. Remind them they will need to listen very closely to the last sound in each word.

✦ Tell students you will say a word and the puppet will say which sound in the word he wants them to take away.

✦ Say a word, have students repeat it, and then have the puppet tell students to take away the ending sound. Everyone will then say the word without the final phoneme. For example:

Teacher: *The word is* fox.
Students: *fox*
Puppet: *Now take away the /ks/. How do you say the word without the /ks/?*
Everyone: *fo …*

✦ Continue with these words:

rib, /b/ ri …	*twig, /g/ twi …*
glad, /d/ gla …	*wax, /ks/ wa …*
puff, /f/ pu …	*room, /m/ roo …*
class, /s/ cla …	*basket, /t/ baske …*
best, /t/ bes …	*battle, /l/ batt …*

Differentiating Instruction | **English Learners**

IF … students have difficulty with phoneme replacement, **THEN …** review the consonant sounds with them, and then have them try the game again.

Teacher Tip

LISTENING SKILLS To focus students on their listening skills at any time, play a brief game of Simon says with them. Ask a volunteer to be the leader, and give directions for others to follow. Play several rounds, and then move into a listening activity such as the one in this lesson.

Teacher Tip

THE SOUND OF *Xx* For students who have difficulty making the /ks/ sound, it may be helpful to have them say the /k/ and /s/ sounds separately. Then you can have them repeat the sounds one after the other with increasing speed until you hear /ks/. Stop students, and congratulate them on making the sound of *Xx*.

Alphabetic Principle

Introducing the Sound of Xx

✦ Refer to Routine 1 for the Introducing Sounds and Letters procedure.

✦ Point to **Alphabet Sound Wall Card** *Xx*, and say its sound: /ks/. Show the picture, and recite the story for the /ks/ sound:

Rex is called the Exiting X.
He runs to guard the door.
To get past Rex,
Make the sound of the x:
/ks/ /ks/ /ks/ /ks/ /ks/.

✦ Ask students *Who can say the sound for* x? Invite several volunteers to say the /ks/ sound. Then ask the class to say it aloud as a group. /ks/ /ks/ /ks/ /ks/ /ks/

Alphabet Sound Wall Card 24

✦ Tell students you will read the story again but this time you want them to make the sound of *x* to "get past Rex." Read the first four lines of the story, and allow students to say the last line.

Listening for /ks/

✦ Hold up and name each of these **Pocket Chart Picture Cards:** 31—box and 7—six. Ask students to listen for the /ks/ sound in the words.

✦ Ask students to listen for where the /ks/ appears in the words: beginning, middle, or end. Hold up and name each **Picture Card** again. Explain to students that *Xx* is a special letter that usually appears at the ends of words.

✦ Give each student an **Alphabet Letter Card** *Xx*. Tell students you are going to say words and you want them to hold up the cards and say the /ks/ sound when they hear a word ending in the /ks/ sound.

✦ Use these words:

flax	flip	*six*	*relax*	box	*ax*
fix	fly	*wax*	wait	mat	*mix*

Technology

Use the **Alphabet Sound Card Stories CD** for practice with the /ks/ sound.

Audio CD

Penmanship

✦ Distribute a sheet of writing paper to each student, or use **White Boards** turned to the sides with writing lines. Place the Supply Icon for *pencil* on the board or in the **Pocket Chart.**

✦ Using the established procedure, review with students how to form a capital *X: Begin here, and make a diagonal line down to the right. Then go back up to the top, and make another diagonal line down to the left so the lines cross in the middle. Capital* X. Also review the steps for making small *x: Begin here, and make a short diagonal line down to the right. Then go back up to the top, and make a short diagonal line down to the left so the lines cross in the middle. Small* x. Remind students the letter *x* makes the /ks/ sound, and have them say the sound as they make the letter in the air.

✦ Now invite students to practice writing capital *X*s across the top row of the paper or board. Have them practice writing small *x*'s across the next row. Then have them proofread by starring their best letters and circling the letter(s) they would like to make better.

Guided Practice

✦ Have students complete **Skills Practice 2** page 13 for additional practice writing the letter *Xx* and identifying the final /ks/ sound.

✦ Have them practice writing capital *X* letters and small *x* letters on the lines at the top of the page. Then say the name of each picture, and have students write an *x* under those whose names end with the /ks/ sound. After students have finished, be sure to review their work. Save student pages for use in penmanship proofreading activities in later lessons.

Monitor Progress to Differentiate Instruction

Formal Assessment ✓

Letter and Sound Identification Observe students' ability to identify the /ks/ sound.

APPROACHING LEVEL

IF ... students are having difficulty, THEN ... help them complete **Reteach** pages 113 and 114.

ON LEVEL

IF ... students need more practice, THEN ... have them continue the activity using **Skills Practice 2** page 14.

ABOVE LEVEL

IF ... students are comfortable, THEN ... have them complete **Challenge Activities** page 86.

 Teacher Tip

USING PROGRAM MATERIALS Use **Transparency** 24 or **Alphabet Sound Wall Card** *Xx* to help you review the shape of *Xx.* Remember that letter-formation procedures are located in the Appendix.

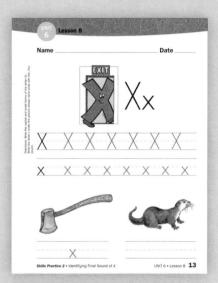

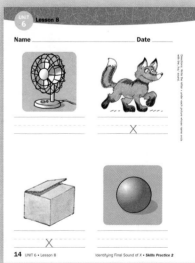

Skills Practice 2, pp. 13–14

Reading and Responding

Students will

✦ develop an understanding of vocabulary words.

✦ review the comprehension strategies Asking Questions and Clarifying.

✦ use the comprehension skill Drawing Conclusions.

✦ analyze the plot structure of the selection.

MATERIALS

✦ *My Shadow Big Book,* pp. 22–41
✦ Routines 5–7

 Preview and Prepare

2nd READ

Preview the Selection **ROUTINE 5**

✦ Display the **My Shadow Big Book** opened to the Table of Contents page. Use Routine 5, the previewing the selection routine, to guide students in understanding and using the Table of Contents to locate the selection. Then point to and say the title and the name of the author and the illustrator.

✦ Prepare to reread the selection. As you turn through the pages, have students use the illustrations to retell the main events in the story and describe characters and setting.

Vocabulary **ROUTINE 6**

✦ Follow Routine 6, the selection vocabulary routine, as you introduce the vocabulary words for this selection.

✦ Explain that when something is *wide*, it is a large distance from side to side. Ask students to stretch their arms as wide as possible.

✦ Tell students the word *sighed* means "made a deep sound with the breath as if tired." Then demonstrate a sigh, and have students sigh all together.

✦ Explain that the word *exclaimed* means "spoke loudly and suddenly." Then write the sentence *You won!* on the board, and ask a volunteer to say it loudly and suddenly. Then say *You won! _____ exclaimed.*

✦ Tell students when they make a *deal* with someone, they make a decision together. Use the following sentence to illustrate: *Let's make a deal to put things where they belong.*

Focus Question Why does Bear talk to his shadow?

Bear Shadow

by Frank Asch

One day Bear went down to the pond with his fishing pole and a big can of worms. While he was putting a worm on his hook, he looked down and saw a big fish. I'm going to catch that fish, thought Bear to himself.

22

My Shadow Big Book, p. 22

Vocabulary

wide	exclaimed
sighed	deal

Read the Selection

ROUTINE **7**

Comprehension Strategies

✦ During the first reading of "Bear Shadow," you modeled the following reading comprehension strategies:

- Asking Questions
- Clarifying

✦ In this second reading of the selection, you will revisit each comprehension strategy model from the first reading.

Comprehension Skills

In this lesson of "Bear Shadow," students will use the comprehension skill Drawing Conclusions.

Reading with a Writer's Eye

✦ In this rereading of "Bear Shadow," you will discuss how the author structures the plot of the story to help students follow and enjoy it.

✦ By discussing the author's writing strategies, students learn how they can be better group writers.

 Teacher Tip

VOCABULARY Encourage students to use a variety of sources to build their vocabulary, such as making word banks, discussing characters and events from a story, talking with other people, and thinking about their own life experiences.

Technology

To promote independent reading, encourage students to use Workshop to listen to the recording of the selection on the *Listening Library CD.* Invite them to follow along and say the words whenever they can.

Audio CD

Comprehension Strategies

Teacher Modeling

1 **Asking Questions** *I asked questions here to help me focus and think about the story. Why is it good to ask questions about what we read?*

2 **Asking Questions** *Remember I wondered if Bear would be able to get rid of his shadow? My question wasn't answered here. But I remember from our last reading that I found my answer at the end of the story. Sometimes we have to wait until the end to see if our questions get answered.*

3 **Clarifying** *I know I can reread other pages to figure out what I don't understand. How were we able to clarify why Bear was wrong about his shadow?*

4 **Clarifying** *How were we able to clarify what a cliff is?*

Differentiating Instruction **English Learners**

IF . . . students have difficulty drawing and expressing conclusions, **THEN . . .** introduce the following linguistic patterns: *I read that _____. I know that _____. I can conclude that _____.*

Focus Question Why does Bear talk to his shadow?

Bear Shadow

by Frank Asch

One day Bear went down to the pond with his fishing pole and a big can of worms. While he was putting a worm on his hook, he looked down and saw a big fish. I'm going to catch that fish, thought Bear to himself.

22

But when Bear stood up to throw his line in the water, his shadow scared the big fish away.

23

"Go away, Shadow!" cried Bear. But Bear's shadow would not go away. **1**

24

"Okay," said Bear. "If you won't go on your own, then I'll just have to get rid of you!" **2**

And he put down his fishing pole and began to run.

25

He ran around the pond. When he got to the other side he kept on running.

He ran through a field of flowers, jumped over the brook and hid behind a tree.
"Good!" thought Bear. "Now Shadow can't find me!"

26

27

But Bear was wrong. When he stepped out **3** from behind the tree the first thing he saw was Shadow.

4 Nearby was a cliff. Bear walked over to the cliff and looked up. I'll climb so high Shadow won't be able to follow me, thought Bear.

28

29

My Shadow Big Book, pp. 22–29

Teacher Tip

DRAWING CONCLUSIONS Use riddles to help students understand the concept of drawing conclusions. Say a riddle, and have students use clues to determine the answer.

Comprehension Skills

Drawing Conclusions

✦ Review with students readers sometimes have to use clues in the story they already know to determine certain things in a story. Remind them this is called drawing conclusions.

✦ Ask students what the author tells us about Bear. *Bear likes to fish in the pond; he fishes by himself; he talks to his shadow.* Then ask them to draw a conclusion about what Bear knows about shadows. *Bear thinks he can run away from his shadow.*

✦ Ask students *What do you know about shadows that Bear doesn't seem to know? Shadows do not disappear simply because you try to hide from them.*

Reading with a Writer's Eye

Plot Structure

✦ Plot is the word we use to describe what happens in a story. Plots sometimes begin with a problem. Ask students what problem Bear faces in the beginning of the story. *Bear wants to catch a fish, but his shadow scares it away.*

✦ Ask students how Bear tries to solve his problem on pages 26–29. Tell students Bear's attempts to solve his problem, or get rid of his shadow, control how the plot develops.

Reading and Responding

2nd READ

Comprehension Strategies

Teacher Modeling

5 **Asking Questions** *Do you remember that I asked why Bear was huffing and puffing? How were we able to answer our question?*

6 **Asking Questions** *We wondered if Bear would be able to nail down his shadow. When we read on, we discovered he could not nail it down even though this is a fantasy, or a make-believe story.*

7 **Asking Questions** *Readers think about what they already know to answer questions they have about a story. When we thought about where the sun is at noon, we were able to answer our own questions about Shadow. We understood why Shadow had disappeared.*

Vocabulary Tip

Review the meanings of the words *wide* and *sighed*. Then have students use the words in sentences.

Bear climbed higher and higher until at last he pulled himself up to the top. Huffing and **5** puffing, he smiled with pride.

30

Then he looked down and saw Shadow.

31

Now Bear was very annoyed, so he went home and got a hammer and some nails to nail his shadow to the ground. **6**

32

He hammered and hammered and hammered, but no matter how many nails he hammered, he couldn't nail his shadow down.

33

If I can't nail him down, thought Bear, maybe I can bury him. So he got his shovel and dug a hole. When the hole was deep and wide, he let his shadow fall in the hole.

34

Then Bear filled in the hole with dirt. When he was finished it was almost noon. The sun was high in the sky and Shadow was nowhere to be seen. **7**

"At last!" sighed Bear. "No more shadow!"

35

But now Bear was very tired. So he went inside and took a little nap.

36

While he slept, time passed and the sun once again cast shadows everywhere.

37

My Shadow Big Book, pp. 30–37

Teacher Tip

ANSWERING QUESTIONS When asking students *why* questions, make sure they explain by discussing the "science" behind shadows and not simply by describing the causal event.

Comprehension Skills

Drawing Conclusions

✦ Ask students what they know about what it takes to make a shadow. Then point to the drawings on pages 32 and 33 in the *Big Book.* Help students draw a conclusion about the illustrations by having them answer the following question: *Why couldn't Bear nail down his shadow? A shadow moves around with the object that casts it.*

✦ Direct students' attention to pages 34 and 35 in the *Big Book.* Ask students *Why did Bear think he had buried his shadow? It was nowhere to be seen. Why couldn't Bear see his shadow when he tried to bury it? It was almost noon, and the sun was high in the sky. When the sun is high in the sky, it does not cast as large a shadow because Bear's body does not block much light.*

Reading with a Writer's Eye

Plot Structure

✦ Ask students how Bear tries to solve his problem on pages 30–37. *He tries to nail his shadow to the ground and bury it.*

✦ Tell students Bear's attempts to solve his problem, or to get rid of his shadow, continue to control how the plot develops.

Comprehension Strategies

Teacher Modeling

8 Clarifying *We were confused about what had happened here. So we thought about what Bear was trying to do by slamming the door. We realized he didn't understand what caused shadows to appear and disappear. We knew why Shadow had stayed with Bear because we remembered how shadows form.*

9 Asking Questions *We wondered how Shadow could let Bear catch a fish. How were we able to answer our question?*

10 Clarifying *We figured out how Shadow kept his part of the deal by thinking about what we knew about shadows. We knew if the sun were in a different part of the sky, Shadow would not be in front of Bear as he was before, and the fish would not be scared away.*

Vocabulary Tip

Review the meanings of the words *exclaimed* and *deal*. Then have students use each word in a sentence.

When Bear got up and opened his door, he saw his shadow on the floor. "Not you again!" exclaimed Bear. And he slammed the door, hoping to lock Shadow inside. But Shadow was too quick. **8**

38

"Mmm," sighed Bear. "How about this . . . If you let me catch a fish, I'll let you catch one, too. Nod your head like this if it's a deal." When Bear nodded his head, Shadow nodded too. **9**

39

So Bear went back to the pond and once again threw his line in the water. By this time the sun was in a different part of the sky, which made it easy for Shadow to keep his part of the deal. **10**

40

And when Bear caught that big fish, Shadow caught one too.

41

My Shadow Big Book, pp. 38–41

Reading with a Writer's Eye

Plot Structure

✦ Ask students how Bear's problem was and how it is solved in the end. Point out to students the sun solves Bear's problem for him.

✦ Point out to students the plot of "Bear Shadow" begins with a problem, continues with efforts to solve the problem, and ends with a solution.

Discussing the Selection

Ask a volunteer to use the illustrations to retell the story. Encourage him or her to use words such as *first, then, next,* and *finally*.

Purposes for Reading

Ask students what they liked best about this selection. Invite students to share what they learned about shadows from this selection.

Vocabulary Review

Review with students the selection vocabulary words *wide, sighed, exclaimed,* and *deal.* Ask students the following questions:

- *What kinds of things can be wide?*
- *When was a time you sighed?*
- *Who is someone you know that has exclaimed something?*
- *Who is someone with whom we might make a deal?*

BIG Idea

Why do shadows come and go?

Write the Big Idea question on the board. Ask students what they have learned about shadows. Ask which selections added something new to their understanding about shadows.

Language Arts

Students will
✦ work in groups to create thank-you cards.
✦ collaborate to extend a story line.

✦ *Story Lines Big Book,* pp. 10–11

Teacher Tip

PLAN AHEAD In preparation for the following activity, have drawing paper and art supplies on hand.

Traits of Good Writing

Ideas Writers use pictures to help readers visualize their ideas.

Writing Process

Draft: Creating Another Card

Teach

✦ Remind students of the thank-you card the class created. Review the steps the class took to create the thank-you card. Write the following on the board:

• Brainstorm a person to send the card to.

• Brainstorm ideas for the card (pictures and words).

• Choose ideas for the card, and put them in order, using the words *first, next,* and *last.*

• Make the card.

• Add ideas to make the card better.

✦ Read steps aloud, and ask students to share what they remember about each. Tell them now it is their turn to follow these steps on their own—they will make a thank-you card for someone else.

Apply

✦ Organize the class into groups of four to five students. Give each group a clean sheet of drawing paper and art supplies.

✦ As students work, remind them periodically of the steps they should be following. Circulate around the room, and offer help as needed. Offer suggestions for the card recipients, or help students spell or write words on their cards.

✦ When they are finished, have each group member sign his or her name to the card.

✦ Collect students' cards, and store them until the next lesson. Tell students they will share their cards with the rest of the class in the next lesson.

Story Crafting ⏱

Story Lines

✦ Display the **Story Lines Big Book,** and open it to pages 10 and 11, "Shadowland."

✦ Review the story, pointing to each frame as you read.

✦ Then draw students' attention to the "Tell Me More" extender frames on pages 14 and 15. Remind students these boxes are just like the story frames they see on the previous pages, except these frames are empty so students can help tell more of Jameena's story.

✦ Review Frame 12, and discuss how the existing story ends. Ask students *What do you think happens after Grandma leaves Jameena's bedroom again?*

✦ To guide students in continuing the story, ask them questions such as the following:

  • *Do you think Jameena fell asleep after Grandma left her bedroom?*

  • *What could Jameena or Grandma do to stop the shadows from coming into Jameena's room?*

✦ Choose one of the students' ideas, and make a simple line drawing in the first extender frame to illustrate it.

✦ Ask students to suggest a sentence describing the action in this new frame. Write the sentences in the space provided.

✦ When students have completed Frames 13–15, review them, and tell students they will finish the story in the next lesson.

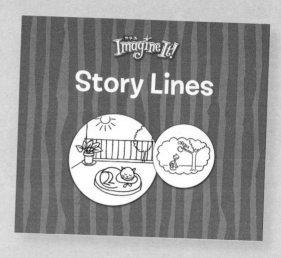

Story Lines Big Book, pp. 10–11

Differentiating Instruction　**English Learners**

IF ... students have limited vocabulary, **THEN ...** help them participate in discussions by asking them questions that can be answered by nodding, by saying *yes* or *no,* or with one or two words.

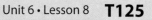

Sounds and Letters

Students will
✦ review the /u/ sound by creating rhyming words.
✦ change the sounds in words by deleting final phonemes.
✦ attach the /ks/ sound to the letter *Xx*.

✦ **Alphabet Flash Cards**
✦ **Alphabet Letter Card** *Xx* for each student
✦ **Alphabet Book Big Book,** pp. 50–51

Calendar

Su	M	T	W	Th	F	S
		1	2	3	4	5
6	7	8	9	10	11	12
13	14	15	16	17	18	19
20	21	22	23	24	25	26
27	28	29	30	31		

Point to the box that represents today. Ask a volunteer to point to the next day that the class will have a special activity such as art class or a field trip. Have everyone say the date aloud.

Differentiating Instruction **English Learners**

IF ... students have difficulty generating rhyming words, **THEN ...** have them play the game by listening carefully to the words their classmates say and, when they catch the ball, repeating the last word they heard rather than generating a new word.

Warming Up

MORNING MESSAGE

Today is _____.

Yesterday we read about _____.

The word *mix* rhymes with *fix*.

Kindergarten News

✦ Copy the text above on the board or on chart paper. Use a self-sticking note to cover the word *rhymes* in the third sentence; it can be today's Secret Word.

✦ Read all three sentences, saying the word *blank* in place of the word *rhymes* in the third sentence. Tell students today's Morning Message has a Secret Word. Explain it is a verb that means "sounds like." Read the third sentence again, and invite students to determine the Secret Word. Discuss the clues that led them to find the correct word.

✦ Discuss the letters and words in the message. You might ask students to identify a few words that have the letter *x*, or you might count the spaces between words in the sentences.

Oral Language

✦ Have students sit in a circle. Give a student something to toss, such as a beanbag.

✦ Tell the student to say a word that has the /u/ sound in the middle, such as *cup*, and then toss the beanbag. Help the student who catches the beanbag say a word that rhymes with the first word. Then have the student toss the beanbag to another student, who says another rhyming word.

✦ Before playing the game, you may want to review some easy-to-rhyme words, such as *bun, cut, duck, dust, gum, hug,* and *rub.*

Phonemic Awareness

Phoneme Manipulation: Final Sounds

✦ Bring out the **Lion Puppet,** and tell students he wants to play the game in which he takes away sounds from words to make new words. Remind them they will need to listen very closely to the last sound in each word.

✦ Tell students you will say a word and the puppet will say which sound in the word he wants them to take away.

✦ Say a word, have students repeat it, and then have the puppet tell students to take away the ending sound. Everyone will then say the word without the final phoneme. For example:

Teacher:	*The word is* mix.
Students:	*mix*
Puppet:	*Now take away the /ks/. How do you say the word now?*
Everyone:	*mi . . .*

✦ Continue with these words:

time, /m/ ti . . .	*job, /b/ jo . . .*
bump, /p/ bum . . .	*pick, /k/ pi . . .*
stand, /d/ stan . . .	*miss, /s/ mi . . .*
stuff, /f/ stu . . .	*oak, /k/ oa . . .*
big, /g/ bi . . .	*bump, /p/ bum . . .*

Teacher Tip

LEARNING THROUGH GAME PLAY Consider modifying popular games to help children learn new letters, sounds, and other concepts. For example, use a modified version of Tic-Tac-Toe to help students practice their familiarity with the letter *Xx*. Write a word that contains *x* on the board, such as *six,* filling in each letter except for *x*. Have students guess which letter is missing. After they guess correctly, guide them in blending the word sound by sound.

Alphabetic Principle

Reviewing the Sound of *Xx*

✦ Use the **Alphabet Flash Cards** to take students through a quick review of the names of the letters of the alphabet.

✦ Hold up the cards in random order, with the capital and small letters showing. Save the *Xx* card for last.

✦ When you come to a card with a letter for which students have learned the sound, review that as well.

✦ End by pointing to **Alphabet Sound Wall Card** *Xx*. Say its sound for students: /ks/. Then review the story for the /ks/ sound, allowing students to say the final line.

Rex is called the Exiting X.

He runs to guard the door.

To get past Rex,

Make the sound of the x:

/ks/ /ks/ /ks/ /ks/ /ks/.

Listening for /ks/

✦ Give each student an **Alphabet Letter Card** *Xx*. Tell students to hold up their cards and say /ks/ when they hear you say a word that contains the /ks/ sound. Ask them where they hear the sound—beginning, middle, or end. *middle*

✦ Use these words:

| **mixer** | **waxing** | scoop | trooper | **extra** |
| blimp | shrimp | **sixty** | **Texas** | popcorn |

Linking the Sound to the Letter

Write the following pairs of words on the board. Read both words, and then repeat the word that has the /ks/ sound. Ask individual students to circle the words you have said, to tell how they know the correct word, and to underline the letter that makes the /ks/ sound. Try these words:

tax ... tap   *extra ... elbow*

ready ... relax   *meadow ... Mexico*

Alphabet Book Big Book—/ks/

✦ Display the **Alphabet Book Big Book,** and turn to pages 50–51, *Xx.* Point to the title letters *Xx,* and have students say the names of the letters. *capital* X, *small* x

✦ Ask students to listen closely for the /ks/ sound while you read the rhyme aloud.

✦ After you finish reading, invite students to mention any words they noticed with the /ks/ sound, such as *box. box, x-ray, ox, mixer, six, T. rex* Write the words on the board in list form under the heading The /ks/ Sound.

✦ Then have volunteers come to the book and point to words that contain the letter *x,* such as *box.* Write those words on the board in a list next to the first list. Use the heading Words with *Xx.*

✦ Remind students that the letter *Xx* make the /ks/ sound. Have students come up to the board and help you draw lines to match the words in each list.

✦ Say the following words from the rhyme, and have students cross their fingers to make an *X* if the word contains the /ks/ sound.

box   **ox**   *Maybe*   **mixer**   **six**   *even*

Alphabet Book Big Book, pp. 50–51

Technology

Each of the rhymes from the **Alphabet Book Big Book** is available on the **Listening Library CD.** Use the **eAlphabet Book** for activities that support the **Alphabet Book Big Book** lessons.

Audio CD

Reading and Responding

Students will

✦ locate the title and the names of the poet and the illustrator.

✦ connect their own life experiences to the text.

✦ develop an understanding of vocabulary words.

✦ use the comprehension strategy Visualizing.

✦ *My Shadow Big Book,* pp. 42–43

✦ Routines 5–7

Focus Question   Why did the shadow hide?

Hide-and-Seek SHADOW

by Margaret Hillert
illustrated by Bob Masheris

I walked with my shadow,

I ran with my shadow,

I danced with my shadow,

I did.

Then a cloud came over

And the sun went under

And my shadow stopped playing

And hid.

42

My Shadow Big Book, pp. 42–43

Technology

To promote independent reading, encourage students to use Workshop to listen to the recording of the selection on the **Listening Library CD.** Invite them to follow along and to say the words whenever they can.

Audio CD

Poetry

Activate Prior Knowledge   ROUTINE 5

✦ Ask students if they have ever watched their shadows as they have moved around. Invite them to share what this was like and how it made them feel. Ask students *Does your shadow ever do something different from what you do? Does it ever disappear and then come back?*

✦ Tell students you will be reading them a poem about a shadow that plays hide-and-seek. Ask students what might make a shadow disappear and then come back. As you read the poem, relate what you already know to what you are reading, and encourage students to do the same.

✦ Have students discuss what they are learning about shadows. This poem conveys the idea that shadows can appear and disappear depending on the light. Key concepts include the following:

• Shadows do what we do and go where we go.

• Shadows appear only when there is some source of light.

Preview the Poem   ROUTINE 5

✦ Display the **My Shadow Big Book** opened to pages 42–43. Follow Routine 5, the previewing the selection routine, as you point to and say the poem's title and the names of the poet and the illustrator. Ask students what a poet and an illustrator do.

✦ Invite students to examine the picture and to share what they see. Ask what the little boy in the picture seems to be doing.

Vocabulary

ROUTINE **6**

◆ Follow Routine 6, the selection vocabulary routine, as you introduce the vocabulary words for this selection.

◆ Tell students a *cloud* is a puffy, white mass floating in the sky.

◆ Explain that the word *hid* means "put something out of sight so you cannot find it." Use the following sentence to illustrate: *The kittens hid when they heard us coming.*

Read the Poem

ROUTINE **7**

◆ Before reading the poem, read the Focus Question above it. Tell students to keep this question in mind as they listen to the poem.

◆ Follow Routine 7, the reading the selection routine, as you read aloud "Hide-and-Seek Shadow." As you read, emphasize the rhythm the words create. Then invite students to clap the rhythm as you read the poem again.

◆ Invite students to ask questions or to think aloud about anything in the poem that interests or puzzles them.

Comprehension Strategies

For this poem, model the comprehension strategy Visualizing to help students use language to make mental pictures of settings, characters, and actions.

Vocabulary

cloud	hid

🍎 Teacher Tip

VISUALIZING Tell students to make mental pictures of what they read. Explain that this technique will help them better understand the poem or story.

Reading and Responding

Focus Question   Why did the shadow hide?

Hide-and-Seek
SHADOW

by Margaret Hillert
illustrated by Bob Masheris

I walked with my shadow,

I ran with my shadow,

I danced with my shadow,

I did.

Then a cloud came over

And the sun went under

And my shadow stopped playing

And hid.

42   43

My Shadow Big Book, pp. 42–43

Teacher Tip

GLOSSARY The words *cloud* and *hid* can be found in the Glossary of the *My Shadow Big Book.*

Comprehension Strategies

Teacher Modeling

❶ **Visualizing** *Close your eyes, and see whether you can make a picture in your mind of the little boy looking for his shadow behind some playground equipment. A cloud is casting a shadow over the playground, so the spot has become shady. The boy's shadow is nowhere to be found.*

Monitor Progress to Differentiate Instruction   Formal Assessment

Visualizing Note how easily students grasp visualizing.

APPROACHING LEVEL	**IF ...** students need help visualizing,	**THEN ...** refer to Unit 6 Lesson 9 of the *Intervention Guide.*
ON LEVEL	**IF ...** students need to practice visualizing,	**THEN ...** have them play the guessing game I'm Thinking of Something… with partners.
ABOVE LEVEL	**IF ...** students are comfortable visualizing,	**THEN ...** give them a scene with shadows to visualize, and have them draw pictures of what they see.

Discussing the Poem

✦ Review the Focus Question with students: Why did the shadow hide? *The sun went behind a cloud.*

✦ Invite students to share their thoughts and ideas about the poem. Discuss how a shadow can appear and disappear.

Purposes for Reading

✦ Remind students they were listening to find out what the poem tells them about shadows. Ask students what they learned about shadows from listening to this poem.

✦ Have students discuss the difference between reading a poem for pleasure and reading something for information.

✦ Have students identify selections in the unit they read for pleasure and which selections provided information.

Vocabulary Review

Review with students the selection vocabulary words *cloud* and *hid*. Ask students the following questions:

• *Where can we see a cloud?*
• *When was a time you hid?*

Language Arts

OBJECTIVES

Students will

✦ share their thank-you cards with the class.

✦ write tongue twisters that repeat sounds.

✦ collaborate to extend a story line.

MATERIALS

✦ *Alphabet Book Big Book,* pp. 6–9

✦ *Pickled Peppers Big Book,* p. 15

✦ *Story Lines Big Book,* pp. 10–11

Writing Process 🕐

Present: Sharing Cards

Teach

✦ Tell students today they will share their thank-you cards with the class.

✦ Have students return to their groups from the previous lesson, and distribute each group's card. Give them a few minutes to plan their presentations. Ask students to look closely at their cards and to decide what they want to say about them. Have them also decide what each group member will say.

Apply

✦ Pointing to the Listening Icons, remind students to listen carefully.

✦ Have groups take turns presenting their cards. If necessary, ask each group questions about the card to initiate discussion.

✦ After each group's presentation, call on an audience member to say one thing he or she likes about the group's card.

✦ After all groups have shared their cards, collect the cards, and facilitate the delivery of each.

Grammar, Usage, and Mechanics 🕐

Teach

✦ Remind students that they studied a unit about patterns, and invite a volunteer to identify a pattern somewhere in the classroom. Explain that patterns appear everywhere, even in sentences.

✦ Display pages 6–7 of the **Alphabet Book Big Book.** Read the rhyme to students once. Have volunteers come up and point to each letter *Bb* in the lines. Explain that all the /b/ sounds in the rhyme create a pattern they can hear. Have students close their eyes while you read the rhyme again, emphasizing the /b/ sound.

✦ Now turn to pages 8–9 in the **Alphabet Book Big Book.** Tell students rhymes can make patterns too. Read the *Cc* rhyme aloud, and have students identify the pattern of rhyming words.

Guided Practice

✦ Display page 15 of the **Pickled Peppers Big Book,** and read the rhyme aloud for students. Remind students that "Peter Piper" is an example of a famous tongue twister.

✦ Challenge students to make patterns with words and sentences by creating tongue twisters from their own names. Ask each student to create a pattern by repeating the sound that begins his or her name.

✦ Invite volunteers to share their tongue twisters with the class.

Story Crafting

Story Lines

✦ Display the **Story Lines Big Book,** and open it to pages 10 and 11, "Shadowland." Have students share what they remember about Jameena and her grandmother.

✦ Review the story, pointing to each story frame as you read its accompanying text.

✦ Turn to page 14, and spend some additional time discussing Frames 13–15—the extender frames students completed in the previous lesson. Ask students *Would you like to change or add anything to these three frames?* Ask volunteers to tell why they think their suggestions will make the story better.

✦ Then turn to page 15, and tell students today they will complete the story of Jameena and the shadow. Guide students by asking questions to spark their creativity. Shape the questions in such a way that they build from Frames 13–15 and lead students to a story resolution. For example, lead them to end the story with Jameena changing bedrooms or with Jameena telling about her shadow experience in school.

✦ Fill the remaining extender frames, and guide the class in crafting story text to accompany the drawings.

✦ When students have completed the story, initiate a class discussion in which students reflect on their experiences with extending Jameena's story.

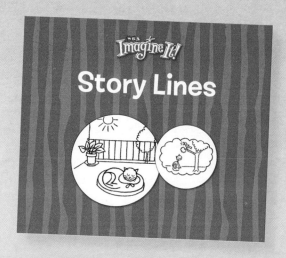

Story Lines Big Book, pp. 10–11

Differentiating Instruction **English Learners**

IF ... students have difficulty verbalizing ideas for completing the story, **THEN ...** encourage them to draw their ideas, and help them put the ideas in their drawings into words.

Students will

✦ create rhyming words by replacing initial phonemes.

✦ identify phoneme positions in words.

✦ attach the /z/ sound to the letter *Zz*.

✦ practice writing the letter *Zz*.

✦ practice sound-by-sound blending.

✦ read and respond to a **Decodable.**

✦ **Pocket Chart Picture Cards** 1, 73, 200, 201

✦ Routines 1, 2, 4

✦ **Alphabet Letter Card** *Zz* for each student

✦ Supply Icons

✦ **Skills Practice 2,** pp. 15–16

✦ **Decodable** 9

Calendar

Su	M	T	W	Th	F	S
		1	2	3	4	5
6	7	8	9	10	11	12
13	14	15	16	17	18	19
20	21	22	23	24	25	26
27	28	29	30	31		

Point to the box that represents today. Then ask students to identify the next weekend day. Invite a volunteer to point to Saturday. If necessary, review the differences between school days and weekend days.

🍎 Teacher Tip

PLAN AHEAD In advance of this lesson, have available three sheets of construction paper in different colors.

Warming Up 🕐

MORNING MESSAGE

Today is _____.

What is your favorite pet?

dog   cat   hamster   fish

Kindergarten News

✦ Copy the text above on the board or on chart paper. Create a simple chart to record students' votes for their favorite pets.

✦ Take a survey of students' favorite pets, count the votes, and record them on the chart. You might ask volunteers to help you count how many students vote for each category.

✦ Use prompts such as the following to discuss the letters and words in the message: *Where is the question in the Morning Message?* the second sentence *Come point to it. What letters make up the word* cat? *c, a, t Let's say each letter's sound all by itself.* /k/, /a/, /t/

Phoneme Replacement

✦ Tell students they are going to play a game in which they will use what they are learning about sounds and letters to make rhymes. Explain that you are going to give them a riddle and that the answer is a word that begins with the sound that you say.

✦ Demonstrate as follows:

Teacher: *What rhymes with* mat *but starts with /h/?*

Students: *hat*

✦ Continue with these riddles:

What rhymes with hit *but starts with /f/?* fit

What rhymes with bet *but starts with /j/?* jet

What rhymes with fix *but starts with /s/?* six

What rhymes with mill *but starts with /f/?* fill

What rhymes with peg *but starts with /l/?* leg

Phonemic Awareness

Phoneme Segmentation

✦ In a row on the floor, tape three sheets of colored construction paper, using three different colors. Display and say aloud the **Pocket Chart Picture Card** for a three-phoneme word such as 73—hat. Have three students stand up. As you say each sound in the word *hat,* have each student step on the first, second, and third sheet of paper, respectively. To help students focus, you may want to tell them, for example, blue is the first sound, red is the middle sound, and yellow is the last sound of the word.

✦ Then ask for a new set of volunteers, and give each volunteer a sound in a word to say. For example, say *Charlie, you are /t/. Ben, you are /m/. Cassie, you are /a/.*

✦ With each student, say the sound several times until he or she can repeat it easily.

✦ Next say the word *mat*, and tell students to stand on the sheets in order so their sounds make the word. When the word has been formed, have each student say her or his sound and then have the class blend the sounds together to say the word.

✦ Ask the class to determine if students have made the correct order of sounds. Tell them to signal thumbs-up if the order is correct and thumbs-down if it is not. If the order is not correct, have the class help students in the row make it correct.

✦ When the order is correct, have students in the row blend the sounds quickly and smoothly to form the whole word. Then have the class blend the sounds to say the word again.

 Teacher Tip

SEGMENTATION In Unit 4, students identified and counted phonemes using blocks. This lesson will begin to advance their understanding of segmentation by counting the number of phonemes in a word and the order in which they come.

Differentiating Instruction **English Learners**

IF . . . students are native speakers of Spanish or an Asian language, **THEN . . .** they may need extra practice pronouncing the letter z, since /z/ does not occur in their native languages.

Technology

Use the *Alphabet Sound Card Stories CD* for practice with the /z/ sound.

Audio CD

Alphabetic Principle

ROUTINE **1**

Introducing the Sound of Zz

+ Refer to Routine 1 for the introducing sounds and letters routine.

+ Display **Alphabet Sound Wall Card** *Zz*, and say its sound. After showing the picture, recite the story for the /z/ sound:

Zack's jacket has a zipper.

Zack zips it up, and it makes this sound:

/z/ /z/ /z/ /z/ /z/ /z/.

Zack zips it down, and it makes this sound:

/z/ /z/ /z/ /z/ /z/ /z/.

+ Read the story once more, this time inviting students to join you on the /z/ /z/ /z/ /z/ /z/ /z/.

Alphabet Sound Wall Card 26

Listening for Initial /z/

+ Hold up and name each of these **Pocket Chart Picture Cards:** 201—zoo, 1—zero, 200—zebra. Ask students to listen for the /z/ sound at the beginnings of the words.

+ Give each student an **Alphabet Letter Card** *Zz*. Tell students you are going to say words and you want them to hold up the cards and say the /z/ sound when they hear you say a word beginning with the /z/ sound.

+ Try the following words:

zip	*hip*	**zipper**	**zag**
lap	*land*	**zany**	**zigzag**
broom	**zoom**	**zone**	*relax*

Linking the Sound to the Letter

Write two words on the board, one that begins with the /z/ sound and one that does not. Say the word that begins with the /z/ sound. Ask individual students to circle the word you said, tell how they knew the correct word, and underline the letter that makes the /z/ sound. Try these words:

boo . . . *zoo*   *zap* . . . tap

zero . . . hero   room . . . *zoom*

Penmanship

✦ Distribute a sheet of writing paper to each student, or use **White Boards** turned to the sides with writing lines. Place the Supply Icon for *pencil* on the board or in the **Pocket Chart.**

✦ Review the formation of capital *Z: Begin here, and make a short horizontal line to the right. Then make a diagonal line to the left. Then make another short horizontal line to the right. Capital* Z. Remind students that the letter *Zz* makes the /z/ sound, and have them say the sound as they make the letter in the air.

✦ Continue by reviewing how to form small *z: Begin here, and make a short horizontal line to the right. Then make a short diagonal line to the left. Then make another short horizontal line to the right. Small* z.

✦ Ask students to write several rows of capital *Z* letters on the front of the sheet or board. Then have them write several rows of small *z* letters. Make sure they are writing from left to right.

Guided Practice

✦ Have students complete **Skills Practice 2** pages 15–16 for additional practice writing the letter *Zz* and identifying the initial /z/ sound.

✦ Have them write a row of capital *Z*s and a row of small *z*'s on the top two lines. Explain that some of the pictures begin with the /z/ sound. Have students write the letter *z* under each picture whose name begins with the /z/ sound.

✦ After students have finished, be sure to review their work.

Teacher Tip

LETTER FORMATION Because the letter *Zz* is a somewhat difficult letter for young writers, students might benefit from extended guided practice. You might begin by having students trace the letter in the air with their fingers as you describe and model the letter-formation steps aloud. Then as they practice writing the letter, walk around the room, and offer struggling students extra support such as hand-over-hand practice.

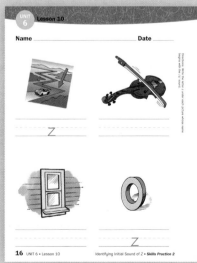

Skills Practice 2, pp. 15–16

Monitor Progress to Differentiate Instruction

Formal Assessment ✓

Penmanship Note how accurately students write the letter *Zz*.

APPROACHING LEVEL	
IF ... students are having difficulty,	**THEN ...** create dot-to-dot letter *Zz*'s, and have them practice tracing the letter before writing more letters on their own.

ON LEVEL	
IF ... students need more practice,	**THEN ...** have them draw a picture of an object beginning with the /z/ sound and then write several letter *Zz*'s beneath the picture.

ABOVE LEVEL	
IF ... students would enjoy a challenging activity,	**THEN ...** have them work independently to complete **Challenge Activities** pages 87 and 88.

Bud and Max

by Tristan Horrom
illustrated by Laura Logan

Decodable 9

Teacher Tip

PRINT AND BOOK AWARENESS Use *Decodable* 9 to help students become familiar with the features of print books. Have students practice locating information and specific page numbers in the book on demand. For example, you might ask them to tell which page has a box in the picture *(page 8)* or to describe what they see on page 5.

Technology

Use **eDecodable** *Bud and Max* to reinforce high-frequency words *but* and *up* and the /u/ and /ks/ sounds.

Audio CD

Reading a Decodable ROUTINE **2** ROUTINE **4**

Decodable 9: Bud and Max

High-Frequency Words: *but, up*

✦ The high-frequency words introduced are *but* and *up*. Write *but* on the board, and read it aloud. Have students repeat it aloud with you. Then have students say the word on their own. Repeat the process with *up*.

✦ Point again to *but* written on the board, and have students read the word independently. Do the same with *up*. Have students work with partners to say a few sentences using the words *but* and *up*.

✦ Tell students they will see the words *but* and *up* very often in books, on posters, and in other print. Ask them to find and point to examples on any classroom posters, bulletin boards, or covers of any books.

✦ Review the high-frequency words introduced in previous lessons.

Blending

Before reading **Decodable** 9, review the sound-by-sound blending procedure with students. Choose words with the /u/ and /ks/ sounds or other sounds students have already learned, such as *fox, jump,* and *mix*. After blending, have students make and extend sentences for each word.

Reading Recommendations

✦ Distribute copies of **Decodable** 9. Ask students to browse through the book and look at the pictures, commenting on what they see and making predictions about what they think the story will be about.

✦ Point to the high-frequency words *but* and *up* in the text, and pronounce them. Then have students point to the words and read them aloud.

✦ Hold up your book, and read the title, pointing to each word. Read the names of the author and the illustrator aloud, pointing to each name as you say it. Ask students to explain the jobs of author and illustrator.

✦ Read the **Decodable,** following the established procedure. (See Routine 4 for a detailed description.) After you have read the story, reread the title, and have students repeat after you. Then have students read it chorally with you. Remind them we read from left to right.

Bud and Max

by Tristan Harrom
illustrated by Laura Logan

Bud and Max pop up!

3

But the sun is up.

4

Dig in, Max! Dig in!

5

Bud and Max pop up!

6

But the sun is not up.

7

Jump on the box, Bud!

8

Decodable 9
Bud and Max

High-Frequency Words Introduced in Decodable 9
but
up

Previously Introduced High-Frequency Words
a
am
and
as
at
can
did
for
girl
go
had
has
have
he
him
his
I
in
is
it
of
on
see
the
to
we
you

Sound-Spelling Correspondences in Decodables
1. /s/, /m/, /d/, /p/, /a/
2. /h/, /t/
3. /n/, /i/
4. /f/
5. /b/, /k/ spelled c
6. /o/, /r/
7. /g/
8. /j/, /f/
9. /u/, /ks/ spelled x

Responding

◆ Display the **High-Frequency Flash Cards** for *but* and *up*. Have students find and point to these high-frequency words in the story. Ask students to identify in the story any of the previously introduced high-frequency words.

◆ Discuss the book. Encourage them to talk about the people (characters) they see in the pictures and the order of events that the pictures illustrate. To engage students, you might use questions such as the following:

- *Why do Bud and Max dig back into their holes?*
- *What do you think Bud and Max will do next? Why do you think so?*
- *What do you know about groundhogs? Tell us about it.*

◆ Write the word *six* on the board, and guide students in segmenting the sounds in the word. After the /ks/ sound has been identified, invite students to search the story for other words that end with the /ks/ sound.

◆ Make copies of the story for students to take home. A black-and-white version of the story is available in **Pre-Decodable and Decodable Takehomes Blackline Masters**.

Decodable Book 9, inside back cover

Reading and Responding

Students will

✦ generate questions about shadows for research.

✦ experiment with making and changing shadows.

✦ describe their observations orally.

✦ *My Shadow Big Book,* pp. 4–43

INQUIRY PLANNER

WEEK 1	✦ Begin discussing and sharing ideas. ✦ Think about a question for the **Concept/Question Board.**
WEEK 2	✦ Begin investigating and collecting information. ✦ Generate a question and/or idea for the **Concept/Question Board.**
WEEK 3	✦ Share your findings with others. ✦ Do you have more questions?

Teacher Tip

CHART Make a chart with a column for student names and a column for what they learned. Have students share what they learned from the experiment. Write their names and what they learned. Discuss the new information on this chart, and talk about how charts in general help us organize our observations.

Inquiry

✦ Discuss with students what they learned in "Bear Shadow." Ask questions such as the following:

• *Why did Bear want to get rid of his shadow?*

• *How did Bear try to get rid of his shadow?*

• *Why did Bear's shadow fall in one direction at one time and in another direction earlier or later in the day?*

✦ Read some questions from the **Concept/Question Board,** and encourage students to answer them if possible. Have volunteers share shadow pictures if they took them or talk about the shadows they saw on the shadow hunt.

Whole-Group Time   Whole Group

✦ Review the experiment from the previous week, and discuss what the class learned. Tell the class they are going to do another experiment today. Attach a large piece of newsprint onto a wall. Fasten a piece of tape onto the floor, leading from a light source toward the newsprint. Mark two spots on the tape, one about one foot from the light source and the other about three feet from the light source.

✦ Gather students around. Have a volunteer stand on the tape at the spot closest to the light source. Turn on the light, and darken the room. Have the volunteer hold a cutout in front of the light. Ask a second volunteer to use a marker and trace around the shadow cast on the newsprint. Then call on a third volunteer to stand on the tape at the second mark on the tape. Give the same cutout to this student, and have him or her hold it in front of the light. Talk about this shadow, and have a volunteer use a marker in a contrasting color to trace around the shape. Turn the lights on, and compare the two outlines. How and why did they change in size?

Small-Group Time Small Group

✦ On a piece of chart paper, draw a light source, such as a lamp or a lightbulb, with a cutout directly above it. On a second piece of paper, draw another light source with the cutout farther from the light source. Point out that in the picture, the light is close to the cutout and in the picture in the second picture, the light is farther from the cutout.

✦ Have students draw the shadow the cutout would make next to each picture. Encourage students to discuss the results of the class experiment before drawing each shadow.

Whole-Group Time Whole Group

Work on a class question-and-answer book about shadows. Encourage students to look at the charts you made as well as the **Concept/Question Board** for ideas. Review good question words. Have magazines and other resources students can look at for ideas. During Workshop have students complete one page for the book using the following two headings: My Question Is and What I Learned about Shadows.

Concept Vocabulary

The second concept vocabulary word for Unit 6, My Shadow, is *darkness*. Write the word on an index card, and post it in your classroom. Explain to students that *darkness* is a state of no or little light. Tell students they are in darkness when they are in their bedrooms at night and the lights are out. Discuss how the word *darkness* relates to the formation of shadows. Use the word in a sentence, and have students practice saying it. Tell students you will use the word *darkness* as often as possible, and encourage them to use it too.

Teacher Tips

RECREATIONAL READING Because it is important to read daily to your students, choose a book from the Additional Reading listed in the Unit Overview, and find a time during the day to read the book aloud to your students.

MATERIALS Activities in this lesson will require sheets of newsprint, masking tape, a lamp, a cardboard cutout, markers, and index cards.

Concept/Question Board

Return to the **Concept/Question Board,** and read each question. Ask students if they have any conjectures or new information that might answer the questions. Invite students to post any new items and to discuss these with the class. As you discuss each idea, invite volunteers to share whether their ideas have changed since the last experiment. Be sure to allow time to help individual students add self-sticking notes to the **Concept/Question Board.**

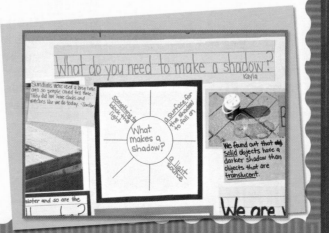

Language Arts

Students will

✦ reflect on their experiences with brainstorming.

✦ practice writing sentences with sound patterns.

✦ review the letters *Xx* and *Zz* through game play.

Writing Process 🕐

Reflection: Illustrating Brainstorming

Teach

✦ Congratulate students on all their hard work while making the thank-you cards.

✦ Remind them before they were able to make the class thank-you card and the ones they made in their groups, they first had to think of ideas for the cards. Invite a volunteer to tell how the class thought of ideas. Remind students brainstorming is one way to think of ideas for writing.

Apply

✦ Have students discuss what it was like to work as a class to brainstorm ideas. Ask them:

  • *What did you like when we brainstormed ideas?*

  • *How do you think brainstorming ideas helped you get ideas for your card?*

✦ After a brief whole-class discussion of brainstorming, ask students to draw pictures in their journals that show how brainstorming helped them when making their thank-you cards.

Grammar, Usage, and Mechanics 🕐

Teach

✦ Remind students certain sounds in words can be repeated to make patterns. Rhyming words can also make sound patterns in writing.

✦ Ask students to recall the tongue twisters they made up about their names in the previous lesson.

Guided Practice

✦ Organize students into pairs. Have partners work together to make up a sentence or two that shows a sound pattern.

✦ Tell students you will write on the board either a letter or a word. If you write a letter, they should use words that begin with the letter to make a sound pattern in a sentence. If you write a word, they should use that word and a rhyming word to make a rhyming sound pattern.

✦ After each round, invite students to share their creations.

 Teacher Tips

HIGH-FREQUENCY WORDS Before students begin this activity, take this opportunity to point out the high-frequency word *up*, appearing three times on page 7 of "Shadows."

PLAN AHEAD In preparation for the following activity, have drawing paper and pencils on hand.

GAME Day

Tic-Tac-Toe Tournament

✦ In advance of the activity, draw a large tournament bracket, such as those used to track sports tournaments, on the board or on chart paper. Create two main brackets, one on the left side of the board and one on the right. In each bracket, write the names of students in pairs, and then draw blank lines to represent the winners at each point in the tournament up to the championship game.

✦ On the day of the activity, have students meet with their first opponents and play three games of tic-tac-toe, using the letters *X* and *Z* instead of *X* and *O*. The student who wins two out of three games advances to the next round.

✦ Have students begin playing and report who should advance after each round. Write the students' names on the appropriate slots in the tournament bracket.

✦ Continue the tournament until only two students remain. Have them play three games to determine the grand champion.

✦ To have the tournament take less time, have students advance after winning one game instead of two out of three.

Teacher Tip

TOURNAMENT BRACKETS If you are unfamiliar with tournament brackets, use the Internet to view examples. (Enter the search terms *tournament bracket encyclopedia* to find reference articles.) The single-elimination tournament, the type suggested for this activity, eliminates one player after each round. It is a basic method of tracking competition.

Lesson Planner

Day 1

Day 2

Sounds and Letters

MATERIALS

- ◆ *Pocket Chart Picture Cards*
- ◆ *Routines 1, 2, 4*
- ◆ *Skills Practice 2,* pp. 17–21
- ◆ *Transparency* 26
- ◆ *Teacher's Resource Book,* p. 37
- ◆ *Alphabet Letter Cards: Ff, Jj, Uu, Xx, and Zz*
- ◆ *Pocket Chart Letter Cards*
- ◆ *Alphabet Book Big Book,* pp. 44–45, 54–55
- ◆ *Decodable* 10

Day 1

Warming Up, pp. T158–T159
Phonemic Awareness
Phoneme Segmentation, p. T159
Alphabetic Principle
- Introducing the Sound of /z/ Spelled *Ss,* p. T160
- Listening for Final /z/, p. T160
- Linking the Sound to the Letter, p. T160
- Penmanship, p. T161

Day 2

Warming Up, p. T168
Phonemic Awareness
Phoneme Segmentation, p. T169
Alphabetic Principle
- Reviewing the Sounds of *Xx* and *Zz,* p. T170
- Listening for Final /ks/ and /z/, p. T170
- *Alphabet Book Big Book*—/z/, p. T171

Reading and Responding

MATERIALS

- ◆ *Science Lap Book,* pp. 20–27
- ◆ *Routines 5–7*
- ◆ *Story Time Collection: Nothing Sticks Like a Shadow*
- ◆ *Skills Practice* 2, p. 22
- ◆ *My Shadow Big Book*
- ◆ *Home Connection,* pp. 49–50
- ◆ *Read Aloud Collection: What Makes a Shadow?*

Science Link, p. T162
Vocabulary, p. T163
Read the Selection, p. T163
Comprehension Strategies, p. T164
Print and Book Awareness, p. T165
Vocabulary Review, p. T165

Science Link, p. T172
Vocabulary, p. T172
Read the Selection, p. T173
Comprehension Strategies, p. T174
Reading with a Writer's Eye, p. T175
Discussing the Selection, p. T175
Vocabulary Review, p. T175

Language Arts

MATERIALS

- ◆ *Language Arts Big Book,* pp. 18, 30, 37, 55
- ◆ *My Shadow Big Book,* p. 44
- ◆ *Transparencies* 38, 48, 48A
- ◆ *Willy the Wisher,* p. 67
- ◆ *Thinking Crowns*
- ◆ *Skills Practice 2,* p. 22

Writing Process
Prewrite: Brainstorming and Sequencing, p. T166
Fine Art
Discussing Fine Art, p. T167

Writing Process
Model: Using Descriptive Words, p. T176
Grammar, Usage, and Mechanics, pp. T176–T177
Willy the Wisher, p. T177

Monitor Progress

✓ = **Formal Assessment**

Ⓑ = **Benchmark Assessment**

✓ *Lesson Assessment Book,* p. 59
✓ **Letter and Sound Identification,** p. T161

✓ *Lesson Assessment Book,* p. 60
✓ **Letter and Sound Identification,** p. T170

Literature Overview

Science Lap Book

Sunny Sky, Starry Sky

by Jeffery Smith

Story Time Collection

Nothing Sticks Like a Shadow

by Ann Tompert

illustrated by Lynn Munsinger

Day 3

Warming Up, pp. T178–T179
Phonemic Awareness
Phoneme Segmentation, p. T179
Alphabetic Principle
• Reviewing the Sounds of *Jj, Ff,* and *Uu,* p. T180
• Listening for /u/ and Initial /j/ and /f/, p. T180
• Linking the Sound to the Letter, p. T180
• Penmanship, p. T181

Preview and Prepare, p. T182
Vocabulary, p. T183
Read the Selection, p. T183
Comprehension Strategies, pp. T184, T186, T188, T190
Print and Book Awareness, pp. T185, T187, T189, T191
Discussing the Selection, p. T191
Vocabulary Review, p. T191

Writing Process
Draft: Collaborating to Create an Advertisement, p. T192
Story Crafting
Working with the New: Problem/Resolution Plots, p. T193

✓ *Lesson Assessment Book,* p. 61
✓ **Letter and Sound Identification,** p. T181

Day 4

Warming Up, pp. T194–T195
Phonemic Awareness
Phoneme Segmentation, p. T195
Alphabetic Principle
• Reviewing the Sounds of *Xx, Zz,* and *Uu,* p. T196
• Listening for /u/ and Final /ks/ and /z/, p. T196
• *Alphabet Book Big Book*—/u/, p. T197

Preview and Prepare, p. T198
Vocabulary, p. T198
Read the Selection, p. T199
Comprehension Strategies, pp. T200, T202, T204, T206
Comprehension Skills, pp. T201, T203, T205
Reading with a Writer's Eye, pp. T201, T203, T205, T207
Discussing the Selection, p. T207
Vocabulary Review, p. T207

Writing Process
Revise: Improving by Adding Ideas, p. T208
Grammar, Usage, and Mechanics, pp. T208–T209
Story Crafting
Working with the New: Thinking about Animals, p. T209

✓ *Lesson Assessment Book,* p. 61
✓ **Letter and Sound Identification,** p. T196
✓ **Describing Words,** p. T209

Day 5

Warming Up, pp. T210–T211
Phonemic Awareness
Phoneme Segmentation, p. T211
Alphabetic Principle
• Reviewing the Sounds of *Jj, Ff, Xx, Zz,* and *Uu,* p. T212
• Listening for Initial /j/ and /f/, p. T212
• Listening for Final /ks/ and /z/, p. T212
• Linking the Sound to the Letter, p. T212
• Penmanship, p. T213
• Proofreading, p. T213
Reading a *Decodable*
Decodable 10: *Liz and Tad,* pp. T214–T215

Theme Wrap-Up and Review, p. T216

Writing Process
Present and Reflect: Displaying Ad and Discussing Writing, p. T217
Grammar, Usage, and Mechanics, p. T217
Benchmark Assessment, pp. T218–T219
Unit Celebration
• Celebrate Shadows!, p. T220
• Inquiry Wrap-Up, p. T221

✓ *Lesson Assessment Book,* p. 62
✓ *Lesson Assessment Annotated Teacher's Edition,* pp. 62A–62B
   Comprehension Observation Log
✓ **Letter and Sound Identification,** p. T213
Ⓑ *Benchmark Assessment,* Benchmark 4

Student Resources

Big Books

Audio CD

Story Time Collection

Nothing Sticks Like a Shadow

by Ann Tompert

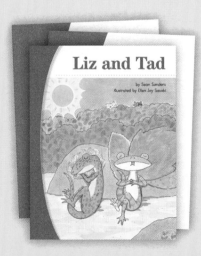

Decodable 10: *Liz and Tad*

Teacher Support

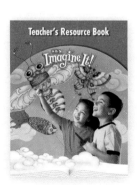

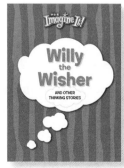

Language Arts Big Book

Teacher's Resource Book

Willy the Wisher

Curriculum Connections

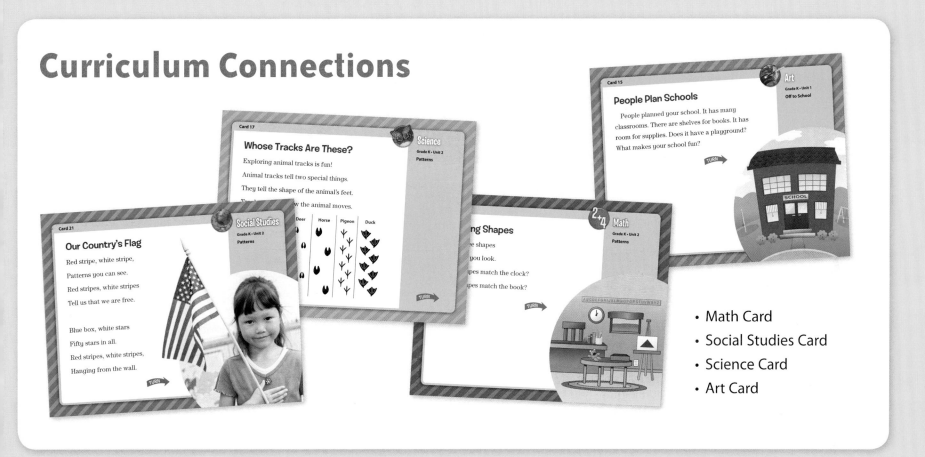

Card 17

Whose Tracks Are These?

Exploring animal tracks is fun!
Animal tracks tell two special things.
They tell the shape of the animal's feet.

Science
Grade K • Unit 2
Patterns

Deer   Horse   Pigeon   Duck

Card 21

Our Country's Flag

Red stripe, white stripe,
Patterns you can see.
Red stripes, white stripes
Tell us that we are free.

Blue box, white stars
Fifty stars in all.
Red stripes, white stripes,
Hanging from the wall.

Social Studies
Grade K • Unit 2
Patterns

ng Shapes

ee shapes
you look.
pes match the clock?
pes match the book?

Math
Grade K • Unit 2
Patterns

Card 15

People Plan Schools

People planned your school. It has many
classrooms. There are shelves for books. It has
room for supplies. Does it have a playground?
What makes your school fun?

Art
Grade K • Unit 1
Off to School

- Math Card
- Social Studies Card
- Science Card
- Art Card

Additional Skills Practice

Approaching Level	On Level	English Learner	Above Level
Reteach	**Skills Practice 2**	**English Learner Support Activities**	**Challenge Activities**
Describing Words, p. 121	Sentence Spacing, p. 22	Lessons 11–15	Letter and Sound Identification, pp. 89–92
Letter and Sound Identification, pp. 115–120, 122	Letter and Sound Identification, pp. 17–21		

Differentiating Instruction
for Workshop

Day 1

Approaching Level	On Level	English Learner	Above Level
Sounds and Letters			
Alphabetic Principle: Students listen to the story for *Zz* on the **Alphabet Sound Card Stories CD,** raising their hands every time they hear the /z/ sound.	**Alphabetic Principle:** Have students browse the ***My Shadow Little Big Book*** for the letter *Zz* and make the /z/ sound each time they find the letter.	**Alphabetic Principle:** Refer to Unit 6 Lesson 11 of the ***English Learner Support Guide.***	**Alphabetic Principle:** Students use the **eSkills** activity for this unit to review letters and their sounds.
Reading and Responding			
Preview: Students browse the illustrations and point out any words they recognize or illustrations that interest them.	**Preview:** Have students discuss the difference between daytime and nighttime and the kinds of things you can see during those times.	**Vocabulary:** Refer to Unit 6 Lesson 11 of the ***English Learner Support Guide.***	**Preview:** Students research with you on the Internet or in the school library about shadows they might find in space. Post their findings on the **Concept/Question Board.**
Language Arts			
Writing: Discuss with students their favorite things.	**Writing:** With your help, students brainstorm lists of things they like.	**Writing:** On the board, write the sentence frame *I like* _____. Read the sentence, and explain it to students with demonstrations and examples. Have students complete the sentence. Write down the things they like on chart paper.	**Writing:** Students brainstorm lists of their favorite things.

Day 2

Approaching Level	On Level	English Learner	Above Level
Sounds and Letters			
Alphabetic Principle: Work with students to use *eGames* for practice identifying letters and their sounds.	**Alphabetic Principle:** Have students use *eSkills* to review letter and sound identification.	**Alphabetic Principle:** Refer to Unit 6 Lesson 12 of the *English Learner Support Guide.*	**Alphabetic Principle:** Students draw pictures of items whose names have the /z/ sound.
Reading and Responding			
Vocabulary: Say each selection vocabulary word, and have students repeat each word after you. If students need further help with definitions, use illustrations and demonstrations.	**Comprehension:** Invite students to talk about "Sunny Sky, Starry Sky" and what they liked best about the selection.	**Comprehension:** Preview the selection *Nothing Sticks Like a Shadow* with students, and have them point to any words or illustrations that interest them.	**Comprehension:** Bring in pictures and information about solar and lunar eclipses and discuss their connection to the unit theme.
Language Arts			
Writing: Students help you create lists of their favorite things. **Grammar:** Students look at simple sentences in books.	**Writing:** With your help, students put the lists in order from most to least favorite. **Grammar:** With your help, students create simple sentences.	**Writing:** Have students draw a picture of something they like. **Grammar:** Refer to Unit 6 Lesson 12 of the *English Learner Support Guide.*	**Writing:** With your help, students title a sheet of paper "Things I Like." **Grammar:** Students find two simple sentences in a book.

Differentiating Instruction
for Workshop

Day 3

Approaching Level	On Level	English Learner	Above Level
Sounds and Letters			
Alphabetic Principle: Work with students to complete the activity on page 119 of **Reteach.**	**Alphabetic Principle:** Have students make a collage of the letters *Jj, Ff,* and *Uu* cut out from magazines and catalogs and then write each of the letters at the bottom of their artwork.	**Alphabetic Principle:** Refer to Unit 6 Lesson 13 of the **English Learner Support Guide.**	**Alphabetic Principle:** Students work independently to complete the activity on page 91 of **Challenge Activities.**
Reading and Responding			
Preview: Have students browse the selection and point out any illustrations that interest them or what they might learn about shadows from the story.	**Preview:** Have students discuss connections between Rabbit's understanding of shadows and what they have learned about shadows.	**Preview:** Refer to Unit 6 Lesson 13 of the **English Learner Support Guide.**	**Preview:** Discuss with students similarities between Bear and Rabbit and what they learned about shadows.
Language Arts			
Writing: With your help, students organize their lists from the most favorite to least favorite things.	**Writing:** Ask students to attach their lists to sheets of paper titled "Things I Like."	**Writing:** Have students show their pictures to the group. Have each student tell the group what they drew by completing the sentence frame. Write their sentences on the board. When they are finished, read the sentences back to them.	**Writing:** Students attach their lists to the title pages.

Day 4

Approaching Level	On Level	English Learner	Above Level

Sounds and Letters

Alphabetic Principle: Guide students in using **eSkills** to practice letter and sound recognition.

Alphabetic Principle: Use **eGames** to practice identifying letters and their sounds.

Alphabetic Principle: Refer to Unit 6 Lesson 14 of the **English Learner Support Guide.**

Alphabetic Principle: Using the **Pocket Chart Picture Cards,** students find pictures of items that have the /ks/, /z/, and /u/ sounds.

Reading and Responding

Comprehension: Have students retell the story *Nothing Sticks Like a Shadow* in their own words. Encourage them to use words such as *first, then,* and *last.*

Comprehension: On chart paper, write the words *real* and *fantasy.* Ask students to discuss each of the unit selections and whether or not they are real or fantasy.

Comprehension: Refer to Unit 6 Lesson 14 of the **English Learner Support Guide.**

Comprehension: Ask students to browse past units and point out selections that are either real or fantasy.

Language Arts

Writing: Students attach their lists to sheets of paper titled "Things I Like."

Grammar: Students add details to their sentences.

Writing: Students write their first and last names on the pages.

Grammar: With your help, students add details to their sentences.

Writing: Display the list of things that students like from Day 1. Have students practice using the sentence frame *I like* _____. with other words on the list. Be sure to read the words to help students select one for their sentence.

Grammar: Refer to Unit 6 Lesson 14 of the **English Learner Support Guide.**

Writing: Students sign their first and last names to their lists.

Grammar: Students make suggestions for how to improve the sentences.

Differentiating Instruction
for Workshop

Lessons 11-15 Overview

AYP

Day 5

Approaching Level	On Level	English Learner	Above Level
Sounds and Letters			
Reading a *Decodable:* Reread **Decodable** 10 with students, reinforcing the high-frequency word all.	**Reading a *Decodable:*** Students review the high-frequency word *all* and blending by using **eDecodable** *Liz and Tad.*	**Reading a *Decodable:*** Reread **Decodable** 10 with students, reviewing the high-frequency word *all* and sound-by-sound blending.	**Reading a *Decodable:*** Students reread **Decodable** 10 with partners, counting how many times the high-frequency word *all* appears.
Reading and Responding			
Review: Have students discuss unit selections they liked best and why.	**Review:** Students group into pairs and retell each selection to one another in their own words.	**Review:** Review the selection *Nothing Sticks Like a Shadow,* and have students talk about any questions or wonderings they have about the selection.	**Review:** Students review each selection and discuss how they relate to the unit theme.
Language Arts			
Writing: Students discuss their lists of favorite things. **Grammar:** Students share their sentences with partners.	**Writing:** Students share their lists with the group. **Grammar:** Students all sign their group sentence and post it in the classroom.	**Writing:** Students show their drawings to the class. If they feel comfortable, they can tell the class about the picture. Otherwise, for each picture say _____ *likes* _____. **Grammar:** Refer to Unit 6 Lesson 15 of the ***English Learner Support Guide.***	**Writing:** Students share their lists with the group. **Grammar:** Students create two new sentences, with you acting as scribe.

Resources for
Differentiating Instruction

English Learner

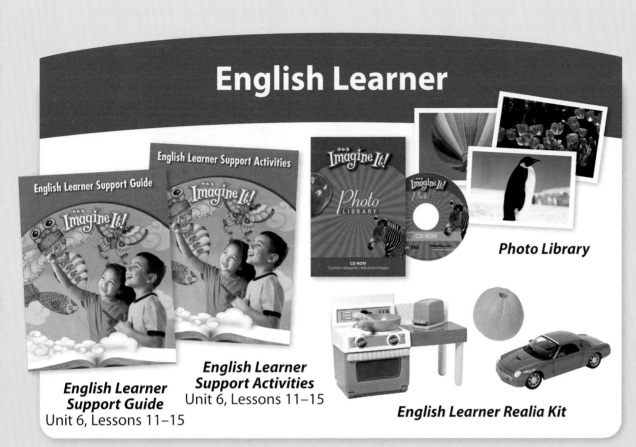

English Learner Support Guide
Unit 6, Lessons 11–15

English Learner Support Activities
Unit 6, Lessons 11–15

Photo Library

English Learner Realia Kit

Approaching Level

Intervention

Intervention Guide

Intervention Workbook

Workshop Kits

- High Frequency Words
- Letter Recognition
- Phonemic Awareness
- Print and Book Awareness
- Sequencing

Technology

Alphabet Sound Card Stories CD
eAlphabet Book
eDecodable Liz and Tad
eSkills & eGames
Listening Library CD

Listening Library Unit 6

Lesson Assessment

Monitor Progress
to Differentiate Instruction

Use these summative assessments along with your informal observations to assess student mastery.

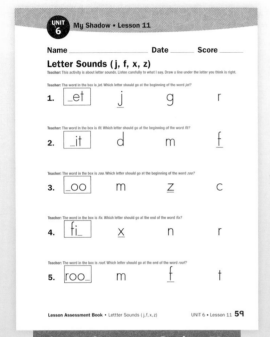

Lesson Assessment Book, p. 59

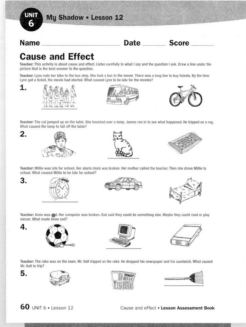

Lesson Assessment Book, p. 60

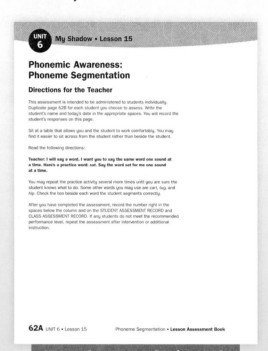

Lesson Assessment Book, p. 62A

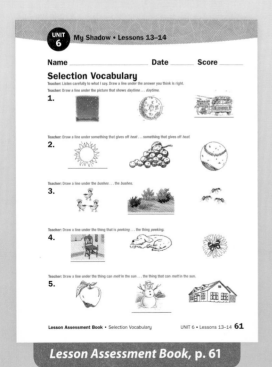

Lesson Assessment Book, p. 61

Lesson Assessment Book, p. 62

UNIT **6** My Shadow • Lesson 15

Name _____ Date _____

Phonemic Awareness:
Phoneme Segmentation

- ☐ band /b/ /a/ /n/ /d/
- ☐ nut /n/ /u/ /t/
- ☐ man /m/ /a/ /n/
- ☐ robin /r/ /o/ /b/ /i/ /n/
- ☐ has /h/ /a/ /z/
- ☐ fill /f/ /i/ /l/
- ☐ just /j/ /u/ /s/ /t/
- ☐ gift /g/ /i/ /f/ /t/
- ☐ ax /a/ /ks/
- ☐ held h/ /e/ /l/ /d/

Phoneme Segmentation total: _____

Lesson Assessment Book • Phoneme Segmentation   UNIT 6 • Lesson 15 **62B**

Lesson Assessment Book, p. 62B

Lesson Assessment Book

Comprehension Observation Log

Student _____ Date _____

Unit _____ Lesson _____ Selection Title _____

General Comprehension
Concepts discussed: _____

Behavior Within a Group
Articulates, expresses ideas: _____

Joins discussions: _____

Collaborates (such as works well with other students, works alone): _____

Role in Group
Role (such as leader, summarizer, questioner, critic, observer, non-participant): _____

Flexibility (changes roles when necessary): _____

Use of Reading Strategies
Uses strategies when needed (either those taught or student's choice of strategy)/Describes strategies used:

Changes strategies when appropriate: _____

Changes Since Last Observation

110   Comprehension Observation Log • Lesson Assessment Book

***Lesson Assessment Annotated
Teacher's Edition, p. 110***

The Comprehension Observation Log, found in the ***Lesson Assessment Annotated Teacher's Edition,*** is a vehicle for recording anecdotal information about individual student performance on an ongoing basis. Information such as students' strengths and weaknesses can be recorded at any time the occasion warrants. It is recommended that you maintain a folder for each student where you can store the logs for purposes of comparison and analysis as the school year progresses. You will gradually build up a comprehensive file that reveals which students are progressing smoothly and which students need additional help.

Use ***Benchmark Assessment,*** Benchmark 4, to target students at risk for reading failure.

Sounds and Letters

Students will
✦ blend initial phonemes.
✦ identify phoneme positions in words.
✦ attach the /z/ sound to the letter *Zz*.
✦ attach the /z/ sound to the letter *Ss*.
✦ practice writing the letters *Zz* and *Ss*.

✦ **Pocket Chart Picture Card** 127
✦ Routine 1
✦ **Alphabet Letter Card** *Zz* for each student
✦ Supply Icons
✦ **Skills Practice 2,** pp. 17–18
✦ **Transparency** 26

Calendar

Su	M	T	W	Th	F	S
		1	2	3	4	5
6	7	8	9	10	11	12
13	14	15	16	17	18	19
20	21	22	23	24	25	26
27	28	29	30	31		

Point to the box that represents today. Take this opportunity to identify any important events that will happen during the coming week, such as students' birthdays, school functions, and national holidays.

Warming Up 🕐

MORNING MESSAGE

Good morning, boys and girls!

Today is _____.

I can see a _____ and a _____ at the zoo.

Kindergarten News

✦ Copy the text above on the board or on chart paper.

✦ Ask students if they can read any words in the message today. Invite students to point to and say any words they can read. Help students identify some high-frequency words such as *is, I, can, see, a,* and others in the third sentence.

✦ Discuss the letters, words, and sentences in the message. For example, have students count the words and the spaces in the third sentence.

Phoneme Blending: Initial Sounds

✦ Tell students the **Lion Puppet** wants to play a blending game again. Tell them you will say the beginning sound of a word and the puppet will say the rest. When the puppet asks what the word is, students should put the parts together and say the word.

✦ Practice with the following word:

Teacher: /z/ (Emphasize the /z/ sound.)

Everyone: /z/

Puppet: *ebra. What is the word?*

Everyone: *zebra*

✦ Continue with words such as *finger, radio, never, dinner, cannot, letter, sample, penny,* and *bottom.*

Phonemic Awareness

Phoneme Segmentation

✦ In a row on the floor, tape three sheets of colored construction paper, using three different colors. Display and say aloud the ***Pocket Chart Picture Card*** for a three-phoneme word such as 127—pig. Then say it again, sound by sound, as you stand on the sheets, left to right from students' perspective.

✦ Ask for volunteers, and give each volunteer a sound in a word to say. For example, say *Nathan, you are /i/. Sam, you are /p/. Bella, you are /g/.*

✦ With each student, say the sound several times until he or she can repeat it easily.

✦ Next say the word *pig,* and tell students to stand on the sheets in order so their sounds make the word. When the word has been formed, have each student say her or his sound.

✦ Ask the class to determine if students have made the correct order of sounds. Tell them to signal thumbs-up if the order is correct and thumbs-down if it is not. If the order is not correct, have the class help students in the row make it correct.

✦ When the order is correct, have students in the row blend the sounds quickly and smoothly to form the whole word. Then have the class blend the word.

Alphabetic Principle

Introducing the Sound of /z/ Spelled *Ss*

✦ Refer to Routine 1 for the introducing sounds and letters procedure.

✦ Point to **Alphabet Sound Wall Card** *Zz*, and ask students what sound the letter *Zz* makes. /z/ /z/ /z/

✦ Tell students the /z/ sound can be spelled another way. Write a small letter *s* on the board. Beneath it, write the words *nose, chose,* and *has*. Say each word, emphasizing the final /z/ sound. Have students repeat the words after you. *nose, chose, has*

Listening for Final /z/

✦ Give each student an **Alphabet Letter Card** *Zz*. Tell students you are going to say words and you want them to hold up their cards and say the /z/ sound when they hear you say a word with the /z/ sound at the end.

✦ Begin with the following words:

buzz	**whiz**	bang	**daze**
fan	**bibs**	**fizz**	quit
trees	**rose**	**jazz**	bluff
graze	juice	wing	**pins**

Linking the Sound to the Letter

✦ Write pairs of words on the board, one word containing the /z/ sound spelled *z*, the other containing the /z/ sound spelled *s*.

✦ Say each word in a pair, and point to the letter in the word that represents the /z/ sound. Have a volunteer underline the letter that makes the /z/ sound for each of the words.

hose . . . froze   *rise . . . prize*

fuzz . . . fins   *maze . . . days*

Penmanship

✦ Distribute a sheet of writing paper to each student, or use **White Boards** turned to the sides with writing lines. Place the Supply Icon for *pencil* on the board or in the **Pocket Chart.**

✦ Use Routine 1 and the established procedure to review how to form capital *Z*, and ask students to write one row of capital *Z* letters on their papers or boards. Then review how to form small *z,* and have students write one row of small *z* letters across the next row.

✦ Ask students to practice making the /z/ sound: /z/ /z/ /z/ /z/ /z/. Say *What other letter can make the /z/ sound?* s

✦ If time permits, have students practice writing rows of capital *S* and small *s* letters on the back of the sheet. Then ask them to proofread, using the procedure from previous lessons.

Guided Practice

✦ Guide students in completing **Skills Practice 2** pages 17–18 for additional practice writing the letters *z* and *s* and in identifying the /z/ sound.

✦ Explain that each picture on the page has a name that includes the /z/ sound. Tell them it is their job to find and circle the letter that makes the /z/ sound in each word.

✦ You might have students work independently, or you might say each word aloud and have them repeat it after you before they circle the letter. After students have finished, be sure to review their work. Save student pages for use in penmanship proofreading activities in later lessons.

Teacher Tip

USING PROGRAM MATERIALS Use **Transparency** 26 or **Alphabet Sound Wall Card** *Zz* to help you review the shape of *Zz.*

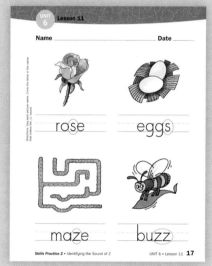

Skills Practice 2, pp. 17–18

Monitor Progress
to Differentiate Instruction

Formal Assessment ✔

Letter and Sound Identification Note how easily students identify the /z/ sound.

APPROACHING LEVEL

IF ... students are having difficulty,　　THEN ... guide them in completing **Reteach** pages 115 and 116.

ON LEVEL

IF ... students need more practice,　　THEN ... lead them in thinking of rhyming words for a few words that end with /z/ spelled *s,* such as *nose, days,* and *rise.*

ABOVE LEVEL

IF ... students are comfortable,　　THEN ... have them work independently to complete **Challenge Activities** page 89.

Students will

✦ connect their own life experiences to the text.
✦ develop an understanding of vocabulary words.
✦ use the comprehension strategies Asking Questions and Making Connections.
✦ make connections to the unit theme.

✦ *Science Lap Book,* pp. 20–27
✦ Routines 5–7

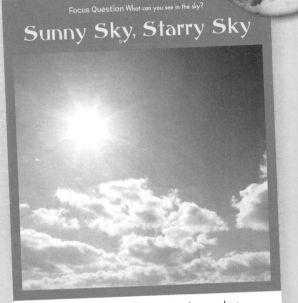

Focus Question What can you see in the sky?

Sunny Sky, Starry Sky

During the daytime we can see the sun shining in the sky.

20

1st READ

Science Lap Book, p. 20

Science Link

Activate Prior Knowledge ROUTINE 5

✦ Remind students readers relate what they already know to what they are reading. Explain that this approach will help them better understand what they read.

✦ Tell students they are going to read about the sky and what they can see there during the day and night. Ask students to think about how a sunny day looks and feels. Ask them what kinds of things they see in the sky on a sunny day. Then ask them if they have ever looked up at the sky at night. Ask them what kinds of things they have seen in the night sky and if this ever changes. Encourage students to think about what they have seen in the sky as they listen to the selection "Sunny Sky, Starry Sky."

Preview the Selection ROUTINE 5

✦ Open the *Science Lap Book* to pages 20–21, the opening pages of "Sunny Sky, Starry Sky." Follow Routine 5, the previewing the selection routine, as you point to and say the title.

✦ Turn through the pages, and focus students' attention on the photographs. Ask them if the photos help them to predict what the story might say.

✦ Encourage students to suggest reasons for reading the selection. Ask them to think what the story might teach them about the unit theme.

✦ Have students discuss what they are learning about shadows as the selection is read. Ask students how the appearance of the day and night skies connects to the unit theme My Shadow.

Technology

To promote independent reading, encourage students to use Workshop to listen to the recording of the selection on the *Listening Library CD.* Invite them to follow along and say the words whenever they can.

Audio CD

Vocabulary

ROUTINE **6**

✦ Follow Routine 6, the selection vocabulary routine, as you introduce the vocabulary words for this selection.

✦ Explain to students that *daytime* is the part of the day between when it is light outside and when it gets dark. Use the following sentence to illustrate: *We go to school in the daytime.*

✦ Tell students the word *heat* means "warmth." Ask students how we get heat.

✦ Explain that the word *twinkle* means "to shine with flashes of light." Use the following sentence to illustrate: *The stars twinkle on a clear night.*

Read the Selection

ROUTINE **7**

✦ Before beginning the selection, read the Focus Question at the top of the first page. Tell students to keep this question in mind as they listen to the story.

✦ Follow Routine 7, the reading the selection routine, as you read the entire selection.

✦ Before, during, and after this first reading, invite students to ask questions or to think aloud about anything in the selection that interests or confuses them.

Comprehension Strategies

✦ As you read, model the following comprehension strategies:
  • Asking Questions
  • Making Connections

✦ Think aloud through each strategy, and encourage students to share their ideas as well.

Vocabulary

daytime	twinkle
heat	

Teacher Tip

VOCABULARY Encourage students to use a variety of sources to build their vocabulary, such as making word banks, discussing characters and events from a story, talking with other people, and thinking about their own life experiences.

Differentiating Instruction **English Learners**

IF ... students need additional help with Vocabulary, **THEN ...** refer to Unit 6 Lesson 11 of the *English Learner Support Guide.*

Comprehension Strategies

Teacher Modeling

1 Making Connections *On a sunny day, I can stay warm in just shorts and a T-shirt. Let's look at this picture. What does the sun make us think about?*

2 Making Connections *Here we see the moon. Last summer we sat on our back porch and watched the moon change each night. At first it was a round ball of light. But each night the light got smaller until it was just a sliver. Then it started to grow again. It looked just like these pictures. When was a time you looked at the moon? What did it look like?*

3 Asking Questions *The moon looks different each night of the month, but does it really change shape? What would make it look different? Hmm ... We're learning about shadows. Maybe part of the moon is covered by a shadow. We'll read on to see if our questions are answered.*

4 Asking Questions *I know what a telescope does. It makes faraway things look bigger and closer. But what does a telescope look like? This picture doesn't show. Maybe if I read on, I'll find an answer to my question. Then I might understand this better.*

Differentiating Instruction **English Learners**

IF ... students have difficulty understanding the concept of making connections,
THEN ... demonstrate concrete examples of connections, such as holding hands with another person. Then use gestures to show that students can also make a connection between the selection and themselves.

Focus Question What can you see in the sky?

Sunny Sky, Starry Sky

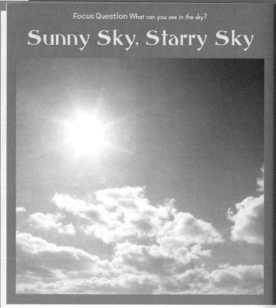

During the daytime we can see the sun shining in the sky.

20

The sun warms us. It provides heat and light energy for the earth.

21

At night we can see the moon in the sky.

22

Its shape looks a little different each night of the month. **3**

23

 Teacher Tip

GLOSSARY The word *twinkle* can be found in the Glossary of the ***Science Lap Book.***

On clear nights, the sky is full of stars that twinkle and shine.

24

If we use a telescope, we can see craters on the moon. 4

25

A telescope can help us see planets like Mars and Jupiter.

26

We can even see galaxies made from billions of stars.

27

Science Lap Book, pp. 20–27

Science Link

Tell students even though we cannot see stars in the sky during the day, they are still there. Ask students why we might be able to see stars better at night than during the day. *During the day, the light from the sun is much brighter than the light from the stars.*

Print and Book Awareness

Picture-Text Relationship

Reread pages 23 and 25–27, and ask students what the photos tell them that the story does not.

High-Frequency Words

Have students find and read any high-frequency words that they have learned. Words they might find include *see, the, a, and, you, of,* and *on.*

Sentences

Ask a volunteer to come to the *Science Lap Book* and to move his or her hand under the first sentence on page 21. Ask students how they know where each sentence begins and ends.

Vocabulary Review

Review with students the selection vocabulary words *daytime, heat,* and *twinkle.* Ask students the following questions:

- *What kinds of things do we do during the* daytime?
- *When is a time we need* heat?
- *What are some things that* twinkle?

OBJECTIVES

Students will
✦ choose a topic for writing an advertisement.
✦ brainstorm ideas for advertisement.
✦ view, appreciate, and react to fine art.

MATERIALS

✦ *Language Arts Big Book,* p. 30
✦ *My Shadow Big Book,* p. 44

Language Arts Big Book, p. 30

Differentiating Instruction

English Learners

IF ... English Learners have difficulty understanding what an advertisement is, **THEN ...** show them examples or pictures of different kinds of ads, including newspaper and magazine ads, handbills or flyers, billboards, television commercials, and Internet ads.

Traits of Good Writing

Vocabulary Writers add details to their sentences to include more descriptive ideas in their work.

Writing Process

Prewrite: Brainstorming and Sequencing

Teach

✦ Tell students for their next writing assignment, they are going to write an advertisement for a school event. Explain that an *advertisement,* or *ad* for short, is a piece of writing that tries to convince someone to do or to buy something.

✦ Display page 30 of the **Language Arts Big Book.** Ask students if they see any advertisements on the page.

Guided Practice

✦ Discuss with students some of the coming events for your class or for the school. Work with students to choose one event for which they would like to write an advertisement. Tell them the goal of their ad is to make people want to come to the event.

✦ Facilitate a class discussion during which students brainstorm a list of ideas— pictures and words—that could be used in the advertisement. Write the list on the board.

✦ Explain to students that they will make their advertisement in the form of a card, similar to the thank-you cards they have been working on. Help students narrow the list to three ideas, and guide them in deciding on the best order for the ideas to appear in the advertisement. Invite volunteers to come to the board and write the numerals *1, 2,* and *3* to show the sequence of ideas on the front and inside pages of the card.

✦ Tell students they will continue working on their advertisement in the next lesson.

Olga Wisinger-Florian. *The First Frost.*
circa 1900. Oil on canvas. 114 x 156 cm.
Vienna, Austria.

Fine Art

Discussing Fine Art

✦ Turn to page 44 in the *My Shadow Big Book.* Focus students'
attention on *The First Frost* by Olga Wisinger-Florian.

✦ Encourage students to freely express their feelings, interpretations,
and opinions about the painting. Use the following questions to start
a discussion about the work:

  • *How does the painting make you feel?*

  • *Does the painting seem cheerful and happy? Is it dark and gloomy?*

  • *Do you like the painting? Why or why not?*

✦ Ask students to describe the setting presented in the painting.
Challenge students to look for clues that tell what time of day it is
and what time of year it is.

✦ Next have them discuss the colors used in the painting. Point out
how the different shades of gray-greens and gray-blues suggest a
cold day, despite the sunlight.

✦ Finally, ask students how the painting relates to the unit theme.
Encourage volunteers to tell about an experience with a
tree's shadow.

Teacher Tip

FINE ART You may want to share with
students other examples of the Impressionists'
interest in light and shadow. One example is
Claude Monet's *Garden at Giverny*.

Background Information

Austrian painter Olga Wisinger-Florian (1844–1926) is considered
one of the finest Impressionist painters the country has produced.
Wisinger-Florian began her career as a pianist but found her
passion for painting in her late twenties. After exhibiting work
in the World's Fairs in Paris and Chicago, the artist won over a
worldwide audience to become one of Austria's most successful
female painters.

Sounds and Letters

OBJECTIVES

Students will
✦ segment and blend initial phonemes in words.
✦ identify and count the phonemes in words.
✦ attach the /ks/ and /z/ sounds to the letters *Xx* and *Zz*.

MATERIALS
✦ **Teacher's Resource Book,** p. 37
✦ **Alphabet Letter Cards** *Xx* and *Zz* for each student
✦ **Alphabet Book Big Book,** pp. 54–55

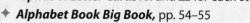

Calendar

Su	M	T	W	Th	F	S
		1	2	3	4	5
6	7	8	9	10	11	12
13	14	15	16	17	18	19
20	21	22	23	24	25	26
27	28	29	30	31		

Point to the box that represents today. Discuss with students the name of the current season and which one comes next. Talk about how the seasons are different from one another in your area.

Differentiating Instruction   English Learners

IF ... students have intermediate or advanced English mastery and have recently moved to the United States, **THEN ...** encourage them to tell something about the weather or climate in their native countries.

Teacher Tip

MATERIALS Have ready three counters for each student in advance of this lesson.

Warming Up

MORNING MESSAGE

Today is _____.

_____ and _____ are things that are yellow.

Kindergarten News

✦ Copy the text above on the board or on chart paper. Have students tell a few items that are normally yellow, such as bananas and dandelions. Invite students to come to the board to write their ideas. You might write the words they suggest first in dotted lines and have students trace them. Or you could help them write the words hand over hand.

✦ To discuss the letters and words in the message, you might ask students *What is the longest word in the message? Come up and point to it. How many letters does it have? Let's count them.*

Phoneme Segmentation and Blending: Initial Sounds

Tell students the **Lion Puppet** will say a word and you want them to say the first sound of that word and then to repeat the whole word. Use these words:

match . . . /m/, *match*   *goal* . . . /g/, *goal*   *boxer* . . . /b/, *boxer*

hold . . . /h/, *hold*   *point* . . . /p/, *point*   *south* . . . /s/, *south*

lion . . . /l/, *lion*   *join* . . . /j/, *join*   *lunch* . . . /l/, *lunch*

dime . . . /d/, *dime*   *rain* . . . /r/, *rain*   *fall* . . . /f/, *fall*

Phonemic Awareness

Phoneme Segmentation

✦ Distribute a copy of **Teacher's Resource Book** page 37 or a **White Board,** along with three counters, to each student.

✦ Tell students you will say a word. Explain that you want each of them to put a counter in a box on the grid for each sound they hear in the word. Remind them to place the counter for the first sound they hear in the box above the arrow. Then using your own grid and markers, model your instructions to students using the word *tap.*

✦ Say the word *sat,* stretching the sounds: /s-s-s-s/ /a-a-a-a/ /t/. Have students place a counter in the correct box for each sound.

✦ Call on volunteers to tell how many sounds the word has. *three* Then have the class blend the word *sat.* *sat*

✦ Continue the activity with the following words: *at, sag, rag, ran, an, in, pin.* Always have students tell how many sounds are in each word; then guide them in identifying each sound and the letters attached to the sounds.

✦ Choose one word, and have students say and write in the boxes on the grid the letter for each sound in the word. Remind them to look at the **Alphabet Sound Wall Cards** if they need help.

 Teacher Tip

ACTIVITY VARIATIONS A simple way to introduce students to counting phonemes is to have them put the tip of a marker on a sheet of paper and to move the marker for each sound they hear in a word.

Teacher Tip

ALPHABET REVIEW To review the names of the letters of the alphabet, have students perform the "Alphabet Rap." (See the Appendix.)

Alphabetic Principle

Reviewing the Sounds of *Xx* and *Zz*

✦ Point to **Alphabet Sound Wall Card** *Xx*, and ask students to say the name of each letter. *capital X, small x* Have students say the sound that goes with the letter. */ks/ /ks/ /ks/*

✦ Repeat with **Alphabet Sound Wall Card** *Zz*, having students say the name of each letter and its corresponding sound. *capital Z, small z; /z/ /z/ /z/*

✦ Recite the stories on each card, and ask everyone to say the /ks/ and /z/ sounds aloud with you.

Listening for Final /ks/ and /z/

Give each student one **Alphabet Letter Card** *Xx* and one **Alphabet Letter Card** *Zz*. Say the following words, and have students hold up their **Alphabet Letter Cards** *Xx* and say */ks/* when they hear you say a word that ends with the /ks/ sound and hold up their **Alphabet Letter Cards** *Zz* and say */z/* when they hear a word that ends with the /z/ sound.

buzz	*whiz*	*tax*	*mix*
sax	*fizz*	*flax*	*quiz*
jazz	*six*	*maze*	*relax*

Monitor Progress to Differentiate Instruction

Formal Assessment

Letter and Sound Identification Note how easily students review the /ks/ and /z/ sounds.

APPROACHING LEVEL

IF ... students have difficulty,

THEN ... guide them in completing **Reteach** pages 117 and 118.

ON LEVEL

IF ... students need more practice,

THEN ... have them draw and decorate a large *Z* on a piece of paper. Then guide them in choosing and writing on the page three words that begin with /z/ and three words that end with /z/.

ABOVE LEVEL

IF ... students are comfortable,

THEN ... have them work independently to complete **Challenge Activities** page 90.

Technology

Use the **Alphabet Sound Card Stories CD** for practice with the /ks/ and /z/ sounds.

Audio CD

Alphabet Book Big Book—/z/

✦ Display the **Alphabet Book Big Book,** and turn to pages 54–55, Zz. Invite a volunteer to help you count how many lines are in the rhyme. *eight* Point out to students that the lines are divided into two groups and that in each group there are four lines. Explain that a blank line is between the two groups of words to show readers where they should take a break before moving on to a new idea. Remind students we read from top to bottom and left to right.

✦ Ask students to listen closely as you read the rhyme aloud to hear words that have the /z/ sound. Remind students the /z/ sound might appear at the beginning, in the middle, or at the end of words.

✦ When you finish reading, invite students to say any /z/ words they remember. Ask them to point to the letter Zz in the rhyme and say its sound. *zoo, fuzzy, buzzy, zebra, zigzagged, zapped, zoomed*

✦ Say the following words from the rhyme, and have students pretend to buzz around like a "fuzzy, buzzy fly" if the word contains the /z/ sound:

day   **zoo**   **fuzzy**   *fly*   **zebra**   *tail*   **zoomed**   *jug*

Alphabet Book Big Book, pp. 54–55

Technology

Each of the rhymes from the **Alphabet Book Big Book** is available on the **Listening Library CD.** Use the **eAlphabet Book** for activities that support the **Alphabet Book Big Book** lessons.

Audio CD

OBJECTIVES

Students will

✦ develop an understanding of vocabulary words.

✦ review the comprehension strategies Asking Questions and Making Connections.

✦ use the comprehension skill Cause and Effect.

✦ analyze the author's use of language.

MATERIALS

✦ *Science Lap Book,* pp. 20–27

✦ Routine 5–7

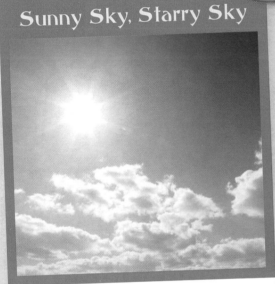

Focus Question What can you see in the sky?

Sunny Sky, Starry Sky

During the daytime we can see the sun shining in the sky.

20

2nd READ

Science Lap Book, p. 20

Vocabulary

telescope   galaxies

planets

Science Link

Preview the Selection [ROUTINE 5]

✦ Display the **Science Lap Book** opened to the Table of Contents page. Use Routine 5, the previewing the selection routine, to guide students in understanding and using the Table of Contents to locate the selection. Then point to and say the title.

✦ Prepare to reread the selection. As you turn through the pages, have students use the photographs to retell the important facts from the selection.

Vocabulary [ROUTINE 6]

✦ Follow Routine 6, the selection vocabulary routine, as you introduce the vocabulary words for this selection.

✦ Explain that a *telescope* is a tool that makes faraway objects seem closer and bigger. Tell students a scientist uses a telescope to study outer space.

✦ Tell students *planets* are bodies, like Earth, that move around the sun. Explain to students that eight planets move around our sun.

✦ Tell students that *galaxies* are huge groups of stars and planets. Use the following sentence to illustrate: *We can see galaxies through our telescope.*

Read the Selection

ROUTINE
7

Comprehension Strategies

✦ During the first reading of "Sunny Sky, Starry Sky," you modeled the following comprehension strategies:

- Asking Questions
- Making Connections

✦ In this second reading of the selection, you will revisit each comprehension strategy model from the first reading.

Comprehension Skills

In this lesson of "Sunny Sky, Starry Sky," students will use the comprehension skill Cause and Effect.

Reading with a Writer's Eye

✦ In this rereading of "Sunny Sky, Starry Sky," students will discuss the author's use of language.

✦ By discussing the writing strategies an author uses, students learn how to be better writers themselves.

Concept/Question Board

Tell students readers keep thinking about any questions that are generated as they are reading. As they read, tell them to keep in mind the questions on the **Concept/Question Board.** Tell them readers are always thinking about what is important in selections and they try to remember this important information.

Technology

To promote independent reading, encourage students to use Workshop to listen to the recording of the selection on the *Listening Library CD.* Invite them to follow along and say the words whenever they can.

Audio CD

Comprehension Strategies

Teacher Modeling

1 Making Connections *What did this picture remind you of? We thought about how the sun keeps us warm and makes our gardens grow. When we connected information from the story with our experiences, we understood better.*

2 Making Connections *We understood these different pictures of the moon when I thought about last summer on our back porch. I remembered how we watched the moon change each night. It looked just like the pictures on this page. Remembering our own experiences helped us understand what the story was saying.*

3 Asking Questions *Here we had some questions about why the moon looks different each night. The story didn't answer our questions. But we got the idea that a shadow might make the moon look different each night. We may have to look at another book to get some answers.*

4 Asking Questions *Here I wondered what a telescope looks like. The picture on this page doesn't show one. I didn't see a picture on the last two pages either. Where can we look to find a picture of a telescope?*

Vocabulary Tip

Review the meanings of the words *telescope*, *planets*, and *galaxies*. Then have students use the words in sentences.

Focus Question What can you see in the sky?

Sunny Sky, Starry Sky

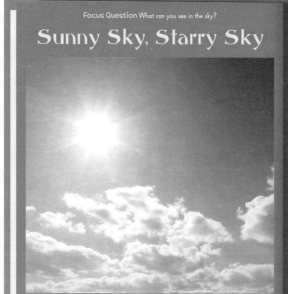

During the daytime we can see the sun shining in the sky.

20

The sun warms us. It provides heat and light energy for the earth.

21

At night we can see the moon in the sky.

22

Its shape looks a little different each night of the month. **3**

23

 Teacher Tip

GLOSSARY The words *telescope* and *planets* can be found in the Glossary of the *Science Lap Book.*

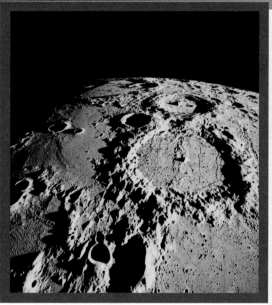

On clear nights, the sky is full of stars that twinkle and shine.

24

If we use a telescope, we can see craters on the moon. **4**

25

A telescope can help us see planets like Mars and Jupiter.

26

We can even see galaxies made from billions of stars.

27

Science Lap Book, pp. 20–27

Science Link

Review with students what makes the night. When the sun shines on the other side of Earth, our side is in the dark. Ask students what shadows might have to do with the way the moon looks at different times of the month.

Reading with a Writer's Eye

Language Use

Explain to students that the author uses some interesting words to tell about the sky. Reread pages 20, 24, and 27, and ask students which words help them picture what the author is saying. *sun shining in the sky, stars that twinkle and shine*

Discussing the Selection

✦ Review the Focus Question with students: What can you see in the sky?

✦ Have students visit the school library and choose a non-fiction or informational selection to read and enjoy.

Vocabulary Review

Review with students the selection vocabulary words *telescope, planets,* and *galaxies.* Ask students the following questions:

• *What kinds of things can we see with a telescope?*

• *What are the names of some of the planets?*

• *Where would we find galaxies?*

Language Arts

Students will
- use descriptive words to add to writing.
- practice extending sentences.
- participate in a Thinking Story experience.

- *Language Arts Big Book,* pp. 18, 30, 55
- *Transparencies* 48, 48A
- *Willy the Wisher,* p. 67

Writing Process

Model: Using Descriptive Words

Teach

- To review describing words, complete the Grammar, Usage, and Mechanics activity on this page before you begin this activity.

- Tell students one important part of writing a good advertisement is to make it very interesting. Ask them *Do you look at boring posters and billboards? Do you pay attention to boring television commercials?*

- Explain that using describing words is a great way to make writing interesting.

Guided Practice

- Return to page 30 of the *Language Arts Big Book.* Remind students that both of the posters on the page are advertisements.

- Demonstrate for students how describing words can make the first poster more interesting. Write on the board *Buy a yummy sandwich!* Discuss how the describing word *yummy* tells more about *sandwich* and how it might make people want to buy the sandwich.

- Invite students to think of other words that might be added to the poster to describe the sandwich. *delicious, great, homemade, peanut butter*

Grammar, Usage, and Mechanics

Teach

- Display page 55 of the *Language Arts Big Book.* Read the sentence at the top of the page: *Words can describe things.* Remind students that describing words tell more about other words.

- Introduce *Transparencies* 48 and 48A to model how to revise by adding.

- Read aloud the base text, and remind students the sentences could be made better by adding more information. Discuss each addition to the original text.

Language Arts Big Book,
pp. 30, 55

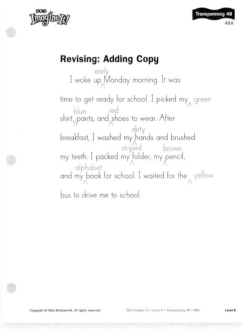

Revising: Adding Copy

I woke up Monday morning. It was time to get ready for school. I picked my green shirt, pants, and shoes to wear. After breakfast, I washed my hands and brushed my teeth. I packed my folder, my pencil, and my book for school. I waited for the yellow bus to drive me to school.

Transparencies 48, 48A

Grammar, Usage, and Mechanics continued

Guided Practice

✦ Turn to page 18 of the **Language Arts Big Book.** Ask students to help you write three simple sentences about what they see on the page; for example, *Doodle is juggling* or *A clown is holding an umbrella.*

✦ Write students' sentences on the board or on chart paper. Then have students close their eyes while you read the sentences aloud. Ask them to think about what part of the sentence needs more information. Tell them to pay attention to what things they wonder about or would like to know more about.

✦ Invite volunteers to suggest describing words that will tell more about the sentences. Change the second sentence to *A tall clown is holding a blue umbrella with stars.*

Language Arts Big Book, p. 18

Differentiating Instruction

English Learners

IF ... students have difficulty extending sentences, **THEN ...** encourage them to listen closely to you and to their classmates and to echo as much of each sentence as they can.

 Teacher Tip

EXTEND THE DISCUSSION Ask students how packing would go faster if Mr. Nosho thought to ask questions. You might also challenge students to think of another **Willy the Wisher** character who would make a good helper for Mrs. Nosho's packing experience. *Mark or Portia would be more helpful than Mr. Nosho.*

Willy the Wisher ⏱

✦ Display the book **Willy the Wisher,** and turn to the story "Mrs. Nosho Gets Ready for a Trip" on page 67 of the book.

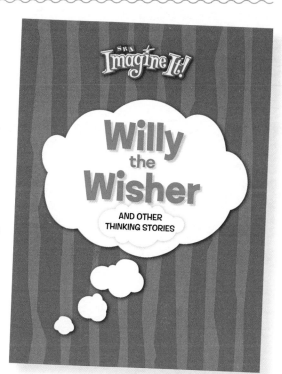

Willy the Wisher, p. 67

✦ Pointing to the Listening Icons, remind students to listen carefully.

✦ Before you begin reading the story, ask students to talk about Mrs. Nosho's thinking problem and to recall what happened in some of the other stories in which she appeared.

✦ Then repeat the title, "Mrs. Nosho Gets Ready for a Trip." Invite students to make predictions—based on what they know about Mrs. Nosho and what they know about getting ready for a trip—about what might happen in the story. Write a few of the students' predictions on the board.

✦ Follow the established procedure for reading from the **Willy the Wisher** book.

✦ After reading the story, discuss Mrs. Nosho's packing experience. Talk about how Mrs. Nosho is often so vague that Mr. Nosho cannot understand her. Students should realize that packing for a trip would go faster if Mrs. Nosho were more specific about what she needed.

✦ Revisit a few of the predictions students made before reading. Discuss which ones were confirmed and which were not. Assure students that just because a prediction did not appear in the story, it is not necessarily a poor prediction.

Sounds and Letters

OBJECTIVES

Students will
+ identify objects that begin with the /f/ sound.
+ identify words in print.
+ identify and count phonemes in words.
+ review the /j/, /f/, and /u/ sounds.
+ practice writing the letters *Jj*, *Ff*, and *Uu*.

MATERIALS
+ **Teacher's Resource Book,** p. 37
+ **Alphabet Letter Cards** *Jj, Ff,* and *Uu* for each student
+ Supply Icons
+ **Skills Practice 2,** pp. 19–20

Calendar

Su	M	T	W	Th	F	S
		1	2	3	4	5
6	7	8	9	10	11	12
13	14	15	16	17	18	19
20	21	22	23	24	25	26
27	28	29	30	31		

Point to the box that represents today. Have students identify the day of the week. Then point to the name of each day of the week, and have students say the individual sounds when possible of the letters that begin each name.

Warming Up

MORNING MESSAGE

Today is _____.

If you like _____ish, swim in the ocean.

If you like _____uice, squeeze an orange.

If you like _____mbrellas, walk in the rain.

Kindergarten News

+ Copy the text above on the board or on chart paper, leaving out letters as indicated.

+ Tell students today a few Mystery Letters are in the Morning Message. Read each sentence, and invite students to identify what letter is missing in each. Have students write the letters in the blanks. Discuss how the clues in the rest of the sentence helped them know the word that was missing a letter.

+ Compare the three Mystery Letter sentences. Have students count words, letters, and spaces.

Oral Language

+ Look around the room until you see something that starts with the /f/ sound. Say *I'm thinking of something that starts with /f/.*

+ Give a clue such as the object's size or color, or direct students' attention to the correct part of the room. Objects you might name include *flag, folder, fan,* and *flowers*.

Phoneme Replacement

✦ Write the words *roast* and *coast* on the board. Say *Which word is* roast?

✦ Have a student come to the board and point to the word. Say *That's right.* /r/ ... oast *has the letter* r *at the beginning.*

✦ Point to the word *coast*, and say *This word rhymes with* roast, *but it starts with* /k/. *What do you think it says?* coast

✦ Continue with these word pairs, this time asking students how they know the correct word: *roll / toll; round / sound; rip / sip; rocket / socket.*

Phonemic Awareness

Phoneme Segmentation

✦ Continue the phoneme-counting activity from the previous lesson, but this time you will focus students' attention more on the position of each sound.

✦ Distribute a copy of **Teacher's Resource Book** page 37 or a **White Board** to each student, along with three counters.

✦ Tell students you will say a word. Explain and model how you want each of them to put a counter in a box on the grid for each sound they hear in the word. Remind them to place the counter for the first sound they hear in the box above the arrow.

✦ Say the word *map,* stretching the sounds: /m-m-m-m/ /a-a-a-a/ /p/. Have students place a counter in the correct box for each sound.

✦ Call on volunteers to tell how many sounds the word has. *three* Then have the class blend the word *map.*

✦ Continue the activity with the following words: *tap, tag, rag, ran, pan, pin.* Have students identify which sound is different in each word change.

✦ Choose one word, and have students say it and write in the boxes on the grid the letter for each sound in the word. Remind them to use the **Alphabet Sound Wall Cards** if they need help.

IF ... students are native Spanish speakers, **THEN ...** they may hold up their *Alphabet Letter Cards* Jj when you say words that begin with *Hh*. In Spanish, the letter *Jj* represents /h/. Review the /j/ sound, and have students practice associating it with the letter *Jj*.

Alphabetic Principle

Reviewing the Sounds of *Jj*, *Ff*, and *Uu*

✦ Point to the **Alphabet Sound Wall Card** for *Jj*. Ask students to tell what they remember about the card and the short story that goes with it. Recite the story with students, stressing the /j/ sound.

✦ Repeat the process for the **Alphabet Sound Wall Cards** for *Ff* and Short *Uu*.

Listening for /u/ and Initial /j/ and /f/

✦ Give each student one *Jj*, one *Ff*, and one *Uu* **Alphabet Letter Card.** Tell students you will say a word and they should repeat it. Say if a word begins with the /j/ sound, on your signal, they should hold up their *Alphabet Letter Cards* Jj and say /j/. If it begins with the /f/ sound, they should hold up their **Alphabet Letter Cards** Ff and say /f/. Tell students a few of the words will not begin with either the /j/ sound or the /f/ sound, so they must listen very carefully.

✦ Try these words:

fun	damp	**jump**	grape	**cup**	fix
five	**hunt**	joy	**just**	feet	hear
jail	milk	four	face	jolly	goose

✦ Reread the first two rows, asking students to hold up their *Alphabet Letter Cards* Uu and say /u/ when they hear a word that has the /u/ sound.

Linking the Sound to the Letter

✦ Write a pair of words on the board, one with the /u/ sound and one without it. Say the word with the /u/ sound for each word pair. Have students identify the word that you said by signaling thumbs-up when you point to it. Then ask them to tell how they know which word you said.

✦ Use these words:

cap ... *cup*   *tuck* ... tick

hint ... *hunt*   *must* ... most

simmer ... *summer*   Timmy ... *tummy*

Penmanship

✦ Distribute a sheet of writing paper to each student, or use **White Boards** turned to the sides with writing lines. Place the Supply Icon for *pencil* on the board or in the **Pocket Chart.**

✦ Model how to write capital and small *Jj* on the board. Then ask students to write one row of capital *J* letters and one row of small *j* letters. Repeat the process for the letters *Ff* and *Uu.* Then have students proofread by correcting any letters that could be made better.

Guided Practice

✦ Have students complete **Skills Practice 2** page 19 for additional practice writing the letters *Jj, Ff,* and *Uu* and identifying the /j/, /f/, and /u/ sounds.

✦ Explain that some of the things in the pictures will begin with the /j/ sound and that some will begin with the /f/ sound. Tell them when a picture has a name that begins with the /j/ sound, they should write a *j* on the line below the picture. If the name begins with the /f/ sound, they should write the letter *f* on the line.

✦ Say the name of each picture, allowing students time to write the letters. When you are finished, tell students you will say each name one more time and you want them to listen for the /u/ sound in any of the words. When they hear a word with the /u/ sound, they should write the letter *u* on the line below that word.

✦ After students have finished, be sure to review their work. Save students' pages for use during a penmanship proofreading activity in later lessons.

Monitor Progress to Differentiate Instruction

Formal Assessment ✓

Letter and Sound Identification Note how readily students identify the /j/, /f/, and /u/ sounds.

APPROACHING LEVEL	
IF ... students are having difficulty,	THEN ... guide them in completing **Reteach** page 119.
IF ... students still have difficulty,	THEN ... refer to Unit 6 Lesson 13 of the **Intervention Guide.**

ON LEVEL	
IF ... students need more practice,	THEN ... continue the review using **Skills Practice 2** page 20.

ABOVE LEVEL	
IF ... students would enjoy a challenging activity,	THEN ... have them work independently to complete **Challenge Activities** page 91.

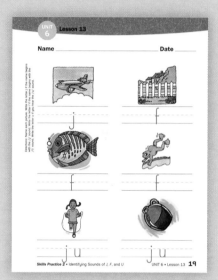

Skills Practice 2, pp. 19–20

MATERIALS

✦ **Story Time Collection:** *Nothing Sticks Like a Shadow*

✦ Routines 5–7

✦ **Home Connection,** pp. 49–50

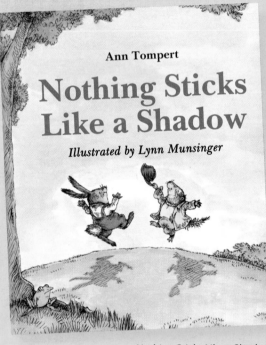

Nothing Sticks Like a Shadow

Differentiating Instruction   **English Learners**

IF ... students do not know the animal names in the story, **THEN ...** as you point to the illustrations, have them say the animal name in their native languages. Then have them repeat the English name of the animal after you.

Technology

To promote independent reading, encourage students to use Workshop to listen to the recording of the selection on the **Listening Library CD.** Invite them to follow along and say the words whenever they can.

Audio CD

1st READ

Preview and Prepare

Activate Prior Knowledge   ROUTINE 5

✦ *Nothing Sticks Like a Shadow* is a fantasy about a character named Rabbit who tries many different ways to get rid of his shadow and to win a bet with Woodchuck. Tell students like the story "Bear Shadow," *Nothing Sticks Like a Shadow* is a made-up story called a fantasy. Explain that the story is not true and could not happen in real life. As you read aloud the selection, relate what you already know to what you are reading, and encourage students to do the same.

✦ Have students note any shadows around them in the classroom. Then briefly turn off the light, and ask students what they see. Turn the light back on, and have students explain what they know about shadows and light. Paraphrase any student responses that are vague to reinforce positive participation.

✦ Encourage students to discuss what they are learning about the unit theme as they listen to the selection. Key concepts include the following:

  • Shadows go where we go and do what we do.

  • Light is necessary for the formation of a shadow.

Preview the Selection   ROUTINE 5

✦ Display the cover of *Nothing Sticks Like a Shadow.* Follow Routine 5, the previewing the selection routine, as you point to and say the title and the names of the author and the illustrator. Ask students what an author and an illustrator do.

✦ Turn through the pages, and focus students' attention on the illustrations. Point out the different animal characters that appear. Invite students to predict what the story might be about.

✦ Encourage students to think of reasons for reading *Nothing Sticks Like a Shadow.* Suggest they might read the story to find out what the characters learn about shadows. Encourage students to wonder how the story might add to the unit theme.

Vocabulary

ROUTINE **6**

- ✦ Follow Routine 6, the selection vocabulary routine, as you introduce the vocabulary words for this selection.

- ✦ Explain to students that a *burrow* is a hole in the ground made by an animal as a home. Tell students a chipmunk, woodchuck, groundhog, fox, and prairie dog live in burrows.

- ✦ Tell students *bushes* are plants with lots of close branches. Ask students if they have any bushes near or around their houses.

- ✦ Explain to students that when they are *peeking* at something, they are looking quickly at it. Use the following sentence to illustrate: *Are you peeking at me from behind the chair?*

- ✦ Tell student if you give someone *advice*, you tell them what you think they should do. Ask students if someone has ever given them advice.

- ✦ Tell students when an object is *coated* with something, it is covered with it. Ask students if they have ever been coated with bubbles when they take baths.

- ✦ Explain to students if something is *handy*, it is useful. Use the following example: *The eraser on my pencil is handy when I make a mistake.*

Vocabulary

burrow	advice
bushes	coated
peeking	handy

Differentiating Instruction **English Learners**

IF ... students need extra help with vocabulary, **THEN** ... help them draw and label pictures that will help them remember the differences between *burrow* and *bushes*.

Read the Selection

ROUTINE **7**

- ✦ Before reading *Nothing Sticks Like a Shadow,* read the Focus Question at the top of the first page. Tell students to keep this question in mind as they listen to the story.

- ✦ Follow Routine 7, the reading the selection routine, as you read the entire selection. Use a different voice for each character to make the story come alive.

- ✦ Before, during, and after the first reading, encourage students to ask questions and to think aloud about anything that interests or puzzles them.

Comprehension Strategies

- ✦ You will introduce and model the following comprehension strategies:
  - Making Connections
  - Clarifying

- ✦ Think aloud through each comprehension strategy, and encourage students to share their ideas as well.

Give each student a copy of *Home Connection* page 49. This same information is also available in Spanish on *Home Connection* page 50. Encourage students to discuss the selection *Nothing Sticks Like a Shadow* with their families and complete the activity.

Comprehension Strategies

Teacher Modeling

1 Clarifying *Here is a word we may not know—fandango. When we come to words we don't understand, we need to reread the sentence to see if it helps. When I reread the sentence, we see that it says that "Rabbit was dancing a wild fandango ... " Now I understand; a fandango is a kind of dance.*

2 Making Connections *Why are Rabbit and Woodchuck arguing like that if they are friends? Have any of you ever argued with a friend? I remember doing that when a friend and I disagreed about something. Thinking about something from our own lives helps us make a connection with the story to understand it better.*

3 Clarifying *Here's the word* burrow *we learned before reading this story. We learned that* burrow *means "a hole in the ground dug by a small animal as a home." Woodchuck went into his burrow, or his underground home. By thinking about what I already knew and the words in the sentence, I figured out what* burrow *meant.*

4 Making Connections *Look at Rabbit taking longer and longer leaps! Why is he doing that? When I am trying to show someone that I can do something, I try extra hard to do it right. I guess that Rabbit is trying extra hard to show Woodchuck that he can lose his shadow.*

Focus Question What does Rabbit do to get rid of his shadow?

1 One day Rabbit was dancing a wild fandango in a field filled with clover. Woodchuck was watching him from the doorway of his burrow.

"Isn't it lonely, playing by yourself?" Woodchuck asked.

"I'm not alone," said Rabbit, pointing. "See my shadow? It goes where I go and does what I do."

5

"I know what you mean," said Woodchuck. "I can't escape my shadow either, no matter how hard I try."

"I can if I want to," said Rabbit.

"Oh, no, you can't," said Woodchuck. "No one can."

"I can too," said Rabbit.

"Can't," said Woodchuck.

2 And they pitched "cans and "can'ts" at each other until Woodchuck said, "I'll bet you my hat you can't."

"Looks as if I'm going to have a new hat," said Rabbit. He ran and hid behind the trunk of a huge tree.

When he looked around, however, he found his shadow standing beside him.

Woodchuck laughed. "You'll have to do better than that," he said.

6   7

Nothing Sticks Like a Shadow, pp. 5–11

Print and Book Awareness

Question Marks

Ask volunteers to point to the question marks on page 5. If necessary, explain that this mark shows that a character in the story has asked a question. Reread page 5, showing the different ways we read questions and statements.

Picture-Text Relationship

Display page 7, and have students describe what they see. Ask them how many shadows they see. Have them count the shadows, not forgetting those of the trees.

Quotation Marks

Point out the quotation marks on pages 8 and 9, and remind students quotation marks show the words a person or story character is saying. Have volunteers run their fingers under the words that Rabbit and Woodchuck say on these pages. Remind students these words fall between the quotation marks.

Comprehension Strategies

Teacher Modeling

❺ Clarifying *We may be confused by the broom. Let me reread what Beaver says. We see that Beaver was trying to be helpful. He thought Rabbit might be able to use the broom to sweep away his shadow. By rereading Beaver's words, I was able to clarify what happened.*

❻ Clarifying *I wonder what jig means. The story says Rabbit danced a* jig. *I think that a* jig *must be a type of dance just like* fandango *was in the beginning of the story.*

Soon Rabbit came to a path beside a river. There he met Beaver carrying a broom over his shoulder.
"Why are you running?" asked Beaver.
"I'm trying to get away from my shadow," said Rabbit. "Woodchuck bet me his hat that I couldn't."

"Well," said Beaver, "it's easy to see you can't run away from it. See if you can sweep it away. Nothing sweeps better than a new broom, you know, and I just bought this one at the market."
"Thank you," said Rabbit. ❺
And he began to sweep the path where his shadow lay.

12   13

Back and forth, back and forth, Rabbit swished the broom. Great whirlwinds of dust filled the air. Soon Rabbit was coated with dust. Dust got into his eyes, making them itch. Dust got into his nose. He sneezed, and then he sneezed again. But he didn't stop sweeping until he could see his shadow no longer.

14   15

 Teacher Tip

CLARIFYING Remind students readers stop reading when some part of the text does not make sense. Model for students the various ways readers clarify difficult ideas or passages. These include rereading, using charts and other graphic organizers, thinking of other comprehension strategies that might help, and asking someone for help.

"I've lost it!" he cried. "I've lost it!"
Dropping his broom, rabbit danced a little jig. As he danced, the dust settled to the ground. And there was his shadow dancing beside him.
"I guess shadows can't be swept away," said Beaver. "I'm sorry I couldn't help you." He picked up his broom and went on his way.

16

No sooner had Beaver left than Skunk came along.
"Goodness!" he exclaimed. "What happened? I've never seen anyone so dirty."
"I was trying to sweep my shadow away," said Rabbit.
"Everyone knows you can't sweep away shadows," said Skunk.
"You can't hide from them or run away from them either," said Rabbit.

17

"Right," said Skunk. "When two things are stuck together, you must pull them apart."
He leaned over, grabbed Rabbit and pulled.

18

Nothing happened. He grabbed Rabbit again and jerked so hard that he tumbled over backward.

19

Nothing Sticks Like a Shadow, pp. 12–19

Print and Book Awareness

Capital Letters

Direct students' attention to page 12. Identify the names of the animals, and ask students if they notice anything special about the words. Remind students we always begin names with capital letters.

Sentences, Directionality

Display page 14 of the **Big Book,** and have volunteers show where to start reading each sentence and where to stop. Remind students we read from left to right, a sentence begins with a capital letter, and some sentences end with periods. Have each volunteer run his or her hand under each line of print.

Word Length

Show students page 17, and point to the words *No sooner.* Ask students which word is longer and how they know. Have them count the letters in each word. Then do the same with the words *stuck together* on page 18.

1st READ

Comprehension Strategies

Teacher Modeling

7 Clarifying *We need to clarify what a Sewing Circle is. Let me read that sentence again. It says Fox was going to a meeting. A meeting is when a group gets together to talk about or to do a certain thing. So a Sewing Circle is a group that gets together to sew. Rereading the sentence helps us clarify that.*

8 Clarifying *Here is an interresting sentence. Clip, clip, clip is written in a different kind of print, and it is not something that Fox is saying. Let's look at this page again. We see Fox has her scissors out and is cutting Rabbit's shadow. The words Clip, clip, clip tell the sounds that the scissors made. By using the picture, we were able to clarify what was read.*

9 Clarifying *I wonder what the word miserable means. Maybe we can figure out its meaning by rereading the words and the sentences around it. Let's see. The story says Rabbit feels miserable. That must mean miserable is a feeling. Rabbit had just been dragged from the water. His skin was soaking wet; his clothes hung on him like wet rags. He probably felt really bad. The word miserable must mean "bad."*

Skunk was ready to try a third time when along came Fox on her way to a meeting of her Sewing Circle. "What in the world is going on?" she asked.

7

"I'm trying to pull Rabbit away from his shadow," said Skunk.

"Woodchuck bet me his hat that I can't get away from it," said Rabbit.

Fox looked at the shadow carefully. Then she took her scissors from her sewing basket. "Some things are too hard to tear apart," she said. "Let me see if I can cut Rabbit's shadow loose."

20

Clip, clip, clip, Fox went with her scissors. *Clip, clip, clip.* Nothing happened. **8**

21

Fox was still clipping when Raccoon came along.

"Well, well," Raccoon said. "What do we have here?"

"I'm trying to get rid of my shadow," Rabbit said.

"Why?" asked Raccoon. "Shadows are handy things to have. Sometimes they show you where you are going, and sometimes they show you where you've been."

"I know," said Rabbit. "But Woodchuck bet me his hat that I can't get rid of mine even if I want to."

"Did you try hiding from it?" asked Raccoon.

"Yes," said Rabbit. "But it didn't work. And I couldn't run away from it or sweep it away."

"I couldn't cut it off," said Fox.

"Let's try soaking it off," said Raccoon. And he ushered Rabbit to the river's edge.

22

23

Differentiating Instruction **English Learners**

IF . . . students have difficulty relating the onomatopoeic word *clip* on page 21 to what it describes, **THEN . . .** demonstrate the meaning of the word as you say it aloud. Encourage students to share the word their native languages use to represent this sound.

Rabbit put one foot into the water, then jerked it out.
"It's cold!" he wailed.
"Go on," urged Raccoon.
Rabbit took a step.
"Keep going," said Raccoon.
Rabbit shivered. "It's too cold!" he cried.
He swung around to leave the river, bumped into Raccoon, and fell into the water with a great so splash. The river swirled around him. He tossed and rolled, trying to get back to his feet.

24

25

Raccoon grabbed him and dragged him to shore. Rabbit was wet to the skin. Water dripped from his ears. His clothes hung on him like wet rags. Never had he felt so miserable. But the water had not washed away his shadow. There it was beside him.
"Looks as if you're stuck with your shadow," said Raccoon.

26

"Why don't you give up?" asked Fox.
"Tell Woodchuck he's right," said Skunk.
"I don't want to," said Rabbit. "But I guess I'll have to."
Rabbit walked slowly across the fields.

27

Nothing Sticks Like a Shadow, pp. 20–27

Print and Book Awareness

Question Marks

Have volunteers point to the question marks on page 22. Ask students what this mark shows. Then reread page 22, showing the different ways we read questions and statements.

Exclamation Points

Display page 24, and have a volunteer point to two exclamation points. Remind students that this sign shows that the speaker is excited. Then read the sentences in both a normal and an excited voice, and invite students to do the same.

Capital Letters

Display page 27, and have students find and point to words that begin with capital *B, But* capital *F, Fox* capital *I, I* capital *R, Rabbit* capital *S, Skunk* and capital *W. Why, Woodchuck* Have students say the names of the letters as they point to them. Tell students to say the rule about capitalizing names and words that begin sentences. Ask another volunteer to point to the words that begin sentences and to the words that are names.

Comprehension Strategies

Teacher Modeling

⑩ Making Connections *I can understand why Rabbit is upset. Sometimes I think I really want something to happen, but when it does happen, I'm very disappointed. Sometimes things don't turn out the way we think they will. When was a time you felt disappointed?*

⑪ Clarifying *Let's see how the hat figures into the story. Let me read these pages again. When we look back, we see that Woodchuck put the hat on Rabbit's head because he thought that Rabbit won the bet. But when Rabbit's shadow came back, Woodchuck knew that Rabbit really lost the bet, so Woodchuck took back the hat. I'm glad that I reread a few pages. That really helped us clarify what happened.*

When he reached Woodchuck's burrow, Woodchuck was not at home. Rabbit stretched out on a flat sunny rock to wait for him. His shadow stretched out beside him. He was tired. The hot sun felt good. Soon steam rose from his drying clothes. He thought about moving to a shady spot, but he was too sleepy to do so.

"Anyway," he said with a yawn, "if I stay here, maybe the sun will melt my shadow away."

Rabbit tried hard to keep his eyes open to watch the sun melt his shadow. But his eyelids grew heavier and heavier until he fell asleep.

28

It was dark when Woodchuck shook Rabbit awake. "You win," said Woodchuck.

Rabbit yawned and stretched and rubbed the sleep from his eyes.

Woodchuck put his hat on Rabbit's head. "Congratulations," he said. "Your shadow is gone."

29

Rabbit turned round and round. "Oh, dear," he wailed. "The sun *did* melt my shadow."

"That's what you wanted, isn't it?" asked Woodchuck.

"No," wailed Rabbit. "I was only trying to show you that I could get rid of it if I wanted to. And now it's gone! What am I going to do without it?"

At that moment, the clouds parted. A full moon shone. And there was Rabbit's shadow.

"Look!" cried Rabbit. "It's back! You were right after all."

30

31

🍎 **Teacher Tip**

COMPREHENSION Ask students one or more of the following questions to make sure they understand what they are reading: *Is anyone confused? Does what you are listening to make sense to you?*

And he and his shadow whirled and twirled in a wild fandango.

"Of course I'm right," crowed Woodchuck, snatching his hat from Rabbit's head. "I told you that nothing sticks like a shadow."

32

Nothing Sticks Like a Shadow, pp. 28–32

Print and Book Awareness

Sentences and End Punctuation: Periods

Display page 28, and have students point to the first and last words in each sentence of the first paragraph. Have them point to the periods at the ends of sentences and say *This is a period.*

Discussing the Selection

Review the Focus Question with students: What does Rabbit do to get rid of his shadow?

Vocabulary Review

Review with students the selection vocabulary words *burrow, bushes, peeking, advice, coated,* and *handy.* Ask students the following questions:

- *What kinds of animals have a burrow in the ground?*
- *Where can we see bushes?*
- *When might you be peeking at something?*
- *Who is someone who might give you advice?*
- *When have you been coated with something?*
- *What are some things that are handy?*

Language Arts

Students will
+ create an advertisement for a school event.
+ identify a character's feelings and ideas.
+ identify the problem and resolution in a story.

+ *Transparency* 38
+ Idea Icon display card
+ Thought Cloud display card

Come to Our Exciting Show!

Teacher Tip

PLAN AHEAD In preparation for the following activity, have drawing paper and art supplies on hand.

Writing Process

Draft: Collaborating to Create an Advertisement

Teach

Remind students they are working as a class to make an advertisement for a school event.

Guided Practice

+ Write on the board the list of sequenced ideas the class created a few lessons ago. Review the list with students, reminding them of the order in which they chose to present the ideas in the ad. Ask students if they would like to make any changes to this writing plan.

+ After students are happy with the writing plan, begin crafting the card as you translate their ideas to paper. You might tape drawing paper onto the board so all students can watch the card take shape.

+ As students decide on what sentences to use, remind them to include some describing words to "spice up" the ad.

+ Tell students they will have the opportunity to revise the card in the next lesson.

Story Crafting

Working with the New: Problem/Resolution Plots

✦ Display *Transparency* 38. Invite students to share what they remember about Rabbit and his experiences.

✦ Collaborate with students to retell the story, pointing to each story frame as you describe the events that are being depicted.

✦ Ask a volunteer to identify the frame in which Rabbit encounters a problem. If necessary, point to Frame 2, in which Rabbit realizes he cannot simply hide from his shadow. Hold up the Thought Cloud display card, and ask students what Rabbit is feeling in Frame 2.

✦ Show students the Idea Icon display card, and remind them the lightbulb shows when a character in a story has an idea. Tell students you are going to tell the story again and stop at some places to hold up the card. Say *When I hold up the card, I want you to tell me what idea a character has.*

✦ Reread the story again, pausing at Frame 3 to hold up the Idea Icon display card. Help students understand Beaver has the idea that Rabbit might brush away his shadow. Continue with other frames in which other characters offer their ideas to Rabbit.

✦ Ask a volunteer to identify the frame in which Rabbit's problem is resolved. If necessary, point to the final frame, and remind students this is where Rabbit realizes he likes his shadow.

✦ Hold up the Thought Cloud display card to the last story frame, and ask students what Rabbit is feeling after his problem is resolved.

Teacher Tip

SKILL REVIEW This activity uses a story plot students know—*Nothing Sticks Like a Shadow*—to review skills students have been studying. This review is in preparation for the Story Crafting activity in Lesson 14, during which students use these skills to craft their own stories.

Differentiating Instruction **English Learners**

IF ... students have difficulty understanding the story terms *problem, idea,* and *solution,* **THEN ...** use comic strips, story illustrations, or your own dramatization to review the words.

Transparency 38

OBJECTIVES

Students will

✦ use letters in different combinations to form words.
✦ segment phonemes in words.
✦ match initial phonemes.
✦ review the /ks/, /z/, and /u/ sounds.

MATERIALS

✦ **Pocket Chart Letter Cards** *f, b, r, s, u, n, i, x, m*
✦ **Teacher's Resource Book,** p. 37
✦ **Alphabet Letter Cards** *Xx, Zz,* and *Uu* for each student
✦ **Alphabet Book Big Book,** pp. 44–45

Calendar

Su	M	T	W	Th	F	S
		1	2	3	4	5
6	7	8	9	10	11	12
13	14	15	16	17	18	19
20	21	22	23	24	25	26
27	28	29	30	31		

Point to the box that represents today. Have students identify the day of the week. Then point to each letter of the day's name, and have volunteers identify each letter and its corresponding sound, if they have learned it.

Differentiating Instruction **English Learners**

IF ... students have difficulty identifying the day of the week, **THEN ...** review the names for the days of the week as you point to them on the calendar. Have students repeat each name after you. Then ask them again to tell what day it is today.

Warming Up 🕐

M☀RNING MESSAGE

Today's date is _____.

Yesterday in class we _____.

Gus the bug made a fuss on the bus.

Kindergarten News

✦ Copy the text above on the board or on chart paper. Cover up the word *Yesterday* with a self-sticking note or a piece of paper, and fill in the blank with an activity students would remember from yesterday's class.

✦ Tell students a Secret Word is in today's Morning Message, and point to the hidden word. Read the sentence aloud, using the word *blank* in place of *Yesterday: Blank in class we drew pictures of a zebra.* Invite students to find the Secret Word.

✦ Use prompts such as the following to discuss the letters and words in the message: *Can someone find the letter* u *in the message? Gus, bug, fuss, bus Come circle it. What sound does the letter* u *make? /u/ How many times do you hear the /u/ sound in the last sentence? four Let's count each time. Can someone hear any words in the message that rhyme with each other? What are they? Gus, fuss, bus*

Grab Bag of Letters

✦ Show students the paper bag that contains the **Pocket Chart Letter Cards** *f, b, r,* and *s.* Tell students you are going to place some letters in the **Pocket Chart** and that you want them to make words by taking letters out of the bag and placing them in front of the letters in the chart.

✦ Place the letters *u* and *n* in the **Pocket Chart,** and say /u/ /n/. Call on a student to reach into the bag for a letter and to place it in the chart in front of -*un*. Ask the volunteer *What is the name of the letter, and what sound does it make?* Ask *What is the word?* Help students blend and read the word if necessary. Then have the entire class blend and read the word.

✦ When students have made all the words *(fun, bun, run,* and *sun),* repeat the activity by putting the letters *i* and *x* in the chart and the letters *f, m,* and *s* in the bag. Have students make, blend, and read the words. *fix, mix, six* Continue with other letters and simple words as time permits.

Phonemic Awareness

Phoneme Segmentation

✦ Distribute one copy of **Teacher's Resource Book** page 37 to each student.

✦ Tell students you will say three words and you want them to listen closely to the three sounds that make up each word. Explain that on the pages you gave them, there is one row of boxes for each word you say. In the first row of boxes, students will write the letters for each sound in the first word you say. In the second row of boxes, they will write the letters for each sound in the second word you say, and so on. After each word, ask students to proofread their work.

✦ Say the word *sad,* stretching the sounds: /s-s-s-s/ /a-a-a-a/ /d/. Repeat the word several times, pausing at least five seconds between each sound. Guide students in writing the letter *s* for the /s/ sound in the first box, the letter *a* for the /a/ sound in the second box, and the letter *d* for the /d/ sound in the third box.

✦ Then repeat the procedure with the words *tap* and *six,* but this time let students try to identify the sounds and letters on their own. Review the letters students should have written in the boxes, and have students correct their work as necessary.

✦ After all students have the correct letters in the grids, ask them to find the words that begin with the same sound. Have them color the boxes for those words.

Teacher Tip

ACTIVITY SUPPORT Make sure the **Alphabet Sound Wall Cards** are clearly displayed for students to reference as they work to determine the sounds and letters for each of the words. Note that when students complete the activity, the first row of boxes *(s-a-d)* and the third row of boxes *(s-i-x)* should be colored.

Teacher Tip

SKILL REVIEW If students still cannot discriminate between the /j/, /f/, /ks/, /z/, and /u/ sounds with ease, note they will have one more review activity in Lesson 15. However, you might want to work with these students individually in Workshop before they move on to learning the sounds of new letters in Unit 7.

Alphabetic Principle

Reviewing the Sounds of *Xx, Zz,* and *Uu*

✦ Point to the **Alphabet Sound Wall Card** for *Xx*. Ask students to tell what they remember about the short story on the card. Read the story aloud, stressing the /ks/ sound. Invite students to join in as you recite the story once more.

✦ Repeat the process with the **Alphabet Sound Wall Cards** for *Zz* and *Uu*.

Listening for /u/ and Final /ks/ and /z/

✦ Give each student one *Xx*, one *Zz*, and one *Uu* **Alphabet Letter Card.** Tell students you will say a word and they should repeat it. Say if a word ends with the /ks/ sound, on your signal, they should say /ks/ as they hold up their **Alphabet Letter Cards** *Xx*. If it ends with the /z/ sound, they should say /z/ as they hold up their **Alphabet Letter Cards** *Zz*. Ask them to listen very carefully. Try these words:

six	**fuzz**	Alex	pox	size	tax
news	wax	**suds**	Rex	quiz	**buzz**
rays	flax	mix	breeze	reflex	cheese

✦ Reread the first two rows, asking students to say /u/ and hold up their **Alphabet Letter Cards** *Uu* when they hear a word that has the /u/ sound.

Monitor Progress to Differentiate Instruction

Formal Assessment

Letter and Sound Review Note how easily students identify the /ks/ and /z/ sounds.

APPROACHING LEVEL

IF ... students are having difficulty,

THEN ... guide them in completing **Reteach** page 120.

ON LEVEL

IF ... students need more practice,

THEN ... continue the listening activity using **Pocket Chart Picture Cards** whose names contain the sounds being reviewed.

ABOVE LEVEL

IF ... students are comfortable,

THEN ... have them walk around the classroom with partners pointing to objects whose names contain the sounds.

Technology

Have students use the **eGames** activity to review the sounds and letters they have learned in this unit.

Audio CD

Alphabet Book Big Book—/u/

✦ Display the **Alphabet Book Big Book,** and turn to pages 44–45, *Uu.*

✦ Tell students you will read the rhyme aloud and you would like them to listen for the words that have the /u/ sound. Ask students to close their eyes as they listen.

✦ Now tell students it is time for them to act like detectives again and to search for all of the capital *U*s and small *u*'s. Arrange the class into three groups, and assign each group one stanza of the rhyme.

✦ Read the first line of the rhyme again, and call on individual students in the first group to tell you where a *U* or a *u* can be found. *up, umpire* Say each word aloud, emphasizing the /u/ sound, and have the class say it aloud after you.

✦ Continue with the rest of the rhyme and the other groups of students.

Teacher Tip

EXTEND THE ACTIVITY You might extend the activity by asking students to think of rhyming words for a few of the /u/ words they have identified in the rhyme on page 44. The words *up, sun, dusty, swung,* and *luck* have rhyming words with which students may be familiar.

Uu

"Batter up!" called the umpire.
I took the batter's stance
And looked up at the pitcher
Who wore some ugly pants.

Underneath the hot sun
Upon the dusty field.
I swung and missed, one, two, three.
And now my luck was sealed.

Maybe I'm unlucky
Or just a little slow,
My baseball bat was upside-down
—How was I to know?

44   45

Alphabet Book Big Book, pp. 44–45

Technology

Each of the rhymes from the **Alphabet Book Big Book** is available on the **Listening Library CD.** Use the **eAlphabet Book** for activities that support the **Alphabet Book Big Book** lessons.

Audio CD

Reading and Responding

Students will
- ✦ develop an understanding of vocabulary words.
- ✦ review the comprehension strategies Making Connections and Clarifying.
- ✦ use the comprehension skill Reality and Fantasy.
- ✦ analyze the characteristics of a story.

- ✦ *Story Time Collection: Nothing Sticks Like a Shadow*
- ✦ Routines 5–7

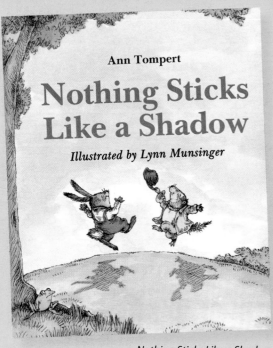

Ann Tompert

Nothing Sticks Like a Shadow

Illustrated by Lynn Munsinger

Nothing Sticks Like a Shadow

Vocabulary

soaking	shady
wailed	melt
shivered	congratulations

Preview and Prepare

Preview the Selection ROUTINE **5**

- ✦ Show students the front cover of *Nothing Sticks Like a Shadow*. Use Routine 5, the previewing the selection routine, as you point to and say the title and the names of the author and the illustrator.

- ✦ Prepare to reread the story. As you turn through the pages, have students use the illustrations to retell the main events in the story.

Vocabulary

ROUTINE **6**

- ✦ Follow Routine 6, the selection vocabulary routine, as you introduce the vocabulary words for this selection.

- ✦ Tell students the word *soaking* means "making completely wet." Use the following sentence to illustrate: "Let's try soaking your socks in bleach to make them whiter."

- ✦ Tell students *wailed* means "cried out in pain." Ask students about a time they wailed.

- ✦ Explain that the word *shivered* means "shook from the cold." Ask students to demonstrate the word *shivered*.

- ✦ Tell students a *shady* place is covered from the sun. Use the following sentence to illustrate: *We found a shady place to sit under a willow tree.*

- ✦ Explain that when things *melt*, they turn into a liquid. Use the following sentence as an illustration: *The ice cubes melt when they are not in the freezer.*

- ✦ Explain to students that when they say *congratulations* to someone, they are saying good wishes for something well done.

Read the Selection

ROUTINE **7**

Comprehension Strategies

✦ During the first reading of *Nothing Sticks Like a Shadow,* you modeled the following comprehension strategies:

- Making Connections
- Clarifying

✦ In this second reading of the selection, you will revisit each comprehension strategy model from the first reading.

Comprehension Skills

In this lesson for *Nothing Sticks Like a Shadow,* students will use the comprehension skill Reality and Fantasy.

Reading with a Writer's Eye

✦ In this rereading of *Nothing Sticks Like a Shadow,* you will discuss genre or the characteristics of a text the author creates.

✦ By discussing the writing strategies the author uses, students become more aware of how they can become better writers.

 Teacher Tip

COMPREHENSION STRATEGIES Readers are also listeners. Reading aloud to students provides an opportunity to teach the reader responses and problem-solving strategies that readers employ. In addition to reading aloud with expression and enthusiasm, model your own comprehension strategies while reading aloud to students. This makes the use of strategies "real" for students and encourages them to begin to respond to text similarly.

Research in Action

Students need multiple exposures to words. Multiple exposures can occur through different learning experiences. Often the word may be used only one or two times in text per grade level, so additional experiences need to be created. Preteaching and post-teaching vocabulary words, using vocabulary words during discussion and for writing, posting and revisiting vocabulary words on a regular basis, and making vocabulary words a part of a personal dictionary that students can refer to throughout the year will give students multiple exposures to new words.

(Marsha Roit)

Technology

To promote independent reading, encourage students to use Workshop to listen to the recording of the selection on the *Listening Library CD.* Invite them to follow along and to say the words whenever they can.

Comprehension Strategies

Teacher Modeling

❶ Clarifying *We had never seen the word* fandango, *and we wanted to know what it meant. Readers know they can reread a sentence to help clarify a word. That's what we did, and we were able to figure out that a* fandango *is a dance.*

❷ Making Connections *We couldn't understand why Rabbit and Woodchuck were arguing. Then we thought about the way we sometimes disagree with our friends. Readers can use information and experiences that they have had themselves to help them understand why things happen in a story.*

❸ Clarifying *Readers can use what they already know and other words in a sentence to figure out what a new word means. We used what we had learned and the words around* burrow *to determine that Woodchuck must live in a burrow.*

❹ Making Connections *When we saw what Rabbit was doing, we didn't understand why he was jumping so high. Then we thought about the way I acted when I was trying to show that I could do something. I used my own experience to make a connection with what was happening in the story.*

Focus Question What does Rabbit do to get rid of his shadow?

❶ One day Rabbit was dancing a wild fandango in a field filled with clover. Woodchuck was watching him from the doorway of his burrow.
"Isn't it lonely, playing by yourself?" Woodchuck asked.
"I'm not alone," said Rabbit, pointing. "See my shadow? It goes where I go and does what I do."

5

"I know what you mean," said Woodchuck.
"I can't escape my shadow either, no matter how hard I try."
"I can if I want to," said Rabbit.
"Oh, no, you can't," said Woodchuck. "No one can."
"I can too," said Rabbit.
"Can't," said Woodchuck.
❷ And they pitched "cans and "can'ts" at each other until Woodchuck said, "I'll bet you my hat you can't."
"Looks as if I'm going to have a new hat," said Rabbit. He ran and hid behind the trunk of a huge tree.

When he looked around, however, he found his shadow standing beside him.
Woodchuck laughed. "You'll have to do better than that," he said.

6   7

Rabbit hurried over to a bunch of bushes and hid behind them. He looked around. No shadow did he see. "I've lost it!" he cried, peeking from behind the bushes at Woodchuck. "Give me your hat."

"Oh, no you haven't," said Woodchuck, pointing. Rabbit looked to where Woodchuck was pointing and saw his shadow's head peeking from behind the bushes, too. "Take my advice," said Woodchuck. "Give it up. Stop wasting time. Nothing sticks like a shadow." With this, he went into his burrow. **3**

8   9

"Woodchuck thinks he knows everything," Rabbit said to his shadow. "But I'll show him. I'll run away from you." And with a great leap, he set out across the field of clover.

Rabbit took longer and longer leaps. His shadow took longer and longer leaps as it followed right behind him. **4**

10   11

Nothing Sticks Like a Shadow, pp. 5–11

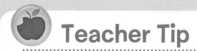

Teacher Tip

RECOGNIZING REALITY AND FANTASY Some students may enjoy making up statements of reality and fantasy for their classmates to judge as real or make-believe.

Comprehension Skills

Reality and Fantasy

✦ Ask students to dictate several facts about shadows as you write them on the board. Then ask them to dictate made-up things about shadows, such as *Shadows want to play with you* or *Shadows like the sunshine.*

✦ Work with students to list things that could be real and things that could never really happen. Ask volunteers which things let them know this story is a *fantasy.*

✦ Explain that even though some stories are made up, the things in the story could really happen. Be sure they understand that a fantasy is about something that could never really happen.

Reading with a Writer's Eye

Genre Knowledge

✦ Explain to students that *Nothing Sticks Like a Shadow* is a fantasy rather than an information book like "Shadows."

✦ Tell students a story has a setting, or a location, where the story takes place. Ask students what the setting of *Nothing Sticks Like a Shadow* is.

✦ Tell students a story also has a plot, or plan, that the story follows. Explain that like most plots, this story begins with a problem. Ask students what problem is stated on page 6.

Comprehension Strategies

Teacher Modeling

5 **Clarifying** *We didn't know why Beaver would give Rabbit his brand-new broom. Then we read Beaver's words again. By rereading, we were able to figure out that Beaver was trying to help Rabbit get rid of the shadow.*

6 **Clarifying** *Remember we were confused about the word* jig? *What good reading strategy did we use to figure out what it means? Did you need to clarify anything else? How did you do that?*

Soon Rabbit came to a path beside a river. There he met Beaver carrying a broom over his shoulder.
"Why are you running?" asked Beaver.
"I'm trying to get away from my shadow," said Rabbit. "Woodchuck bet me his hat that I couldn't."

"Well," said Beaver, "it's easy to see you can't run away from it. See if you can sweep it away. Nothing sweeps better than a new broom, you know, and I just bought this one at the market."
"Thank you," said Rabbit. **5**
And he began to sweep the path where his shadow lay.

12   13

Back and forth, back and forth, Rabbit swished the broom. Great whirlwinds of dust filled the air. Soon Rabbit was coated with dust. Dust got into his eyes, making them itch. Dust got into his nose. He sneezed, and then he sneezed again. But he didn't stop sweeping until he could see his shadow no longer.

14   15

Nothing Sticks Like a Shadow, pp. 12–19

Teacher Tip

REALITY AND FANTASY You may need to work individually with students who seem confused about the differences between reality and fantasy.

Comprehension Skills

Reality and Fantasy

Work together to create a chart in which students keep track of things in the story that could be real and things that could never really happen.

Reading with a Writer's Eye

Genre Knowledge

✦ Tell students a story often has several characters. Ask students which characters have appeared so far in the story. *Rabbit, Woodchuck, Beaver, and Skunk*

✦ Explain that the plot of the story continues as Rabbit tries to find a way to solve his problem or win his bet with Woodchuck and escape his shadow. How has Rabbit tried so far to win his bet with Woodchuck? *He has tried to hide from his shadow, run away from it, sweep it away, and pull it away.*

Comprehension Strategies

Teacher Modeling

7 Clarifying *When we needed to clarify what a Sewing Circle was, we knew readers use the words and sometimes what they already know to help them figure something out. I reread the sentence and recognized the word* meeting. *Then we remembered we already knew what a meeting was. By using these two things, we were able to figure out what we needed to know.*

8 Clarifying *When the words* Clip, clip, clip *confused us, I reread the sentence and looked at the picture. We could see the words were in a different kind of type. Then we knew readers can also use the pictures to help them clarify something. When we saw what Fox was doing, I realized what* Clip, clip, clip *meant.*

9 Clarifying *Remember we were confused about the word* miserable? *To figure out what the word means, we did what readers do: I reread the words and the sentences around it. By rereading, we were able to understand that* miserable *means "to feel very unhappy."*

Clip, clip, clip, Fox went with her scissors. *Clip, clip, clip.* **8** Nothing happened.

7 Skunk was ready to try a third time when along came Fox on her way to a meeting of her Sewing Circle. "What in the world is going on?" she asked.

"I'm trying to pull Rabbit away from his shadow," said Skunk.

"Woodchuck bet me his hat that I can't get away from it," said Rabbit.

Fox looked at the shadow carefully. Then she took her scissors from her sewing basket. "Some things are too hard to tear apart," she said. "Let me see if I can cut Rabbit's shadow loose."

20

21

Fox was still clipping when Raccoon came along.

"Well, well," Raccoon said. "What do we have here?"

"I'm trying to get rid of my shadow," Rabbit said.

"Why?" asked Raccoon. "Shadows are handy things to have. Sometimes they show you where you are going, and sometimes they show you where you've been."

"I know," said Rabbit. "But Woodchuck bet me his hat that I can't get rid of mine even if I want to."

"Did you try hiding from it?" asked Raccoon.

"Yes," said Rabbit. "But it didn't work. And I couldn't run away from it or sweep it away."

"I couldn't cut it off," said Fox.

"Let's try soaking it off," said Raccoon. And he ushered Rabbit to the river's edge.

22

23

Vocabulary Tip

Review the meaning of the word *soaking*. Then have students use the word in a sentence.

Rabbit put one foot into the water, then jerked it out.
"It's cold!" he wailed.
"Go on," urged Raccoon.
Rabbit took a step.
"Keep going," said Raccoon.
Rabbit shivered. "It's too cold!" he cried.
He swung around to leave the river, bumped into Raccoon, and fell into the water with a great splash. The river swirled around him. He tossed and rolled, trying to get back to his feet.

24

25

Raccoon grabbed him and dragged him to shore. Rabbit was wet to the skin. Water dripped from his ears. His clothes hung on him like wet rags. Never had he felt so miserable. But the water had not washed away his shadow. There it was beside him. ⑨
"Looks as if you're stuck with your shadow," said Raccoon.

26

"Why don't you give up?" asked Fox.
"Tell Woodchuck he's right," said Skunk.
"I don't want to," said Rabbit. "But I guess I'll have to."
Rabbit walked slowly across the fields.

27

Nothing Sticks Like a Shadow, pp. 20–27

Teacher Tip

SHARING FANTASY STORIES Students may enjoy sharing fantasy stories with one another.

Comprehension Skills

Reality and Fantasy

Have volunteers tell what they have learned about the differences between *reality* and *fantasy*. Then ask students to add information from these pages to the chart.

Reading with a Writer's Eye

Genre Knowledge

✦ *What new characters did the author have enter the story on pages 20–27?* Fox and Raccoon

✦ *What other things does Rabbit do to try to solve his problem and win his bet with Woodchuck?* Rabbit lets Fox try to cut loose his shadow, and he tries to wash it away in the river.

✦ *How do these pages help us understand this story is a fantasy?*

Vocabulary Tip

Review the meanings of the words *wailed* and *shivered*. Then have students use the words in sentences.

2nd READ

Comprehension Strategies

Teacher Modeling

⑩ Making Connections *We remembered readers can use their own experiences to help them understand what is happening in a story. We thought about times when we really wanted something to happen like Rabbit did. Then we remembered when things didn't turn out to be what we expected, we felt disappointed and sad. I'm glad we were able to use something that happened to us to help us understand what was happening to Rabbit.*

⑪ Clarifying *This was a little confusing for me. To figure out what was happening, I knew we could go back a few pages and read them again. That helped us remember Woodchuck first thought Rabbit won the bet. By rereading, we were able to clarify something that was confusing us.*

When he reached Woodchuck's burrow, Woodchuck was not at home. Rabbit stretched out on a flat sunny rock to wait for him. His shadow stretched out beside him. He was tired. The hot sun felt good. Soon steam rose from his drying clothes. He thought about moving to a shady spot, but he was too sleepy to do so.

"Anyway," he said with a yawn, "if I stay here, maybe the sun will melt my shadow away."

Rabbit tried hard to keep his eyes open to watch the sun melt his shadow. But his eyelids grew heavier and heavier until he fell asleep.

28

It was dark when Woodchuck shook Rabbit awake. "You win," said Woodchuck.

Rabbit yawned and stretched and rubbed the sleep from his eyes.

Woodchuck put his hat on Rabbit's head. "Congratulations," he said. "Your shadow is gone."

29

Rabbit turned round and round. "Oh, dear," he wailed. "The sun *did* melt my shadow."

"That's what you wanted, isn't it?" asked Woodchuck.

"No," wailed Rabbit. "I was only trying to show you that I could get rid of it if I wanted to. And now it's gone! What am I going to do without it?"

At that moment, the clouds parted. A full moon shone. And there was Rabbit's shadow.

"Look!" cried Rabbit. "It's back! You were right after all."

30

⑩

31

🍎 **Teacher Tip**

MAKING CONNECTIONS Encourage students to be active readers who make connections as they read. Invite students to share their connections with the class.

And he and his shadow whirled and twirled in a wild fandango.

"Of course I'm right," crowed Woodchuck, snatching his hat from Rabbit's head. "I told you that nothing sticks like a shadow."

32

Nothing Sticks Like a Shadow, pp. 28–32

Reading with a Writer's Eye

Genre Knowledge

Have students discuss the differences between a story and an information book, using *Nothing Sticks Like a Shadow* and "Shadows" as examples. Review the characteristics of a story (setting, plot, problem/solution, and characters) and an information book (shares facts about a subject).

Discussing the Selection

Help students use the illustrations to retell the sequence of events in the story as you turn through the pages.

Purposes for Reading

Ask students what they liked best about *Nothing Sticks Like a Shadow* and what they learned about shadows from this selection.

Vocabulary Review

Review with students the selection vocabulary words *soaking, wailed, shivered, shady, melt,* and *congratulations.* Ask students the following questions:

- *When would be a time we could have something soaking?*
- *When was a time you wailed?*
- *What did it feel like when you shivered?*
- *Where could we find a shady place?*
- *What kinds of things melt?*
- *When might you say congratulations?*

OBJECTIVES

Students will
✦ revise the advertisement by adding ideas.
✦ improve sentences by adding describing words.
✦ collaborate with partners to craft a story about animals.

MATERIALS

✦ *Language Arts Big Book,* pp. 37, 55
✦ Class advertisement
✦ *Transparency* 38
✦ *Thinking Crowns*

Writing Process 🕐

Revise: Improving by Adding Ideas

Teach

✦ Remind students the class is working together to create an advertisement for a school event. Display the card the class created during the previous lesson. Invite students to offer their suggestions about how to revise the card, or how to make it better.

✦ Choose several of the students' ideas, and implement the changes on the card.

✦ Explain to students that the card has now become a first draft, or a first try. Tell them you will use the notes you added to the first draft to create a new card. This new card is called the final draft.

Guided Practice

✦ Display a new blank sheet of drawing paper on the board. Tell students to watch as you make the final draft and to tell you if you forget something. When drawing the first page, omit a few of the pictures or words that are supposed to appear there.

✦ Tell students you are ready to begin working on the inside of the card. Ask if you have forgotten anything on the front page. If students do not identify your omissions, tell them you should double-check your work before you move on. Point to the items you omitted.

✦ Complete the advertisement, and tell students in the next lesson they will decide where to put the card so people will see it.

Grammar, Usage, and Mechanics 🕐

Teach

Display page 55 of the *Language Arts Big Book.* Remind students describing words tell more about other words. Describing words can also make sentences more interesting.

Language Arts Big Book, p. 55

 ## Teacher Tip

PLAN AHEAD In preparation for the Writing Process activity, have drawing paper, art supplies, and blank index cards on hand.

Grammar, Usage, and Mechanics continued

Guided Practice

✦ Display page 37 of the **Language Arts Big Book,** pointing to the sentences on the right-hand side of the page.

✦ Tell students you want them to close their eyes while you read the sentences aloud. Ask them to think about what part of each sentence needs more information.

✦ Invite volunteers to suggest describing words that will tell more about the sentences.

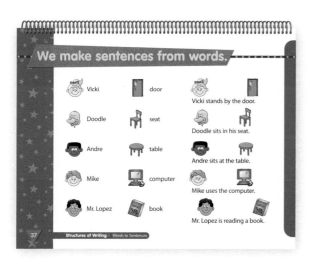

Language Arts Big Book, p. 37

Monitor Progress

Formal Assessment ✔

to Differentiate Instruction

Grammar Note how easily students use describing words.

APPROACHING LEVEL	
IF . . . students are having difficulty,	**THEN . . .** have them complete **Reteach** page 121.

ON LEVEL	
IF . . . students need more practice,	**THEN . . .** let them work with partners and extend some simple sentences that they see around the classroom.

ABOVE LEVEL	
IF . . . students are comfortable ,	**THEN . . .** have them work with partners challenging each other to extend simple sentences they have created.

Story Crafting

Working with the New: Thinking about Animals

✦ Display **Transparency** 38. Remind students about Rabbit's experiences with his shadow.

Transparency 38

✦ Hold up a **Thinking Crown,** and tell students they are going to wear the crowns to show everyone what they are thinking.

✦ Call for a volunteer, and place a **Thinking Crown** on his or her head. Ask the student to close his or her eyes and think of a favorite animal. Make a quick, simple drawing of the animal on a blank index card, and place it in the student's crown.

✦ Continue with each student, distributing the **Thinking Crowns** one at a time and inserting quick sketches of the animals they name.

✦ After each student is wearing a **Thinking Crown,** assign partners. Make sure students are partnered with someone who has a different animal in his or her **Thinking Crown.**

✦ Ask students to work with their partners to make up a story that has both students' favorite animals as the main characters. Suggest the story could have something to do with shadows. Remind them that the best stories have a problem, an idea, and a solution.

✦ Circulate around the room, and have students tell you about the stories they are creating. Provide guidance as necessary.

✦ If possible, allow time for pairs to share their original stories with the class.

Sounds and Letters

Students will

✦ segment phonemes in words.
✦ match initial phonemes.
✦ review the /j/, /f/, /ks/, /z/, and /u/ sounds.
✦ proofread their penmanship from the unit.
✦ practice sound-by-sound blending.
✦ read and respond to a **Decodable.**

✦ **Teacher's Resource Book,** p. 37; 3 copies for each student
✦ **Alphabet Letter Cards** *Jj, Ff, Xx,* and *Zz* for each student
✦ Supply Icons
✦ **Skills Practice 2,** p. 21
✦ **Decodable** 10
✦ Routines 2, 4

Calendar

Su	M	T	W	Th	F	S
		1	2	3	4	5
6	7	8	9	10	11	12
13	14	15	16	17	18	19
20	21	22	23	24	25	26
27	28	29	30	31		

Point to the box that represents today. Ask a volunteer to say the name of the month. Then have other volunteers identify each of the letters that make up the month's name.

Warming Up

MORNING MESSAGE

Today is _____.

Let's do a letter hunt!

Joey the funny fox sneezed six times in January.

Kindergarten News

✦ Copy the above text on the board or on chart paper.

✦ Ask the class to identify any letters or sounds they learned in this unit.
Jj, Ff, Xx, Zz, Uu; /j/, /f/, /ks/, /z/, /u/

✦ Have students tell which sentences end with periods and which ends with an exclamation point. *first, third; second*

Phoneme Replacement

✦ Tell students they are going to play the rhyme game. Remind them in the game they use what they are learning about sounds and letters to make rhymes. Say you are going to give them a riddle and the answer is a word that begins with the sound you say.

✦ Demonstrate as follows:

Teacher: *What rhymes with* fun *but starts with* /b/?

Everyone: *bun*

✦ Continue with these riddles:

• *What rhymes with* boom *but starts with* /z/? *zoom*

• *What rhymes with* six *but starts with* /f/? *fix*

- *What rhymes with* cart *but starts with /d/?* dart
- *What rhymes with* bump *but starts with /j/?* jump
- *What rhymes with* lace *but starts with /f/?* face

Phonemic Awareness

Phoneme Segmentation

✦ Distribute three copies of **Teacher's Resource Book** page 37 to each student. Continue the phoneme segmentation and matching activity that students practiced in Lesson 14.

✦ Remind students that you will say three words and that you want them to listen closely to the three sounds that make up each word. In the first row of boxes on the page, they will write each sound in the first word you say; in the second row of boxes, they will write each sound in the second word you say; and so on.

✦ Say the word *big,* stretching the sounds: */b-b-b/ /i-i-i/ /g/.* Repeat the word several times, and guide students in writing the letters for each of the sounds in the boxes for this first word.

✦ Repeat the procedure with the words *bus* and *pot,* but have students try to identify the sounds on their own. Review the letters students should have written in the boxes, and have students correct their work as necessary.

✦ After all students have the correct letters in the grids, ask them to find the words that begin with the same sound. Have them color the boxes for those words.

✦ Repeat two more times with the new sheets and these sets of words: *jam / hat / hug* and *fig / fan / dog.*

 Teacher Tip

PHONOLOGICAL AND PHONEMIC AWARENESS Remember to move quickly through these activities. Even though students are progressing to more difficult skills, they will still have several opportunities to practice each one. Plan to work with struggling students individually during Workshop.

Differentiating Instruction **English Learners**

IF ... students have difficulty with the Phoneme Segmentation activity, **THEN ...** refer to Unit 6 Lesson 15 of the **English Learner Support Guide.**

Teacher Tip

SKILL REVIEW Remember this is the final review of the /j/, /f/, /ks/, /z/, and /u/ sounds before students move on to learning the sounds of new letters in Unit 7. During Workshop, take time to help students who are still struggling with differentiating sounds and linking the sounds to the proper letters. You might guide these students in redoing a few of the **Skills Practice 2** or **Reteach** pages they completed in this unit.

Alphabetic Principle

Reviewing the Sounds of *Jj, Ff, Xx, Zz,* and *Uu*

Review once more the **Alphabet Sound Wall Cards** for *Jj, Ff, Xx, Zz,* and short *Uu.* Have students make each sound aloud and discuss what they remember about the story on each card.

Listening for Initial /j/ and /f/

Give each student one *Jj* and one *Ff* **Alphabet Letter Card.** Tell students you will say a word and they should repeat it. Then students should hold up the **Alphabet Letter Cards** and say the sound of the letter that begins the word. Try these words:

jam jam /j/	*fork* fork /f/	*fan* fan /f/
jelly jelly /j/	*jury* jury /j/	*finish* finish /f/

Listening for Final /ks/ and /z/

Repeat the previous activity with **Alphabet Letter Cards** *Xx* and *Zz,* asking students to listen for words that end with /ks/ or /z/ and then raise their cards and say the word's ending sound.

box box /ks/	*quiz* quiz /z/	*freeze* freeze /z/
index index /ks/	*hex* hex /ks/	*jazz* jazz /z/

Linking the Sound to the Letter

Write a pair of words on the board, one with the short *u* sound and the other with a different vowel sound. Say the words, and have students identify the word with the /u/ sound by signaling thumbs-up when you point to it. Then have a volunteer tell how he or she knows the correct word and to circle the letter that makes the /u/ sound in the word. Try these words:

tag … **tug**	**duck** … *deck*
study … *steady*	*match* … **much**

Technology

Have students use the **eSkills** activity for this unit to review the sounds of /j/, /f/, /ks/, /z/, and /u/. Students can use one of the **eGames** activities for this unit for a comprehensive review.

Audio CD

Penmanship

✦ Distribute a sheet of writing paper to each student, or use **White Boards** turned to the sides with writing lines.

✦ Place the Supply Icon for *pencil* on the board or in the **Pocket Chart.**

✦ Model how to write the letter *Xx* on the board. Then ask students to write one row of capital *X* letters and one row of small *x* letters. Repeat the process for the letter *Zz*.

Guided Practice

✦ Have students complete **Skills Practice 2** page 21 for a review of *Jj, Ff, Xx, Zz,* and *Uu* and the /j/, /f/, /ks/, /z/, and /u/ sounds.

✦ Tell students one letter is missing from each word on the page. Explain that you will say the names of the pictures aloud and they should listen closely to the sounds in the words to discover which letter is missing from each.

✦ Review each picture, repeating the names as necessary and allowing students plenty of time to write the letters.

✦ After students have finished, review and proofread the page as a class. Have students use colored pencils to circle any mistakes and make them better.

Proofreading

✦ Tell students they are going to proofread the work they did in this unit. Distribute a few of students' completed **Skills Practice 2** pages. Also give each student a colored pencil with which to circle and correct their work.

✦ Ask students to look at the letters they wrote and to choose a few they think they can write better. Have them circle the letters with their colored pencils and then write the new letters above them.

✦ Continue with as many of the unit's **Skills Practice 2** pages as you think would benefit students, but try to review at least one page for each new letter they learned in this unit.

✦ After students have finished, invite volunteers to show off their "better letters" to their classmates.

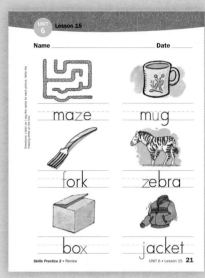

Skills Practice 2, p. 21

Monitor Progress

to Differentiate Instruction
Formal Assessment

Letter and Sound Review Observe how easily students review the letters and sounds.

APPROACHING LEVEL

| IF ... students are having difficulty, | THEN ... guide them in completing **Reteach** page 122. |

ON LEVEL

| IF ... students need more practice, | THEN ... write the letters/sounds being reviewed on the board, and have them hunt in the **My Shadow Little Big Book** for objects that match those letters/sounds. |

ABOVE LEVEL

| IF ... students are comfortable, | THEN ... have them complete **Challenge Activities** page 92. |

Liz and Tad
by Sean Sanders
illustrated by Ellen Joy Sasaki

Decodable 10

Teacher Tips

HIGH-FREQUENCY WORDS Take every opportunity to focus students' attention on the word *all,* as well as the previously introduced high-frequency words, in the context of their daily **Big Book** reading and in other classroom print. Tell students these are words they will see often in books and in other print.

STUDENT PRACTICE Before sending home the takehome versions of the **Decodables,** listen to students read a page or two during Workshop to be sure they are comfortable and confident reading their books.

Technology

Use **eDecodable** *Liz and Tad* to reinforce the high-frequency word *all* and the /z/ sound.

Audio CD

Reading a Decodable
ROUTINE **2** ROUTINE **4**

Decodable 10: Liz and Tad

High-Frequency Word: *all*

✦ The high-frequency word introduced is *all.* Write *all* on the board, and read it aloud. Have students repeat it aloud with you. Then have students say the word on their own.

✦ Explain to students that the word *all* is used when talking about a group of people or things. *All* means "each and every one in the group." You might use this sentence as an example: *All the students in my class are wonderful!*

✦ Point again to *all* written on the board, and have students read the word independently.

✦ Have students work with partners to say a few sentences using the word *all.*

✦ Review the high-frequency words introduced in previous lessons.

Blending

Before reading **Decodable** 10, review the sound-by-sound blending procedure with students. Choose words with the /z/ sound or other sounds students have already learned, such as *zip, fan,* and *jug.* After blending, have students make and extend sentences for each word.

Reading Recommendations

✦ Distribute copies of **Decodable** 10. Ask students to browse the books and look at the pictures, commenting on what they see and making predictions about what they think the story will be about.

✦ Point to the high-frequency word *all* in the text, and pronounce it. Then have students point to the word and read it aloud.

✦ Hold up your book, and read the title, pointing to each word. Read the names of the author and the illustrator aloud, pointing to each name as you say it. Ask students to explain the jobs of author and illustrator.

✦ Read the **Decodable,** following the established procedure. (See Routine 4 for a detailed description.) After you have read the story, reread the title, and have students repeat after you. Then have students read it chorally with you.

Liz and Tad

by Sean Sanders
illustrated by Ellen Joy Sasaki

Liz and Tad nap.

3

All the cats run!

4

Liz and Tad zig and zag.

5

Can the cats tag Liz and Tad?

6

Liz and Tad run in the mud!

7

All the cats zip in. Fun!

8

Decodable 10
Liz and Tad

High-Frequency Word
Introduced in Decodable 10
all

Previously Introduced
High-Frequency Words
a
am
and
as
at
but
can
did
for
girl
go
had
has
have
he
him
his
I
in
is
it
of
on
see
the
to
up
we
you

Sound-Spelling Correspondences in Decodables
1. /s/, /m/, /d/, /p/, /a/
2. /h/, /t/
3. /n/, /l/
4. /i/
5. /b/, /k/ spelled *c*
6. /o/, /r/
7. /g/
8. /j/, /f/
9. /u/, /ks/ spelled *x*
10. /z/

Responding

✦ Display the *High-Frequency Flash Card* for *all*. Have students find and point to the high-frequency word *all* in the story. Ask students to identify in the story any of the previously introduced high-frequency words.

✦ Ask students to tell about any difficult words they saw in the story. Ask students to explain how they figured out the words. Review each word that students identify.

✦ Have volunteers take turns reading pages of the story aloud. Guide them as necessary.

✦ Invite students to connect the story to their personal experiences. Ask volunteers to share stories about a time they had fun playing tag. You might ask them to describe how to play tag and to share any secrets they have for being good at playing the game.

✦ Make copies of the story for students to take home. A black-and-white version of the story is available in *Pre-Decodable and Decodable Takehomes Blackline Masters.*

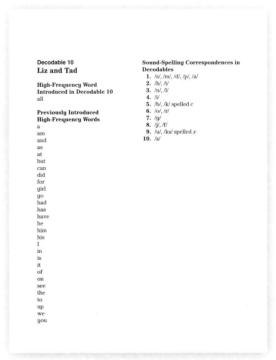

Decodable 10, inside back cover

Students will
+ present the class advertisement.
+ discuss the writing process.
+ review sentence skills.
+ participate in a celebration of the unit theme.

MATERIALS

+ **Skills Practice 2,** p. 22
+ **My Shadow Big Book**
+ **Read Aloud Collection:** *What Makes a Shadow?*
+ **Story Time Collection:** *Nothing Sticks Like a Shadow*

Differentiating Instruction **English Learners**

IF ... students have difficulty understanding questions about the stories, **THEN ...** break down the questions into simple sentences that require brief answers. For example: *Do you remember the story* What Makes a Shadow? *It told about night. What makes the night?*
a shadow

Theme Wrap-Up and Review 🕐

+ Show students *What Makes a Shadow?*, "Shadows," "Bear Shadow," and *Nothing Sticks Like a Shadow*. Assist students in retelling each story. Invite them to share any comments, and then ask the following questions:
  • *What did you learn about the night in* What Makes a Shadow?
  • *Name three things you need to make a shadow from "Shadows."*
  • *What does Bear not know about shadows in "Bear Shadow"?*
  • *How does Rabbit try to get rid of his shadow in* Nothing Sticks Like a Shadow?

+ Encourage students to use complete sentences in answering the above questions. Invite them to ask other questions they have and to discuss them as a group. Encourage students to discuss their thoughts and feelings about the unit theme My Shadow. Begin a discussion by asking the following questions:
  • *What kinds of objects make shadows?*
  • *Why is your shadow sometimes behind you and other times in front of you?*
  • *Can the shape of shadows change? How?*

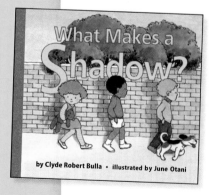

Read Aloud Collection: *What Makes a Shadow?*

My Shadow Big Book

Story Time Collection: *Nothing Sticks Like a Shadow*

Language Arts

Writing Process

Present and Reflect: Displaying Ad and Discussing Writing

Teach

Remind students that they have completed making an advertisement card that tells about a school event. Tell them it is now time to present their work.

Apply

✦ Take out the class ad, and ask students to give their opinions on where they would like to display the card. Have them also tell why they chose the spots they suggest.

✦ Write no more than five suggestions on the board, and have the class vote to find the winner.

✦ Next ask students to think about their experiences writing the advertisement. Have students generate a list of words that tell about their experiences using describing words in their writing.

Monitor Progress to Differentiate Instruction

Formal Assessment ✓

Grammar Note how easily students understand spacing.

APPROACHING LEVEL

IF ... students are having difficulty,

THEN ... refer to Unit 6 Lesson 15 of the *Intervention Guide* for additional support of this Grammar activity.

ON LEVEL

IF ... students need more practice,

THEN ... let them work with partners and review any one of the *Read Aloud Collection* selections and discuss spacing.

ABOVE LEVEL

IF ... students are comfortable,

THEN ... have them look at a paragraph without spaces between sentences and words and make slash marks where they should be.

Grammar, Usage, and Mechanics

Teach

✦ Review with students some of the things they have learned about sentences during the past few weeks. Write the following list on the board:

- Sentences have spaces between them.
- Two neighboring sentences should begin in two different ways.
- Sound patterns make sentences interesting.
- Describing words make sentences interesting.

✦ Spend a few moments discussing each point on the list to refresh students' memories.

Guided Practice

✦ Have students open *Skills Practice 2* to page 22.

✦ Read the paragraph aloud to students. Explain that some mistakes are in the sentences and that there are ways to make the sentences better.

✦ Begin by saying *First let's make sure a space is between sentences. Does anyone see any mistakes?* Ask students to place a slash mark where a space should be.

Skills Practice 2, p. 22

Monitor Progress ✓
Formal Assessment Options

You will need the following materials, along with your informal observations and **Lesson Assessment** results, to monitor student progress throughout the year.

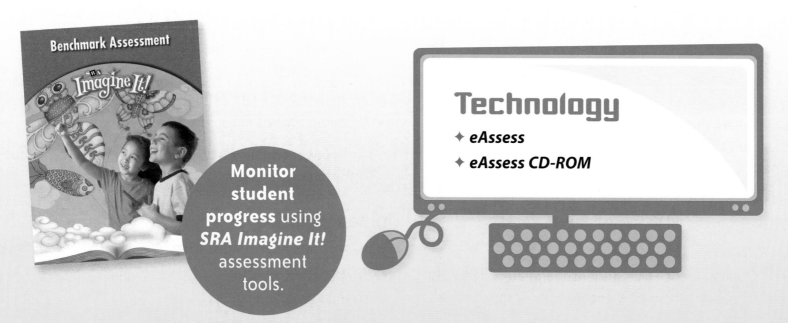

Benchmark Assessment

Imagine It!

Monitor student progress using *SRA Imagine It!* assessment tools.

Technology
✦ **eAssess**
✦ **eAssess CD-ROM**

Benchmark Assessment for Unit 6 addresses the following skills:

- **Phonemic Awareness**
- **Letter Recognition**
- **Phonics/Word Reading**
- **Comprehension**
- **Grammar, Usage, and Mechanics**

Results on **Benchmark Assessment** will serve as a performance indicator that shows how well students are prepared to take an end-of-the-year standardized test. **Benchmark Assessment** results also will allow you to intervene with students who are at risk for failure.

Monitor Progress with Benchmark Assessment

Below are two sets of **Benchmark Assessment** cutoffs that can be used for predicting student performance—one for Benchmark Skills Assessments and the other for Oral Fluency Assessments. Each cutoff begins with a baseline score under Benchmark 1, which is given at the beginning of the year and ends with Benchmark 6, which is given at the end of the year. The cutoffs are determined by finding the amount of growth a student must make over the course of the year to ensure he or she will not be at risk for reading failure.

Benchmark Skills Assessment

The Benchmark Skills Assessment is a 100-point test, consisting of questions covering phonemic awareness; letter recognition; phonics/word reading; comprehension; and grammar, usage, and mechanics. The table below shows how many points out of 100 kindergarten students should score on a particular Benchmark Skills Assessment over the course of the year. The highlighted score indicates where your students should be at this time.

Benchmark 1	Benchmark 2	Benchmark 3	Benchmark 4	Benchmark 5	Benchmark 6
7	23	38	54	70	85

Oral Fluency Assessment: Letter Sounds

The Oral Fluency Assessment is an individually administered assessment, consisting of letter sounds, phonetically regular words, and high-frequency words that students read aloud to the teacher to assess fluency. The table below shows how many letter sounds and words kindergarten students should read on a particular Oral Fluency Assessment over the course of the year. The highlighted score indicates where your students should be at this time.

Benchmark 1	Benchmark 2	Benchmark 3	Benchmark 4	Benchmark 5	Benchmark 6
0	6	12	18	24	30

Independent Tools to Monitor Progress

DIBELS and TPRI

Based on your DIBELS or TPRI scores, use manipulatives from the **Workshop Kit** to practice letter sounds and letter recognition.

BIG Idea

Why do shadows come and go?

Write the Big Idea question on the board. Ask students what they learned about shadows. Ask which selections added something new to their understanding of shadows. Encourage students to share their thoughts about the unit.

Teacher Tip

UNIT CELEBRATION Remember, the goal of this celebration is to allow students to take ownership of their learning. Your role is to guide them toward success. You must take the lead with certain elements of the celebration, but rely on student input for all major decisions.

Celebrate Shadows!

✦ In advance of the activity, prepare the materials students will need to share their final product of inquiry. The necessary materials will depend on the method students chose for sharing.

✦ Congratulate students on all their hard work in this unit as they learned about shadows. Remind them the unit celebration is a special way to recognize their hard work.

✦ Support students through each step of their preparation for the celebration. For example, if students have decided to perform a demonstration of how shadows form and how they move and change, help them choose and procure the best materials for presenting such a demonstration.

✦ Help students as they plan individual roles in the celebration; in this way you can ensure that all students are taking part. Each student may want to read his or her special page.

✦ Help students create a forum for sharing the final product of their inquiry. Encourage them to generate new ideas for sharing their inquiry with people outside the classroom. If students need help sparking their creativity, make suggestions for how students might share their celebration with others.

Inquiry Wrap-Up

✦ Have students assemble their question-and-answer book. Talk about how to organize the pages and what should be on the title page.

✦ Have students come up and read their questions and answers to the class.

✦ Make copies of the class book for each student to take home and share with their families. Talk with your librarians, and put one copy in the library.

Concept/Question Board

Invite students to discuss what they have learned about shadows. Encourage them to share how their ideas about shadows have changed since the beginning of the unit. Direct students' attention to the postings on the **Concept/Question Board,** and "peel back the layers" of self-sticking notes to see how their knowledge has changed. Read each question aloud, and determine if it has been answered and can be moved to the Concept side of the Board. Invite volunteers to add ideas to the questions that have not been answered.

 Teacher Tips

SCHEDULING Some of these suggestions may warrant extra time that is not available in this lesson. Perhaps another part of the day could be set aside to devote to some of the suggested activities.

RECREATIONAL READING Because it is important to read daily to your students, choose a book from the Additional Reading listed in the Unit Overview, and find a time during the day to read the book aloud to your students.

B

bury
My dog likes to **bury** his bone.

C

cloud
The **cloud** is big and white.

H

hid
Manuel **hid** behind the tree.

R

railing
We hold onto the **railing** when we walk down the stairs.

46

47

race

We run in the **race**.

S

shines

The sun **shines** brightly through the window.

Z

zigzags

Michael **zigzags** around the neighborhood on his bike.

48

49

SRA Imagine It!

The Program Appendix includes a step-by-step explanation of procedures for research-based, effective practices in reading instruction that are repeatedly used throughout *SRA Imagine It!* These practices may also be used in other instructional materials.

Table of Contents

Phonological and Phonemic Awareness

The key to learning to read is the ability to identify different sounds and to connect those sounds to the letters of the alphabet. The basic purpose of providing structured practice in phonemic awareness is to help students hear and understand the sounds from which words are made. Before students can be expected to understand the sound/symbol correspondence that forms the base of written English, they need to have a strong working knowledge of the sound relationships that make up the spoken language. This understanding of spoken language lays the foundation for the transition to written language.

Phonological awareness is an umbrella term. It incorporates a range of oral language skills that involve the ability to notice, think about, and manipulate individual sounds in words. Phonological awareness involves working with sentences, words, rhyme, syllables, and sounds. The objective is for students to be able to manipulate words, word parts, and sounds without regard to meaning.

Phonological and phonemic awareness activities initially provide students with the opportunity to think about sentences and to break them into words and then to play with words and to break them into parts. It involves easy and fun activities that engage students in playing with and exploring the parts and sounds of language. The goal of these gamelike activities is to help students understand that speech is made of distinct, identifiable sounds. The playful nature of the activities makes them appealing and engaging, while giving students practice and support for learning about language. When students begin reading and writing, this experience with manipulating sounds will help them use what they know about sounds and letters to sound out and spell unfamiliar words when they read and write.

Developing phonological awareness engages students in activities that move from working with words and syllables — the larger units of language — to individual sounds (phonemes). Students progress by

- Identifying sentences
- Identifying words
- Working with rhymes
- Exploring compound words
- Listening for syllables

- Blending syllables
- Oral blending
- Deleting and substituting sounds
- Segmenting phonemes

As students progress through various phonemic awareness activities, they will become proficient at listening for and reproducing the sounds they hear. It is essential for their progression to phonics and reading that they are able to hear the sounds and the patterns used to make up recognizable words. The phonemic awareness activities support the phonics instruction. Initially students are not expected to read the words they are exploring and manipulating, so any consonant and vowel sounds may be used, even if students have not been formally taught the sounds and their spellings.

> *As students progress through various phonemic awareness activities, they will become proficient at listening for and reproducing the sounds they hear.*

After students have an awareness of phonemes, they can begin to connect sounds to letters and to engage in a variety of activities in which sounds and letters are substituted to make new words. Students begin to understand that if a sound changes, a letter must change, and a new word is created. As students move into phonics, research suggests that connecting sounds to spellings actually heightens their awareness of language. Phonological and phonemic awareness is both a prerequisite for and a consequence of learning to read.

Research suggests that the majority of instructional time should be focused on two critical phonemic awareness formats: phoneme or oral blending and phoneme

segmentation. These are supported by discrimination and elision activities (deleting and substituting sounds) and general wordplay. Oral blending encourages students to combine sounds to make words and lays the foundation for decoding and reading. Segmentation, conversely, requires students to break words into discrete sounds and lays the foundation for spelling. Other activities support discrimination, or recognition, of particular sounds. Sometimes simple songs, rhymes, or games engage students in wordplay. In these, students manipulate words in a variety of ways. From these playful activities, students develop serious knowledge about their language.

Oral Blending
Purpose

In oral blending, students are led through a progression of activities designed to help them hear how sounds are put together to make words.

Until students develop an awareness of the component parts of words, they have no tools with which to decode words or to put letters together to form words. Oral blending helps students understand these component parts of words, from syllables down to single sounds, or phonemes. Oral blending is not to be confused with the formal blending of specific sounds whose spellings students will be taught through phonics instruction. Oral blending does not depend on the recognition of written words; it focuses instead on hearing the sounds.

Oral blending focuses on hearing sounds through a sequence that introduces the most easily distinguished word parts and then systematically moves to oral blending of individual sounds that contains all the challenges of phonic decoding (except letter recognition). This sequence provides support for the least-prepared student—one who comes to school with no concept of words or sounds within words. At the same time, the lively pace and playful nature of oral blending activities hold the interest of students who already have some familiarity with words and letters.

Oral blending prepares students for phonics instruction by developing an awareness of the separate sounds that make up speech. Oral blending activities then continue in concert with phonics instruction to reinforce and extend new learning. And because these activities involve simply listening to and reproducing sounds, oral blending need not be restricted to the sounds students have been or will be taught in phonics.

The tone of the activities should be playful and informal and should move quickly. Although these activities will provide information about student progress, they are not diagnostic tools. Do not expect mastery. Those students who have not caught on will be helped more by varied experiences than by more drilling on the same activity.

Procedure

The following is a description of the progression of oral blending activities.

Word-Part Blending

Syllables are easier to distinguish than individual sounds (phonemes), so students can quickly experience success in forming meaningful words. Tell students that you are going to say some words in two parts. Tell them to listen carefully so they can discover what the words are. Read each word, pronouncing each part distinctly with a definite pause between syllables. The lists of words that follow are arranged in sequence from easy to harder. They cover different types of cues. Whenever they fit into the sequence, include multisyllabic names of students in the class.

Model

Teacher: dino . . . saur. What's the word?
Students: dinosaur

Example Words

✦ First part of the word cues the whole word:
vita . . . min
vaca . . . tion
hippopot . . . amus
ambu . . . lance

✦ Two distinct words easily combined:
butter. . . fly
straw. . . berry
surf . . . board
basket . . . ball

✦ Two distinct words, but first word could cue the wrong ending:
tooth . . . ache
tooth . . . paste
water . . . fall
water . . . melon

✦ First part, consonant + vowel, not enough to guess whole word:
re . . . member
re . . . frigerator
bi . . . cycle
bi . . . ology

✦ Identifying cues in second part:
light . . . ning
sub . . . ject
in . . . sect

✦ Last part, consonant + vowel sound, carries essential information:
yester . . . day
rain . . . bow
noi . . . sy
pota . . . to

✦ Changing the final part changes the word:
start . . . ing
start . . . er
start. . . ed

Initial Consonant Sounds

Initial consonant blending prepares students for consonant replacement activities that will come later. Tell students that you will ask them to put some sounds together to make words. Pronounce each word part distinctly, and make a definite pause at the breaks indicated. When a letter is surrounded by slash marks, pronounce the letter's sound, not its name. When you see /s/, for example, you will say "ssss," not "ess." The words that follow are arranged from easy to harder. Whenever they fit into the sequence, include names of students in the class.

Model

Teacher: /t/ . . . iger. What's the word?
Students: tiger

Example Words

✦ Separated consonant blend, with rest of word giving strong cue to word identity:
/b/ . . . roccoli   */k/ . . . racker*
/f/ . . . lashlight   */k/ . . . reature*

✦ Held consonant that is easy for students to hear, with rest of word giving strong cue:
/s/ . . . innamon   */l/ . . . adybug*
/s/ . . . eventeen   */n/ . . . ewspaper*

✦ Stop consonant that is harder for students to hear preceding vowel, with rest of word giving strong cue:
/t/ . . . adpole   */p/ . . . iggybank*
/d/ . . . ragonfly   */b/ . . . arbecue*

✦ Single-syllable words and words in which the second part gives a weaker cue:
/s/ . . . ing   */l/ . . . augh*   */v/ . . . ase*

Final Consonant Sounds

In this phase of oral blending, the last sound in the word is separated.

Model

Teacher: cabba . . . /j/. What's the word?
Students: cabbage

Example Words

✦ Words that are easily recognized even before the final consonant is pronounced:
bubblegu . . . /m/   *Columbu . . . /s/*
crocodi . . . /l/   *submari . . . /n/*

✦ Multisyllabic words that need the final consonant for recognition:
colle . . . /j/ (college)   *come . . . /t/ (comet)*

✦ Single-syllable words:
sa . . . /d/   *gra . . . /s/ (grass)*   *snai . . . /l/*

Initial Consonant Sound Replacement

This level of oral blending further develops awareness of initial consonant sounds. The activity begins with a common word then quickly changes its initial consonant sound. Most of the words produced are nonsense words, which helps keep the focus on the sounds in the word. Note that the words are written on the board, but students are not expected to read them. The writing is to help students see that when the sounds change, the letters change, and vice versa.

Model

Teacher: [Writes word on board.] This word is *magazine*. What is it?
Students: magazine
Teacher: Now I'm going to change it. [Erases initial consonant.] Now it doesn't start with /m/; it's going to start with /b/. What's the new word?
Students: bagazine
Teacher: That's right . . . [Writes *b* where *m* had been.] It's *bagazine*. Now I'm going to change it again. . . .

Repeat with different consonant sounds. Then do the same with other words such as *remember, Saturday, tomorrow, lotion,* and *million*. Continue with single-syllable words such as *take, big, boot, cot, seat, look, tap, ride,* and *late*. There are two stages in using written letters:

✦ The replacement letter is not written until **after** the new "word" has been identified.

✦ Later, the replacement letter is written at *the same time* the change in the initial phoneme is announced. For example, erase *d* and write *m* while you say, "Now it doesn't start with /d/; it starts with /m/."

When the consonants used have already been introduced in phonics, you may wish to alter the procedure by writing the replacement letter and having students sound out the new word. Feel free to switch between the two procedures within a single exercise. If students are not responding orally to written spellings that have been introduced in phonics, do not force it. Proceed by saying the word before writing the letter, and wait until another time to move on to writing before pronouncing.

One-Syllable Words

Students now begin blending individual phonemes to form words. This important step can be continued well into the year. Continued repetitions of this activity will help students realize how they can use the sound/spellings they are learning to read and write real words.

At first, the blended words are presented in a story context that helps students identify the words. They soon recognize that they are actually decoding meaningful words. However, the context must not be so strong that students can guess the word without listening to the phonemic cues. Any vowel sounds and irregularly spelled words may be used because there is no writing involved.

Model

Teacher: When I looked out the window, I saw a /l/ /ī/ /t/. What did I see?
Students: A light.
Teacher: Yes, I saw a light. At first I thought it was the /m/ /o͞o/ /n/. What did I think it was?
Students: The moon.
Teacher: But it didn't really look like the moon. Suddenly I thought, maybe it's a space /sh/ /i/ /p/. What did I think it might be?
Students: A spaceship!

When students are familiar with this phase of oral blending, they can move to blending one-syllable words without the story context.

Example Words

✦ CVC (consonant/vowel/consonant) words beginning with easily blended consonant sounds (/sh/, /h/, /r/, /v/, /s/,

/n/, /z/, /f/, /l/, /m/):
nip   nap
✦ CVC words beginning with any consonant:
ten   bug   lip
✦ Add CCVC words:
flap   step
✦ Add CVCC words:
most   band   went
✦ Add CCVCC words:
stamp   grand   scuffs

Final Consonant Sound Replacement

Final consonant sounds are typically more difficult for students to use than initial consonants.

✦ Begin with multisyllabic words, and move to one-syllable words.
✦ As with initial consonants, first write the changed consonant after students have pronounced the new word.
✦ Then write the consonant as they pronounce it.
✦ For sound/spellings introduced in phonics instruction, write the new consonant spelling, and have students identify and pronounce it.

Model

Teacher: [Writes word on board.] This word is *teapot*. What is it?
Students: teapot
Teacher: Now I'm going to change it. [Erases final consonant.] Now it doesn't end with /t/; it ends with /p/. What's the word now?
Students: teapop
Teacher: That's right . . . [Writes *p* where *t* had been.] It's *teapop*. Now I'm going to change it again. . . .

Example Words

✦ Words that are easily recognized even before the final consonant is pronounced:
picnic   picnit   picnis   picnil   picnid
airplane   airplate   airplabe   airplafe
✦ Multisyllabic words that need the final consonant for recognition:
muffin   muffil   muffim   muffip   muffit
amaze   amate   amake   amale   amade
✦ Single-syllable words:
neat   nean   neap   neam   neaj   nead   neaf
broom   broot   brood   broof   broop   broon

Initial Vowel Replacement

Up to now, oral blending has concentrated on consonant sounds because they are easier to hear than vowels. As you move to vowel play, remember that the focus is still on the sounds, not the spellings. Use any vowel sounds.

Model

Teacher: [Writes word on board.] This word is *elephant*. What is it?
Students: elephant
Teacher: Now I'm going to change it. [Erases initial vowel.] Now it doesn't start with /e/; it starts with /a/. What's the word now?
Students: alephant
Teacher: That's right . . . [Writes *a* where *e* had been.] It's *alephant*. Now I'm going to change it again. . . .

Example Words

✦ Multisyllabic words:
angry   ingry   oongry   ungry   engry
ivy   avy   oovy   evy   ovy   oivy
✦ One-syllable words:
ink   ank   oonk   unk   onk   oink
add   odd   idd   oudd   edd   udd

Segmentation

Purpose

Segmentation and oral blending complement each other: Oral blending puts sounds together to make words, while segmentation separates words into sounds. Oral blending will provide valuable support for decoding when students begin reading independently.

Procedure

Syllables

The earliest segmentation activities focus on syllables, which are easier to distinguish than individual sounds, or phonemes. Start with students' names, and then use other words. As with the oral blending activities, remember to move quickly through these activities. Do not hold the class back waiting for all students to catch on. Individual progress will vary, but drilling on one activity is less helpful than going on to others. Return to the same activity often. Frequent repetition is very beneficial and allows students additional opportunities to catch on.

- Say, for example, "Let's clap out Amanda's name. A-man-da."
- Have students clap and say the syllables along with you. Count the claps.
- Tell students that these word parts are called syllables. Don't try to explain; the idea will develop with practice. After you have provided the term, simply say, "How many syllables?" after students clap and count.
- Mix one-syllable and multisyllabic words: *fantastic   tambourine   good   imaginary   stand   afraid*

> *Oral blending will provide valuable support for decoding when students begin reading independently.*

Comparative Lengths of Words

Unlike most phonemic awareness activities, this one involves writing on the board or on an overhead transparency. Remember, though, that students are not expected to read what is written. They are merely noticing that words that take longer to say generally look longer when written.

- Start with students' names. Choose two names, one short and one long, with the same first letter (for example, *Joe* and *Jonathan*).
- Write the two names on the board, one above the other, so that the difference is obvious.
- Tell students that one name is *Jonathan* and that one is *Joe*. Have them pronounce and clap each name. Then have them tell which written word they think says *Joe*.
- Move your finger under each name as students clap and say it syllable by syllable.
- Repeat with other pairs of names and words such as *tea/telephone, cat/caterpillar, and butterfly/bug*. Be sure not to give false clues. For example, sometimes write the longer word on top, sometimes the shorter one; sometimes ask for the shorter word, sometimes the

longer; sometimes ask for the top word, sometimes the bottom; and sometimes point to a word and ask students to name it, and sometimes name the word and ask students to point to it.

Listen for Individual Sounds

Activities using a puppet help students listen for individual sounds in words. Use any puppet you have on hand. When you introduce the puppet, tell students that it likes to play word games. Each new activity begins with the teacher speaking to and for the puppet until students determine the pattern. Next, students either speak for the puppet or correct the puppet. To make sure all students are participating, alternate randomly between having the whole group or individuals respond. The activities focus on particular parts of words, according to the following sequence:

1. Repeating last part of word. Use words beginning with easy-to-hear consonants such as *f, l, m, n, r, s,* and *z*. The puppet repeats only the rime, the part of the syllable after the initial consonant.

Model

Teacher: farm
Puppet: arm
After the pattern is established, students respond for the puppet.
Teacher: rope
Students: ope

Example Words
Use words such as the following:
mine . . . ine   soup . . . oup   feet . . . eet

2. Restoring initial phonemes. Now students correct the puppet. Be sure to acknowledge the correction.

Model

Teacher: lake
Puppet: ake
Teacher: No, lllake. You forgot the /l/.
Teacher: real
Puppet: eal
Teacher: What did the puppet leave off?
Students: /r/. It's supposed to be *real*.
Teacher: That's right. The word is *real*.

Example Words
Use words such as the following:
*look . . . ook   mouse . . . ouse
sand . . . and*

3. Segmenting initial consonants. The puppet pronounces only the initial consonant.

Model

Teacher: pay
Puppet: /p/

Example Words
Use words such as the following:
moon . . . /m/   nose . . . /n/   bell . . . /b/

4. Restoring final consonants. Students correct the puppet. Prompt if necessary: "What's the word? What did the puppet leave off?"

Model

Teacher: run
Puppet: ru
Students: It's run! You left off the /n/.
Teacher: That's right. The word is *run*.

Example Words
Use words such as the following:
meet . . . mee   cool . . . coo   boot . . . boo

5. Isolating final consonants. The puppet pronounces only the final consonant.

Model

Teacher: green
Puppet: /n/

Example Words
Use words such as the following:
glass . . . /s/   boom . . . /m/   mice . . . /s/

6. Segmenting initial consonant blends. The sounds in blends are emphasized.

Model

Teacher: clap
Puppet: lap
Next have students correct the puppet.
Teacher: stain
Puppet: tain
Students: It's stain! You left off the /s/.
Teacher: That's right. The word is *stain*.

Example Words
Use words such as the following:
*blaze . . . laze   draw . . . raw
proud . . . roud*

Discrimination

Purpose

Discrimination activities help students focus on particular sounds in words.

Listening for long-vowel sounds is the earliest discrimination activity. Vowel sounds are necessary for decoding, but young students do not hear them easily. This is evident in students' invented spellings, where vowels are often omitted. Early in the year, students listen for long-vowel sounds, which are more easily distinguished than short-vowel sounds:

✦ Explain to students that vowels are special because sometimes they say their names in words.

✦ Tell students which vowel sound to listen for.

✦ Have them repeat the sound when they hear it in a word. For example, if the target-vowel sound is long *e*, students will say long *e* when you say *leaf*, but they should not respond when you say *loaf*.

✦ Initially students should listen for one long vowel sound at a time. Later they can listen for two vowel sounds. All Example Words, however, should contain one of the target vowels.

Procedure

Listening for short-vowel sounds

These discrimination activities should be done after the short vowels /a/ and /i/ have been introduced. Short vowels are very useful in reading. They are generally more regular in spelling than long vowels, and they appear in many short, simple words. However, their sounds are less easily distinguished than those of long vowels. Thus, the activities focus only on /a/ and /i/. All the words provided have one or the other of these sounds. Either have students repeat the sound of a specified vowel, or vary the activity as follows: Write an *a* on one side of the board and an *i* on the other. Ask students to point to the *a* when they hear a word with the /a/ sound and to point to the *i* when they hear a word with the /i/ sound. Use words such as the following:

> bat mat sat sit spit
> pit pat pan pin spin

Consonant sounds in multisyllabic words

Discriminating these sounds helps students attend to consonant sounds in the middle of words.

✦ Say the word *rib,* and have students repeat it. Ask where they hear the /b/ in *rib*.

✦ Then say *ribbon,* and ask students where they hear the /b/ in *ribbon*.

✦ Tell students that you will say some words and that they will repeat each word.

✦ After they repeat each word, ask what consonant sound they hear in the middle of that word. Use words such as the following:
> famous message picky
> jogger flavor zipper

Phonemic Play

Purpose

Wordplay activities help students focus on and manipulate sounds, thus supporting the idea that words are made of specific sounds that can be taken apart, put together, or changed to make new words. Through wordplay, students gain important knowledge about language.

Procedure

Producing rhymes

Many phonemic play activities focus on producing rhymes. A familiar or easily learned rhyme or song is introduced, and students are encouraged to substitute words or sounds. An example is "Willaby Wallaby Woo," in which students change the rhyming words in the couplet "Willaby Wallaby Woo/ An elephant sat on you" so that the second line ends with a student's name and that the first line ends with a rhyme beginning with *W;* for example, "Willaby Wallaby Wissy/An elephant sat on Missy."

Generate alliterative words

Students can also say as many words as they can think of that begin with a given consonant sound. This is a valuable complement to discrimination activities in which the teacher produces the words and students identify them.

The Alphabetic Principle: How the Alphabet Works

The Alphabetic Principle

Purpose

A major emphasis in the kindergarten program is on letter recognition and attending to sounds. Students need to learn the alphabetic principle: that letters work together in a systematic way to connect spoken language to written words. This understanding is the foundation for reading. Students are not expected to master letter/sound correspondence at the beginning of kindergarten, nor are they expected to blend sounds into words themselves. They are expected to become an "expert" only on their Special Letters as they learn how the alphabet works. Through this introduction to the alphabetic principle, students will have the basic understanding required to work through the alphabet letter by letter, attaching sounds to each.

Key concepts of the alphabetic principle include the following:

✦ A limited number of letters combine in different ways to make many different words.

✦ Words are composed of sounds, and letters represent those sounds.

✦ Anything that can be pronounced can be spelled.

✦ Letters and sounds can be used to identify words.

✦ Meaning can be obtained by using letters and sounds to determine words.

Procedures for Kindergarten

The following steps can be used for introducing letters and sounds in kindergarten. These steps may be adapted for students at other grades if they do not understand the alphabetic principle. The tone of these activities should be informal, fun, and fast-paced. The purpose of these activities is to familiarize students with how the alphabet works by having them participate in group play with letters and sounds.

I Can Spell Anything

✦ Reinforce the idea that anything that can be pronounced can be spelled with the letters of the alphabet.

✦ Tell students that you can spell any word. Have them give you words to spell.

✦ Write the words on the board, naming each letter as you write it. This shows students that the words contain the letters displayed on the **Alphabet Sound Wall Cards.**

✦ Have students help you spell the words again by pointing to letters as you say them.

✦ Encourage students to spell each word letter by letter.

> The alphabetic principle is the understanding that speech sounds can be mapped onto print.

Letter Expert Groups

✦ Have **Alphabet Letter Cards** (Levels K and 1) available for the following set of letters: b, d, f, h, l, m, n, p, s, t. You will need two or three cards for each letter. (You will not need the **Alphabet Sound Cards** until later.)

✦ You will be the letter expert for the vowels.

✦ Organize the class into groups of two or three, and assign each group a letter. Give each student the appropriate **Alphabet Letter Card.**

✦ Tell students that they are now in their Letter Expert groups and that they are going to become experts on their Special Letter's name, shape, and sound.

Making Words

✦ Begin each lesson with a rehearsal of each group's letter name.

✦ Demonstrate how letters work by writing a word in large letters on the board.

✦ Tell students the experts for each letter in the word should hold up their **Alphabet Letter Cards** and name the letter. One member of the group should stand in front of their letter on the board.

✦ Continue until all letters in the word are accounted for. Remember that you are responsible for the vowels.

✦ Demonstrate that you can make different words by changing a letter or by changing the letter order.

Identifying Sounds in Words

✦ Use the **Alphabet Sound Cards** to demonstrate that every letter has at least one sound.

✦ Give each student the **Alphabet Sound Card** for his or her Special Letter.

✦ Point out the pictures on the cards. Explain that each card has a picture of something that makes the letter's sound. The picture will help them remember the sound.

✦ Tell each group the sound for its letter. (Remember, you are the expert for the vowels.)

✦ Quickly have each group rehearse its letter's name and sound.

✦ Write a word on the board in large letters. First say the word sound by sound, and then blend the word.

✦ For each letter/sound in the word, have one student from each Letter Expert group come forward, stand in front of the appropriate letter, and hold his or her card. Although only one member of the group may come forward with the **Alphabet Letter Card** or **Alphabet Sound Card,** all students in a Special Letter group should say the name or sound of their letter when it occurs in words.

✦ Say the word again, pointing to the **Alphabet Sound Cards.**

✦ Ask students who are not already standing to help you hold the vowel cards.

✦ Vary the activity by changing one letter sound and having an expert for that letter come forward.

✦ End the activity for each word by saying the sounds in the words one by one and then saying the entire word. Encourage students to participate.

Tips

✦ Remind students to use the picture on the **Alphabet Sound Card** for their Special Letter to help them remember the letter's sound. Students are expected to "master" only their own Special Letter and to share the information with their classmates. At this point in the year, they are not expected to blend and read the words by themselves. These are group activities in which you work with students to help them gain insight into the alphabet.

✦ Be sure to connect what students learn about the letters and words to the words they work with in **Big Book** selections.

✦ Occasionally, have students find their special letters in a **Big Book** selection. Play some of the letter replacement and rearrangement games with words encountered in the **Big Books.**

Developing the Alphabetic Principle

Purpose

The alphabetic principle is the understanding that speech sounds can be mapped onto print. It is the association of sounds with letters and the understanding that speech can be turned into print and that print can be turned into speech sounds. Activities associated with the alphabetic principle help kindergarten students develop a more thorough understanding of how sounds "work" in words. In this group of activities, students are introduced to specific letter/sound correspondences, consonants, and short vowels. While students have previously been introduced to vowels and their special characteristics, students' understanding is extended by introducing students to the convention that a vowel has a short sound in addition to its long sound. With this information and a carefully structured set of activities, students can begin to explore and understand the alphabetic principle in a straightforward and thorough manner. Students not only listen for sounds in specified positions in words, they also link sounds to their corresponding letters. The

activities in this group of lessons lay the groundwork for students to work their way through the entire alphabet as they learn letter-sound associations and to understand the purpose and the value of this learning.

Move students quickly through these activities. Do not wait for all students to master each letter/sound correspondence before going on. They will have more opportunities to achieve mastery. The goal of these activities is for students to obtain a basic understanding of the alphabetic principle.

> *Students need to learn the alphabetic principle: that letters work together in a systematic way to connect spoken language to written words. This understanding is the foundation for reading.*

Procedures

Introducing Consonant Letters and Sounds

✦ Point to the **Alphabet Sound Wall Card** and ask students what they know about the card (the letter name, the capital and lowercase letter, and so on).

✦ Turn the card, and point to the picture. Name the picture, and point to and name the letter. Tell students the sound of the letter and how the picture helps them remember the sound. Repeat the sound several times.

✦ Tell students you will read them the short story or an alliterative sentence to help them remember the sound of the letter. Read the story several times, emphasizing the words with the target sound. Have students join in and say the sound.

✦ After introducing and reviewing a letter/sound correspondence, summarize the information on the **Alphabet Sound Wall Card:** the name of the card, the sound, and the letter.

Generating Words with the Target Sound

Brainstorm to create a list of words that begin with the target sound. Write the words on the board or on a chart. Include any of the students' names that begin with the target sound.

Listening for Initial Sounds

✦ Give each student an **Alphabet Letter Card** for the target sound.

✦ Point to the picture on the **Alphabet Sound Wall Card,** and have students give the sound.

✦ Tell students to listen for the first sound in each word you say. If it is the target sound, they should hold up their cards. Establish a signal so that students know when to respond.

✦ Read the list of words, some beginning with the target sound and some beginning with other sounds.

Listening for Final Sounds

The procedure for listening for the final sound of a word is the same as that for listening for the initial sound. Students may need to be reminded throughout the activity to pay attention to the final sound.

Read a list of words, some ending with the target sound and some ending with other sounds. Avoid words that begin with the target sound.

Linking the Sound to the Letter

✦ **Word Pairs (initial sounds).** Write pairs of words on the board. One of each pair should begin with the target sound. Say the word beginning with the target sound, and ask students to identify it. Remind them to listen for the target sound at the beginning of the word, to think about which letter makes that sound, and to find the word that begins with that letter. For example,
Target sound: /s/
Word pair: *fit sit*
Which word is *sit*?

✦ **Word Pairs (final sounds).** Follow the same procedure used for initial sounds, and direct students to think about the sound that they hear at the end of the word. Because it is often more difficult for students to attend to the ending sound, you may need to lead them through several pairs of words. Remind students to listen for the target sound and to think about which letter makes that sound.

✦ **Writing Letters.** Using either of the handwriting systems outlined in this Program Appendix or the system in use at your school, have students practice writing uppercase and lowercase letters. Remind students about the letter sound, and have them repeat it.

Other activities that support the development of the alphabetic principle include the following:

Comparing Initial Consonant Sounds

This activity is exactly like Listening for Initial Sounds except that students must discriminate between two sounds. They are given **Alphabet Letter Cards** for both sounds and must hold up the appropriate card when they hear the sound.

Comparing Final Consonant Sounds

This activity is exactly like Listening for Final Sounds except that students must discriminate between two sounds. They are given **Alphabet Letter Cards** for both sounds and must hold up the appropriate card when they hear the sound.

Linking the Consonant Sound to the Letter

In these activities students will link beginning and ending sounds and letters.

✦ **I'm Thinking of Something That Starts (Ends) with ___ Game.** Begin with the target sound, and add clues until students guess the word. If students give a word that does not begin with the target sound, emphasize the beginning sound, and ask if the word begins with the target sound.

✦ **Silly Sentences.** Make silly sentences with students that include many words with the target sound. Encourage students to participate by extending the sentences: Mary mopes. Mary mopes on Monday. Mary and Michael mope on Monday in Miami. For older students, have them make silly sentences using the sound at the beginning of their first

name. Have them use the dictionary to find more words beginning or ending with the target sound.

Introducing Short-Vowel Sounds

✦ Tell students that the vowels are printed in red to remind them that they are special letters. (They are not special because they are printed in red.) They are special because they have more than one sound, and every word in English must have a vowel sound.

✦ Point to the long *Aa* **Alphabet Sound Wall Card,** and remind students that this letter is called a vowel. Tell them vowels sometimes say their names in words (for example, *say, day, tray*). When the vowel says its name, the sound is long. Tell them this vowel sound is called long *a*.

✦ Have students repeat the sound.

✦ Tell students sometimes vowels say different sounds. Point to the picture of the lamb on the short *Aa* card, and tell students that *a* also makes the sound heard in the middle of *lamb*. This is the short *a*. Read the short vowel story to help students remember the short *a*.

✦ Have all students join in saying /a/ /a/ /a/.

Listening for Short-Vowel Sounds Versus Long-Vowel Sounds

✦ Tell students that you will read words with long *a* and short *a*. Review the two sounds.

✦ Give students a signal to indicate when they hear the vowel sound. You may want one signal for short *a,* such as scrunching down, and another for long *a,* such as stretching up tall.

✦ Continue with lists of words such as *add, back, aid, tan, bake,* and *tame.*

Linking the Vowel Sound to the Letter

✦ **Writing Letters.** Have students practice writing the letter and review the sound of the letter.

✦ In this activity to help students link sounds and letters, students will make words either by adding initial consonants to selected word parts or by adding a different final consonant to a consonant-vowel-consonant

combination. Change the beginning of the word or the word ending, but retain the vowel sound to make new words:

at	hat	mat	pat
ap	map	tap	sap
am	Sam	Pam	ham

Comparing Short-Vowel Sounds

This activity requires students to discriminate between short-vowel sounds in the middle of words. Review the short-vowel sounds.

✦ Say a word, and have students repeat it. Establish a signal to indicate whether they hear short *a* or short *o* in the middle of the word. For example, they can hold up the appropriate **Alphabet Letter Card** when they hear a sound. Sample words: *cap, cot, rat, rot, rack,* and *rock.*

Linking the Sound to the Letter

✦ In this activity, write a word on the board, and help students say it.

✦ Change the word by changing the vowel. Help students say the new word, for example, *map, mop; hot, hat; pot, pat.*

✦ For a variation of this activity, write the pairs of words, and simply have students say which word is the target word. For example, students see *tap* and *top.* Ask which word *top* is, directing students' attention to the vowel.

Introducing Long-Vowel Sounds

The introduction of short vowels and consonants helps students internalize the alphabetic principle—a sound can be mapped onto a letter. In English, however, some sounds are represented by more than one letter, for example, the /ē/ can be represented by the letter *e* as in *me* but also represented by e_e as in *Pete.* Toward the end of kindergarten, students will be introduced to long vowels and two common representations of those sounds. These include the single vowel such as *a* or *e* and the vowel consonant silent *e* (VCe). The introduction of the VCe pattern or unit gives students a wide range of common words to read by the end of kindergarten and sets a solid foundation for first grade.

✦ If necessary, remind students that vowels are written in red. Point to the long *Aa* card, and tell students that the sound of long *a* is /ā/.

- ✦ Have students say the sound with you.
- ✦ Tell students that long *a* can be written in more than one way; it can be written as *a* just like short *a* but it can also be written as *a_e*. When we see the blank, it is a clue that another sound and letter needs to be put on the blank or line to make a word.
- ✦ Write *a_e*, and have students give the sound: /ā/. Then write a *t* on the blank, say the sound, and blend the word: *ate*.
- ✦ The goal is to have students see the *a_e* or any of the other VCe patterns as a unit.
- ✦ While students have been blending and reading short-vowel words, long vowels create a shift in thinking: Combinations of letters can be used to represent a sound. Here are some easy tips when you are first working with the VCe patterns:
  - The VCe patterns are not written on the **Alphabet Sound Cards.** You may want to write the *a_e, e_e, i_e, o_e,* and *u_e* units on the respective long-vowel cards as a reminder for students. Do this as you introduce

each long vowel unit. Use an erasable marker so you can reintroduce these special patterns each year.

- Provide maximum support when first using the long-vowel units in blending.
- Write the letter for the first sound, for example, /m/, and have students give the sound.
- Write the unit for /ā/: *a_e*. Tell students this says /ā/. Be sure to write the whole unit.
- Write the final letter ON the blank, for example, *k*. Give the sound for the *k*, and then blend the word.
- Let students hear your voice during the blending, but gradually reduce it so they are doing more of the thinking.
- Help students blend long vowel words as they are reading their **Decodables.**

Tips

- ✦ Model and support the activities as necessary until students begin to catch on and can participate with confidence.
- ✦ To keep students focused on the various activities, have them tell you the task for each activity. For example, after telling students to listen for final sounds, ask students what they will be listening for.
- ✦ Actively involve students by giving them opportunities to tell what they know rather than supplying the information for them. *What is the letter name? What is the sound? What words begin with the sound?*
- ✦ Keeping students focused on the idea that they are learning about sounds and letters so they can read books themselves makes the lessons more relevant for students.

Introducing Sounds and Letters

Purpose

In **SRA Imagine It!** students learn to relate sounds to letters in kindergarten through the use of thirty-one **Alphabet Sound Wall Cards.** In the upper grade levels, **Sound/ Spelling Wall Cards** (Levels 1–3) are used to relate sounds and spellings. The purpose of the **Alphabet Sound Wall Cards** is to remind students of the sounds of the English language and their letter correspondences. These cards are a resource for students to use to remember sound-letter associations for both reading and writing.

Each card contains the capital and small letter and a picture that shows the sound being produced. For instance, the Sausage card introduces the /s/ sound and shows sausages sizzling in a pan. The sound the sausages make sizzling in the pan is /s/ /s/ /s/. The name of the picture on each card contains the target sound at the beginning of the word for the consonants and in the middle for the vowels. Vowel letters are printed in red, and consonants are printed in black. In addition, the picture associates a sound with an action. This action-sound association is introduced through a short, interactive story found in the **Teacher's Edition,** in which the pictured object or character "makes" the sound of the letter. Long vowels are represented by a tall—or "long"—picture of the letters themselves rather than by a picture for action-sound association. Short vowels have a green background, and long vowels have a yellow background.

Procedures

✦ Display Cards 1–26 with the picture sides to the wall. Initially post the first twenty-six cards in alphabetical order so that only the alphabet letters on the back show. The short-vowel cards may be posted as they are introduced later. As you introduce the sound of each letter, you will turn the card to show the picture and the letter on the other side. Because students will be referring to these cards for reading and writing, post them where all students can easily see them.

✦ Before turning a card, point to the letter. Ask students to tell what they know about the letter. For example, they are likely to know its name if the letter is one with which they have already worked. They might also note that there is an upper- and lowercase for the letter or that the letter is a consonant or a vowel.

✦ Turn the card, and point to the picture. Tell students the name of the picture (card), and explain that it will help them remember the sound the letter makes.

✦ Tell students the name and the sound of the letter.

✦ Read the story that goes with the card. Read it expressively, emphasizing the words with the target sound and the isolated sound when it occurs. Have students join in to produce the sound.

*The purpose of the **Alphabet Sound Wall Cards** is to remind students of the sounds of the English language and their letter correspondences.*

✦ Repeat the story a few times, encouraging all students to say the sound along with you.

✦ Repeat the name of the letter and the sound.

✦ Follow the story with the cards for the target sound. (These are listed within the lessons.)

✦ Name each picture, and have students listen for the target sound at the beginning of the word. Ask students to repeat the words and the sound.

✦ Listening for the sound in different positions in words provides additional work with phonemic awareness. Give each student the letter card for the introduced sound and letter. Read the words from Listening for the Sound, and have students raise their letter card if they hear the target sound at the beginning of the word. For many letters, students will also listen for the sound at the end of words as well.

✦ To link the sound and the letter, demonstrate how to form the uppercase and lowercase letters by writing on the board or on an overhead transparency. Have students practice forming the letter and saying the sound as they write.

Alphabet Sound Cards

The pictures and letters on the **Alphabet Sound Wall Cards** also appear on the small sets of individual **Alphabet Sound Cards.** The **Teacher's Edition** specifically suggests that you use the individual **Alphabet Sound Cards** for Workshop and small-group activities for review, reteaching, and practice sessions. Place sets of the cards in the appropriate Workshop area for students to use alone or with partners. Add each small card to the Activity Center after you have taught the lesson in which the corresponding individual **Alphabet Sound Card** is introduced. Here are some suggestions for activities using the individual **Alphabet Sound Cards:**

1. **Saying sounds from pictures.** The leader flashes pictures as the others say the sound each picture represents.

2. **Saying sounds.** The leader flashes the letters on the cards as the others say the sound that the letters represent.

3. **Naming words from pictures.** The leader flashes pictures. The others say the sound and then say a word beginning with that sound.

4. **Writing letters from the pictures.** Working alone, a student looks at a picture and then writes the letter for the sound that picture represents.

5. **Making words using the pictures.** A student uses the pictures (Sausages, Pig, Timer for *sit*) or the letters to make words.

Tips

✦ Throughout the beginning lessons, help students remember that vowels are special by reminding them that vowels sometimes say their names in words. For example, tell them the picture of the *a* on the long *a* ***Alphabet Sound Wall Card*** is long because the long *a* says its name. The short *a* ***Alphabet Sound Wall Card*** pictures the lamb because the lamb makes the short *a* sound, and you can hear the sound in the word *lamb*.

✦ From the very beginning, encourage students to use the ***Alphabet Sound Wall Cards*** as a resource to help them with their work.

✦ Mastery of letter recognition is the goal students should reach so that they will be prepared to link each letter with its associated sound. If students have not yet mastered the names of the letters, it is important to work with them individually in Workshop, or at other times during the day.

✦ Both the *Cc* and the *Kk* cards have the same picture—a camera. A camera makes the /k/ sound when it clicks, and the word *camera* begins with the /k/ sound. However, the word *camera* is not spelled with a *k*. Remember, the first sound of the word helps students remember the sound of the letter.

✦ The picture on the *Qq* card depicts quacking ducks. Make sure that students consistently call them quacking ducks, not ducks, and that they focus on the /kw/ sound.

Explicit, Systematic Phonics

The purpose of phonics instruction is to teach students the association between the sounds of the language and the written symbols—spellings—that have been chosen to represent those sounds.

As with all alphabetic languages, English has a limited number of symbols—twenty-six—that are combined and recombined to make the written language. These written symbols are a visual representation of the speech sounds we use to communicate. This is simply a code. The faster students learn the code and how it works, the faster the whole world of reading opens up to them.

Beginning at the kindergarten level, students are introduced to sounds and letters. Students learn that sounds can be mapped onto letters and that those sounds and letters can be blended to read words.

In Grade 1, students make the shift from mapping sounds onto letters to mapping sounds onto spellings. The introduction of both sounds and letters in kindergarten and the sounds and spellings in Grade 1 is done in a very systematic, sequential manner. This allows students to continually build on what they learned the day before. As each sound/symbol relationship is introduced, students learn about and practice with words containing the target sound and letter in kindergarten and sound/spelling in Grade1. This new knowledge is then reinforced through the use of engaging text specifically written for this purpose.

It can be very difficult for students to hear the individual sounds, or phonemes, that make up words. When phonics instruction is explicit—students are told the sounds associated with the different written symbols—there is no guesswork involved. They know that the sound /b/ is spelled b. Therefore, students in an **SRA Imagine It!** classroom spend time learning to discriminate individual speech sounds, and then they learn the spellings of those sounds. This systematic, explicit approach affords students the very best chance for early and continuing success.

Sound/Spelling Wall Cards

(Grade 1 on) See The Alphabetic Principle for information on the introduction of sounds and letters in pre-kindergarten and kindergarten.

Purpose

The purpose of the **Sound/Spelling Wall Cards** (Levels 1–3) is to remind students of the sounds in English and their spellings. The name of the picture on each card contains the target sound at the beginning of the name for consonants and in the middle for the short vowels. Long vowels are represented by elongated pictures of the vowel. The variant vowels such as /aw/ and /oi/ contain the vowel sound in the name as well. In addition, the picture associates a sound with an action. This association is introduced through an interactive story in which the pictured object or character "makes" the sound. This "action" cue is particularly helpful for students whose primary language is not English. In some cases, the name of the card and the initial sound may be similar to words in other languages. For example, the word for *lion* in Spanish is *león,* which begins with the same sound as the English word. This is not true for other languages. In Russian the word for *lion* is *лев* and in Japanese it is *raion*. The word for *zipper* in Spanish is *cremallera,* in Russian it is *застежка-молния* and in Japanese it is *jippa*. But all students can remember the actions and sounds and use them as a resource for both reading and writing.

> *The faster students learn the code and how it works, the faster the whole world of reading opens up to them.*

Procedure

Posting the Cards

In Grade 1, initially post the first twenty-six cards with the picture to the wall so that only the alphabet letters on the backs show. As you introduce each card, you will turn it to show the picture and the spellings on the front of the card. Some Grade 1 teachers who have students who are familiar with the cards from kindergarten choose to place the first twenty-six cards (the alphabet) with the pictures facing the class. Because students are familiar with the cards and how to use them, this provides support for writing. Even these first-grade teachers, however, cover the spellings not introduced in kindergarten. In second- or third-grade classrooms in which students are reviewing what they learned the year before, place all the cards with the pictures and the spellings facing forward so students can use these as a resource from the beginning of the school year. Make sure that the cards are positioned so that you can touch them with your hand or with a pointer when you refer to them and so that all students can see them easily. The cards should be placed where students can readily see and reference them throughout the day.

Special Devices

✦ Vowel spellings are printed in red to draw attention to them. It is the vowels and their different spellings that challenge us all. Consonants are printed in black. The blank line in a spelling indicates that a letter will take the place of the blank in a word. For example, the replacement of the blank with *t* in the spelling *a_e* makes the word *ate*. The blank lines may also indicate the position of a spelling in a word or a syllable. The blank in *h_,* for example, means that the sound /h/ spelled *h_* occurs at the beginning of a word or a syllable.

✦ The blanks in *_ie_* indicate that the *ie* spelling will not come at the beginning or the end of a word or a syllable as in *babies,* while the blank in *_oy* shows that the *oy* spelling comes at the end of a word or a syllable as in *toy*. Uses of blanks in specific spellings are discussed in the lessons. Please note now, however, that when you write a spelling of a sound on the board or an overhead transparency, you should include the blanks.

✦ The color of the background behind the spellings also has a meaning. Consonants have a white background. The colors behind vowel spellings are pronunciation clues. Short-vowel spellings have a green background, which corresponds to the green box that appears before some consonant spellings. Thus, before *ck, tch,* or *x,* you will see a green box, which indicates that a short vowel always precedes that spelling. Long-vowel spellings have a yellow background; other vowel spellings such as *r*-controlled vowels, diphthongs, and variant vowels have a blue background. The color code reinforces the idea that vowels are special and have different pronunciations.

Introducing the Sound/ Spelling Wall Cards

In first grade, each sound and spelling is introduced by using a see/hear/say/write sequence. In Grades 2 and 3 the same sequence is used in the review of the cards.

1. *See:* Students see the spelling or spellings on the **Sound/Spelling Wall Card** and the board or an overhead transparency.

2. *Hear:* Students hear the sound used in words and in isolation in the story. The sound is, of course, related to the picture (and the action) shown on the **Sound/ Spelling Wall Card.**

3. *Say:* Students say the sound.

4. *Write:* Students write the spelling(s) for the sound.

There are a number of important points to remember about this routine.

✦ Take down the **Sound/Spelling Wall Card,** tell the class the name of the card, the sound, and the spelling.

✦ Read the alliterative story so students hear the sound used in words as well as in isolation, and say the sound.

✦ After you present the sound and spelling, have several students go to the board to write the spelling. Have them say the sound as they write the spelling. After they have written the spelling of the sound, give them an opportunity to proofread their own work. Then give

the other students the opportunity to help with proofreading by noting what is good about the spelling and then suggesting how to make it better.

✦ Difficulty in blending may be the result of not knowing the sounds or not being able to pronounce the sounds. Teach the sounds thoroughly during the introduction of the **Sound/Spelling Wall Card** and during initial sounding and blending. To help ensure success for all students, make certain that every student is able to see the board or screen.

Introducing the Sound /s/ spelled *s*

✦ Point to the back of **Sound/Spelling Wall Card** 19—Sausages, and have students tell you what they know about the card: it is a consonant and there is an upper and lowercase *s* on the card. Turn the card, and tell the class the name of the card: Sausages. Point to the sausages in the picture, and say the word *sausages,* emphasizing the initial consonant sound—*sssssssausages.* Note: teachers usually place a sticky note over the other spellings of /s/—the *ce, ci_,* and *cy*—in order to help students focus on the single spelling being introduced in the lesson.

✦ Point to the spelling *s.* Tell students that /s/ is spelled *s.*

✦ Read the alliterative story. In Grades 2 and 3, the stories for the card are printed in the Level Appendix of the **Teacher's Edition.** If your students in Grades 2 and 3 are familiar with the cards, have them tell you the name of the card, the sound, and the spelling and tell the story.

✦ If students had **SRA Imagine It!** before, you can ask them if they learned an action to help them remember the sound. If your students do not already have an action they associate with the sound, make some up with your students. They will have fun, and it will be another way for them to remember the sound/spelling relationships.

✦ Write *s* on the board or on an overhead transparency, and say the sound. Write the spelling again and ask students to say the sound with you as they write the spelling on slates, on paper, or with their index fingers in the air or in the palm of their hands. Repeat this activity several times.

✦ Have several students come to the board and write the upper- and lowercase spelling while the others continue to write them on slates or with their fingers. Be sure to encourage students to say the sound as they make the spelling. For students writing at the board, take time to have them proofread their work.

✦ Have students listen for words beginning with /s/, indicating by some signal, such as thumbs-up or thumbs-down, whether they hear the /s/ sound and saying /s/ when they hear it in a word. Repeat with the sound in various positions in words. Encourage students to tell you and the class words with /s/ at the beginning, as well as at the ends of words.

✦ Check students' learning by pointing to the card. Have students identify the sound, name the spelling, and discuss how the card can help them remember the sound.

Remember that saying the sound, listening to the alliterative story, and listening for the sound (discriminating it from other sounds) in different positions in words are all phonemic awareness activities that have been integrated into phonics.

Individual Sound/Spelling Cards

Use the individual **Sound/Spelling Cards** for review and for small-group reteaching and practice sessions. Students can use them alone or with partners. Here are some suggestions for activities using the individual **Sound/Spelling Cards:**

1. **Saying sounds from pictures.** The leader flashes pictures as the others say the sound each picture represents.

2. **Saying sounds.** The leader flashes the spellings on the cards as the others say the sound that the spellings represent.

3. **Naming spellings from pictures.** The leader flashes pictures. The others name the card, say the sound, and then name as many spellings as they can.

4. **Writing spellings from the pictures.** Working alone, a student looks at a picture and then writes as many spellings for that **Sound/Spelling Card** as he or she can remember.

5. **Saying words from pictures.** The leader presents a series of individual cards, for example, Sausages, Lamb, Timer. The others tell the word by blending the sounds represented—*sat.*

Blending

Purpose

The purpose of blending is to teach students a strategy for figuring out unfamiliar words. Initially students will be blending sound by sound as they learn how to blend. After they understand the process, they will move to whole-word blending and develop the strategy they will use to read unfamiliar words. Ultimately students will sound and blend only those words that they cannot read. Eventually the blending process will become quick and comfortable for them.

Procedure

Learning the sounds and their spellings is only the first step in learning to read and write. The second step is learning to blend the sounds into words.

Blending Techniques

Blending lines are written on the board or an overhead transparency as students watch and participate. The lines and sentences should not be written out before class begins. It is through the sound-by-sound blending of the words and the sentences that students learn the blending process.

Sound-by-Sound Blending

✦ Write the spelling of the first sound in the word. Point to the spelling, and say the sound. For example, the word students will be blending is *sat*.

✦ Have students say the sound with you as you say the sound again. Write the spelling of the next sound. Point to the spelling, and say the sound. Have students say the sound with you as you say the sound again. After you have written the vowel spelling, blend through the vowel (unless the vowel is the first letter of the word), making the blending motion—a smooth sweeping of the hand beneath the sounds, linking them from left to right, for example, *sa.* As you make the blending motion, make sure that your hand is under the letter that corresponds to the sound you are saying at the moment.

✦ Write the spelling of the next sound—*t.* Point to the spelling, and have students, say the sound with you as you touch the spelling. If this is the last sound and spelling in the word, then have students

blend and read the word—*sat.* If this is not the final sound and spelling, continue pointing to the spelling and asking for the sound. For example, in the word *sand,* you would blend through the vowel then ask for the sounds for the spellings *n* and *d* before blending the word. After pronouncing the final sound in the word, make the blending motion from left to right under the word as you blend the sounds. Then have students blend the word. Let them be the first to pronounce the word normally.

✦ Ask a student to read the word again naturally, as he or she would say or speak it. Then have a student use it in a sentence. Ask another student to extend the sentence, that is, make it more interesting by giving more information. Help the student by asking an appropriate question about the sentence, using, for example, *How? When? Where?* or *Why?* Continue blending the rest of the words in the blending line. At the end of each line, have students reread the words naturally.

> *Blending is the heart of phonics instruction and the key strategy students must learn to open the world of written language.*

Whole-Word Blending

When students are comfortable with sound-by-sound blending, they are ready for whole-word blending.

✦ Write the whole word to be blended on the board or display the overhead transparency.

✦ Ask students to blend the sounds as you point to each spelling.

✦ Then have students say the whole word.

✦ Ask students to use the word in a sentence and then to extend the sentence.

✦ After blending each line, have students read the words naturally, as they would say them.

✦ When all of the words have been blended, point to words randomly, and ask individuals to read them.

Blending Syllables

In reading the **Student Readers,** students will often encounter multisyllabic words. Some students are intimidated by long words, yet many multisyllabic words are easily read by reading and blending the syllables rather than the individual sounds. Beginning in first grade, students will learn about different syllable generalizations, open and closed syllables, consonant -*le*, and the like. Following a set of rules for syllables is difficult because so many of the rules have exceptions. Students need to remember that each syllable in a word contains one vowel sound. Early in the process, you will need to provide support.

✦ Have students identify the vowel sounds and spellings in the word.

✦ Have students blend the first syllable sound by sound if necessary or read the first syllable.

✦ Handle the remaining syllables the same way.

✦ Have students blend the syllables together to read the word.

Blending Sentences

Blending sentences is the logical extension of blending words. Blending sentences helps students develop fluency, which is critical to comprehension. Encourage students to reread sentences with phrasing and natural intonation.

Write the sentence on the board, underlining any high-frequency sight words—words that students cannot decode either because they are irregular or because they contain sounds or spellings that students have not yet learned or reviewed—or display the transparency. High-frequency sight words are taught before blending. Write the word or words on the board or the overhead transparency, and introduce them before writing the sentence. Read the word, and have students repeat the word then spell the word. Use each word in a sentence. Point to the word or words, and have students read them again. These words should not be blended but read as whole words.

Tips

✦ The goal of blending in first grade is not to have students blend words sound by sound for the whole year. Sound-by-sound instruction should begin with maximum instructional support—with teachers and students blending together. As students understand the sound-by-sound blending routine, drop the verbal cues (sound, sound, blend, sound, blend), and simply point to the spellings after they are written, and have the class give the sounds.

♦ How do you know when to move from sound-by-sound to whole-word blending? When you are writing the final spelling and students are reading the word, it is time to move on to whole-word blending. This often occurs around Unit 3 in first grade.

♦ Keep in mind, however, that when you introduce more complex long-vowel and variant vowel spellings, you can always drop back to sound-by-sound blending for the first couple of blending lines in the lesson.

♦ Even though the entire class may be doing whole-word blending, sound-by-sound blending is an excellent preteaching tool for students needing extra help. After all the sounds and spellings have been introduced, students may be ready to move just to reading the words in the blending line. Have them read the words, stopping to blend only words they cannot read fluently and automatically.

♦ In Grades 2 and 3, teachers often begin the phonics review in the Getting Started lessons with sound-by-sound blending and then quickly move into whole-word blending. Again, the goal is to have students reading the words as quickly and automatically as possible. If the majority of the class can do this, then use whole-word blending. Use sound-by-sound blending to preteach the blending lines with students who need more support.

Building for Success

A primary cause of students' blending failure is their failure to understand how to use the **Sound/Spelling Cards.** Students need to practice sounds and spellings when the **Sound/Spelling Cards** are introduced and during initial blending. They also need to understand that if they are not sure of how to pronounce a spelling, they can check the cards. You may need to lead the group almost constantly. Soon, however, leaders in the group will take over. Watch to see whether any students are having trouble

during the blending. Include them in small-group instruction sessions. At that time you may want to use the vowel-first procedure to reteach blending lines.

Extra Help

In working with small groups during Workshop, you may want to use some of the following suggestions to support students who need help with blending.

Vowel-First Blending

Vowel-first blending is an alternative to sound-by-sound and whole-word blending for students who need special help. Used in small-group sessions, this technique helps students who have difficulty with the other two types of blending focus on the most important part of each word—the vowels—and do only one thing at a time. These students are not expected to say a sound and blend it with another at virtually the same time. The steps to use in vowel-first blending follow:

1. Across the board or on an overhead transparency, write the vowel spelling in each of the words in the line. For a short vowel, the line may look like this:
   a   a   a
   For a long vowel, the line may look like this: *ee   ea   ea*

2. Point to the spelling as students say the sound for the spelling.

3. Begin blending around the vowels. In front of the first vowel spelling, add the spelling for the beginning sound of the word. Make the blending motion, and have students blend through the vowel, adding a blank to indicate that the word is still incomplete. Repeat this procedure for each partial word in the line until the line looks like this:
   ma__   sa__   pa__
   see__   mea__   tea__

4. Have students blend the partial word again as you make the blending motion, and then add the spelling for the ending sound.

5. Make the blending motion, and have students blend the completed word—for example, *mat* or *seed*.

6. Ask a student to repeat the word and to use it in a sentence. Then have another student extend the sentence.

7. Repeat steps 4, 5, and 6 for each word in the line, which might look like this:
   mat   sad   pan
   or
   seed   meat   team

Tips

♦ In the early lessons, blend with as much direction and dialogue as is necessary for success. Reduce your directions to a minimum as soon as possible. You have made good progress when you no longer have to say, "Sound—Sound—Blend," because students automatically sound and blend as you write.

♦ Blending is more than just reading words; it is an opportunity to build vocabulary and to develop oral language.

Always ask students to use less familiar words in sentences and then to extend the sentences. This sentence extension is a technique that can be applied to writing as well. Students will naturally extend sentences by adding phrases to the ends of the sentences. Encourage them to add phrases at the beginning or in the middle of the sentence as well.

♦ Use the vowel-first procedure in small-group preteaching or reteaching sessions with students who are having a lot of trouble with blending. Remember that you must adapt the blending lines in the lessons to the vowel-first method.

♦ The sight words in the sentences cannot be blended. Students must approach them as sight words to be memorized. If students are having problems reading sight words, tell them the words.

♦ Cue marks written over the vowels may help students.

  • Straight line cue for long vowels
    EXAMPLES: āpe, mē, fīne, sō, ūse

  • Curved line cue for short vowels
    EXAMPLES: căt, pĕt, wĭn, hŏt, tŭg

  • Tent cue for variations of *a* and *o*
    EXAMPLES: âll, ôff

  • Dot cue for schwa sound with multisyllabic words
    EXAMPLES: saläd, planėt, pencil, wagȯn

Dictation and Spelling

Purpose

The purpose of dictation is to teach students to segment words into individual sounds and to spell words by connecting sounds to spellings. In addition, learning dictation gives students a new strategy for reflecting on the sounds they hear in words to help them with their own writing.

As students learn about sounds and spellings, they begin to learn the standard spellings that will enable others to read their writing. As students learn to encode, they develop their visual memory for spelling patterns and words (spelling ability) and hence increase their writing fluency. Reinforcing the association between sounds and spellings and words through dictation gives students a spelling strategy that provides support and reassurance for writing independently. Reflecting on the sounds they hear in words will help students develop writing fluency as they apply the strategy to writing unfamiliar words.

A dictation activity is a learning experience; it is not a test. Students should be encouraged to ask for as much help as they need. The proofreading technique is an integral part of dictation. Students' errors lead to self-correction and, if need be, to reteaching. The dictation activities must not become a frustrating ordeal. Students should receive reinforcement and feedback.

There are two kinds of dictation: Sounds-in-Sequence Dictation and Whole-Word Dictation. The two types differ mainly in the amount of help they give students in spelling the words. The instructions vary for each type.

Procedure

Sounds-in-Sequence Dictation

Sounds-in-Sequence Dictation gives students the opportunity to spell words sound by sound, left to right, checking the spelling of each sound as they write. (Many students write words as they think they hear and say the words, not as the words are actually pronounced or written.)

✦ Pronounce the first word to be spelled. Use the word in a sentence, and say the word again (word/sentence/word). Have students say the word.

✦ Tell students to think about the sounds they hear in the word. Ask, "What's the first sound in the word?"

✦ Have students say the sound.

✦ Point to the *Sound/Spelling Card,* and direct students to check the card. Ask what the spelling is. Students should say the spelling and then write it.

✦ Proceed in this manner until the word is complete.

✦ **Proofread.** You can write the word on the board as a model, or have a student do it. Check the work by referring to the *Sound/Spelling Cards.* If a word is misspelled, have students circle the word and write it correctly, either above the word or next to it.

Whole-Word Dictation

Whole-Word Dictation gives students the opportunity to practice this spelling strategy with less help from the teacher.

✦ Pronounce the word, use the word in a sentence, and then repeat the word (word/sentence/word). Have students repeat the word. Tell students to think about the word and each sound in the word. Remind students to check the *Sound/Spelling Cards* for spellings and to write the word.

✦ **Proofread.** Write or have a volunteer write the word on the board as a model. Check the word by referring to the *Sound/Spelling Cards.*

Sentence Dictation

Writing dictated sentences. Help students apply this spelling strategy to writing sentences. Dictation supports the development of fluent and independent writing. Dictation of a sentence will also help students apply conventions of written language, such as capitalization and punctuation.

✦ Say the complete sentence aloud.

✦ Dictate one word at a time, following the procedure for Sounds-in-Sequence Dictation.

Continue this procedure for the rest of the words in the sentence. Remind students to put a period at the end. Then proofread the sentence sound by sound or word by word. When sentences contain sight words, the sight words should be dictated as whole words, not sound by sound. Students should be encouraged to check the high-frequency sight words posted in the room if they are unsure how to spell them. As students learn to write more independently, the whole sentence can be dictated word by word.

Proofreading

Whenever students write, whether at the board or on paper, they should proofread their work. Proofreading is an important technique because it allows students to learn by self-correction, and it gives them an immediate second opportunity for success. It is the same skill students will use as they proofread their writing. Students should proofread by circling—not by erasing—each error. After they circle an error, they should write the correction beside the circle. This type of correction allows you and students to see the error as well as the correct form. Students also can see what needs to be changed and how they have made their own work better.

You may want to have students use a colored pencil to circle and write in the correction. This will make it easier for them to see the changes.

Procedure for Proofreading

✦ Write—or have a student write—the word or sentence on the board or on an overhead transparency.

✦ Have the other students tell what is good; for example, it is spelled correctly.

✦ Have students check their words and identify whether anything can be made better, the word needs to be spelled differently, or the handwriting needs to be improved.

✦ If there is a mistake, have the student circle it and write it correctly—make it better.

✦ Have the rest of the class proofread their own work.

The Word Building Game (Grades K and 1)

The major reason for developing writing alongside reading is that reading and writing are complementary communicative processes. Decoding requires that students blend the phonemes together into familiar cohesive words. Spelling requires that students segment familiar cohesive words into separate phonemes. Both help students develop an understanding of how the alphabetic principle works.

The Word Building game gives students a chance to exercise their segmentation abilities and to practice using the sounds and spellings they are learning. The game is a fast-paced activity in which students spell related sets of words with the teacher's guidance. (Each successive word in the list differs from the previous one by one sound.)

For the Word Building game, students use their **Alphabet Letter Cards** (Levels K and 1) to build the words. (As an alternative they can use pencil and paper.) You will be writing at the board.

Give students the appropriate **Alphabet Letter Cards.** For example, if the list for the Word Building game is *am, at,* and *mat,* they will need their *a, m,* and *t* **Alphabet Letter Cards.**

✦ Say the first word, such as *am.* (Use it in a sentence if you wish.) Have students repeat the word. Say the word slowly sound by sound. Tell students to look at the **Alphabet Sound Cards** to find the letters that spell the sounds. Touch the first sound's card, in this case the Lamb card, and have students say the sound. Continue the process with the second sound. Write the word on the board while students use their **Alphabet Letter Cards** to spell it. Have students compare their words with your word, make changes as needed, and then blend and read the word with you.

✦ Students will then change the first word to make a different word. Say the next word in the list, (at). Segment the sounds of the word, and have students find the **Alphabet Letter Cards** that correspond. Write the new word *(at)* under the first word *(am)* on the board, and have students change their cards to spell the new word. Have them compare their words to yours and make changes as needed. Blend and read the word with students. Continue in a like manner through the word list.

Word Structure

Purpose

As students move into the upper grades, there is a shift from Phonics to Word Structure. Phonology is the study of the sounds that make up words. In the early grades, students learn to map sounds with spellings to read words. However, as students move into the upper grades and encounter more complex and longer words, the understanding of morphology and the morphological units that make up words is important for fluent reading, vocabulary development, and comprehension.

Morphology is the study of Word Structure. Word Structure activities support the development of fluency as students learn to identify and read meaningful chunks of words rather than individual spellings. Word Structure also supports the development of vocabulary as students learn how inflectional endings change a word's tense, number, and so on and how affixes can be added to a base word to create or derive a new but related meaning.

Morphemes are the smallest units that have semantic meaning. Morphemes may be free or bound. A free morpheme can stand alone, such as the words *dog, man,* or *woman.* A bound morpheme, on the other hand, is a unit of meaning that must be combined with another morpheme to make a meaningful word. For example, in *rewrite* the prefix *re-* means "to do again", and in *dogs* the *-s* changes the meaning to plural. Both re- and -s are bound morphemes because they must combine with other words to create new words.

Learning about word structure helps the reader on several levels. Being able to identify key-word parts not only helps with the pronunciation of longer, unfamiliar words but it also helps with meaning. In Word Structure, students learn how to deconstruct words—to identify the root of the word as well as the affixes. When affixes occur at the beginning of a word, they are called prefixes, and when they occur at the end of a word they are called suffixes. The prefix, root word, and suffix are all morphemes.

In the word *restatement,* there are three morphemes: the prefix *re-,* the root *state* and the suffix *-ment.*

prefix	root	suffix
re-	state	-ment

Suffixes, in particular, can impact the root word in different ways. Suffixes such as *-s* and *-ed* can change the tense of a verb; suffixes such as *-s* can change the number of a noun to make it a plural. Derviational morphemes, in contrast, can be added to words to create or derive another word, for example the addition of *-ness* to *sad* creates the new word *sadness,* or the addition of *-ly* changes *sad* to an adverb, *sadly.*

Word structure includes the study of the following:

✦ **Compound words** are made of two words that combine to form a new word. Compounds can be open or closed.

✦ **Root words** focus on learning about the basic element of words. Root words are the foundations upon which the meaning of a word is formed. A root may be a real word as in *audio,* meaning "sound," but it can also used with a suffix to become *audible,* changing the noun to an adjective. Although *audible* can have other elements, it does not need other elements to be complete. Most roots, however, do need other elements. Roots such as *duct, anthrop,* and *cred* require affixes to form the words *deduct, anthropology,* and *incredible,* respectively. Knowledge of root words and affixes provides students with critical tools for understanding derived words.

✦ **Prefixes** include any morpheme that is attached to the beginning of a root or word and changes the meaning of that word. Prefixes do not change the form of the word, only the meaning. Common prefixes include: *con-, com-, ad-, de-, di-, dis-, per-, re-, sub-, hyper-, un-,* and so on as well as numbers *(bi-, tri-, uni-, mono-, octo-,* and so on.)

✦ **Suffixes** include any morpheme that is attached to the end of a word or root and that changes the meaning of that word. Suffixes often change the function of the word and often require a spelling change in the root as well. For example, the addition of *-ial* to *colony* changes a noun to an adjective.

Common Latin Roots

Aud: auditory, auditorium, inaudible, audible, audition

Dict: dictate, predict, contradict, prediction

Ject: reject, inject, project, object, projection, objection

Port: transport, import, export, portable, support, report

Rupt: rupture, erupt, eruption, disrupt, interruption

Scrib/script: scribe, describe, manuscript, inscription, transcript, description, prescription

Spect: spectator, inspect, inspector, respect, spectacle, spectacular

Struct: structure, construct, instruct, destruction, reconstruction

Tract: tractor, traction, attract, subtraction, extract, retract, attractive

Vis: vision, visual, visit, supervisor, invisible, vista, visualize, visionary

Common Greek Roots

Auto: automatic, autograph, autobiography, automobile

Bio: biology, biography

Graph: graphite, geography, graphic, photograph, phonograph

Hydr: hydrogen, hydrant

Meter: speedometer, odometer, thermometer, metronome

Ology: geology, zoology, phonology

Photo: photography, photocopy, photosynthesis, photogenic

Scope: telescope, stethoscope, microscope, microscopic, periscope

Tele: telephone, television, telegraph

Therm: thermos, thermostat

Other examples of suffixes that change the word form include the following:

- Noun suffixes: *-age, -al, -ance, -ant, -ate, -ee, -ence, -ent, -er, -or, -ar, -ese, -ess, -hood, -ice, -isn, -ist, -ment, -ness, -sion, -tain, -tion, -ure*
- Suffixes that form adjectives: *-able, -al, -er, -est, -ette, -let, -ful, -fully, -ible, -ic, -ical, -ish, -ive, -less, -ous, -some, -worthy*
- Suffixes that form adverbs: *-ly, -wards, -ways, -wide, -wise*
- Suffixes that create verb forms: *-ate, -ed, -en, -ing, -ise, -ize, -yze*
- Inflectional endings are a special set of suffixes that change the number (singular to plural), case, or gender when added to nouns and change tense when added to verbs.

Teaching Word Structure

- ✦ *Have students read the words in a line.
- ✦ Tell students that words can be made of several individual parts.
- ✦ Examine the words in each line for meaningful parts, roots, and affixes.
- ✦ Identify the root or base word, and discuss the meaning.
- ✦ Underline and discuss the meaning of the prefix or suffix or both. If there is a prefix and a suffix, begin with the prefix. Tell students a prefix is a group of letters that is attached to the beginning of a base or root word. These letters have a specific meaning. For example, *un-* means "not" or "the opposite of," *non-* means "not," and *re-* means "again." A suffix is a group of letters that comes at the end of the base or root word and changes the meaning of the word. For example, *-er* changes a verb to a noun or the person doing the action as in *sing* and *singer*, or *-al* or *-ial* change nouns to adjectives as in *colony* and *colonial*.
- ✦ Reassemble the word, thinking about the meaning of the word parts.
- ✦ Say the word.
- ✦ Use the word in a sentence.

*Sometimes students are intimidated by longer words. Understanding syllable breaks helps when reading these longer words. The following chart includes information on syllable "generalizations." These may help your students when reading longer words during Word Structure activities and in the reading.

Word	Break into Syllables	Syllable Generalizations
Puppet	Pup-pet	Closed. If a word has two consonants in the middle, divide the word between the two consonants. The first syllable is closed, and the vowel pronunciation is short.
Music	Mu-sic	Open. If a word has a VCV pattern, break the syllables before the consonant, which makes the first syllable an open syllable and the first vowel long.
Closet	Clos-et	Some VCV patterns have the break after the consonant, which makes the first syllable a closed syllable and the vowel pronunciation short.
Hundred	Hun-dred	When there is a VCCCV pattern, the break is usually between the consonants. The first syllable is closed, and the vowel pronunciation is short.
Coward	Cow-ard	When there are two diphthongs, the syllable break comes between them.
Chaos	Cha-os	When there is a VV pattern, the syllable break comes between the vowels, and the first vowel is usually long.
Handle	Han-dle	Consonant plus *-le*. If a word has an *-le* (or *-el*) at the end, it usually forms a separate syllable and is pronounced with the consonant and /ə/ /l/.
Excitement Reform	Ex-cite-ment Re-form	Prefixes and suffixes are separate syllables.
Entertain Hurdle	En-ter-tain Hur-dle	*R*-controlled vowels. In most syllables where the vowel is followed by an *r*, the vowel sound is *r*-controlled.
Complete	Com-plete	Final *e*. When there is a vowel, consonant, and then an *e* at the end, the vowel before the consonant is pronounced long, and the *e* is silent.

Developing Vocabulary

For students to develop a deeper understanding of words, they should have multiple experiences with them. There are any number of activities that students can do to help them use words and internalize their meanings. The following activities can be used with the whole class or in small groups during Workshop.

- ✦ Give a word, and ask the student to find it in the line and to give a definition.
- ✦ Give a word, and ask the student to add a prefix or a suffix and to tell the meaning of the new word and the new part of speech.

- ✦ If the word is a multiple-meaning word, have the student point to the word, and then have the student give one meaning and use it in a sentence. Then have a second student give another meaning and use it in a sentence. (Be sure that the words that are used are truly multiple-meaning words and not words that can be used as different parts of speech, for example, a verb and a noun that have the same basic meaning.)
- ✦ Give two words, and have the student point to them. Ask what is the difference between these two words. For example, *hot* and *cold* are antonyms. The same could be done for synonyms, homonyms,

and homophones. This gets students to use the vocabulary and do the thinking. Point to two words, and have students tell how they are alike and different. For example, *history, historical,* and *historian* all have the same roots. All three words have a common root, but *history* and *historian* are nouns, and *historical* is an adjective.

✦ Give students a word, and have them point to the word. If it is a singular noun, have them change it to a plural or vice versa. If it is a verb, have students change the tense, or if it is an adjective, change it into an adverb if appropriate. In all cases, be sure that students spell the new word.

✦ Give students a word, have them point to and read the word, and then give the part of speech.

✦ Give a student a word, and have him or her use the word in a sentence. Have the class decide if the sentence truly shows the meaning of the word. For example, if the word is *camouflage,* and the student says, "Animals use camouflage," have the class add to the sentence to show the meaning: "Animals use camouflage to protect themselves from predators."

✦ Give students a word with a base word, and ask them to point to the word and read it and then to tell the root of the word.

✦ Give students a word with a Greek or Latin root. Have them point to and read the word, and then have them identify the root. Challenge students to think of other words that have the same root.

✦ Give students a word with a prefix or suffix. Have a student point to and read the word and then identify the prefix or suffix and tell the meaning of the affix. Then, if appropriate, have the student or a different student replace the affix with a different one and tell the meaning of the new word.

✦ When appropriate, give students a word, and have them give a synonym or antonym. When appropriate, work on gradations of words. For example, if the word is *hot* then the opposite is *cold*. Gradations would be *hot, warm, tepid, cool, cold*. These kinds of activities expand vocabulary.

✦ Give two words that are connected in some way, for example, *colony* and *colonial*. Have students come to the board, point to the words, and read them. Then have them tell why or how the words are connected.

✦ Have students find other words that follow comparable patterns to those taught in the lesson. If *colony, colonial, colonist* is a line in Word Structure, many students could find related nouns and use them with affixes, *(history, historical, historian)*. Challenge students to think more about words.

Tips

✦ Be sure students understand the limits of structural analysis. The *un-* in *unhappy* is a prefix, but the *un* in *under* and *uncle* is not.

✦ Help students realize that many words are related and that using their knowledge of a word can help them understand related words.

✦ Encourage students to use their knowledge of word structure during all reading to clarify unfamiliar words.

Fluency

Fluency is the ability to read or access words effortlessly with seemingly little attention to decoding. Fluent readers decode words not only automatically but accurately. In addition, fluent readers group words into meaningful units, utilize punctuation to guide their voices, and use expression appropriately to help them comprehend what they are reading. Fluent readers also adjust their reading rate as necessary.

To become proficient readers who fully understand what they read, the whole process of decoding must become automatic. Readers need to be so familiar with the sound/spellings, with common meaningful units like prefixes and suffixes and with the most common nondecodable sight words that they automatically process the spellings and word chunks. This enables them to read the word effortlessly and expend most of their energy on comprehending the meaning of the text. Automaticity is a key component of fluency.

The concept of fluency is introduced in the early grades, even before students are reading. When reading aloud, teachers are modeling fluency and using expression and intonation to support meaning. In pre-kindergarten and kindergarten, emergent readers learn about concepts of print that support fluency: learning about spaces and ending punctuation, reading from left to right, and automatically recognizing high-frequency sight words. Students apply this knowledge to reading **Pre-Decodables.** These skills are then applied to reading **Decodables.** While fluency begins in first grade, many students will continue to need practice in building fluency in second and third grades. Initially students can use the **SRA Imagine It! Decodable Stories** in Grades 2 and 3, but fluency practice should include using materials from a variety of different sources, including selections from the **Student Readers, Leveled Readers,** and the **Leveled Science** and **Social Studies Readers.** At all grade levels using **Pre-Decodables, Decodables, Readers,** or any other materials, students need to appreciate that fluency is about meaning. Take time to ask questions after students have read, talk about new and interesting words, and discuss any problems students encountered.

Building Fluency: Reading Pre-Decodables (K–1)

Purpose

Pre-Decodables play an important role in students' early literacy development by providing them with meaningful "reading" experiences before they are actually reading on their own and by expanding their awareness of the forms and uses of print. By following along as you read aloud a **Pre-Decodable,** students learn about the left-to-right and top-to-bottom progression of print on a page, the clues that indicate the beginnings and endings of sentences, the connections between pictures and words, and important book conventions such as front and back covers, authors' and illustrators' names, title pages, and page numbers.

The **Pre-Decodables** provide students with opportunities to apply their growing knowledge of letter names, shapes, and sounds and to become familiar with individual words. In addition, students practice reading high-frequency sight words. The automatic recognition of these words, the identification of ending punctuation, and reading with expression support the development of foundational fluency skills.

Through retelling the story in a **Pre-Decodable,** predicting or wondering about what will happen, and asking and responding to questions about the book, students not only learn about the relationship between spoken and written language, they learn to think about what they have read.

About the Pre-Decodables

Each **Pre-Decodable** contains a story that engages students' interest as it provides them with opportunities to practice what they are learning in their lessons. These "pre-decodable" stories each contain several high-frequency words that most students already have in their spoken vocabularies and that are a basic part of all meaningful stories. Learning to identify high-frequency words quickly, accurately, and effortlessly is a critical part of students' development as fluent, independent readers. The inside back cover of each **Pre-Decodable** contains a list of high-frequency words.

How to Use the Pre-Decodables

✦ Before reading a **Pre-Decodable,** take time to familiarize students with any new high-frequency words in the book and to review previously introduced words. To reinforce the idea that it is important to know these words because they are used so often in print, always point out the words in context. For example, focus students' attention on the words in **Big Book** selections or on signs and posters around the classroom.

✦ Give each student a copy of the book. Tell students that you will read the book together. Hold up your book. Read the title. If the title has a rebus picture, point to it, and tell students what it is. Then point to the word beneath it, and explain that the picture represents that word. Point to and read the names of the author and illustrator, reminding students that an author writes a book, and an illustrator draws the pictures. Page through the book, pointing to and naming the rebus pictures. Have students say the name of each rebus. To avoid confusion, always tell them the exact word that a rebus represents. Do not encourage them to guess at its meaning.

✦ Allow students time to browse through the book on their own, commenting on what they see in the illustrations and making predictions about what they think the book will be about. Encourage them to comment on anything special they notice about the story, the illustrations, or the words in the book.

✦ Help students find page 3. Read the book aloud without stopping. As you read, move your hand beneath the words to show the progression of print. Pause at each rebus as you say the word it represents, pointing first to the rebus then to the word beneath it.

✦ Reread the book. This time, ask students to point to and read the high-frequency words.

✦ Tell students to follow along in their books as you read the story again. Read the title aloud, and then have students read it with you. Reread page 3. Point to each rebus picture, and ask a volunteer to "read" it. Point to the word beneath the picture, and remind students that the picture shows what the word is. Continue through each page of the book, calling on volunteers to "read" and stopping as necessary to clarify and help students with words.

✦ After reading, answer any questions students might have about the book. Encourage them to discuss the illustrations and to explain what is happening in each one.

Building Fluency: Reading Decodables (K–3)

Purpose

The most urgent task of early reading instruction is to make written thoughts intelligible to students. This requires a balanced approach that includes systematic instruction in phonics as well as experiences with authentic literature. Thus, from the very beginning, *SRA Imagine It!* includes the reading of literature. At the beginning of first grade, when students are learning phonics and blending as a tool to access words, the teacher reads aloud. During this time students are working on using comprehension strategies and skills and discussing stories. As students learn to code and blend words, recognize critical sight words, and develop some level of fluency, they take more responsibility for the actual reading of the text.

This program has a systematic instruction in phonics that allows students to begin reading independently. This instruction is supported by *SRA Imagine It! Decodables.*

About the Decodables

The *SRA Imagine It! Decodables* are designed to help students apply, review, and reinforce their expanding knowledge of sound/spelling correspondences. Each story supports instruction in new phonic elements and incorporates elements and words that have been learned earlier. There are eight-page and sixteen-page *Decodables.* Grade K has eight-page *Decodables.* In Grade 1, the eight-page books focus on the new element introduced in the lesson, while the sixteen-page books review and reinforce the elements that have been taught since the last sixteen-page book. They review sounds

from several lessons and provide additional reading practice. Grades 2–3 have eight-page *Decodable Stories* in Getting Started, and eight- and sixteen-page stories in Units 1–3 in Grade 3 and Units 1–6 in Grade 2. The primary purpose is to provide practice reading the words. It is important that students also attach meaning to what they are reading. Questions are often included in the *Teacher's Edition* to check both understanding and attention to words.

How to use Decodables

Preparing to Read

✦ Introduce and write on the board or cards any nondecodable high-frequency or story words introduced or reviewed in the story. Tell students how to pronounce any newly introduced high-frequency words. Then point to each new word, and have students spell and say it. Have them read any previously introduced sight words in the Word Bank list. All the *SRA Imagine It! Decodables* contain high-frequency words that may not be decodable. For example, the word *said* is a common high-frequency word that is not decodable. Including words such as *said* makes the language of the story flow smoothly and naturally. Students need to be able to recognize and read these words quickly and smoothly.

✦ Read the title. At the beginning of the year, you may need to read the title of the book to students, but as the year goes on, you should have a student read it whenever possible. In Grade 1, selected sixteen-page *SRA Imagine It! Decodables* contain two related chapters, each using the same sounds and spellings. In such cases, read the title of the *Decodable,* and then point out the two individual chapter titles. Have volunteers read the title of the chapter you are about to read.

✦ Browse the story. Have students look through the story, commenting on whatever they notice in the text or illustrations and telling what they think the story will tell them.

Reading the Story

After this browsing, students will read the story a page at a time. Again, these stories are designed to support the learning of sounds and spellings. The focus should not

be on comprehension. Students should understand what they are reading, and they should feel free to discuss anything in the story that interests them. Any areas of confusion are discussed and clarified as they arise, as described below.

✦ Have students read a page to themselves. Then call on one student or groups of students to read the page aloud, or have the entire group read it aloud.

✦ If a student has difficulty with a word that can be blended, help her or him blend the word. Remind the student to check the *Sound/Spelling Cards* for help. If a word cannot be blended using the sound/spellings learned so far, pronounce the word for the student.

✦ If a student has trouble with a word or sentence, have the reader call on a classmate for help and then continue reading after the word or sentence has been clarified. After something on a page has been clarified or discussed, have a different student reread that page before moving on to the next page.

✦ Repeat this procedure for each page.

✦ Reread the story twice more, calling on various students to read or reading it in unison. These readings should go more quickly, with fewer stops for clarification.

Responding to the Story

After the story has been read aloud a couple of times, have students respond as follows:

✦ Ask students which difficult words they found in the story and how they figured them out. They may mention high-frequency words they did not recognize, words they had to blend, and words whose meanings they did not know.

✦ Have students tell about the story, retelling it in their own words, describing what they liked about it, or citing what they found interesting or surprising. Specific suggestions to use are listed in the *Teacher's Edition.*

✦ Questions are often provided in the *Teacher's Edition.* They are designed to focus students' attention on the words and not just the pictures. Ask students the questions, and have all students point to the answer in the story rather than having one student respond orally. Having students point to the answers is important. First, it ensures that all students are engaged in finding the answer, not just one. Second, by pointing to the answer, you know that students know the answer from reading and not just from having heard it read. Third, locating information in a text is an important skill. Finally, by pointing to the answer, you can quickly monitor who is understanding the story and who may still need more support during Workshop.

◆ Have students reread the story with partners. Circulate among the pairs, listening to individual students read. This allows you to monitor students' reading and to identify any students who may need additional help during Workshop.

Building Fluency beyond Decodables (middle of grade 1 on)

For some students, fluency develops naturally, seemingly without instruction. Other students, however, can benefit from more explicit instruction. There are students who can decode and read words but lack the critical phrasing, intonation, and expression that support meaning. Teach the text characteristics that support fluency, model them for students, and then provide students regular opportunities to practice fluency. Instruction can focus on any or all of the following areas:

◆ Discuss and model ending punctuation and what this means in terms of expression and intonation. This should be modeled and then discussed with students. Begin with ending punctuation, and then move to internal punctuation such as commas and semicolons. During modeling,

- pause longer at a period or other ending punctuation.
- raise your voice at a question mark.
- use expression when you come to an exclamation point.
- pause at commas or other internal punctuation such as semicolons.
- when you come to quotation marks, think of the character and how he or she might say his or her words.
- pause at an ellipsis.
- pause at dashes.

◆ Discuss and model words written in a

special way—typographical signals such as underlined words, boldfaced words, or those in all caps—need to be read with expression and changed in intonation for emphasis.

◆ Talk about reading rate. Oral reading should be done at a normal speaking rate. Students should not be reading so fast that someone listening could not hear the individual words and make sense of what is being read.

◆ Discuss and model intonation. Let students hear how voices change with different ending punctuation, how voices change when reading dialogue, and how intonation changes with cues from the author. In dialogue, think of the difference between "screamed Jennifer" versus "pleaded Jessie."

◆ Work on phrase cue boundaries. A good way to teach this is by using an overhead of what students are reading. Mark natural phrase boundaries—for example, clauses, prepositional phrases, subject phrases, verb phrases, and so on, with slashes. For example, *In the summertime,/Josh likes to play baseball/ at the park/down the street from his house.* Have students listen to you read the text, noticing how you paused at the markers. Then have students read the sentences naturally, using the markers as guides. Scaffold the instruction. In the beginning, mark the boundaries, and have students practice reading using the already marked passages. As students become comfortable, have them mark what they are reading with boundary markers. Gradually fade out the markers or slashes.

Fluency develops over time, and students should be given repeated opportunities to practice fluency with a variety of different texts. After students have read a text, take time to go back and discuss any new vocabulary or interesting words that students encountered while reading. Fluency is not an isolated activity; it is about supporting comprehension.

There are a number of techniques for practicing fluency: repeated readings, partner reading, tape-assisted reading, and Reader's Theater. All of these techniques can be done with a variety of different reading materials, including selections from the *Student Readers,* the *Leveled Readers,* and the *Science* and *Social Studies Leveled Readers.*

◆ Repeated readings increase reading rate, accuracy, and comprehension by providing students with multiple exposures to words and spelling patterns. In addition, it helps students improve their ability to break sentences into meaningful phrases and to use intonation. It is effective with both older and younger students. Repeated readings involve the students reading segments of text between 50 to 200 words, depending upon students' ability. Students should practice repeated readings with a variety of different text types. While repeated readings can be done with materials from *SRA Imagine It!* using segments from science and social studies texts helps students in the upper grades apply their reading knowledge across the curriculum. The goal is to have students read the text fluently and automatically at a per-minute rate commensurate with grade-level norms.

◆ CD-assisted readings help build confidence and are excellent support for second-language learners. Tape-assisted reading allows students to hear good models of reading and to develop their awareness of phrasing and prosody, or expressive reading. Tapes should provide students with experiences from a variety of text types. Tape selections should be read at approximately 80–100 words per minute by fluent readers with natural intonation, phrasing, and expression. Students read along with the text, aloud or subvocalizing. When the student is comfortable with the text, the student should practice reading the text independently and then read a portion of it to the teacher. The CDs in *SRA Imagine It!* can help students develop fluency with selections in the *Student Readers.*

◆ Reader's Theater legitimizes practicing fluency because it involves reading a script. While students do not memorize the script the way actors do in a play, they must be able to read the script fluently so the audience—the rest of the class—can enjoy the play. Several students can work together on a single play or playlet. They will need to practice reading the script several times before presenting it to the class. Reader's Theater also provides students with a writing opportunity. They can use a selection from their *Student Readers,* write a playlet, and then practice it for Reader's Theater.

+ Radio Reading, like Reader's Theater, connects reading aloud to real-life situations. Students, with copies of the text, read aloud in front of the class as if they were news broadcasters. Expository text works particularly well for this. Students can practice, and then once a week, several students can be the radio announcers. Students can also write weekly news reports and read them.

+ Partner Reading involves students reading with a partner. They can take turns reading pages or the entire selection. While one student reads, the listening-partner should note misread words and then discuss them with the partner after the reading. If the pairs are reading for one-minute-fluency checks, the nonreading partner can be responsible for timing the reading. Selections should be read multiple times with the goal being that students achieve a higher fluency rate on successive readings.

Assessing Fluency

Fluency should be assessed periodically to determine students' growth and to monitor progess. Listening to students read regularly is key. Fluency assessment should include not just reading rate but decoding accuracy, prosody (phrasing and intonation), and expression. In addition, checks should be done using various text types.

Generally accepted procedures for assessment include the following:

+ Use a passage of approximately 250 words at student's reading level. In the first half of first grade, use the appropriate **Decodable** in the Practice set. Have two copies—one for the student and one for you to mark.

+ Have the student read the passage for one minute. Use a timer, if possible, so you do not have to keep watching a stopwatch or the minute hand on a clock. You can also tape-record the reading. The goal is to have students read the text aloud in a natural way, the

way they would speak the words. This is not a race! Use the following scoring conventions. Mark any errors made by the reader.

+ Draw a line through any misread word, and count it as an error.

+ Circle any words the student omits or refuses to read, and count them as errors.

+ Indicate with a caret any extra words the student inserts.

+ Draw an arrow between words that student reverses, and count as one error.

+ Put two check marks above a word that a student repeats, but do not count it as an error.

+ Draw a box around the last word student reads in the one-minute time frame.

To calculate the student's accuracy rate, count the total number of words read in one minute. Subtract the number of errors from the total number of words read, and use that number to find the number of correct words read per minute.

For example, to calculate the rate:
Total words read – errors = words correct per minute
75 words read – 10 errors = 65 words per minute

For example, to calculate the accuracy:
Number of words ÷ the total number of words = percent of accuracy
145 (words correct) ÷ 156 (total number of words) = 93%

Descriptive Statistics for Oral Reading Fluency by Season for Grades 1–6 (Medians)			Fall	Winter	Spring
Grade	Percentile		WCPM[2]	WCPM	WCPM
1	75			46.75	82
	50			23	53
	25			6	15
2	75		79	100	117
	50		51	72	89
	25		25	42	61
3	75		99	120	137
	50		71	92	107
	25		44	62	78
4	75		119	139	152
	50		94	112	123
	25		68	87	98
5	75		139	156	168
	50		110.25	127	139
	25		85	99	109
6	75		153	167	177
	50		127	140	150
	25		98	111	122

[2]WCPM = words correct per minute

SOURCE
From "Curriculum-Based Oral Reading Fluency Norms for Students in Grades 1 Through 6" (2005) by Jan E. Hasbrouck and Gerald Tindal. *Behavioral Research and Teaching.*

In addition, watch for and note the following:

✦ Expression

✦ Ability of the reader to read words in natural syntactic clusters

Assessing accuracy, pace or rate, and expression provide information for instruction.

In addition to the qualitative information, some teachers like to use rubrics in their evaluation of fluency.

✦ **Level 1:** Reads basically word by word with limited phrasing, little expression. Reading is labored with difficulty in reading words automatically and fluently.

✦ **Level 2:** Reads in limited phrases of two words, but grouping of words is not natural. There is little or no appropriate expression or intonation.

✦ **Level 3:** Reads in phrases with most having appropriate breaks. Most of the reading has appropriate expression and intonation. There is limited comprehension.

✦ **Level 4:** Reads with appropriate phrasing, intonation, and expression and demonstrates understanding of the piece.

Interpreting Fluency Data

First compare the student's number of correct words per minute with accepted fluency norms.

Then examine the student's accuracy percentage. Reading accuracy should remain constant or gradually increase within and between grades until it stabilizes at 90 percent or higher. Compare the student's accuracy percentage after each assessment to ensure that his or her accuracy percentage is holding constant or improving.

Next examine the types of errors the student made, and consider what they mean for instruction.

✦ Inserting extra words suggest that the student understands what is being read but is reading perhaps impulsively or carelessly.

✦ Refusing to attempt to read words suggests that the student may be uncertain of his or her abilities, unwilling to take risks, or needs additional work with decoding at the sound/spelling or morpheme level. Look at the words the student does not read. Are they one-syllable words or multisyllabic words?

✦ Misreading routine CVC and CVCe words suggest that the student may need more work with the sounds and spellings. In some cases, a student may be able to read words with common sounds and spellings but needs more work with long vowels, diphthongs, and diagraphs.

✦ Looking for patterns in errors is key.

✦ Using or not using intonation, expression, and phrasing but reading quickly and accurately suggests that students need to think about how words combine to make meaning and how our expression can support understanding.

Tips

✦ Use Workshop time for building fluency. Introduce different ways to practice fluency one at a time.

✦ Set up a listening area for Workshop that students can use for tape-assisted instruction.

✦ Make sure *Pre-Decodables, Decodables,* and *Leveled Readers* are available to students.

✦ Have simple timers available for students to check their fluency rate.

✦ Encourage students to chart their fluency growth. If students are doing repeated reading, have them chart the number of words read each day for several days so they can see their fluency improving.

✦ When students have developed some degree of fluency with a *Pre-Decodable, Decodable,* or *Leveled Reader,* send the materials home for additional practice.

✦ Use a range of materials to practice building fluency throughout the day. Remember, fluency practice can be as short as one minute several times a day.

Reading Aloud

Purpose

Adults read aloud a variety of materials to students. In this program there are **Big Books**, picture books, novels, and excerpts for reading aloud. Research has shown that students who are read to are more likely to develop the skills they need to read successfully on their own.

In kindergarten and Grade 1, there are **Big Books**. In every grade level of **SRA Imagine It!** there are opportunities for teachers to read aloud to students. At the beginning of each unit is a Read Aloud selection tied to the unit theme. This Read Aloud selection allows students the opportunity to think about the unit theme before reading selections on their own.

Reading aloud at any age serves multiple purposes. Reading aloud

+ provokes students' curiosity about text.
+ conveys an awareness that text has meaning.
+ demonstrates the various reasons for reading text (to find out about the world, to learn useful new information and new skills, or simply for pleasure).
+ exposes students to the "language of literature," which is more complex than the language they ordinarily use and hear.
+ provides an opportunity to teach the problem-solving strategies that good readers employ. As students observe you interacting with the text, expressing your own enthusiasm, and modeling your thinking aloud, they perceive these as valid responses and begin to respond to text in similar ways.

Procedures

The following set of general procedures for reading aloud is designed to help you maximize the effectiveness of any Read Aloud session.

+ **Read-Aloud sessions.** Set aside time each day to read aloud.
+ **Introduce the story.** Tell students that you are going to read a story aloud to them. Tell its title, and briefly comment on the topic. To allow students to anticipate what will happen in the story, be careful not to summarize.

+ **Activate prior knowledge.** Ask whether anyone has already heard the story. If so, ask them to see if this version is the same as the one they have heard. If not, activate prior knowledge by saying, "First, let's talk a little about _____." If the story is being read in two (or more) parts, before reading the second part, ask students to recall the first part.
+ **Before reading.** Invite students to interrupt your reading if there are any words they do not understand or ideas they find puzzling or to ask questions. Throughout the reading, encourage them to do this.
+ **Read the story expressively.** Occasionally react verbally to the story by showing surprise, asking questions, giving an opinion, expressing pleasure, or predicting events. Expressive reading not only supports comprehension but serves as a model for fluency. Think-aloud suggestions are outlined below.
+ **Use Comprehension Strategies.** While reading aloud to students, model the use of comprehension strategies in a natural, authentic way. Remember to try to present a variety of ways to respond to text. These include visualizing, asking questions, predicting, making connections, clarifying, and summarizing.
+ **Retell.** When you have finished reading the story, call on volunteers to retell it.
+ **Discuss.** After reading, discuss with students their own reactions: how the story reminded them of things that have happened to them, what they thought of the story, and what they liked best about the story.
+ **Reread.** You may wish to reread the selection on subsequent occasions, focusing the discussion on the unit theme.

Think-Aloud Responses

The following options for modeling thinking aloud will be useful for reading any story aloud. Choose responses that are most appropriate for the selection you are reading.

+ React emotionally by showing joy, sadness, amusement, or surprise.

+ Ask questions about ideas in the text. This should be done when there are points or ideas that you really do wonder about.
+ Identify with characters by comparing them to yourself.
+ Show empathy with or sympathy for characters.
+ Relate the text to something you already know or something that has happened to you.
+ Show interest in the text ideas.
+ Question the meaning or clarity of the author's words and ideas.

Questions to Help Students Respond

At reasonable stopping points in reading, ask students general questions to get them to express their own ideas and to focus their attention on the text. These types of generic questions will help students discuss their reactions to the reading and demonstrate their comprehension.

+ What do you already know about this?
+ What seems really important here? Why do you think so?
+ Was there anything that you did not understand? What?
+ What did you like best about this?
+ What did you not like about this?
+ What new ideas did you learn from this?
+ What does this make you wonder about?
+ What surprised you in the story?

Vocabulary

Purpose

Strong vocabulary skills are correlated to achievement throughout school. The purpose of vocabulary instruction is to introduce students to new words (and ideas) and to teach students a range of strategies for learning, remembering, and incorporating unknown vocabulary words into their existing reading, writing, speaking, and listening vocabularies.

Words chosen for inclusion in **SRA Imagine It!** are based upon the vocabulary research of Andrew Biemiller, who has developed a comprehensive database of words students with large vocabularies know by the end of sixth grade. Biemiller's work identifies words that all students need to know and provides evidence that students from various backgrounds acquire these word meanings in roughly the same order. It appears that for students with small vocabularies, improving vocabulary mainly means moving them through the sequence faster. Because vocabulary knowledge is so critical to comprehension, vocabulary instruction is integrated throughout **SRA Imagine It!**

Vocabulary is taught throughout every part of the lesson.

Part 1: Preparing to Read

✦ In Grades 2–6, Word Structure develops vocabulary and the understanding that words can be deconstructed and related through known elements to determine meaning. In addition, students are learning about Greek and Latin roots, antonyms, synonyms, and multiple-meaning words. The emphasis on root words and affixes, in particular, serves to expand students' knowledge of words and their vocabulary.

✦ In Grades K–1, students are using words they blend in sentences to develop vocabulary and oral language. Learning about inflectional endings also helps children see the relationship between root words and various forms of the root. Reviews of blending lines focus on using words based on teacher clues as well as finding synonyms and antonyms.

Part 2: Reading and Responding

✦ The selection vocabulary instruction in this part of the lesson focuses on teaching specific vocabulary necessary for understanding the literature selection more completely.

✦ In kindergarten and the first half of Grade 1, the teacher introduces the selection vocabulary orally before reading the selection. Suggestions are made throughout the reading to discuss new and interesting words as the class reads the **Big Books.** Work from Biemiller suggests that clarifying words in the context of reading is an effective technique for expanding student vocabulary. Suggestions for which words to stop and clarify are suggested throughout the lessons. Vocabulary review activities are found throughout the lesson.

✦ From the middle of Grade 1 on, critical word meanings needed to understand the story are pre-taught as students read the Vocabulary Warm-Up in the **Student Reader.** This provides an initial exposure to the selection vocabulary. This is followed by guided vocabulary practice in which students discuss the definitions of critical words; learn to apply critical skills such as context, structure and apposition; use the vocabulary words in a variety of activities, and then return to the Vocabulary Warm-Up to reread the sentences containing the vocabulary words and to discuss the words. The clarification of additional vocabulary words is highlighted throughout the reading of each selection. Vocabulary review activities are found throughout the lesson.

✦ Students write the words and their definitions in their Writer's Notebooks.

✦ Vocabulary words, along with any other words students find interesting, are posted on charts to remind students to use these words in discussion of their reading as well as in their writing.

Part 3: Language Arts

During writing, students are encouraged to use their new vocabulary.

General Strategies

There is no question that having students read and reading to students are effective vocabulary instructional strategies. Most word learning occurs through exposure to words in listening and reading. Multiple exposures to words, particularly when students hear, see, say, and write words, is also effective. Wordplay, including meaning and dictionary games, helps develop a word consciousness as well.

Vocabulary Strategies for Unknown Words

Different strategies have been shown to be particularly effective for learning completely new words. These strategies are included in the Vocabulary Warm-Up lessons and **Skills Practice** activities.

Key Word This strategy involves providing or having students create a mnemonic clue for unknown vocabulary. For example, the word *mole* is defined in chemistry as a "gram molecule." By relating *mole* to *molecule*, students have a key to the meaning of the word.

Definitions Copying a definition from a dictionary is somewhat effective in learning new vocabulary. Combining this with using the word in writing and speaking adds to the effectiveness of this strategy. Requiring students to explain a word or to use it in a novel sentence helps ensure that the meaning is understood. It is not uncommon when students use words in sentences that the meaning of the vocabulary word is not clear. For example, a typical sentence a student might give for the word *camouflage* is "The octopus uses camouflage." The word *camouflage* is correctly used, but there is no real indication that the student knows the meaning of the word. Having students extend the sentence to explain why or how in the sentence helps: "The octopus uses camouflage to protect itself from predators." Or "The camouflage an octopus uses when it is in danger is to change its shape and color."

Context Clues Some words can be inferred from context and can be learned with repeated exposure to words in reading and listening. While using context can be useful, it is not the most effective way to learn new words. Also, as students move into content area reading, context becomes a less effective tool for determining the meaning of unfamiliar words.

✦ **Syntax** How a word is used in a sentence may provide some clue as to its meaning. This is particularly effective with homographs. "The lead pipe is a hazard to the community." Here lead is an adjective and is pronounced with a short e. In the sentence "He will lead the troops into battle," *lead* has a very different meaning, is a verb, and is pronounced with a long e.

✦ **Apposition** Sometimes the word is actually defined within the text. In an appositive, the definition of a word is often set off by commas for the reader.

Word Structure Examining the affixes and roots of a word often provides clues to its meaning. Knowing the meaning of at least part of the word can provide a clue as to its meaning. For example, *unenforceable* can be broken down into meaningful word parts. This is a particularly important tool in content area reading.

Developing Vocabulary

Purpose

Vocabulary is closely connected to comprehension. Considerable vocabulary growth occurs incidentally during reading. A clear connection exists between vocabulary development and the amount of reading a person does, and there are strong indications that vocabulary instruction is important and that understanding the meanings of key words helps with comprehension.

In **SRA Imagine It!** vocabulary is addressed before, during, and after reading. Before reading, the teacher presents vocabulary words from the selection. Students use skills such as context clues, apposition, and structural analysis to determine the meanings of the words. These selection vocabulary words are not only important to understanding the text but are also high-utility words that can be used in discussing and writing about the unit theme.

During reading, students monitor their understanding of words and text. When they do not understand something, they stop and clarify what they have read. Students will use these same skills—context clues, apposition, structural elements, and so on—to clarify the meanings of additional words encountered while reading. Determining the meanings of words while reading prepares students for the demands of independent reading both in and out of school.

After reading, students review the vocabulary words that they learned before reading the selection. They also review any interesting words that they identified and discussed during reading. Students record in their Writer's Notebooks both the selection vocabulary words and the interesting words they identified during their reading and are encouraged to use both sets of words in discussion and in writing.

Procedure

Before students read the selection, they read the Vocabulary Warm-Up in the **Student Reader.** As they read, students use context clues, word structure, or apposition to figure out the highlighted selection vocabulary. If students cannot determine the meaning of a word using one of the skills, they can consult the glossary or dictionary. After reading the Vocabulary Warm-Up, the teacher displays an overhead transparency to review the selection vocabulary.

Below are suggestions for modeling the use of context clues, apposition, or word structure to determine the meaning of a word.

Modeling Using Context Clues

Write the following sentences on the board or on a transparency. Explain to students that

they will use context clues, or other words in the sentence, to determine the meaning of the underlined word.

1. Mrs. Frisby must undertake a <u>treacherous</u> journey to take her son some medicine.

2. We took a <u>treacherous</u> walk near a swamp filled with crocodiles.

Have students look for clues in the sentences that might help them understand the meaning of the underlined word. Point out that a good clue in the second sentence is "near a swamp filled with crocodiles." This clue should help them understand that *treacherous* probably has something to do with danger. Guide students until they can give a reasonable definition of *treacherous*. To consolidate understanding of the word, ask another student to use the definition in a sentence.

Modeling Using Apposition

Write the following sentences on the board or on a transparency. Explain to students that they will use apposition to determine the meaning of the underlined word. In apposition, the word is followed by the definition, which is set off by commas.

1. The conductor thought he was an <u>abolitionist,</u> a person who wanted to end slavery.

2. John Brown was a famous <u>abolitionist</u>, a person who wanted to end slavery.

It should be clear to students using apposition that the definition of the word *abolitionist* is "a person who wanted to end slavery."

Modeling Using Word Structure

Write the following sentences on the board or on a transparency. Explain to students that they will use word structure, or parts of the word, to determine the meaning of the underlined word.

1. The strong wind blew Ivan's ship away into <u>uncharted</u> seas.

2. The explorers Lewis and Clark went into <u>uncharted</u> territory.

Have students look at the word *uncharted* and break it into parts: the prefix *un-*, *chart,* and the suffix *-ed.* Students should know that the suffix *un-* means "not" and that the suffix *-ed* usually indicates the past tense of a verb. However, you may need to remind students about the meanings of these affixes. Ask students for the meaning of the word *chart.* Students should know that a chart could be a map or a table. Guide them as they put together the definitions of the word parts: *un-* (not), *charted* (mapped or tabled). They should be able to come up with the definition "not mapped" or "unmapped" or even "unknown." Have them substitute their definition in the sentences to see if the definition makes sense. For instance, the first sentence would read, "The strong wind blew Ivan's ship away into unmapped (or unknown) seas." Confirm with students that the new sentence makes sense, and then repeat the same process for the second sentence.

Everything students learn about phonemic awareness, phonics, word structure and decoding has one primary goal—to help them understand what they are reading. Without comprehension, there is no reading.

Take time to review words and their meanings. Help students connect new words to familiar words. Each unit in **SRA Imagine It!** revolves around a theme, and there are key words. In every lesson, there is a concept.

Semantic Mapping Having students create a semantic map of an unknown word after learning its definition helps them learn it. Have students write the new word and then list in a map or web all words they can think of that are related to it.

Semantic Feature Analysis A semantic feature analysis helps students compare and contrast similar types of words within a category to help secure unknown words. Have students chart, for example, the similarities and differences between various types of sports, including new vocabulary such as *lacrosse* and *cricket.*

Reading Comprehension

Purpose

The primary aim of reading is comprehension. Without comprehension, neither intellectual nor emotional responses to reading are possible—other than the response of frustration. Reading is about problem solving. Expert readers bring their critical faculties to bear on everything they read. They generally understand most of what they read, but just as importantly, they recognize when they do not understand, and they have at their command an assortment of strategies for monitoring and furthering their understanding.

The goal of comprehension strategy instruction is to turn responsibility for using strategies over to students as soon as possible. Research has shown that students' comprehension and learning problems are not a matter of mental capacity but rather their inability to use strategies to help them learn. Expert readers use a variety of strategies to help them make sense of the text and to get the most out of what they read. Trained to use a variety of comprehension strategies, students dramatically improve their learning performance. To do this, the teacher models strategy use and gradually incorporates various kinds of prompts and possible student think-alouds as examples of the types of thinking students might do as they read to comprehend what they are reading.

Setting Reading Goals

Even before they begin reading and using comprehension strategies, good readers set reading goals and expectations. Readers who have set their own goals and have definite expectations about the text they are about to read are more engaged in their reading and notice more in what they read. Having determined a purpose for reading, they are better able to evaluate a text and to determine whether it meets their needs. Even when the reading is assigned, the reader's engagement is enhanced when he or she has determined ahead of time what information might be gathered from the selection or how the selection might interest him or her.

Comprehension Strategies

Descriptions of strategies expert readers use to comprehend the text follow.

> *Good readers continually monitor their speed and ability to understand throughout reading.*

Summarizing

Periodically it is important to summarize and check our understanding as we read. Sometimes readers reread to fill in gaps in their understanding. They use the strategy of summarizing to keep track of what they are reading and to focus their minds on important information. The process of putting the information in one's own words not only helps good readers remember what they have read but also prompts them to evaluate how well they understand the information. Sometimes the summary reveals that one's understanding is incomplete, in which case it might be appropriate to reread the previous section to fill in the gaps. The strategy of summarizing is particularly helpful when readers are reading long or complicated text. When to stop and summarize depends on the difficulty of the text as well as the type of text. Often in content area reading, it makes sense to stop and summarize the key ideas after each section. In narratives, the reader often stops to summarize after an episode has been read. Many of us will automatically summarize what has happened if we have put down a book and are about to continue reading it again. Students should think to themselves the following:

✦ Does this make sense? What is this selection about?

✦ What are the big ideas the writer is trying to get at?

✦ What can I delete from my summary? What is not important?

✦ Have I said the same thing more than once in my summary?

✦ How can I put what I just read into my own words?

✦ What is unclear? What is the meaning of the word or sentence? How can I determine this?

Clarifying

Monitoring understanding is key to reading. It allows readers to make sure they understand what they read. They note the characteristics of the text, such as whether it is difficult to read or whether some sections are more challenging or more important than others are. In addition, when readers become aware that they do not understand, they stop and take appropriate action, such as rereading, to understand the text better. As they read, good readers stay alert for problem signs such as loss of concentration, unfamiliar vocabulary, or lack of sufficient background knowledge to comprehend the text. This ability to self-monitor and identify aspects of the text that hinder comprehension is crucial to becoming a proficient reader. Clarifying may occur at the word, the sentence, the paragraph, or at the whole-text level. Students should think to themselves the following:

✦ What does not make sense? If it is a word, how can I figure it out? Do I use context, structure, or apposition, or do I need to ask someone or look it up in the dictionary or glossary?

✦ What does not make sense? The paragraph is long and full of details. What can I do? I can take some notes, I can reread it more slowly; I can discuss it with someone.

✦ These sentences are endless. How can I deal with long, complicated sentences?

✦ What is the main idea of what I just read?

✦ Can I summarize what I just read?

Asking Questions

Asking questions allows the reader to constantly check his or her understanding and to follow the writer's train of thought. Good readers ask questions that may prepare them for what they will learn. If their questions are not answered in the text, they may try to find answers elsewhere and thus add even more to their store of knowledge. Certain kinds of questions occur naturally to a reader, such as to clear up confusion or to wonder why something in the text is as it is. Intentional readers take this somewhat informal questioning one step further by formulating questions with the specific intent of checking their understanding. They literally test themselves by thinking of questions a teacher might ask and then by determining answers to those questions. Students should think to themselves the following:

✦ Why is this the way it is? What else is there to know about this?

✦ What question can I ask to check if I have understood what I just read?

✦ How does this connect to the unit theme? What new information will I learn?

✦ What questions do I think the author will answer as I read this selection?

✦ Do I understand the author? What is not making sense?

✦ What is interfering with my understanding?

Predicting

Predicting what will happen in the story allows the reader to summarize what has been read so far, to identify clues and events in the text, and to use prior knowledge and personal experience to make inferences about what will happen next. When reading fiction, readers make predictions about what they are reading and then confirm or revise those predictions as they go. Predictions are not wild guesses. They are made based on information provided by the author as well as the reader's background knowledge. Students should think to themselves the following: What do I already know that will help me predict? What are the clues in the text that will help me predict?

✦ Why was my prediction confirmed?

✦ Why was my prediction not confirmed?

✦ What clues did I miss that would have helped me make a better prediction?

> *The responsibility for using strategies by students should begin as soon as they understand that reading is about problem solving and making sense of text and that these strategies will help them do both.*

Making Connections

Making connections between the text and what is known from personal experience or previous reading deepens our understanding of text and expands our understanding. Comprehension is enhanced when we relate what is read to what is known. Students should think to themselves the following:

✦ What does this remind me of? What else have I read like this?

✦ What does this remind me of in my own life? In my own experiences?

✦ How does this connect with other selections I have read?

✦ How does this connect with what is going on in the world today?

Visualizing

Creating a mental image about the text involves not just the literal interpretation of the author's word but going beyond the literal to incorporating prior knowledge and experiences that deepen understanding. Readers form mental images as they read. They picture the setting, the characters, and the action in a story. Visualizing can also be helpful when reading expository text. Visualizing helps readers understand descriptions of complex activities or processes. When a complex process or an event is being described, the reader can follow the process or the event better by visualizing each step or episode. Sometimes an author or an editor helps the reader by providing illustrations, diagrams, or maps. If no visual aids have been provided, it may help the reader to create one. Creating mental images helps the reader create pictures that can be stored efficiently in his

or her long-term memory. Students should think to themselves the following:

✦ What picture does the words create in my mind? How do the words suggest feelings, actions, and settings?

✦ Would a drawing help me understand the process?

✦ How does my mental picture extend beyond the words in the text?

✦ How did this picture help me understand what I am reading?

Adjusting Reading Speed

Some texts are easy to read; others are more challenging. How difficult a text is to read depends on both author and reader variables. Good readers understand that not all text is equal. Because of this, they continuously monitor what they are reading and adjust their reading speed accordingly. Efficient readers skim parts of the text that are not important or relevant to their reading goals, and they purposely slow down when they encounter difficulty in understanding the text. Students should think to themselves the following:

✦ When I reread does this make sense?

✦ This is a long and involved sentence. Rereading may help.

Procedures

Modeling and Thinking Aloud

One of the most effective ways to help students understand and use critical comprehension is to make strategic thinking public. Modeling these behaviors and encouraging students to think aloud as they attempt to address comprehension problems and to understand text can demonstrate for everyone in a class how these behaviors are put into practice. Suggestions for think-alouds are provided throughout the ***Teacher's Edition.***

The most effective models you can offer will be those that come from your own reading experiences. What kinds of questions did you ask yourself? What kinds of things surprised you the first time you read a story? What kinds of new information did you learn? What kinds of things were confusing until you reread or read further? Drawing on these questions and on your students' questions and comments as they read will make the strategic reading process more meaningful to students. Below are suggestions for modeling each of the comprehension strategies.

Before Reading

✦ **Modeling Setting Reading Goals.** To model setting reading goals, engage students in the following:

- **Activate prior knowledge.** As you approach a new text, consider aloud what you already know about the subject or what your experiences have been in reading similar material.

- **Browse the text.** To get an idea of what to expect from a text, look at the title and the illustrations. When students are reading fiction, they will browse the text to look for Clues, Problems and Wonderings. Possible clues will support comprehension— for example, genre, content, author, setting, and so on—potential problems might include things such as difficult words or dense paragraphs as well as unfamiliar concepts; and wonderings are the things students are curious to find out about from their reading— questions about the selection. Wonderings are students' purposes for reading. When students read nonfiction, they will use a KWL chart— this is what I know (K), this is what I want to find out (W), and this is what I have learned (L). Both these activities— Clues, Problems, and Wonderings and KWL—engage students in thinking before reading the selection by having them activate their own background knowledge, identify potential problems, and set purposes for reading. Have students glance quickly at the selection, looking briefly at the illustrations and the print. Have them tell what they think they might be learning about as they read the selection. Early in the year, model the thinking involved with these activities and then begin to turn the responsibility for completing them over to students.

During Reading

Modeling— or thinking aloud— about how to use strategies to solve problems is a powerful tool for teaching comprehension. While think-aloud models are included in

all lessons, relate your own thinking and experiences to the lesson and the think-alouds. Early in the process you will need to model thinking about how, when, and why to use the strategies. Encourage students to stop and use them as well; engage them in thinking!

✦ **Modeling Summarizing.** Just as the strategy of summarizing the plot and then predicting what will happen next can enhance a student's reading of fiction, so too can the same procedure be used to the student's advantage in reading nonfiction. In expository text, it is particularly logical to stop and summarize at the end of a chapter or section before going on to the next. One way to model the valuable exercise of making predictions and at the same time to expand knowledge is to summarize information learned from a piece of expository writing and then to predict what the next step or category will be. Appropriate times to stop and summarize include the following:

- When a narrative text has covered a long period of time or a number of events

- When many facts have been presented

- When an especially critical scene has occurred

- When a complex process has been described

- Any time there is the potential for confusion about what has happened or what has been presented in the text

- When returning to a selection

✦ **Modeling Clarifying.** A reader may need clarification at any point in the reading. Model this strategy by stopping at points that confuse you or that may confuse your students. Indicate that you are experiencing some confusion and need to stop and make sure you understand what is being read. Difficulty may arise from a challenging or unknown word or phrase. It may also stem from the manner in which the information is presented. Perhaps the author did not supply needed information. As you model this strategy, vary the reasons for stopping to clarify so that students understand that good readers do not simply skip over difficult or confusing material—they stop and determine what they do not understand.

✦ **Modeling Asking Questions.** Learning to ask productive questions is not an easy task. Students' earliest experiences with this strategy take the form of answering teacher-generated questions. However, students should be able to move fairly quickly to asking questions like those a teacher might ask. Questions that can be answered with a simple *yes* or *no* are not typically very useful for helping them remember and understand what they have read. Many students find it helpful to ask questions beginning with *Who? What? When? Where? How?* and *Why?* As students become more accustomed to asking and answering questions, they will naturally become more adept at phrasing their questions. As their question asking becomes more sophisticated, they progress from simple questions that can be answered with explicit information in the text to questions that require making inferences based on the text.

✦ **Modeling Predicting.** Predicting can be appropriate at the beginning of a selection—on the basis of the titles and the illustrations—or at any point while reading a selection. At first, your modeling will take the form of speculation about what might happen next, but tell students from the start what clues in the text or illustrations helped you predict to make it clear that predicting is not just guessing. When a student makes a prediction—especially a far-fetched one—ask on what in the selection or in his or her own experience the prediction is based. If the student can back up the prediction, let the prediction stand; otherwise, suggest that the student make another prediction on the basis of what he or she already knows. Often it is appropriate to summarize before making a prediction. This will help students consider what has come before as they make their predictions about what will happen next. When reading aloud, stop whenever a student's prediction has been confirmed or contradicted. Have students tell whether the prediction was correct. If students seem comfortable with the idea of making predictions but rarely do so on their own, encourage them to discuss how to find clues in the text that will help them.

Modeling Making Connections. To model making connections, share with students any thoughts or memories that come to mind as you read the selection. Perhaps a character in a story reminds you of a childhood friend, allowing you to better identify with interactions between characters. Perhaps information in an article on Native American life in the Old West reminds you of an article that you have read on the importance of the bison to Native Americans. Sharing your connections will help students become aware of the dynamic nature of reading and show them another way of being intentional, active learners.

Modeling Visualizing. Model visualizing by describing the mental images that occur to you as you read. A well-described scene is relatively easy to visualize, and if no one does so voluntarily, you may want to prompt students to express their own visualizations. If the author has not provided a description of a scene, but a picture of the scene would make the story more interesting or comprehensible, you might want to model visualizing as follows: "Let's see. The author says that the street was busy, and we know that this story is set during the colonial period. From what I already know about those times, there were no cars, and the roads were different from the roads of today. The street may have been paved with cobblestones. Horses would have been pulling carriages or wagons. I can almost hear the horses' hoofs going clip-clop over the stones." Remind students that different readers may picture the same scene quite differently, which is fine. Every reader responds to a story in her or his own way.

Modeling Adjusting Reading Speed. Just as readers need to monitor for problems, they need to be aware that various texts can be approached in various ways. For example, if reading a story or novel for enjoyment, the reader will typically read at a relaxed speed that is neither so fast as to miss information nor as slow as they might read a textbook. If on the other hand, the reader is reading a textbook, he or she will probably decrease speed to assure understanding and make sure that all important information is read and understood. When modeling this strategy, be sure you indicate why you,

as the reader, have chosen to slow down or speed up. Good readers continually monitor their speed and ability to understand throughout reading.

If your students have not previously engaged in the sort of strategic thinking aloud that is promoted throughout *SRA Imagine It!,* you will have to do all or most of the modeling at first, but encourage students to participate as soon as possible. Remember, however, the goal is for students to use these strategies independently as they read both in and out of school. In addition to the think-alouds for the teachers, there are also prompts to encourage students to do the thinking. The responsibility for using strategies by students should begin as soon as they understand that reading is about problem solving and making sense of text and that these strategies will help them do both.

Reading Aloud

At the beginning of the year, students should be encouraged to read selections aloud. This practice will help you and them understand some of the challenges posed by the text and how individual students approach these challenges.

Reading aloud helps students build fluency, which in turn will aid their comprehension. Students in Grades K–3 can use *Decodables* to build fluency, while students in Grades 4–6 can use the literature from the *Student Readers. Leveled Readers* are also available for Grades 1–6. Fluent second graders read between 79 and 117 words per minute with accuracy and understanding, depending on the time of the year (fall/spring). Fluent third graders can be expected to read between 99 and 137 words per minute; fourth (119/152); fifth (139/168); sixth (123/177).

Make sure that you set aside time to hear each student read during the first few days of class—the days devoted to Getting Started are perfect for this—so that you can determine students' abilities and needs. Workshop is also a good time to listen to any students who do not get to read aloud while the class is reading the selection together.

As the year progresses, students should continue reading aloud often, especially with particularly challenging text. Model your own use of strategies, not only to help students better understand how to use strategies but also to help them understand that actively using strategies is something that good, mature readers do constantly.

Most students are unaccustomed to thinking aloud. They will typically stand mute as they try to determine an unfamiliar word or to deal with a confusing passage. When this happens, students should be encouraged to identify specifically with what they are having difficulty. A student might identify a particular word, or he or she may note that the individual words are familiar but that the meaning of the passage is unclear.

Active Response

Not only are good readers active in their reading when they encounter problems, but they respond constantly to whatever they read. In this way they make the text their own. As students read they should be encouraged to

- make as many connections as they can between what they are reading and what they already know.

- visualize passages to help clarify their meanings or simply to picture appealing descriptions.

- ask questions about what they are reading. The questions that go through their minds during reading will help them examine, and thus better understand, the text. Doing so may also interest them in pursuing their own investigations. The questions may also provide a direction for students' research or exploration.

- summarize and make predictions as a check on how well they understand what they are reading.

Tips

- Remember that the goal of all reading is comprehension. If a story or article does not make sense, the reader needs to choose whatever strategies will help make sense of it. If one strategy does not work, the reader should try another.

- Always treat problems encountered in text as interesting learning opportunities rather than something to be avoided or dreaded.

- Encourage students to think aloud about text challenges.

- Encourage students to help each other build meaning from text. Rather than telling each other what a word is or what a passage means, students should tell each other how they figured out the meanings of challenging words and passages.

✦ Assure students that these are not the only strategies that can be used while reading. Any strategy that they find helpful in understanding text is a good, useful strategy.

✦ Encourage students to freely share strategies they have devised on their own. You might want to write these on a large sheet of paper and tape them onto the board.

✦ An absence of questions does not necessarily indicate that students understand what they are reading. Be especially alert to students who never seem to ask questions. Be sure to spend tutorial time with these students occasionally, and encourage them to discuss specific selections in the context of difficulties they might have encountered and how they solved them as well as their thoughts about unit concepts.

✦ Observing students' responses to text will enable you to ascertain not only how well they understand a particular selection but also their facility in choosing and applying appropriate strategies. Use the strategy rubrics to evaluate students' understanding of and ability to use the different reading strategies. Take note of the following:

• Whether the strategies a student uses are effective in the particular situation.

• Whether the student chooses from a variety of appropriate strategies or uses the same few over and over.

• Whether the student can explain to classmates which strategies to use in a particular situation and why.

• Whether the student can identify alternative resources to pursue when the strategies she or he has tried are not effective.

• Whether students' application of a given strategy is becoming more effective over a period of time.

✦ Encourage students to use the reading strategies throughout the day in all their reading activities.

Becoming familiar and comfortable with these self-monitoring techniques gives readers the confidence to tackle material that is progressively more difficult. A good,

mature reader knows when understanding what he or she is reading is becoming a problem and can take steps to correct the situation. He or she has internalized the strategies, values them, and uses strategies automatically.

Comprehension Skills

Purpose

An important purpose of writing is to communicate thoughts from one person to another. The goal of instruction in reading comprehension skills is to make students aware of the logic behind the structure of a written piece. If the reader can discern the logic of the structure, he or she will be more able to understand the author's logic and to gain knowledge both of the facts and the intent of the selection. By keeping the organization of a piece in mind and considering the author's purpose for writing, the reader can go beyond the actual words on the page and make inferences or draw conclusions based on what was read. Strong, mature readers utilize these "between the lines" skills to get a complete picture of not only what the writer is saying but what the writer is trying to say.

Effective comprehension skills include the following:

Author's Point of View

Point of view involves identifying who is telling the story. If a character in the story is telling the story, that one character describes the action and tells what the other characters are like. This is first-person point of view. In such a story, one character will do the talking and use the pronouns *I, my,* and *me.* All other characters' thoughts, feelings, and emotions will be reported through this one character.

If the story is told in third-person point of view, someone outside the story who is aware of all of the characters' thoughts, feelings, and actions is relating them to the reader. All of the characters are referred to by their names or the pronouns *he/she, him/her,* and *it.*

If students stay aware of who is telling a story, they will know whether they are getting the full picture or the picture of events as seen through the eyes of only one character.

Sequence

The reader cannot make any decisions about relationships or events if he or she has no idea in which order the events take place. The reader needs to pay attention to how the writer is conveying the sequence. Is it simply stated that first this happened and then that happened? Does the writer present the end of the story first and then go back and let the reader know the sequence of events? Knowing what the sequence is and how it is presented helps the reader follow the writer's line of thought.

Fact and Opinion

Learning to distinguish fact from opinion is essential to critical reading and thinking. Students learn what factors need to be present for a statement to be provable. They also learn that an opinion, while not provable itself, should be based on fact. Readers use this knowledge to determine for themselves the validity of the ideas presented in their reading.

Main Idea and Details

An author always has something specific to say to his or her reader. The author may state this main idea in different ways, but the reader should always be able to tell what the writing is about.

To strengthen the main point or main idea of a piece, the author provides details to help the reader understand. For example, the author may use comparison and contrast to make a point, to provide examples, to provide facts, to give opinions, to give descriptions, to give reasons or causes, or to give definitions. The reader needs to know what kinds of details he or she is dealing with before making a judgment about the main idea.

Compare and Contrast

Using comparison and contrast is one of the most common and easiest ways a writer gets his or her reader to understand a subject. Comparing and contrasting unfamiliar thoughts, ideas, or things with familiar thoughts, ideas, and things gives the reader something within his or her own experience base to use in understanding.

Cause and Effect

What made this happen? Why did this character act the way he or she did? Knowing the causes of events helps the reader see the whole story. Using this information to identify the probable outcomes (effects) of events or actions will help the reader anticipate the story or article.

Classify and Categorize

The relationships of actions, events, characters, outcomes, and such in a selection should be clear enough for the reader to see the relationships. Putting like things or ideas together can help the reader understand the relationships set up by the writer.

Author's Purpose

Everything is written for a purpose. That purpose may be to entertain, to persuade, or to inform. Knowing why a piece is written— what purpose the author had for writing the piece—gives the reader an idea of what to expect and perhaps some prior idea of what the author is going to say.

If a writer is writing to entertain, then the reader can generally just relax and let the writer carry him or her away. If, on the other hand, the purpose is to persuade, it will help the reader understand and keep perspective if he or she knows that the purpose is to persuade. The reader can be prepared for whatever argument the writer delivers.

Drawing Conclusions

Often, writers do not directly state everything—they take for granted their audience's ability to "read between the lines." Readers draw conclusions when they take from the text small pieces of information about a character or event and use this information to make a statement about that character or event.

Reality and Fantasy

Students learn to distinguish reality from fantasy as they read different genres, including expository text, realistic fiction, fables, fairy tales, and so on. As students read, they note that a fantasy contains people, animals, and objects that do things that could not happen in the real world. Reality contains people, animals, and objects that can exist and do things in the real world.

Making Inferences

Readers make inferences about characters and events to understand the total picture in a story. When making inferences, readers use information from the text, along with personal experience or knowledge, to gain a deeper understanding of a story event and its implications.

Procedures

Read the Selection

First, have students read the selection using whatever skills they need to help them make sense of the selection. Then discuss the selection to assure that students did, indeed, understand what they read. Talk about any confusion they may have, and make any necessary clarifications.

Reread

Revisiting or rereading a selection allows the reader to note specific techniques that authors use to organize and present information in narratives and expository genres. When students have a basic understanding of the piece, have them reread the selection in whole or in part, concentrating on selected skills. Students learn to appreciate that writers use different structures, for example, cause and effect or compare/contrast, to organize their work and that recognizing these structures can help readers understand what they have read. It is these same structures that students will use in their own writing.

Limit this concentration on specific comprehension/writing skills to one or two that can be clearly identified in the piece. Trying to concentrate on too many things will just confuse students and make it harder for them to identify any of the organizational devices used by the writer. If a piece has many good examples of several different aspects, then go back to the piece several times over a span of days.

Write

Solidify the connection between how an author writes and how readers make sense of a selection by encouraging students to incorporate these organizational devices into their own writing. As they attempt to use these devices, they will get a clearer understanding of how to identify them when they are reading.

Remind students often that the purpose of any skill exercise is to give them tools to use when they are reading and writing. Unless students learn to apply the skills to their own reading—in every area of reading and study—then they are not gaining a full understanding of the purpose of the exercise.

Writing is a complicated process. A writer uses handwriting, spelling, vocabulary, grammar, usage, genre structures, and mechanics skills with ideas to create readable text. In addition, a writer must know how to generate content, or ideas, and understand genre structures to effectively present ideas in writing. Many students never progress beyond producing a written text that duplicates their everyday speech patterns. Mature writers, however, take composition beyond conversation. They understand the importance of audience and purpose for writing. They organize their thoughts, eliminating those that do not advance their main ideas, applying what they have learned in reading, and elaborating on those that do so that their readers can follow a logical progression of ideas in an essay or story. Mature writers also know and can use the conventions of grammar, usage, spelling, and mechanics. They proofread and edit for these conventions, so their readers are not distracted by errors.

Reading Big Books

Purpose

Many students come from homes where they are read to often, but a significant number of other students have not had this valuable experience. **Big Books** (Levels K and 1) offer all students crucial opportunities to confirm and expand their knowledge about print and reading, to develop vocabulary, and to enjoy literacy experiences. They are especially useful for shared reading experiences in the early grades.

The benefits of reading **Big Books** include engaging even nonreaders in

- unlocking the books' messages.
- developing print awareness.
- participating in good reading behaviors.
- observing what a good reader does: remarking on the illustrations and the title, asking questions about the content and what might happen, making predictions, and clarifying words and ideas.
- promoting the insights about print, for example, that a given word is spelled the same way every time it occurs as high-frequency words are identified.
- reinforcing the correspondence between spoken and written words and spelling patterns.
- enjoying the illustrations and connecting them to the text to help students learn to explore books for enjoyment and information.
- learning about different genre and the language of print.
- developing vocabulary and academic language.
- interpreting and responding to literature and expository text before they can read themselves.

Procedure for Reading Big Books

During the first reading of the **Big Books,** you will model reading behaviors and comprehension strategies similar to those that will later apply to their own reading. This focus on strategies encourages students to think about the ideas in the stories, to ask questions, and to learn new vocabulary. During the second reading, you will address print awareness and teach comprehension skills such as classifying and categorizing or sequencing, which help the reader organize information and focus on the specifics in the selection. In addition, you will teach skills such as making inferences and drawing conclusions, which help the reader focus on the deeper meaning of the text. At first, teachers should expect to do all of the reading but should not prevent students from trying to read on their own or from reading words they already know.

- **Activate Prior Knowledge.** Read the title of the selection and the author's and illustrator's names. At the beginning of each **Big Book,** read the title of the book and discuss what the whole book is about before going on to reading the first selection. Initiate a brief discussion of any prior knowledge students have that might help them understand the selection.

> **Big Books** *offer all students opportunities to confirm and expand their knowledge about print and reading.*

- **Browse the Selection.** Explain to the class that browsing means to look through the pages of the story to get a general idea of what the story is about, to see what interests them, and to ask questions. Ask students to tell what they think the story might be about just from looking at the illustrations. This conversation should be brief so that students can move on to a prereading discussion of print awareness.

- **Develop Print Awareness.** The focus of browsing the **Big Books** is to develop awareness of print. Urge students to tell what words or letters they recognize rather than what they expect the selection to be about.

  To develop print awareness, have students look through the selection page by page and to comment on whatever they notice in the text. Some students may know some of the words, while others may recognize only specific letters or sounds. The key is to get students to look at the print separately from the illustrations even before they have heard the actual text content. This process isolates print awareness so that it is not influenced by content. It also gives you a clearer idea of what your students do or do not know about print.

- **Read Aloud.** Read the selection aloud expressively, using intonation and pauses at punctuation. Not only does this enable students to hear and enjoy the text as it is read through once, it serves as an early model for fluency. Good fluency and expression support comprehension. As you read, you will stop periodically to model behaviors and comprehension strategies that all students will need to develop to become successful readers—for example, asking questions; clarifying unfamiliar words, first by using the pictures and later by using context; or predicting what might happen next.

- **Reread.** Read the selection expressively again. During the second reading of the stories, you will focus on teaching comprehension skills. Also, to develop print awareness, point to each word as it is read, thus demonstrating that text proceeds from left to right and from top to bottom and helping advance the idea that words are individual spoken and written units. Invite students to identify the rhyming words in a poem or to chime in on repetitive parts of text as you point to the words. Or students can read with you on this second reading, depending on the text. As students' knowledge of words and phonics grows, they can participate in decoding words and reading high-frequency sight words.

✦ **Discuss Print.** Return to print awareness by encouraging discussion of anything students noticed about the words. Young students should begin to realize that you are reading separate words that are separated by spaces. Later, students will begin to see that each word is made of a group of letters. Students should be encouraged to discuss anything related to the print. For example, you might ask students to point to a word or to count the number of words on a line. Or you might connect the words to the illustrations by pointing to a word and saying it and then asking students to find a picture of that word.

✦ **Responding.** Responding to a selection is a way of insuring comprehension. Invite students to tell about the story by asking them what they like about the poem or story or calling on a student to explain in his or her own words what the poem or story tells about. Call on others to add to the telling as needed. For nonfiction selections, this discussion might include asking students what they learned about the topic and what they thought was most interesting.

Tips for Using Big Books

✦ Make sure the entire group is able to see the book clearly while you are reading.

✦ If some students are able to read words, encourage them to do so during the rereading.

✦ Encourage students to use their knowledge of print.

✦ Encourage students' use of academic language as they talk about reading. Students should be comfortable using strategic reading words such as *predict* and *clarify* and book and print words such as *author* and *illustrator*.

✦ Allow students to look at the **Big Books** whenever they wish.

✦ Provide small versions of the **Big Books** for students to browse through and to try to read at their leisure.

✦ The reader of the **Big Book** should try to be part of the collaborative group of learners rather than the leader.

Strategic Reading

Purpose

Reading is a complex process that requires students not only to decode automatically and correctly what they read but also to understand and respond to it. The purpose of this section is to help you identify various reading behaviors used by good readers and to encourage those behaviors in your students.

Reading Behaviors and Comprehension Strategies

There are four basic behaviors that good readers engage in during reading: Setting Reading Goals and Expectations, Responding to Text, Checking Understanding, and Monitoring and Clarifying Unfamiliar Words and Passages. Engaging in these behaviors involves the application of certain comprehension strategies. These strategies are initially modeled while reading the **Big Books** (Level K and the first half of Level 1) and **Student Readers** (Levels 1–6). The goal of strategy instruction, however, is to ultimately turn over responsibility for using strategies to students so they set their own goals for reading, respond to text, and check their own understanding and solve problems while reading. Students need to take responsibility for doing the thinking and making sense of text.

Setting Reading Goals and Expectations

Good readers set reading goals and expectations before they begin reading. This behavior involves a variety of strategies that will help students prepare to read the text.

- **Activate prior knowledge.** When good readers approach a new text, they consider what they already know about the subject or what their experiences have been in reading similar material.

- **Browse the text.** To get an idea of what to expect from a text, good readers look at the title and the illustrations. They may look for potential problems, such as difficult words. When browsing a unit, have students glance quickly at each selection, looking briefly at the illustrations and the print. Have them tell what they think they might be learning about as they read the unit.

- **Decide what they expect from the text.** When reading for pleasure, good readers anticipate enjoying the story or the language. When reading to learn something, they ask themselves what they expect to find out.

Responding to Text

Good readers are active readers. They interact with text by using the following strategies:

- **Making connections.** Good readers make connections between what they read and what they already know. They pay attention to elements in the text that remind them of their own experiences. Readers make connections to personal experiences, to other stories they have read, and to world knowledge.

- **Visualizing, or picturing.** Good readers visualize what is happening in the text. They not only form mental images as they read but make inferences based on their own experiences. Visualizing goes beyond the words in text. They imagine the setting and the emotions it suggests, they picture the characters and their feelings, and they visualize the action in a story. When reading expository text, good readers picture the objects, processes, or events described. Visualizing helps readers understand descriptions of complex activities or processes.

- **Asking questions.** Good readers ask questions that may prepare them for what they will learn. If their questions are not answered in the text, they may try to find answers elsewhere and thus add even more to their store of knowledge.

- **Predicting.** Good readers predict what will happen next. When reading fiction, they make predictions about what they are reading and then confirm or revise those predictions as they go.

- **Thinking about how the text makes you feel.** Well-written fiction touches readers' emotions; it sparks ideas.

Checking Understanding

One of the most important behaviors good readers exhibit is the refusal to continue reading when something fails to make sense. Good readers continually assess their understanding of the text with strategies such as the following:

- **Interpreting.** As they read, good readers make inferences that help them understand and appreciate what they are reading.

- **Summarizing.** Good readers summarize to check their understanding as they read. Sometimes they reread to fill in gaps in their understanding.

- **Adjusting reading speed.** Good readers monitor their understanding of what they read. They slow down as they come to difficult words and passages. They speed up as they read easier passages.

Monitoring and Clarifying Unfamiliar Words and Passages

Monitoring understanding involves knowing when meaning is breaking down. The reader needs to stop and identify what the problem or source of confusion is. It might be an unfamiliar word, complex and hard-to-understand sentences or unfamiliar concepts that need clarifying. At the word level, the reader might

- apply decoding skills to sound out unknown words.

- apply context clues in text and illustrations to figure out the meanings of words.

- use structural elements to figure out the meaning of the word.

- ask someone the meaning of the word.

- reread the passage to make sure the passage makes sense.

- check a dictionary or the glossary to understand the meanings of words not clarified by clues or rereading.

Complex sentences may require the reader to look for the main idea in the sentence, to pull out clauses that may interfere with the main idea, or to ask for help. When faced with unfamiliar concepts, readers often ask for clarification from someone.

These cognitive activities engage the reader in thinking about text before, during, and after reading. Readers think about text before they read by activating background knowledge, anticipating content, setting purposes, and wondering about the text and what they will learn. During reading, the reader is constantly checking understanding—asking whether what is being read makes sense and constructing conclusions or summary statements. When the text is not making sense, the reader uses strategies to clarify words, ideas, and larger units of text or may reread more slowly for clarification. After reading, the reader reflects on what was read, connecting new information to prior knowledge, evaluating purposes, and connecting the relevance of the new information to the purpose.

Procedures

Modeling and Thinking Aloud

Modeling and encouraging students to think aloud as they attempt to understand text can demonstrate for everyone how reading behaviors are put into practice. Modeling and thinking aloud helps students learn how to process information and learn important content. It is more than asking students questions; it is letting students in on the thinking that helps readers make sense of text, solve problems while reading, and use strategies differentially and intentionally. The most effective models will be those that come from your own reading. As you model the different strategies, let students know what strategy you are using and why you are using it.

Model comprehension strategies in a natural way, and choose questions and comments that fit the text you are reading. Present a variety of ways to respond to text.

✦ Pose questions that you really do wonder about.

✦ Identify with characters by comparing them with yourself.

✦ React emotionally by showing joy, sadness, amusement, or surprise.

✦ Show empathy with or sympathy for characters.

✦ Relate the text to something that has happened to you or to something you already know.

✦ Show interest in the text ideas.

✦ Question the meaning or clarity of the author's words and ideas.

Encourage Students' Responses and Use of Strategies

Most students will typically remain silent as they try to figure out an unfamiliar word or a confusing passage. Encourage students to identify specifically with what they are having difficulty. When the problem has been identified, ask students to suggest a strategy for dealing with the problem. Remind students to

✦ treat problems encountered in text as interesting learning opportunities.

✦ think aloud about text challenges.

✦ help each other build meaning. Rather than tell what a word is, students should tell how they figured out the meanings of challenging words and passages.

✦ consider reading a selection again with a partner after reading it once alone. Partner reading provides valuable practice in reading for fluency.

✦ make as many connections as they can between what they are reading and what they already know.

✦ visualize to clarify meanings or enjoy descriptions.

✦ ask questions about what they are reading.

✦ notice how the text makes them feel.

In addition, using open-ended questions such as the following, as well as your students' questions and comments, will make both the text and the strategic reading process more meaningful to students.

✦ What kinds of things did you wonder about?

✦ What kinds of things surprised you?

✦ What new information did you learn?

✦ What was confusing until you reread or read further?

Discussion

The more students are able to discuss what they are learning, to voice their confusions, and to compare perceptions of what they are learning, the deeper and more meaningful their learning becomes.

Purpose

Through discussions, students are exposed to points of view different from their own and learn how to express their thoughts and opinions coherently. Through discussion, students add to their own knowledge that of their classmates and learn to explain themselves coherently. They also begin to ask insightful questions that help them better understand what they have read and all that they are learning through their inquiry/research and explorations. The purpose of classroom discussion is to provide a framework for learning.

Procedure

Reflecting on the Selection

After students have finished reading a selection, provide an opportunity for them to engage in discussion about the selection. Students should

✦ check to see whether the questions they asked before reading as part of Clues, Problems, and Wonderings and KWL (What I Know, What I Want to Know and What I Have Learned) have been answered. Encourage them to discuss whether any unanswered questions should still be answered. If unanswered questions are related to the theme, add those questions to the **Concept/Question Board.**

✦ discuss any new questions that have arisen because of the reading. Encourage students to decide which of these questions should go on the **Concept/Question Board.**

✦ share what they expected to learn from reading the selection and tell whether expectations were met.

✦ talk about whatever has come to mind while reading the selection. This discussion should be an informal sharing

of impressions of, or opinions about, the selection; it should never take on the aspects of a question-and-answer session about the selection.

✦ give students ample opportunity to ask questions and to share their thoughts about the selection. Participate as an active member of the group, making your own observations about information in a selection or modeling your own appreciation of a story. Be especially aware of unusual and interesting insights suggested by students so that these insights can be recognized and discussed. To help students learn to keep the discussion student-centered, have each student choose the next speaker instead of handing the discussion back to you.

> *The purpose of classroom discussion is to provide a framework for learning.*

Recording Ideas

As students finish discussions about their reactions to a selection, they should be encouraged to record their thoughts, feelings, reactions, and ideas about the selection or the subject of the selection in their Writer's Notebooks. This will not only help keep the selections fresh in students' minds; it will strengthen their writing abilities and help them learn how to write about their thoughts and feelings.

Students may find that the selection gave them ideas for their own writing, or it could have reminded them of some person or incident in their own lives. Perhaps the selection answered a question that has been on their minds or raised a question they had never thought before. Good, mature writers—especially professional writers—learn the value of recording such thoughts and impressions quickly before they fade. Students should be encouraged to do this also.

Handing Off

Handing off (Levels 1–6) is a method of turning over to students the primary responsibility for controlling discussion. Often, students who are taking responsibility for controlling a discussion tend to have all "turns" go through the teacher. The teacher is the one to whom attention is transferred when a speaker finishes, and the teacher is the one who is expected to call on the next speaker—the result being that the teacher remains the pivotal figure in the discussion.

Having students "hand off" the discussion to other students instead of the teacher encourages them to retain complete control of the discussion and to become more actively involved in the learning process. When a student finishes his or her comments, that student should choose (hand off the discussion to) the next speaker. In this way, students maintain a discussion without relying on the teacher to decide who speaks.

When handing off is in place, the teacher's main roles are to occasionally remind students to hand off, to help students when they get stuck, to encourage them to persevere on a specific point, and to get them back to a discussion, and to monitor the discussion to ensure that everyone gets a chance to contribute. The teacher may say, for example, "Remember, not just boys (or girls)." or "Try to choose someone who has not had a chance to talk yet." It is not unusual early in the process for students to roam from the topic and selection. To bring the discussion back to the topic and selection, be a participant, raise your hand, and ask a question or make a statement that refocuses students' thinking and discussion.

For handing off to work effectively, a seating arrangement that allows students to see one another is essential. It is hard to hold a discussion when students have their backs to each other. A circle or a semicircle is effective. In addition, all students need to have copies of the materials being discussed.

Actively encourage this handing-off process by letting students know that they, not you, are in control of the discussion.

If students want to remember thoughts about, or reactions to, a selection, suggest that they record these in the Response Journal section of their Writer's Notebooks.

Encourage students to record the thoughts, feelings, or reactions that are elicited by any reading they do.

Exploring Concepts within the Selection

To provide an opportunity for collaborative learning and to focus on the concepts, you may want to have students form small groups and spend time discussing what they have learned about the concepts from this selection. Topics may include new information that they have acquired, new ideas that they have had, or new questions that the selection raised.

Students should always base their discussions on postings from the **Concept/Question Board** as well as on previous discussions of the concept. The small-group discussions should be ongoing throughout the unit; during this time, students should continue to compare and contrast any new information with their previous ideas, opinions, and impressions about the concepts. How does this selection help confirm their ideas? How does it contradict their thinking? How has it changed their outlook?

As students discuss the concepts in small groups, circulate around the room to make sure that each group stays focused upon the selection and the concepts. After students have had some time to discuss the information and the ideas in the selection, encourage each group to formulate some statements about the concept that apply to the selection.

Sharing Ideas about Concepts

Have a representative from each group report and explain the group's ideas to the rest of the class. Then have the class formulate one or more general statements related to the unit concepts and write these statements on the **Concept/Question Board.** As students progress through the unit, they will gain more and more confidence in suggesting additions to the **Concept/Question Board.**

✦ **Visual Aids** During this part of the discussion, you may find it helpful to use visual aids to help students as they build the connections to the unit concepts. Not all units or concepts will lend themselves to this type of treatment; however, aids such as time lines, charts, graphs, and pictographs may help students see how each new selection adds to their growing knowledge of the concepts.

Encourage students to ask questions about the concepts that the selection may have raised. Have students list on the **Concept/Question Board** those questions that cannot be answered immediately and that they want to explore further.

> *Through discussions, students are exposed to points of view different from their own and learn how to express their thoughts and opinions coherently.*

Exploring Concepts across Selections

As each new selection is read, encourage students to discuss its connection with the other selections and with the unit concepts. Also encourage students to think about selections that they have read from other units and how they relate to the concepts for this unit.

Ultimately, this ability to make connections between past knowledge and new knowledge allows any learner to gain insights into what is being studied. The goal of the work with concepts and the discussions is to help students to start thinking in terms of connections—how is this like what I have learned before? Does this information confirm, contradict, or add

a completely different layer to that which I already know about this concept? How can the others in the class have such different ideas than I do when we just read the same selection? Why is so much written about this subject?

Learning to make connections and to delve deeper through self-generated questions and substantive discussions give students the tools they need to become effective, efficient, lifelong learners.

Tips

✦ Create an environment that facilitates discussion. Have students sit in circles or some other configuration so everyone can see each other.

✦ When students are discussing the selection, they should have their books with them, and students should feel free to refer to them throughout the discussion.

✦ Discussions offer a prime opportunity for you to introduce, or seed, new ideas about the concepts. New ideas can come from a variety of sources: Students may draw on their own experiences or on the books or videos they are studying; you may introduce new ideas into the discussion; or you may at times invite experts to speak to the class.

✦ If students do not mention an important idea that is necessary to the understanding of some larger issue, you may "drop" that idea into the conversation and, indeed, repeat it several times to make sure that it does get picked up. This seeding may be subtle ("I think that might be important here") or quite direct ("This is a big idea, one that we will definitely need to understand and one that we will return to regularly").

✦ To facilitate this process for each unit, you must be aware of the unit concepts and be able to recognize and reinforce them when they arise spontaneously in discussions. If central unit concepts do not arise naturally, then, and only then, will you seed these ideas by direct modeling. The more you turn over discussions to students, the more involved they will become, and the more responsibility they will take for their own learning. Make it your goal to become a participant in, rather than the leader of, class discussions.

✦ Help students see that they are responsible for carrying on the discussion. After a question is asked, always wait instead of jumping in with a comment or an explanation. Although this wait time may be uncomfortable at first, students will come to understand that the discussion is their responsibility and that you will not jump in every time there is a hesitation.

✦ As the year progresses, students will become more and more adept at conducting and participating in meaningful discussions about what they have read. These discussions will greatly enhance students' understanding of the concepts that they are exploring.

Discussion Starters and Questions

The following examples of discussion starters can be modeled initially, but then the responsibility for using them should be turned over to students. The starters provide the opportunity for open-ended discussions by students.

✦ I didn't know that . . . .

✦ Does anyone know . . . .

✦ I figured out that . . . .

✦ I liked the part where . . . .

✦ I'm still confused about . . . .

✦ This made me think . . . .

✦ I agree with _____ because . . . .

✦ I disagree with _____ because . . . .

✦ The reason I think _____ is . . .

✦ I found _____ interesting because . . . .

✦ I learned . . .

✦ What I learned in this selection reminds me of what we read in _____ because . . .

✦ This author's writing reminds me of . . .

✦ I had problems understanding _____ because . . .

✦ I wonder why the author chose to . . .

✦ I still do not understand . . .

✦ I was surprised to find out . . .

✦ I like the way the author developed the character by . . .

✦ The author made the story really come alive by . . .

In addition to these open-ended discussion starters, students should be encouraged to ask open-ended questions. When students ask questions, other students should respond to the question before moving on to another idea or topic. One student asking a question often helps to clarify something for the whole class and places a value on asking questions as a critical part of learning.

✦ Why did the author . . . ?

✦ What did the author mean when he or she wrote . . . ?

✦ Who can help me clarify . . . ?

✦ Who can help me figure out . . . ?

✦ How does this piece connect to the unit theme?

✦ What does this section mean?

Writing

Purpose

The writing program in **SRA Imagine It!** teaches students how to write skillfully. This is essential, as writing is a powerful tool that fosters learning, communication, creativity, and self-discovery. **SRA Imagine It!** writing teaches students how to use writing effectively for these purposes.

Writing is a complex process. It involves deftly juggling a variety of skills, strategies, and knowledge. Writers must make plans, consider the reader, draw ideas from memory, develop new ideas, organize thoughts, consider the conventions of the genre, translate ideas into words, craft sentences, evaluate decisions, make needed revisions, transcribe words into correctly spelled print, and monitor the writing process, among other things.

SRA Imagine It! writing is designed to ensure that students acquire the skills, knowledge, strategies, and dispositions they need to become skilled writers. This includes the following:

✦ Knowledge about the qualities of good writing, characteristics of different genres, intended audience, and writing topics. Skilled writers know how to obtain information about their topics, are familiar with basic features of different genres, and possess basic schemas or frameworks for accomplishing common writing tasks.

✦ The writing strategies involved in basic composing processes such as prewriting, drafting, monitoring, evaluating, revising, editing/proofreading, and publishing. Skilled writers flexibly employ these strategies to create text.

✦ Command of basic writing skills such as handwriting, spelling, sentence construction, grammar, and usage. Skilled writers execute these basic writing skills with little conscious effort.

✦ Interest and motivation to write as well as perceptions of competence as a writer. Skilled writers possess an "I can do" attitude.

Procedures

With **SRA Imagine It!** writing, evidence-based practices are used to teach students to write skillfully. These evidence-based practices are drawn from research on the effectiveness of specific writing interventions that show that the quality of students' writing can be improved by

✦ explicitly teaching strategies for prewriting, drafting, revising, editing/proofreading, and publishing.

✦ modeling effective use of writing strategies.

> *Children start school wanting to learn how to write and enjoying writing. The goal of **SRA Imagine It!** writing is for children to become lifelong writers—people who enjoy writing and use writing effectively at work as well as in their personal lives.*

✦ having students work together to prewrite, draft, revise, edit/proofread, and publish their compositions.

✦ using prewriting tools such as graphic organizers to gather information.

✦ involving students in inquiry activities designed to help them further develop their ideas for writing.

✦ making the goals for writing assignments clear and specific.

✦ teaching students how to construct more sophisticated sentences.

✦ providing students with the opportunity to read, evaluate, and emulate models of good writing.

✦ teaching students how to use word processing as a tool for composing.

The evidence-based practices in **SRA Imagine It!** are also based on the study of expert teachers who

✦ make sure their students are engaged, spending most of their writing time doing something that involves thoughtfulness, such as crafting a story or learning how to construct a complex sentence.

✦ teach basic writing skills, strategies, and knowledge balanced by ample opportunity to apply what is learned.

✦ involve students in writing for a variety of different purposes.

✦ create a writing classroom environment that is supportive, pleasant, and motivating.

✦ encourage students to accomplish as much as possible on their own (to act in a self-regulated fashion), but who are ready to offer support and instruction as needed.

✦ use reading to support writing development and vice versa.

✦ monitor students' growth in writing and encourage students to monitor their own growth.

✦ provide extra assistance to students who experience difficulty.

✦ are passionate about writing.

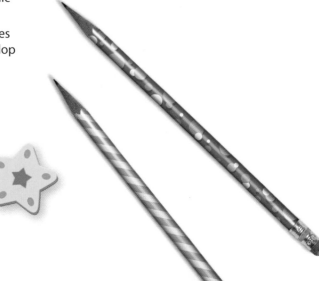

Knowledge about Writing

Purpose

Writing can be used to communicate, entertain, inform, reflect, persuade, and learn. To take full advantage of this flexible tool, students must acquire knowledge about the qualities of good writing and the various purposes and forms of writing. They must also carefully consider their audience and be knowledgeable about the topics they write about.

Procedures

Qualities of Good Writing

One way students learn about the qualities of good writing is by directly teaching them that good writing is characterized by the following seven traits:

- Clearly presented and fully developed ideas
- Writing that is easy to follow and logically organized
- Effective and precise word choice
- Varied use of sentence structure to promote fluency, rhythm, and natural speech patterns
- Writing that captures appropriate tone or mood to make the desired impact on the reader
- Correct spelling, usage, and grammar
- A written product that is legible, attractive, and accessible

For each writing assignment, teachers concentrate on one or more of these traits, teaching students strategies for enhancing the trait(s) in their writing. For example, students are taught to circle words that are vague in their writing and to replace them with more precise ones.

Another way that students learn about the qualities of good writing is through reading. The reading material in *SRA Imagine It!* provides concrete models that illustrate the characteristics of good writing, such as how authors

- present, develop, and organize ideas.
- use words to evoke specific images and feelings.
- manipulate sentences to speed up or slow down the flow of text.

- set and change the mood to match the action of the characters.
- use illustrations to reinforce and sharpen readers' understanding.

This knowledge is fostered in *SRA Imagine It!* through Reading with a Writer's Eye. Teachers and students discuss what the author of a reading selection did to achieve certain purposes. For example, after reading a mystery, the class discusses how the author planted a false lead to make the story more interesting and complex. Students are then encouraged to use the same technique in a mystery they write.

Different Purposes and Forms of Writing

Students learn the purposes and forms of a wide range of genres they need to master for success both in and out of school. This includes using writing to do the following:

- Communicate with others (personal letters, business letters, notes, cards, and e-mail)
- Create personal narratives (journal writing, autobiography, writing about a personal event, and so on)
- Entertain (stories, plays, poems, and so on)
- Learn (learning logs, reports, journal entries, summarizing, and biographies)
- Inform (writing lists, explaining how to do something, describing objects or places, describing events, news reports, reports, and biographies)
- Respond to literature (book evaluations, book reports, and book reviews)
- Persuade (advertisements, opinions about controversial topics)
- Demonstrate knowledge (for example, traditional classroom tests, high-stakes tests involving writing, high-stakes tests involving multiple-choice answers)

In *SRA Imagine It!* writing, students learn to write stories, poetry, plays, journal entries, summaries, book reviews, informative reports, descriptions, explanations, letters, critiques, and e-mail. They also use these various forms of writing to gather, think about, and report what they have learned when doing extended Inquiry projects.

One way they learn about the purposes and forms of these various genres is through the use of models of each type of writing. As students begin working on a new genre, the class analyzes an exemplary

model of this type of writing to determine its characteristics and functions. They are encouraged to incorporate these features in their writing. In addition, what they write is frequently tied to what they read, so their reading material provides a model and source of information on the purpose and form of their writing.

Students are also asked to carefully consider the purpose for each of their compositions and include this determination as part of the planning process. As they plan, the form and purpose of their compositions is further emphasized through the use of graphic organizers, in which students typically generate and organize ideas for each of the basic elements included in the type of composition they are composing.

Knowledge of Writing Topics

To write well, students must have something to write about. Good writers typically know a lot about their topics or have strategies for acquiring such information. With *SRA Imagine It!* writing, students are taught effective strategies for gathering information to write about. This includes how to

- locate information in written and electronic sources.
- obtain information through interviews or surveys.
- summarize information in notes.
- reference informational sources.

Developing a Sense of Audience

While writing is often viewed as a solitary activity, it is typically meant to be read by others. Children and adults most often use writing to communicate, persuade, or inform others. Because the writer is usually not present when the composition is read, he or she must carefully consider the needs of the readers. *SRA Imagine It!* writing helps students develop a sense of audience by asking them to identify their audience when they write collaboratively or independently. Students are also encouraged to share what they write with their peers and others. The following are procedures for presenting and sharing:

- Before presenting, have the writer
  - decide what will be shared.
  - practice what will be shared.
- During presenting,
  - have the writer tell what is to be shared and why.

- have the writer read aloud his or her work or idea.
- remind students to listen carefully.

✦ After presenting,
  - have students tell what they like.
  - have students offer the writer helpful suggestions.
  - take notes of students' comments to share with the writer.

Tips

✦ Have students keep a log of new information they have learned about the attributes of good writing.

✦ Develop wall charts that specify the purpose and attributes of specific writing genres.

✦ Ask students to evaluate their writing and the writing of others based on seven traits of good writing.

✦ Before students begin work on a writing assignment, hold a class discussion on the topic to share information, clarify misperceptions, and identify information students still need to locate.

Mastering the Writing Process

Purpose

To write skillfully, young writers must master the basic processes involved in writing. These processes include the strategic "know-how" involved in writing and include the following:

✦ **Prewriting:** Writers spend time thinking about and planning their topics. They consider their purposes, audience, and the focus of their topics. Writers make plans to guide the composing process, establishing goals for what to do and say. They gather possible ideas for their writing, drawing on memory and external sources such as books, interviews, articles, and the Internet. Writers make decisions about which information to include and how to organize it.

✦ **Drafting:** Writers draft or put their ideas into words, using the initial plans they developed as a guide. These plans are expanded, modified, and even reworked as writers create a first draft of their composition, often in a rough form.

✦ **Revising:** While some revising may occur during prewriting and drafting, writers revisit and revise their first drafts. They reread them to see whether the drafts say what the writers intended. Writers check to be sure the drafts make sense and that the meaning is clear for the audience. They consider whether their writing will have the desired impact on the audience. As they make changes in their text, they discover new things to say and new ways to present their ideas.

> *Writers need feedback throughout the writing process. Feedback is one of our most powerful tools for helping developing writers.*

✦ **Editing/Proofreading:** Writers edit/proofread their work. They recognize that spelling, grammar, and usage errors make it harder for others to understand and enjoy their published work. Writers know that readers are more likely to value their message when they correct these mistakes.

✦ **Publishing:** Writers share their writing by reading their entire work, or part of their work, to others. They publish their work in books, newspapers, magazines, anthologies, and so on.

Skilled writers move back and forth through these processes—from prewriting to drafting to revising and back—to create their final pieces.

Procedures

Much of what happens during writing is not visible. It occurs inside the writer's head. *SRA Imagine It!* writing makes the processes involved in writing concrete and visible in the following four ways:

✦ Establishing a predictable writing routine during which students are expected to prewrite, draft, revise, edit/proofread, and publish.

✦ Using graphic organizers and revising, editing/proofreading, and publishing checklists that help developing writers carry out basic writing processes.

✦ Teaching strategies for prewriting, drafting, revising, editing/proofreading, and publishing.

✦ Providing feedback throughout the writing process through writing conferences and students' presentation of their works in progress and completed compositions.

Establishing a Predictable Writing Routine

One way to make the basic writing processes more concrete is to create a predictable classroom writing routine, during which students plan, draft, revise, edit, proofread, and publish their work. This establishes that these processes are important and ensures that time is provided for each process. It also allows students to work with minimum teacher direction and at their own pace.

Tips

✦ Guide students through the steps of the writing routine. Model each step of prewriting, drafting, revising, editing/proofreading, and publishing.

✦ Make sure students learn that the processes of writing do not always occur in the same order but are recursive. For example, revising may occur at any stage of the composing process. You should not only model this by showing how this is done, but the predictable routine should vary at times to reflect this flexibility.

Using Graphic Organizers and Revising, Editing/Proofreading, and Publishing Checklists

Graphic organizers and revising, editing/proofreading, and publishing checklists provide students with assistance in carrying out the thinking activities involved in a writing assignment. They provide structure and information for how to carry out the process. The graphic organizer typically includes a series of prompts that ask the student to think about the purpose for writing a particular piece and the intended audience. It also provides prompts designed to help the student generate and organize possible writing ideas. This frequently involves generating possible content for each part of the target composition. The revising, editing/proofreading, and publishing checklists direct students' attention to specific features or aspects of text that would be useful to consider while writing.

Tips

It is important to be sure that students understand how to use graphic organizers and revising, editing/proofreading, and publishing checklists. Be sure to

+ explain the purpose of the graphic organizer or revising, editing/ proofreading, and publishing checklist.

+ describe how students are to use the graphic organizer or revising, editing/ proofreading, and publishing checklist.

+ model aloud how to carry out the basic activities on the graphic organizer or revising, editing/proofreading, and publishing checklist.

+ make sure students understand each part of the graphic organizer or revising, editing/proofreading, and publishing checklist.

Teaching Strategies for Carrying Out Basic Writing Processes

A strategy involves a series of actions a writer undertakes to achieve a desired goal. In **SRA Imagine It!** students are taught strategies to help them carry out each of the basic writing processes—prewriting, drafting, revising, editing/proofreading, and publishing. Each strategy is also designed to enhance one or more of the seven traits of good writing. These include clearly presented and fully developed ideas; writing that is easy to follow and logically organized; effective and precise word choice; varied use of sentences to promote fluency, rhythm, and natural speech patterns; writing that captures appropriate tone or mood to make maximum impact on readers; correct spelling, usage, and grammar; and a written product that is legible, attractive, and accessible.

The goal is for students to be able to use the strategy independently and to make it part of their writing tool kit. The steps for teaching writing strategies are to

+ describe the strategy.

+ tell why the strategy is important.

+ tell students when they should use the strategy.

+ model how to use the strategy when writing, making your thoughts visible by saying aloud each thing you are doing and thinking.

+ make sure students understand why the strategy is important, when to apply it, and how to use it.

+ provide students with assistance in applying the strategy until they can do it on their own.

+ remind students to use the strategy when they write.

Tips

+ Ask students to evaluate their progress and how the strategy improved their writing.

+ Be enthusiastic about learning the strategy.

+ Establish the importance of effort in learning and using the strategy.

+ Provide opportunities for students to see how the strategy improves their writing.

+ Praise and reinforce students' use of the strategy.

+ Foster students' ownership of the strategy.

Providing Feedback through Conferencing and Presentation

Writers need feedback throughout the writing process. They need reactions to ideas, drafts, and revisions. Feedback is one of our most powerful tools for helping developing writers. Writers want to know how their works-in-progress sound to someone else, whether their compositions make sense, whether they contain any incorrect or misleading information, and where and how to make changes.

Regular feedback encourages developing writers to solve problems and make meaningful changes throughout the writing process.

One way of providing feedback is through conferences. Teachers may initiate conferences, but students should also be encouraged to call conferences on an as-needed basis. Because conferences can be held at various times throughout the writing process, the focus will vary. Conferences held during the early stages of the writing process help students identify and refine a topic or identify research references. During the revision process, conferences help students

learn to elaborate and reorganize their writing. During the final stages, students learn to edit and proofread stories before they are published. Conferences offer an excellent opportunity for the teacher and student to evaluate jointly the student's progress and set goals for future growth.

The basic procedures for writing conferences are as follows:

+ Have the student read aloud his or her work.

+ Review any feedback the student has received so far.

+ Identify positive elements of the work.

+ Use one or more of these strategies to help the student improve his or her work.

  · Have the student explain how he or she got his or her ideas.

  · Have the student think aloud about how he or she will address the feedback he or she has received.

  · Ask the student to help you understand any confusion you may have about his or her writing.

  · Have the student add, delete, or rearrange something in the work, and ask how it affects the entire piece.

  · Think aloud while you do a part of what the student was asked to do. Then ask the student to compare what you did to what he or she did.

  · Have the student prescribe as if to a younger student how to revise the work.

+ Ask two or three questions to guide the student through revising (see below).

+ Conclude the conference by having the student state his or her plan for continuing work on the piece of writing.

Tips

+ Set aside a special area of the classroom for you to work with students or for students to work with each other.

+ You don't have to meet with every student every day.

+ Conferences should be brief; don't overwhelm students with too many comments or suggestions. Several short conferences are often more effective than one long one.

+ If appropriate, suggest that students take notes to help them remember where changes are to be made.

- Don't take ownership of the students' work. Encourage students to identify what is good and what needs to be changed, and let the students make the changes.
- Focus on what is good about the students' work; discuss how to solve problems rather than telling students what to do.
- Peer conferencing should be encouraged during Workshop.
- As students engage in peer conferencing, note which students are participating, the types of questions they ask, and the comments they make. Use this information to help students become more effective in peer conferencing.
- You may need to structure peer conferences by asking students to first explain what they liked about the composition, and then teaching them how to give constructive feedback.

Having students present or share their work provides another opportunity for them to receive feedback about their writing. Student presentations can involve

- presenting an initial idea or plan for a writing assignment.
- sharing a first draft of a paper.
- presenting orally part or all of a final piece of writing.

Tips

- Everyone must listen carefully and provide constructive feedback. Focus on what is good about a piece and ways to make it better.
- The student author has ownership and can decide which suggestions to use. The author does not have to incorporate all suggestions from the audience.
- Have a chair designated as the "Author's Chair" from which the student author can read his or her work or share ideas. This lends importance to the activity.
- The student author should be encouraged to give a bit of background, including where he or she is in the process, why he or she chose a particular part, or what problem he or she is having. This helps orient the audience.

- Short pieces of writing can be read in their entirety. As students become more proficient and write longer papers, they should be encouraged to read just a part of their writing; for example, a part they need help with, a part that has been revised, or a part they particularly like.
- Take notes during the presentations, and encourage older students to do the same.
- Be sensitive to the attention span of the class and the feedback being given. Students have a tendency to repeat the same comments to each author.

Word Processing and Other Aspects of Electronic Composing

Using a word processor to compose a piece of writing makes many aspects of the writing process easier. Text can easily be changed, deleted, or moved during drafting or revising. Software such as spell-checkers or word prediction provides assistance with basic writing skills. Information for writing can be obtained on-line or through other electronic sources, such as encyclopedias. Students can use publishing software to develop a more polished and attractive final product by adding pictures to their composition, developing a cover, changing fonts, and so on. *SRA Imagine It!* supports the use of these technologies.

Teaching Basic Writing Skills

Purpose

Young writers need to learn many basic writing skills to the point that the skills can be executed with minimal effort so they do not interfere with other writing processes. Correct handwriting, spelling, and grammar should be mastered to the point that they require little attention on the part of the writer. While sentences cannot and should not be constructed without conscious attention and effort, developing writers need to become familiar with different sentence types, and they need to become proficient at building them.

Procedures

Sentence Construction

SRA Imagine It! teaches sentence construction skills through the use of sentence frames, sentence expansion, and sentence combining.

- **Sentence Frames** With sentence frames, students are given part of a sentence and asked to generate the rest of it. For example, students can be taught to write a simple sentence, with a single subject and predicate, by giving them a frame containing the subject (The dog _____ _____.) and asking them to complete the sentence by telling what happened (The dog ran.).
- **Sentence Expansion** With sentence expansion, students are given a kernel sentence and asked to expand it by adding additional words. For example, students can be taught to make sentences more colorful by adding descriptive words to a kernel sentence: *Rewrite **The cat and dog like the toy** so the sentence tells more about the cat and dog and the toy — The big dog and gray cat like the fuzzy little toy.*
- **Sentence combining** With sentence combining, students learn how to combine two or more kernel sentences into a more complex single sentence. For example, you can lead students to produce sentences with relative clauses by combining the following two sentences:

  John will win the race.

  John is very fast. (who)

  John, who is very fast, will win the race.

When teaching sentence construction skills, the following three steps should be followed:

- Describe the skill, establish why it is important, and model how to use it.
- Provide students with assistance until they can apply the skill correctly and independently.
- Ask students to apply the skill when they write.

Tips

+ Use more than one method to teach a sentence construction skill.
+ Ask students to monitor how often they use the sentence construction skill.
+ Encourage students to set goals to use sentence construction skills in their writing.

Handwriting

Students need to develop both legible and fluent handwriting. An important aspect of meeting this goal is to teach them an efficient pattern for forming individual letters (both lowercase and uppercase letters). Effective teaching procedures include

+ modeling how to form the letter.
+ describing how the letter is similar to and different from other letters.
+ using visual cues, such as numbered arrows, as a guide to letter formation.
+ providing practice tracing, copying, and writing the letter from memory.
+ keeping instructional sessions short, with frequent review and practice.
+ asking students to identify or circle their best formed letter or letters.
+ encouraging students to correct or rewrite poorly formed letters.
+ monitoring students' practice to ensure that letters are formed correctly.
+ reinforcing students' successful efforts and providing corrective feedback as needed.

In addition to learning how to write the letters of the alphabet correctly, students must be able to produce them quickly. Fluency generally develops as a consequence of writing frequently, but it can also be fostered by having students copy short passages several times, and trying to write them a little faster each time.

Tips

+ Make sure that each student develops a comfortable and efficient pencil grip.
+ Encourage students to sit in an upright position, leaning slightly forward, as they write.
+ Show students how to place or position their papers when writing.

+ Implement appropriate procedures for left-handed writers, such as how to properly place or position their papers when writing.
+ Monitor students' handwriting, paying special attention to their instructional needs in letter formation, spacing, slant, alignment, size, and line quality.
+ Encourage students to make all final drafts of their papers neat and legible.

Spelling

Purpose

To become good spellers, students must learn to spell correctly and easily the words they are most likely to use when writing. They need to be able to generate and check plausible spellings for words whose spellings are uncertain. They also need to learn to use external sources such as spell-checkers to ensure correct spelling during writing. In **SRA Imagine It!** students are taught how to spell words they frequently use when writing as well as spelling patterns that help them spell untaught words.

Tips

+ Teach students an effective strategy for studying spelling words.
+ Reinforce the correct spelling of taught words in students' writing.
+ Have students build words from letters or letters and phonograms, for example, c - at.
+ Teach strategies for determining and checking the spelling of unknown words.
+ Model the use of correct spelling and how to correct spelling errors when you write in front of the class.
+ Encourage students to correct misspelled words in all final drafts of their writing.
+ Provide instruction and practice in proofreading.
+ Encourage students to use spell-checkers, dictionaries, and so on to determine the correct spelling of unknown words.

Grammar and Usage

Traditional methods of teaching grammar and usage skills are not effective. With such instruction, students are initially provided with an abstract definition, such as an adjective is a word that describes a noun or pronoun. This is often followed by asking students to practice applying the skill correctly without actually generating any textual material longer than a word or a phrase. For example, students might be asked to complete the following sentence: The _____ wagon rolled through the _____ town. It is not surprising that many students do not understand the rules they are taught or how to use them in their writing, because such instruction is abstract and decontextualized.

To make grammar instruction effective, **SRA Imagine It!** applies the following five principles. To make these principles concrete, the program illustrates each as it would apply to the rule for capitalizing the first letter in a person's name.

+ Grammar and usage skills need to be defined in a functional and concrete manner. The rule of capitalizing the first letter in a person's name can be introduced by writing a sentence with two or three familiar names on the board. With the students' help, identify each name in the sentence, and ask them what they notice about the first letter in each name—They are capital letters. Repeat this process with a second sentence, and then establish the "capitalization rule" with students' help.

+ As soon as the skill is functionally described or defined, establish why it is important—Capitalizing the first letter in a person's name makes the name stand out and shows respect for the person named. This is an important rule for writing.

+ Show students how to use the skill when writing. Generate a sentence using the names of students in the class, or have your students help you generate such a sentence. Write it on the board, capitalizing the first letter while simultaneously telling the class what you are doing.

◆ Provide students with guided practice in applying the skill when writing. Generate with the class another sentence that includes three of your students' names. Tell the class you will write the sentence on the board, but they will need to tell you when to capitalize a word. Next, have students work together in pairs to generate two sentences using names of their friends, capitalizing the first letter in each name. Provide support as needed. Finally, have each student generate one sentence of his or her own containing two names. Monitor to ensure that students capitalize the first letter in each name. Have them share their sentences with a peer.

◆ Ask students to apply the skill in their compositions. Have students look at one of the papers in their writing portfolio and correct any capitalization mistakes involving people's names. Remind students to capitalize people's names when writing and revising subsequent writing assignments.

Tips

◆ Ask students to correct other students' papers, focusing on specific grammar and usage rules and mistakes.

◆ Encourage students to read their papers aloud when revising. This will help them spot grammar and usage mistakes.

Fostering Motivation

Purpose

Children start school wanting to learn how to write and enjoying writing. Too quickly, however, many begin to view writing as a chore or something to be avoided. The goal of *SRA Imagine It!* writing is for children to become lifelong writers—people who enjoy writing and use writing effectively at work as well as in their personal lives.

Procedures

One way to foster an interest in writing is to have students write for real purposes and audiences. This includes having students identify why they are writing and what they hope to accomplish. Likewise, students need to share their writing with others. They are more likely to do their best writing when there is an audience. Students can share their plans, an initial draft, a portion of their

composition, or the completed paper with you, their peers, or other children or adults.

Students are also likely to give their best effort when the writing environment is supportive and pleasant. This can be accomplished by the following:

◆ Establishing clear rules for student behavior during the writing period. Keep the rules simple and reasonable in number and consistently reinforce them. Students are not likely to enjoy writing, or learn well, if the classroom environment is chaotic.

◆ Creating a low-risk environment in which students feel comfortable taking risks with their writing. This means being accepting and encouraging of students' efforts and encouraging them to act in the same manner. For example, make it a rule in your class that when someone shares his or her writing, the first thing that you or other students do is say what you liked most about it.

◆ Supporting students as they begin to apply the knowledge, skills, or strategies you teach them. This can include reteaching, providing hints and reminders, giving useful feedback, and initially helping students apply what was taught.

◆ Having students help each other as they plan, draft, revise, edit/proofread, and publish their work. This is most effective when the process of working together is structured. For instance, students are more likely to give good advice for revising if they are asked to focus on specific aspects of the composition, such as identifying places where the writing is unclear or more detail is needed.

◆ Celebrating student success by displaying their work. This can be done by prominently displaying student work in the classroom or in other places in the school. Students can also be asked to publish their work in a class or school newspaper or to read their compositions aloud to younger children, in other classes, or at a special event.

◆ Fostering an "I can do" attitude among your students. Consistently emphasize that the key to good writing is effort and the use of what they have learned.

◆ Setting a positive mood during writing time. Be enthusiastic about writing and what your students write.

Tips

◆ Allow students to make their own decisions and to accomplish as much on their own as possible.

◆ Increase students' ownership of a writing topic by allowing them to develop unique interpretations of the topic.

◆ Encourage students to take ownership of their writing. This includes allowing them to arrange a suitable writing environment, construct a personal plan for accomplishing the writing task, to work at their own pace when possible, and to decide what feedback from you and their peers is most pertinent for revising their writing.

◆ Look for opportunities to give students positive feedback about their work. Let them know when they have done something well in their writing.

◆ Encourage students to monitor their progress. For example, have students select their best writing to keep in a writing portfolio, identifying why they selected each piece.

◆ Show your students that you are a writer too. Share your writing with them. Talk about the various ways you use writing each day.

◆ Connect writing to students' lives and the world in general. Have them document the types of writing they do outside school. Develop a wall chart on which the class can identify how they use writing away from school.

◆ Provide incentives for writing at home. For example, have parents document that their child writes for twenty minutes at home a set number of nights for a month. Provide a special party for these children, allowing each one to select a book to keep from an array of books donated by parents or a sponsoring business partner.

Spelling Strategies

Spelling

Many people find English difficult, because English sound/spelling patterns seem to have hundreds of exceptions. The key to becoming a good speller, however, is not just memorization. The key is recognizing and internalizing English spelling patterns. Some people do this naturally as they read and develop large vocabularies. They intuitively recognize spelling patterns and apply them appropriately. Others need explicit and direct teaching of vocabulary and spelling strategies and spelling patterns before they develop spelling consciousness.

Purpose

Spelling is a fundamental skill in written communication. Although a writer may have wonderful ideas, he or she may find it difficult to communicate those ideas without spelling skills. Learning to spell requires much exposure to text and writing. For many it requires a methodical presentation of English spelling patterns.

English Spelling Patterns

A basic understanding of English spelling patterns will help provide efficient and effective spelling instruction. Just as the goal of phonics instruction is to enable students to read fluently, the goal of spelling instruction is to enable students to write fluently so they can concentrate on ideas rather than spelling.

Sound Patterns Many words are spelled the way they sound. Most consonants and short vowels are very regular. When a student learns the sound/spelling relationships, he or she has the key to spelling many words.

Structural Patterns Structural patterns are employed when adding endings to words. Examples of structural patterns include doubling the final consonant, adding -s or -es to form plurals, and dropping the final e before adding -ing, -ed, -er, or -est. Often these structural patterns are very regular in their application. Many students have little trouble learning these patterns.

Meaning Patterns Many spelling patterns in English are morphological; in other words, the meaning relationship is maintained regardless of how a sound may change. Prefixes, suffixes, and root words that retain their spellings regardless of how they are pronounced are further examples of meaning patterns.

Foreign Language Patterns Many English words are derived from foreign words and retain those language patterns. For example, kindergarten (German), boulevard (French), and ballet (French from Italian) are foreign-language patterns at work in English.

Developmental Stages of Spelling

The most important finding in spelling research in the past thirty years is that students learn to spell in a predictable developmental sequence, much as they learn to read. It appears to take the average student three to six years to progress through the developmental stages and emerge as a fairly competent, mature speller.

Prephonemic The first stage is the prephonemic stage, characterized by random letters arranged either in continuous lines or in wordlike clusters. Only the writer can "read" it, and it may be "read" differently on different days.

Semiphonemic As emergent readers learn that letters stand for sounds, they use particular letters specifically to represent the initial consonant sound and sometimes a few other very salient sounds. This marks the discovery of phonemic awareness that letters represent speech sounds in writing.

Phonemic When students can represent most of the sounds they hear in words, they have entered the phonemic stage of spelling. They spell what they hear, using everything they know about letter sounds, letter names, and familiar words. Many remedial spellers never develop beyond this stage and spell a word the way it sounds whenever they encounter a word they cannot spell.

Transitional or Within-Word Pattern As they are exposed to more difficult words, students discover that not all words are spelled as they sound. They learn that they must include silent letters, spell past tenses with -ed, include a vowel even in unstressed syllables, and remember how words look. The transitional stage represents the transition from primarily phonemic strategies to rule-bound spelling.

Derivational The derivational stage occurs as transitional spellers accumulate a large spelling vocabulary and gain control over affixes, contractions, homophones, and other meaning patterns. They discover that related or derived forms of words share spelling features even if they do not sound the same. As spellers gain control over these subtle word features and spell most words correctly, they become conventional spellers.

Procedures

The spelling lessons are organized around different spelling patterns, beginning with phonetic spelling patterns and progressing to other types of spelling patterns in a logical sequence. Word lists including words from the literature selection focus on the particular patterns in each lesson. In general, the sound patterns occur in the first units at each grade, followed by structural patterns, meaning patterns, and foreign-language patterns in the upper grade levels.

✦ As you begin each new spelling lesson, have students identify the spelling pattern and how it is like and different from other patterns.

✦ Give the pretest to help students focus on the lesson pattern.

✦ Have students proofread their own pretests immediately after the test, crossing out any misspellings and writing the correct spelling.

✦ Have them diagnose whether the errors they made were in the lesson pattern or in another part of the word. Help students determine where they made errors and what type of pattern they should work on to correct them.

✦ As students work through the spelling pages from *Skills Practice,* encourage them to practice the different spelling strategies in the exercises.

Sound Pattern Strategies

Pronunciation Strategy As students encounter an unknown word, have them say the word carefully to hear each sound. Encourage them to check the *Sound/Spelling Cards.* Then have them spell each sound. (/s/ + /i/ + /t/: sit). This strategy builds directly on the Dication and Spelling introduced in kindergarten and taught in Levels 1–3.

Consonant Substitution Have students switch consonants. The vowel spelling usually remains the same. (bat, hat, rat, flat, splat) This is a natural extension of Phonemic Awareness activities begun in prekindergarten and kindergarten.

Vowel Substitution Have students switch vowels. The consonant spellings usually remain the same. (CVC: hit, hat, hut, hot; CVCV: mane, mine; CVVC: boat, beat, bait, beet) This is a natural extension of Phonemic Awareness activities begun in prekindergarten and kindergarten.

Rhyming Word Strategy   Have students think of rhyming words and the rhymes that spell a particular sound. Often the sound will be spelled the same way in another word. (cub, tub, rub) This is a natural extension of Phonemic Awareness activities begun in prekindergarten and kindergarten.

Structural Pattern Strategies

Conventions Strategy   Have students learn the rules and exceptions for adding endings to words (dropping *y*, dropping *e*, doubling the final consonant, and so on).

Proofreading Strategy   Many spelling errors occur because of simple mistakes. Have students check their writing carefully and specifically for spelling.

Visualization Strategy   Have students think about how a word looks. Sometimes words "look" wrong because a wrong spelling pattern has been written. Have them double-check the spelling of any word that looks wrong.

Meaning Pattern Strategies

Family Strategy   When students are not sure of a spelling, have them think of how words from the same base word family are spelled. (critic, criticize, critical; sign, signal, signature; nation, national, nationality)

Meaning Strategy   Have students determine a homophone's meaning to make sure they are using the right word. Knowing prefixes, suffixes, and base words will also help.

Compound Word Strategy   Tell students to break apart a compound and to spell each word. Compounds may not follow convention rules for adding endings. (homework, nonetheless)

Foreign-Language Strategy   Have students think of foreign-language spellings that are different from English spelling patterns. (ballet, boulevard, sauerkraut)

Dictionary Strategy   Ask students to look up the word in a dictionary to make sure their spelling is correct. If they do not know how to spell a word, have them try a few different spellings and look them up to see which one is correct. (fotograph, photograph) Have students use the *Sound/Spelling Cards* to help them look up words. This develops a spelling consciousness.

Use the post test to determine understanding of the lesson spelling pattern and to identify any other spelling pattern problems. Encourage student understanding of spelling patterns and use of spelling strategies in all their writing to help transfer spelling skills to writing.

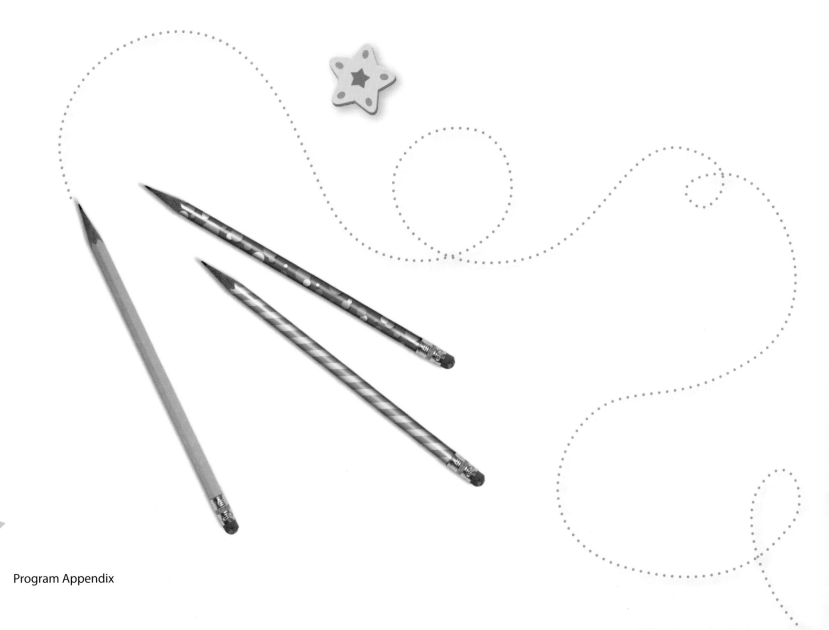

Grammar, Usage, and Mechanics

Purpose

The Study of English Conventions

Over the years the study of grammar, usage, and mechanics has gone in and out of favor. In the past century much research has been done to demonstrate the effectiveness of traditional types of instruction in the conventions of English. Experience and research have shown that learning grammatical terms and completing grammar exercises have little effect on the student's practical application of these skills in the context of speaking or writing. These skills, in and of themselves, do not play a significant role in the way students use language to generate and express their ideas—for example, during the prewriting and drafting phases of the writing process. In fact, emphasis on correct conventions has been shown to have a damaging effect when it is the sole focus of writing instruction. If students are evaluated only on the proper use of spelling, grammar, and punctuation, they tend to write fewer and less complex sentences.

Knowledge of English conventions is, however, vitally important in the editing and proofreading phases of the writing process. A paper riddled with mistakes in grammar, usage, or mechanics is quickly discounted. Many immature writers never revise or edit. They finish the last sentence and turn their papers in to the teacher. Mature writers employ their knowledge of English language conventions in the editing phase to refine and polish their ideas.

The study of grammar, usage, and mechanics is important for two reasons.

1. Educated people need to know and understand the structure of their language, which in large part defines their culture.

2. Knowledge of grammar gives teachers and students a common vocabulary for talking about language and makes discussions of writing tasks more efficient and clearer.

Procedure

The key issue in learning grammar, usage, and mechanics is how to do it. On the one hand, teaching these skills in isolation from writing has been shown to be ineffective and even detrimental if too much emphasis is placed on them. On the other hand, not teaching these skills and having students write without concern for conventions is equally ineffective. The answer is to teach the skills in a context that allows students to directly apply them to a reading or writing activity. Students should be taught proper use of punctuation or subject/verb agreement at the same time they are taught to proofread for those conventions. As they learn to apply their knowledge of conventions during the final stages of the writing process, they will begin to see that correcting errors is an editorial rather than a composition skill.

> *A paper riddled with mistakes in grammar, usage, or mechanics is quickly discounted.*

History of English

A basic understanding of the history and structure of the English language helps students understand the rich but complex resource they have for writing.

Old English

The English language began about A.D. 450 when the Angles, Jutes, and Saxons––three tribes that lived in northern Europe–– invaded the British Isles. Much of their language included words that had to do with farming (*sheep, dirt, tree, earth*). Many of their words are the most frequently used words in the English language today. Because of Latin influences, English became the first of the European languages to be written.

Middle English

In 1066 William the Conqueror invaded England and brought Norman French with him. Slowly Old English and Norman French came together, and Middle English began to appear. Today forty percent of Modern English comes from French. With the introduction of the printing press, English became more widespread.

Modern English

With the Renaissance and its rediscovery of classical Greek and Latin, many new words were created from Greek and Latin word elements. This continued intensively during the Early Modern English period. This rich language was used in the writings of Shakespeare and his contemporaries and profoundly influenced the nature and vocabulary of English. With dictionaries and spelling books, the English language became more standardized, although it continues to be influenced by other languages and new words and trends. These influences continue to make English a living, dynamic language.

Punctuation

Early writing had no punctuation or even spaces between words. English punctuation had its beginning in ancient Greece and Rome. Early punctuation reflected speaking rather than reading. By the end of the eighteenth century, after the invention of printing, most of the rules for punctuation were established, although they were not the same in all languages.

The Structure of English

Grammar is the sound, structure, and meaning system of language. People who speak the same language are able to communicate because they intuitively know the grammar system of that language, the rules to make meaning. All languages have grammar, and yet each language has its own grammar.

Traditional grammar study usually involves two areas:

✦ **Parts of speech** (nouns, verbs, adjectives, adverbs, pronouns, prepositions, conjunctions) are typically considered the content of grammar. The parts of speech involve the form of English words.

✦ **Sentence structure** (subjects, predicates, objects, clauses, phrases) is also included in grammar study. Sentence structure involves the function of English.

Mechanics involves the conventions of punctuation and capitalization. Punctuation helps readers understand writers' messages. Proper punctuation involves marking off sentences according to grammatical structure. In speech students can produce sentences as easily and unconsciously as they can walk, but in writing they must think about what is and what is not a sentence.

In English there are about fourteen punctuation marks (period, comma, quotation mark, question mark, exclamation point, colon, semicolon, apostrophe, hyphen, ellipsis, parenthesis, bracket, dash, and underscore). Most immature writers use only three: period, comma, and question mark. The experienced writer or poet with the command of punctuation adds both flexibility and meaning to his or her sentences through his or her use of punctuation.

Usage is the way in which we speak in a given community. Language varies over time, across national and geographical boundaries, by gender, across age groups, and by socioeconomic status. When the variation occurs within a given language, the different versions of the same language are called dialects. Every language has a prestige dialect associated with education and financial success. In the United States,

this dialect is known as Standard English and is the language of school and business.

Usage involves the word choices people make when speaking certain dialects. Word choices that are perfectly acceptable in conversation among friends may be unacceptable in writing. Usage is often the most obvious indicator of the difference between conversation and composition. Errors in word usage can make a writer seem ignorant and thus jeopardize his or her credibility, no matter how valid or important his or her overall message might be. Usage depends on a student's cultural and linguistic heritage. If the dialect students have learned is not the formal language of school settings or if it is not English, students must master another dialect or language in order to write Standard English.

The Grammar, Usage, and Mechanics lessons in **SRA Imagine It!** are structured to focus on skills presented in a logical sequence. A skill is introduced with appropriate models and then practiced in reading and writing on subsequent days to ensure that skills are not taught in isolation. Encourage students to use the focused English language convention presented in each lesson as they complete each Writing Process Strategies activity. Also encourage them to reread their writing, checking for proper use of the conventions taught. With practice, students should be able to apply their knowledge of conventions to any writing they do.

Tips

✦ Some of the errors students make in writing are the result simply of not carefully reading their final drafts. Many errors occur because the writer's train of thought was interrupted and a sentence is not complete or a word is skipped. These may look like huge errors that a simple rereading can remedy. Most

often the writer can correct these types of errors on his or her own. A major emphasis of any English composition program should be to teach the editing and proofreading phases of the writing process so students can eliminate these types of errors themselves. This involves a shift in perception—from thinking of grammar as a set of discrete skills that involve mastery of individual rules to understanding grammar as it applies to the act of communicating in writing.

✦ As students learn English language conventions, they should be expected to incorporate them into their written work.

✦ Sometimes, students write sentences that raise grammatically complex problems that require a deep understanding of English grammar. Use the Sentence Lifting strategies outlined in the Proofreading part of the Appendix to identify and discuss these more sophisticated types of errors that can include the following:

✦ **Faulty Parallelism.** Parts of a sentence parallel in meaning are not parallel in structure.

✦ **Nonsequiturs.** A statement does not follow logically from something said previously.

✦ **Dangling Modifiers.** A phrase or clause does not logically modify the word next to it.

✦ **Awkwardness.** Sentences are not written simply.

✦ **Wordiness.** Thoughts are not written in as few words as possible. Precise words are not used.

Listening/Speaking/Viewing

Some people are naturally good listeners, and others have no trouble speaking in front of groups. Many people, however, need explicit instruction on how to tune in for important details and how to organize and make an oral presentation. While some people naturally critique what they read, hear, and see, many others need specific guidance to develop skills for analyzing what they encounter in images and the media. The abilities to listen appropriately and to speak in conversations and in groups, as well as to critically evaluate the information with which they are presented, are fundamental skills that will serve students throughout their lives.

Purpose

In addition to reading and writing, listening, speaking, and viewing complete the language arts picture. Through the development of these language arts skills, students gain flexibility in communicating orally, visually, and in writing. When speaking and listening skills are neglected, many students have difficulty speaking in front of groups, organizing a speech, or distinguishing important information they hear. A top anxiety for many adults is speaking in front of groups. Much of this anxiety would not exist if listening, speaking, and viewing skills were taught from the early years.

The Listening/Speaking/Viewing instruction focuses on the literature selection or the Writing Process Strategies to provide context, to reinforce other elements of the lesson, and to integrate the other language arts. Many of the listening, speaking, and viewing skills are very similar to reading or writing skills. For example, listening for details is the same type of skill as reading for details. Preparing an oral report employs many of the same skills as preparing a written report. Learning to use these skills effectively gives students flexibility in how they approach a task. Furthermore, listening and speaking are naturally integrated into all aspects of learning as students listen and respond to each other during discussions, writing, and Inquiry.

Procedure

Listening, speaking, and viewing skills are presented with increasing sophistication throughout every grade level of **SRA Imagine It!** in the Language Arts part of each lesson. Every unit includes at least one lesson on each of the following skills so that students encounter the skills again and again throughout a grade level:

+ **Listening.** Listening skills include comprehending what one hears and listening for different purposes, such as to identify sequence or details, to summarize or draw conclusions, or to follow directions.

+ **Speaking.** Speaking skills include speaking formally and conversationally, using appropriate volume, giving oral presentations, and using effective grammar. Speaking skills also include using descriptive words, figurative language, and formal and informal language.

+ **Viewing.** Viewing skills include comprehending main ideas and messages in images, mass media, and other multimedia.

+ **Interaction.** Interaction instruction focuses on a combination of listening and speaking skills. These include asking and responding to questions; nonverbal cues such as eye contact, facial expression, and posture; and contributing to and interacting in group settings.

+ **Presenting Information.** The last Listening/Speaking/Viewing lesson in every unit usually focuses on presentation skills. These include sharing ideas, relating experiences or stories, organizing information, and preparing for speeches. These lessons often parallel the Writing Process Strategies instruction so that students can prepare their information in written or oral form. These skills are an integral part of the Inquiry process as students share their ideas, questions, conjectures, and findings.

Tips

+ Identify the parallels among the language arts skills: providing written and oral directions, telling or writing a narrative, and so on. Encourage students to see that they have choices for communicating. Discuss the similarities and differences between different forms of communication, and determine whether one is preferable in a given situation.

+ Ensure that all students have opportunities to speak in small groups and whole-class situations.

+ Provide and teach students to allow appropriate wait time before someone answers a question.

+ Encourage students (when they are able) to take notes to help them remember what they heard so they can better respond.

+ Remind students to use visuals when appropriate in their presentations to support their presentations and to help keep the listeners' attention.

+ Set up simple class rules to show respect for the listener and speaker. These rules should be used during Inquiry or handing off or any time of the day and should foster respect for the speaker and listeners.

  - Students should speak in a voice loud and clear enough for everyone in the class to hear.

  - Students should raise their hands and not interrupt.

  - If someone asks a question, then the person who responds should address the question before going on to another idea or topic.

  - The speaker should look at the audience, and the audience should look at the speaker.

Inquiry

Even in elementary school, students can produce works of genuine research—research that seeks answers to real questions or solutions to real problems.

Inquiry—research, investigation, and exploration—forms the heart of the *SRA Imagine It!* program. To encourage students to understand how reading and writing are tools for learning that can enhance their lives and help them become mature, educated adults, they are asked in each unit to use the content they are learning in the unit as the basis for further inquiry, exploration, and research. The unit information is simply the base for their investigations.

There are two types of units in the *SRA Imagine It!* program—units based on universal topics of interest such as friendship, heritage, and courage and content units that provide students a very solid base of information upon which they can begin their own inquiry and research. Units delving into science-related areas such as camouflage, energy, and ecology or into social studies units that address American history, geography, or money invite students to become true researchers by exploring personal areas of interest driven by problems or questions raised by students. Based upon common areas of interest, students conduct Inquiry in small collaborative groups and then present their findings to their classmates. In this way, students recognize the importance of sharing knowledge and gain much more knowledge of the unit theme than they would have simply by reading the selections in the unit.

The selections in the units are organized so that each selection will add more information or a different perspective to students' growing bodies of knowledge.

Inquiry through Reflective Activities

Purpose

The units in *SRA Imagine It!* that deal with universal topics tend to be explored through reflective activities. These units—such as Courage, Friendship, and Risks and Consequences—are organized to help students expand—perhaps even change— their perspectives of familiar concepts. As they explore and discuss the concepts that emerge from reading selections related to each unit topic, students are involved in activities that extend their experiences and offer opportunities for reflection. Such activities include writing, drama, art, interviews, debates, and panel discussions. Students will choose the activities and presentation format best suited to explore or investigate their research questions. Throughout each unit, students may be involved in a single ongoing investigative activity, or they may participate in a number of different activities. They may choose to produce a final written project or a multimedia presentation. They will share with the rest of the class the new knowledge that they have gained from their investigations. Workshop provides an ideal time for students to work individually or in collaborative groups on their investigation and/or projects.

The Inquiry activities will be those of students' own choosing, thereby allowing them to explore the unit concepts more fully. They are free, of course, to make other choices or to devise activities of their own.

Procedure

Choosing an Area to Investigate

Students may work on activities alone, in pairs, or in small groups. They have the option of writing about or using other methods for presenting their findings to the entire group. Students should decide what concept-related question or problem they wish to explore. Generally, it is better for students to generate wonderings, questions, or problems after they have engaged in some discussion at the beginning of each unit. This should be done, however, before they have had a chance to consult source materials. The goal is to have students ask questions that will drive their inquiry. This approach is more likely to bring forth ideas that students actually wonder about or wish to understand. Students may also look at the questions posted on the **Concept/Question Board** or introduce fresh ideas inspired by material they have just finished reading.

Inquiry pairs or groups are developed based upon common areas of interest or common questions that appear on the **Concept/Question Board.** Students who share a common interest for inquiry should work together to develop a common question to explore. Some of students may need your assistance in deciding upon, or narrowing down, a question or a problem so that it can be explored more easily. A good way to model this process for students is to make webs for a few of your own ideas on the board and to narrow down these ideas to a workable question or problem.

Organizing the Group

After a question or a problem has been chosen, students may choose an activity that will help them investigate that problem or question. For example, if students in Grade 3 are exploring the question "What are the common characteristics that define friendship?" they may want to develop and conduct a survey of classmates, friends, and so on. To develop the survey, group participants may want to do some additional reading about friendship, explore resources on the Internet, and so on to have a sense of the kinds of questions to include in the survey. Students' next responsibility is to decide who is going to investigate which facet of the question or the problem (when they are conducting a literature search, for example) or who is going to perform which activity related to the particular reflective activity (when they are writing and performing an original playlet or puppet show, for example). Lastly, students need to decide how, or if, they want to present their findings. For instance, after conducting a literature search, some students may want to read and discuss passages from a book with a plot or theme that relates to a unit concept. Other students may prefer performing and discussing scenes from the book.

Deciding How to Investigate

The following suggestions may help you and your students choose ways in which to pursue their investigations. For units on universal topics that are more literary in nature, students may want to do one of the following activities to pursue answers to their questions.

✦ Conduct a literature search to pursue a question or a problem. Discussion or writing may follow.

- Write and produce an original playlet or puppet show based on situations related to the concepts.

- Play a role-playing game to work out a problem related to the concepts.

- Stage a panel discussion with audience participation on a question or problem.

- Hold a debate on an issue related to the concept.

- Write an advice column dealing with problems related to the concepts.

- Write a personal-experience story related to the concepts.

- Invite experts to class. Formulate questions to ask.

- Conduct an interview with someone on a subject related to the concepts.

- Produce and carry out a survey on an issue or a question related to the concept.

- Produce a picture or photo-essay about the concept.

You may want to post this list in the classroom so that groups have access to it as they decide what they want to investigate and how they want to proceed. Encourage students to explore other possibilities as well and to add these ideas to the list.

EXAMPLE: In the Heritage unit in Grade 5 of *SRA Imagine It!,* students read "In Two Worlds: A Yup'ik Eskimo Family." This selection is about how three generations of Eskimos living in Alaska near the Arctic strive to adopt the best of modern ways without abandoning their traditional values. During the class discussion, some students may note that Alice and Billy Rivers want their students to learn both the new and the old ways of living. As the discussion continues, many students may conclude from the story that the older generations hope that future generations will continue to value their roots and their cultural traditions. Students then relate this story to their own heritage. Some students may share information about their customs or traditions.

Students choose some reflective activities that will help them learn more about family heritage and that will answer some of their questions about the unit concepts. These questions may relate to the value of maintaining traditional customs and values versus. adopting contemporary ones. Other students may ask exploring questions related to how to maintain traditional

values in the face of contemporary changes. Some students may be interested in interviewing family members or close family friends about their cultural traditions and heritages or interviewing students in their class about their cultural heritage and then looking for commonalities and differences. These students review what they know about interviewing. They should proceed by performing the following:

- Researching examples of interviews to see what they might look like and how to build in space to write answers

- Preparing a list of questions to ask

- Preparing a list of subjects to interview, deciding how to record the interview (by audiotape, videotape, or taking notes)

- Contacting in advance the person(s) they want to interview

- Deciding whether to photograph the person and, if so, getting permission to do so in advance—collecting the equipment necessary for conducting the interview

- After they conduct the interviews, students decide how they wish to present the information that they have collected.

EXAMPLE: Another group of students in the same fifth-grade class may be more interested in planning a photo-essay about one family or about a neighborhood with many families belonging to a particular culture. These students may decide to reexamine "In Two Worlds" in terms of how the text and the photographs complement each other and what information is conveyed in each photograph. They may also decide to examine some photo-essays listed in the unit bibliography. These students will need to make some advance preparations as well. They should proceed by performing the following:

- Determining which neighborhood and which family or families to photograph

- Contacting in advance the persons to be interviewed and photographed

- Touring the neighborhood in advance of the photo shoot

- Making a list of questions to ask the family or families about their heritage or about their neighborhood

- Thinking about what information to include in their essay so that they can

determine what photographs to take

- Collecting the equipment necessary for conducting interviews and photographing subjects

After students collect the information and take photographs, they may write and organize the photo-essay and present it to the class. The teacher should remind students of the phases of the writing process and encourage them to plan, draft, revise, and edit/proofread their work until they are completely satisfied with it.

Not all questions on the **Concept/ Question Board** will be explored in depth. Throughout the unit, students can continue discussing family heritage and raising and posting new questions. The teacher should remind them that as they read further, they may think of additional ways to explore the unit concepts. Students should sign or initial their questions or ideas so that they can identify classmates with similar interests and exchange ideas with them. The teacher should encourage students to feel free to write an answer or a note on someone else's question or to consult the Board for ideas for their own explorations. From time to time, the teacher should post his or her own questions on the **Concept/Question Board.**

Tips

- The *Leveled Readers* contain books related to the unit concepts. Remind students that these are good sources of information and that they should consult them regularly—especially when they are investigating concept-related ideas and questions.

- Some students work better within a specified time frame. Whenever they are beginning a new activity, discuss with students a reasonable period of time within which they will be expected to complete their investigations. Post the completion date somewhere in the classroom so that students can refer to it and pace themselves accordingly. At first, you may have to help them determine a suitable deadline, but eventually they should be able to make this judgment on their own.

- Some teachers like to do the Inquiry for the first unit with a common question decided upon by the whole class. Then students break into small groups and work on different ways to explore the question. One group may do a literature search while another might conduct a survey. The end results in students sharing new knowledge that addresses the common research question.

Inquiry through Research

Purpose

Students come to school with a wealth of fascinating questions. Educators need to capitalize on this excitement for learning and natural curiosity. A classroom in which the teacher is the only person who asks the questions and defines the assignments, only correct answers are accepted, and students are not allowed to make errors and consider alternative possibilities to questions can quickly deaden this natural curiosity and enthusiasm. The purpose of the inquiry and research aspect of this program is to capitalize on students' questions and natural curiosity by using a framework or structure based upon the scientific method. This structure helps students ask questions and preserve the open-ended character of real research, which can lead to unexpected findings and to questions that were not originally considered.

The conventional approach to school research papers can be found, with minor variations, in countless textbooks and instructional resources. This approach consists of a series of steps such as the following: Select a topic or choose a topic from a list suggested by the teacher, narrow the topic to something of interest, collect materials, take notes, outline, and write. By following these steps, a student may produce a presentable paper, but the procedure does not constitute research in a meaningful sense. Indeed, this restrictive approach gives students a distorted notion of what research is about. We see students in universities and even in graduate schools still following this procedure when they do library research papers or literature reviews; we see their dismay when their professors regard such work as mere cutting and pasting and ask them where their original contribution is.

Elementary school students can produce works of genuine research—research that seeks answers to real questions or solutions to real problems—when they are provided the opportunity, taught how to ask good questions and develop conjectures, and work collaboratively to find information or data that will support or refute their conjecture. Being able to collect, analyze, and evaluate information are critical twenty-first century skills. In the adult world, as knowledgeable consumers, productive members of a sophisticated workforce, and lifelong learners, students will be expected to constantly identify problems, raise questions, analyze new information, and make informed decisions on the basis of this information. Preparing students for the analytic demands of adult life and teaching them how to find answers to their questions are goals of education.

Procedure

To make the research productive, the following important principles are embodied in this approach:

1. Research is focused on problems, not topics.

2. Questions and wonderings are the foundation for inquiry and research.

3. Conjectures—opinions based on less than complete evidence or proof—are derived from questions and guide the research; the research does not simply produce conjectures.

4. New information and data are gathered to test and revise conjectures.

5. Discussion, ongoing feedback, and constructive criticism are important in all phases of the research but especially in the revising of problems and conjectures.

6. The cycle of true research is essentially endless, although presentations of findings are made from time to time; new findings give rise to new problems and conjectures and thus to new cycles of research.

Following a Process

While working with the science and social studies units, students are encouraged to use this framework to keep their research activities focused and on track. Within this framework, there is flexibility. Students may begin with a question, develop a conjecture, and begin collecting information only to find that they need to redefine their conjecture. Like the writing process, there is a recursive nature to this framework. Students may go through these steps many times before they come to the end of their research. Certainly for adult researchers, this cycle of question, conjecture, research, and reevaluation can go on for years and, in some cases, lifetimes.

This cycle uses the following process:

1. Decide on a problem or question to research. Students should identify a question or problem that they truly wonder about or wish to understand and then form research groups with other students who have the same interests.
   - My problem or question is _____.

2. Formulate an idea or conjecture about the research problem. Students should think about and discuss with classmates possible answers to their research problems or questions and meet with their research groups to discuss and record their ideas or conjectures.
   - My idea/conjecture/theory about this question or problem is _____.

3. Identify needs and make plans. Students should identify knowledge needs related to their conjectures and meet with their research groups to determine which resources to consult and to make individual job assignments. Students should also meet periodically with the teacher, other classmates, and research groups to present preliminary findings and to make revisions to their problems and conjectures on the basis of these findings.
   - I need to find out _____.
   - To do this, I will need these resources: _____
   - My role in the group is _____.
   - This is what I have learned so far: _____
   - This is what happened when we presented our findings _____

4. Reevaluate the problem or question based on what we have learned so far and the feedback we have received.
   - My revised problem or question is _____.

5. Revise the idea or conjecture.
   - My new conjecture about this problem is _____.

6. Identify new needs and make new plans.
   - Based on what I found out, I still need to know _____.
   - To do this, I will need these resources: _____
   - This is what I have learned: _____
   - This is what happened when we presented our new findings: _____

Procedure for Choosing a Problem to Research

1. Discuss with students the nature of the unit. Explain to students that the

unit they are reading is a research unit and that they will produce and publish in some way the results of their explorations. They are free to decide what problems or questions they wish to explore, with whom they want to work, and how they want to present their finished products. They may publish a piece of writing, produce a poster, write and perform a play, or use any other means to present the results of their investigations and research. They may work individually, with partners, or in small groups.

2. Discuss with students the schedule you have planned for their investigations: how long the project is expected to take, how much time will be available for research, when the first presentation will be due. This schedule will partly determine the nature of the problems that students should be encouraged to work on and the depth of the inquiry students will be encouraged to pursue.

3. Have students talk about things they wonder about that are related to the unit subject. For example, in the Grade 3 unit Money, students might wonder where money in the money machine comes from or how prices are determined. Conduct a free-floating discussion of questions about the unit subject.

4. Brainstorm possible questions for students to think about. It is essential that students' own ideas and questions be the starting point of all inquiry. Helpful hint: For the first research unit, you might wish to generate a list of your own ideas, having students add to this list and having them choose from it.

5. Using their wonderings, model for students the difference between a research topic and a research problem or question by providing several examples. For example, have them consider the difference between the topic *California* and the problem *Why do so many people move to California?* Explain to them that if they choose to research the topic *California,* everything they look up under the subject heading or index entry *California* will be related in some way to their topic. Therefore, it will be quite difficult to choose which information to record. This excess of information also creates problems in organizing their research. Clearly, then, this topic is too broad and general. Choosing a specific question or problem, one that particularly interests them, helps them

narrow their exploration and advance their understanding. Some possible ideas for questions can be found in the unit introduction. Ideas can also be generated as you and your students create a web of their questions or problems related to the unit concept. For example, questions related to the topic *California* might include the following: Why do so many people move to California? How have the different groups of people living in California affected the state?

6. A good research problem or question not only requires students to consult a variety of sources but is engaging and adds to the groups' knowledge of the concepts. Furthermore, good problems generate more questions. Help students understand that the question *Why do so many people move to California?* is an easy one to research. Many sources will contribute to an answer to the question, and all information located can be easily evaluated in terms of usefulness in answering the question. Helpful hint: Students' initial responses may indeed be topics instead of problems or questions. If so, the following questions might be helpful: What aspect of the topic really interests you? Can you turn that idea into a question?

7. Remember that this initial problem or question serves only as a guide for research. As students begin collecting information and collaborating with classmates, their ideas will change, and they can revise their research problem or question. Frequently, students do not sufficiently revise their problems until after they have had time to consider their conjectures and to collect information.

8. As students begin formulating their research problems, have them elaborate on their reasons for wanting to research their stated problems. They should go beyond simple expressions of interest or liking and indicate what is puzzling, important, or potentially informative, and so forth about the problems they have chosen.

9. At this stage, students' ideas will be of a very vague and limited sort. The important thing is to start them thinking about what really interests them and what value it has to them and the class.

10. Have students present their proposed problems or questions, along with reasons for their choices, and have

an open discussion of how promising proposed problems are. As students present their proposed problems, ask them what new things they think they will be learning from their investigations and how that will add to the group's growing knowledge of the concepts. This constant emphasis on group knowledge building will help set a clear purpose for students' research.

11. Form research groups. To make it easier for students to form groups, they may record their problems on the board or on self-sticking notes. Final groups should be constituted in the way you find best for your class—by self-selection, by assignment on the basis of common interests, or by some combination of methods. Students can then meet during Workshop to agree on a precise statement of their research problem, the nature of their expected research contributions, and lists of related questions that may help later in assigning individual roles. They should also record any scheduling information that can be added to the planning calendar.

Using Technology

Students and teachers can access the Web site **www.SRAonline.com** to find information about the themes in their grade level.

What does Inquiry look like in the classroom?

Inquiry is a new concept for many students and is performed over an extended period of time. The following series of vignettes are an example of what Inquiry might look like in a third-grade classroom that is studying the third-grade unit Money.

Lesson 1

Developing questions

For the unit on money, Ms. Hernandes introduced the theme through "A New Coat for Anna" and now is focusing on having her students generate some questions. To maximize the number of resources available to her students to do their inquiry, she talked with the librarian at her local library as well as local high school teachers who are knowledgeable in the area. Both were able to provide resources for the class. Ms. Hernandes began with a discussion of money. She had prepared some basic questions to get the class started.

- Why do you think it is important to have a system of money like ours?
- What is money?
- Why do you think we have both paper money and coins?
- How have you learned about money?
- How would your life change if suddenly there were no money in the world?
- When people are using credit cards to pay for something, are they paying with real money?
- When someone writes a check, are they paying with real money?
- What is the difference between credit cards and checks and cash, or actual money?
- Why do you think people use credit cards and checks instead of cash?

The teacher felt that using open-ended questions like these would help get her students talking about what they know about money as well as give her an opportunity to informally assess students' background knowledge.

Students were able to provide some basic information such as the following:

- Money is used to buy things.
- There was not always money in the world.
- Some people used things such as animals instead of money.
- Sometimes people traded things to get something they wanted.
- Coins are made of metal.
- Some things cost more than other things.
- Sometimes you need to determine ways to get things when you do not have money.

But there were some basic misunderstandings that arose during the conversation, such as the following:

- All countries use dollars and cents.
- Everything costs the same no matter where you live.

- Money is made of paper.
- You can use credit cards whenever you want.

By discussing money in such general terms, students were able to share basic information.

To move students to the next level—asking questions—Ms. Hernandes began by thinking aloud about things related to the unit that interested her.

"I really am curious about how money is made. And another thing I've wondered about is how the government knows how much money to print." Ms. Hernandes encouraged her students to share some of their wonderings or things they are curious about. Some student wonderings included the following:

- What kind of money do people in other countries use?
- Does everyone make the same amount of money?
- What would happen if there were only credit cards and no money?
- How much money do people make?
- Does ripped money get thrown away?
- How come we cannot make our own money?

Lesson 2

Forming groups based on shared interest

Developing good research questions

Ms. Hernandes and her class have been reading about money for the past week. Many students read different trade books during Workshop to learn more about money. Every day at the end of Workshop, they shared some of their new questions. Some students even started bringing in articles from newspapers and magazines and posting them on the **Concept/Question Board.**

By now there are a number of questions on the **Concept/Question Board** and Ms. Hernandes wants to work with the class to generate more questions that will help students connect what they are learning in school to the real world. She began by modeling or thinking aloud and sharing some of her own thoughts: "I know that at the checkout stand in stores, you can buy plastic cards that have a dollar amount printed on them. I wonder how might this change our whole idea about money. Maybe instead of getting cash from the automatic

money machines, we'll get a coded card."

The focus is on asking questions. She recognized that students' questions needed to be refined to lead to functional conjectures. The class discussed what makes a good question.

- Questions or wonderings should be things that students are truly curious about.
- Questions should be generated without consulting an encyclopedia or a reference source.
- Good questions cannot be answered with a simple *yes* or *no.*
- Questions should help students deepen their understanding of the unit theme rather than focus on a character or incident in a specific story.
- A good research question often begins with *how.*

Ms. Hernandes and the class talked about their questions and how to refine them. For example, one question the class raised earlier was "Does money change?" The class decided to change the question to "How does money change over time?"

- What possible changes might we see in the future?
- Given the changes in technology today, how might our use of money change over time?

Based on the selections the class has read, students generated the following questions to add to their existing ones on the **Concept/Question Board:**

- I wonder when and how the government decided to change coins and bills.
- I wonder if the government can ever run out of money.
- What happens when people make fake money?
- How do people choose the metals they use to make coins?
- How can money be made so people cannot copy it or make counterfeits?
- What do other countries use for money?
- Where do you save money?

To help move students toward developing some good questions for inquiry, the class reviewed all the questions and grouped them together. They discussed these groups of questions and decided to think of a good representative question. The class worked over the next couple of days to think of a question they were all interested in.

Lesson 3

Forming Conjectures

Identifying Needs and Making Plans

A goal of Inquiry is to have students move from asking questions to forming conjectures. Ms. Hernandes explained to the class that they were now going to take their question and develop a conjecture. Developing a conjecture simply means thinking of what they think the best answer is, given what they know now and have read so far.

Ms. Hernandes modeled this by using one of the questions students raised in the earlier lesson. The question was "How do people choose the metals to make coins?" Ms. Hernandes thought aloud about possible answers to this question: "I think that people choose a strong metal that will last a long time but that is not too heavy for people to carry."

Then Ms. Hernandes wrote the question the class thought of last week. They discussed the question and talked about what possible answers they might find. The question the class decided to focus on was "How is money made so that people cannot copy it?"

The class conjecture was "Special paper and really detailed pictures are used so no one can copy it." However, Ms. Hernandes realized that there could be other conjectures for the same question. She arranged the class into small groups and had them think about other possible conjectures. Some additional conjectures included the following:

- Every dollar has a different number that is recorded in a computer.
- Special ink is used so colors cannot be duplicated.
- When you hold up a bill to the light, you can see a special band in it that maybe only a special government machine can make.

At the end of the lesson, Ms. Hernandes created a chart with the question and all the conjectures students developed.

During the week, Ms. Hernandes continued working with the class on Inquiry. To help the group get started on identifying needs and materials related to their conjecture, Ms. Hernandes asked the following questions:

- What information will we need to help us decide if our conjecture is accurate?
- Where can we find this information?
- Who can help us find information related to our conjecture?
- What people in our school might be able to help us?
- What family members might know something about this?
- What words could we plug in on the Internet to help us get more information?

During the rest of this week, students started collecting different resources and reading various books during Workshop. Students were encouraged to take notes and to share with their groups each day.

Lesson 4

Revising Plans as Necessary

Collecting Data and Information

Now that students have started collecting material, they need to identify individual job assignments so they are not duplicating efforts. At the beginning of this week, Ms. Hernandes took time to have students meet in their groups. During this time she met with the small groups to track their progress, discuss any problems, and help them focus their research efforts.

The group working with the conjecture "Every dollar has a different number that is recorded in a computer" was having trouble finding information to support or refute their conjecture. They had looked in books but did not really find anything. As they talked with the teacher, someone mentioned the term *mint*. As they discussed what happened in the mint, someone suggested that they write the mint with their question to see if they could get some help. This simple activity led students to the Internet to find out the address of the mint. They then spent the rest of that period composing a letter.

At the end of Inquiry that day, Ms. Hernandes made time for each group to present a summary of what it had done. If the group had any unsolved problems, it shared them with the class to get possible suggestions on how to solve the problems. When the group who wrote to the mint shared its problem and solution, several other groups realized that the Internet would be a good resource for them to use as well.

Lesson 5

Continuing Working and Planning Final Presentation

At this point students are beginning to conclude their investigations. Several of the groups realized as they collected information that they really needed to change or revise their conjectures. Ms. Hernandes asked in what ways their ideas have changed—what do they know now that they did not know before? For example, the group that had the conjecture that special ink was used so colors cannot be duplicated revised its conjecture by broadening it. After doing some research, their new conjecture was that there are many different things that the government does in addition to using special ink to protect money from being copied.

As groups presented their conjectures and progress, Ms. Hernandes modeled constructive comments such as the following: "Your points are clearly made." "Your charts and graphs help us understand each of your points." "Each one of you presented different pieces of information that all connect to your conjecture." "How was your conjecture supported?" After the lesson, Ms. Hernandes took time to reflect and realized that it was very hard for her students to give constructive feedback. She knew that this is an area they would need to work on. She would have to continue modeling but also thought about having groups exchange conjectures and provide feedback in writing to each other. This might reduce anxiety as well as give students time to reflect on the questions and conjectures and to develop some thoughtful feedback.

During this week, Ms. Hernandes took time to discuss possible ways that students could present their findings. The class brainstormed other ideas including the following:

- Writing a series of articles on their information for a magazine
- Creating a poster with diagrams of a process
- A panel discussion
- A computer presentation

Students returned to their groups to decide how they wanted to present their findings.

Final Presentation

Students have been busy working on completing their investigations and developing their presentations. While the class decided on a single research question at the beginning of the unit, different groups developed their own conjectures. Because their conjectures guided their research, each group will be presenting different information. Ms. Hernandes has created a simple web with the class's research question in the center and circles around the question. After groups present their work, the class will discuss what information was found to address the research question. As presentations are made, students will also be encouraged to make connections not only to the question but to each other's findings.

Throughout the unit, Ms. Hernandes recognized that students need more work on asking questions of each other and providing constructive feedback. She plans on modeling questions and comments as groups complete their presentations. Some examples include the following:

- How does what you presented support or refute your conjecture?
- Would you clarify . . .
- It would be helpful if . . .
- Have you thought about . . .
- Your visuals really helped me better understand your ideas.
- That was a great idea. Where can we find more information on it so we can learn more about it?
- What other questions did you think of as you were researching your conjecture?

Overall, Ms. Hernandes felt that this first attempt at Inquiry with the entire class focusing on a single question but generating multiple conjectures made Inquiry manageable for students and herself. Ms. Hernandes is now thinking about how to plan the next Inquiry unit so there are multiple questions as well as multiple conjectures. From the final presentations, she has really begun to appreciate how Inquiry incorporates all the reading and writing skills she has been teaching and how it takes students to the next level of learning—delving deeper into ideas that personally interest them, taking time and responsibility to learn about something, working collaboratively, and sharing new ideas and information.

Tips

- ✦ Inquiry takes time to develop. You may want to do the first unit as an entire class.
- ✦ Provide time throughout the unit for students to work on Inquiry. Use Workshop as well as computer and library time to support Inquiry.
- ✦ If students are careful about the problems or questions they choose to research, they should have few problems in following through with the research. If the problem is too broad or too narrow, they will have problems.

- ✦ Have students take sufficient time in assessing their needs—both knowledge needs and physical needs in relation to their research. Careful preplanning can help the research progress smoothly with great results.
- ✦ Encourage students to reevaluate their needs often so they are not wasting time finding things they already have or ignoring needs that they have not noticed.
- ✦ Interim presentations of material are every bit as important, if not more so, than final presentations. It is during interim presentations that students have the opportunity to rethink and reevaluate their work and change direction or to decide to carry on with their planned research.
- ✦ Connect Inquiry to learning in the content areas. Have students apply their Inquiry skills to learning science, social studies, and the arts.

Assessment

Assessment can be your most effective teaching tool if it is used with the purpose of informing instruction and highlighting areas that need special attention.

Purpose

The assessment components of **SRA Imagine It!** are designed to help you make informed instructional decisions, make adequate yearly progress, and help ensure you meet the needs of all your students. The variety of assessments is intended to be used continuously and formatively. That is, students should be assessed regularly as a follow-up to instructional activities, and the results of the assessment should be used to inform subsequent instruction.

You can use assessment as a tool to monitor students' progress, to diagnose students' strengths and weaknesses, to prescribe forms of intervention as necessary, and to measure student outcomes. Both formal and informal assessment can be used, though formal assessment will be your main assessment tool. Formal assessment of student learning consists of performance assessment (both reading and writing), objective tests (multiple choice, short answer, and essay), progress assessment (through students' everyday oral and written work), and assessment rubrics (used for writing, inquiry, and comprehension strategies). Informal assessment can be done by observing or listening to students as they work and jotting down notes either in the Comprehension Observation Log or in a notebook.

Procedure

Formal Assessment

Formal assessment is addressed in **SRA Imagine It!** in the form of **Benchmark Assessments** and **Lesson Assessments.** Both will help you use the results to differentiate instruction, especially for students needing some type of intervention to ensure they will not be at risk for reading failure.

Benchmark Assessments

The **Benchmark Assessments** are a form of general outcome measurement that offer an overall framework for assessment and serve as a predictor of how well students will perform at the end of the school year. Each **Benchmark Assessment** has material that students will learn over the course of the school year, and each **Benchmark Assessment** is of equivalent difficulty. Students are not expected to score high on the initial screening benchmark; instead, students are expected to show growth as they move on to each subsequent benchmark. Only at the end of the year are students expected to have mastered the materials on these assessments.

> *Observing students as they go about their regular classwork can be an effective way to learn your students' strengths and areas of need.*

One **Benchmark Assessment** will be administered at the beginning of the year for screening. This can serve as a baseline score against which you can measure students' progress throughout the year. Subsequent benchmarks will also be given at regular intervals—at the end of every other unit in grades K–1, for a total of six assessments, and at the end of each unit for students in grades 2–6, for a total of seven assessments. Since the tests are of equivalent difficulty and contain the same types of items, students' higher scores will reflect their increasing mastery of the curriculum over the course of the year. Use the data from the **Benchmark Assessments** to identify students who are at risk for reading failure, to identify strengths and weaknesses of students, and to gauge student progress toward high-stakes tests.

Depending upon the grade level, tested benchmark skills include the following:

- letter recognition,
- phonemic/phonological awareness,
- phonics,
- high-frequency word recognition,
- vocabulary,
- spelling,
- grammar, usage, and mechanics,
- comprehension,
- oral fluency, and
- maze fluency.

In addition, a writing assessment is given in the initial screening, at midyear, and also again at the end of the year for students in grades 3–6. This assessment is the type of on-demand writing performance students will encounter in high-stakes tests. Each writing assessment is of equal difficulty, and student outcomes should reflect an increased mastery of writing convention and genre expectations.

Lesson Assessments

The **Lesson Assessments** cover the most important skills featured in the lesson of a given unit—skills that are closely related to reading success and are typically in state and national standards. These assessments will help you determine how well students are grasping the skills and concepts as they are taught and will help inform you about any additional instruction they might need.

The **Lesson Assessments** are easily administered and scored. They feature the same language used in the instructional components of **SRA Imagine It!** and correspond to its sequence of instruction. The format of these weekly assessments range from multiple choice questions to short answer to an extended writing response. Depending upon the grade level, skills assessed include the following:

- letter and number recognition
- phonological and phonemic awareness
- phonics
- print and book awareness
- high frequency words

- selection vocabulary
- spelling
- grammar, usage, and mechanics skills
- comprehension skills
- oral fluency
- writing

The *Lesson Assessments* are offered in several formats so that students can demonstrate their knowledge of content in a number of developmentally appropriate ways. Wherever possible, the assessments are designed to be administered to the whole class or small groups of students. In some cases, however, individually administered assessments are included, such as the oral fluency assessments, as well as critical pre-literacy skills such as phoneme blending or segmentation as well as letter and number recognition.

The *Lesson Assessments* will allow you to monitor students' progress as they are assessed on the specific skills taught in a given lesson. The results will provide instructionally relevant information that you can use to differentiate instruction for students who may need additional learning opportunities.

Progress Assessment

Written Practice

Students work on several different skills throughout the day. Each of these assignments can provide you with valuable information about your students' progress. One very helpful resource that students will work in daily is the *Skills Practice Book* (Levels K–6). The *Skills Practice Books* include lessons that act as practice and reinforcement for the skills lessons taught before and during the reading of the lesson as well as in conjunction with the Language Arts lesson. These skills pages give you a clear picture of students' understanding of the skills taught. Use them as a daily assessment of student progress in the particular skills taught through the program.

Also included in the *Skills Practice Books* are lessons that help students with their Inquiry activities. Students can record what they know about the concepts and what they learn, they can keep a record of their research, and they can practice study and research skills that will help them in all of their schooling. You will be able to monitor their growing ability to make connections, find resources, and enhance their knowledge base as they find the answers to the research questions they have posed.

Dictation

In grades 1–3, students use dictation to practice the sound/spelling associations they are learning and/or reviewing. Collect the dictation papers and look through them to see how the students are doing with writing and with proofreading their words. Record notes on the papers and keep them in the student portfolios.

Portfolios

Portfolios are more than just a collection bin or gathering place for student projects and records. They add balance to an assessment program by providing unique benefits to teachers, students, and families.

✦ Portfolios help build self-confidence and increase self-esteem as students come to appreciate the value of their work. More importantly, portfolios allow students to reflect on what they know and what they need to learn. At the end of the school year, each student will be able to go through their portfolios and write about their progress.

✦ Portfolios provide the teacher with an authentic record of what students can do. Just as important, portfolios give students a concrete example of their own progress and development. Thus, portfolios become a valuable source of information for making instructional decisions.

✦ Portfolios allow families to judge student performance directly. Portfolios are an ideal starting point for discussions about a student's achievements and future goals during teacher/family conferences.

You will find that there are many opportunities to add to students' portfolios.

Fluency

✦ During partner reading, during Workshop, or at other times of the day, invite students, one at a time, to sit with you and read a story from an appropriate *Decodable* (grades 1–3), *Leveled Readers* (grades 1–6), *Leveled Readers for Science* or *Social Studies* (grades 1–6), or the *Student Reader.*

✦ As each student reads to you, follow along and make note of any recurring problems the student has while reading. Note students' ability to decode unknown words as well as any attempt—successful or not—to use strategies to clarify or otherwise make sense of what they are reading. From time to time,

check students' fluency by timing their reading and noting how well they are able to sustain the oral reading without faltering.

✦ If a student has trouble reading a particular *Decodable* or *Leveled Reader,* encourage the student to read the story a few times on her or his own before reading it aloud to you. If the *Decodable* has two stories, use the alternate story to reassess the student a day or two later.

✦ If after practicing with a particular Decodable Book or Leveled Reader and reading it on his or her own a few times, a student is still experiencing difficulty, try the following:

- Drop back two *Decodables.* (Continue to drop back until the student is able to read a story with no trouble.) If the student can read that book without problems, move up one book. The same is true for *Leveled Readers.*

- Continue the process until the student is able to read the current *Decodable* or *Leveled Readers.*

Assessment Rubrics

In addition to the formal assessment opportunities available in *Benchmark Assessments, Lesson Assessments,* and progress assessment, *SRA Imagine It!* provides rubrics for you to evaluate students' performance in comprehension, Inquiry, and writing. Rubrics provide criteria for different levels of performance. Rubrics established before an assignment is given are extremely helpful in evaluating the assignment. When students know what the rubrics for a particular assignment are, they can focus their energies on the key issues. Rubrics can be found in the Level Appendix.

Informal Assessment

Observation

Informal assessment is a part of the everyday classroom routine. Observing students as they go about their regular classwork can be an effective way to learn your students' strengths and areas of need. The more students become accustomed to you jotting down informal notes about their work, the more it will become just another part of classroom life that they accept and take little note of. This gives you the opportunity to assess their progress constantly without the interference and possible drawback of formal testing situations.

One tool that will help you make

informal assessment of student progress a part of your everyday classroom routine is the Comprehension Observation Log. You can record information quickly on this observation sheet and even extend your observations over several days, until you have had a chance to observe each student's performance in a particular area.

✦ Enter students' names in the Comprehension Observation Log, found in the **Lesson Assessment Books.**

✦ Before each day's lesson begins, decide which students you will observe.

✦ Keep the Comprehension Observation Log available so that you can easily record your observations.

✦ Decide what aspect of the students' learning you wish to monitor.

✦ During each lesson, observe this aspect in the performances of several students.

✦ When observing students, do not pull them aside; rather, observe students as part of the regular lesson, either with the whole class or in small groups.

✦ Record your observations.

✦ It may take four to five days to make sure you have observed and recorded the performance of each student. If you need more information about performance in a particular area for some of your students, you may want to observe them more than once.

Responding to Assessment Results

The point of assessment is to monitor progress in order to inform instruction, diagnose students' strengths and weaknesses, and differentiate instruction for students who need extra practice in certain skills or an extra challenge. **SRA Imagine It!** offers you opportunities to diagnose areas that may cause problems for students, differentiate instruction according to their abilities, monitor their progress on an ongoing basis, and measure student outcomes through **Lesson Assessments** or **Benchmark Assessments,** in addition to high-stakes state assessments. **SRA Imagine It!** also provides several ways to differentiate instruction based on the results of the various assessments. These include the following:

✦ Reteach lessons are available for students who are approaching level and appear to grasp a given concept but need more instruction and practice to solidify their learning. Many skills taught in the **Skills Practice Books** are available in a **Reteach** format.

✦ Intervention lessons provide options for you to use with students who need more intensive support and who are struggling to understand the on-level material. In addition to the support for the weekly lesson, controlled vocabulary lessons and specific skills lessons can help bring students up to grade level.

✦ **English Learner Support** lessons are available for students who are having difficulty with the concepts because they lack the necessary English language background. These resources will provide English Learners with the vocabulary, phonics, comprehension, grammar, and writing support they need to access the **SRA Imagine It!** lessons.

✦ **Challenge Activities** provide continued stimulation for those students who are doing well and working above grade level. Many skills covered in the **Skills Practice Books** are also available in **Challenge Activities.**

✦ **Workshop Resource Book** activities give students alternative activities to strengthen or extend their skills in areas such as letter recognition, phonics, vocabulary, comprehension, fluency, word structure, and grammar.

✦ **Leveled Readers** provide students at all different levels of instruction— Approaching Level, On Level, Above Level, and English Learners—with additional opportunities to practice fluency, vocabulary, and comprehension skills. Besides the general **Leveled Readers, Leveled Readers for Science** and **Leveled Readers for Social Studies** provide students cross-curricular opportunities.

These materials, along with formal and informal assessments, help ensure that assessment and instruction work together to meet every student's needs.

Workshop

Every teacher and every student needs time during the day to organize, to take stock of work that is done, to make plans for work that needs doing, and to finish up incomplete projects. In addition, teachers need time for differentiating instruction, for holding conferences with students, and for doing fluency checks.

Purpose

Workshop is the period of time each day in which students work independently or collaboratively to practice and review material taught in the lessons.

A variety of activities may occur during this time. Students may work on a specific daily assignment, complete an ongoing project, work on unit inquiry activities, focus on writing, or choose from a wide range of possibilities. With lots of guidance and encouragement, students gradually learn to make decisions about their use of time and materials and to collaborate with their peers.

A goal of Workshop is to get students to work independently and productively. This is essential because Workshop is also the time during which the teacher can work with individuals or groups of students to reinforce learning, to provide extra help for those having difficulties, to extend learning, or to assess the progress of the class or of individuals.

Procedure

Initially for many students you will need to structure Workshop carefully. Eventually students will automatically go to the appropriate areas, take up ongoing projects, and get the materials they will need. Workshop will evolve slowly from a very structured period to a time when students make choices and move freely from one activity to the next.

Setting up Workshop guidelines is key. By the time students have completed the first few weeks of school, they should feel confident during Workshop. If not, continue to structure the time and limit options. For young students, early periods of Workshop may run no more than five to eight minutes. The time can gradually increase to fifteen minutes or longer as students gain independence. Older students may be able to work longer and independently from the very beginning of the school year.

Introducing Workshop

Introduce Workshop to students by telling them that every day there will be a time when they are expected to work on activities on their own or in small groups. For younger students explain that in the beginning there may be just a couple of activities but that gradually new ones will be introduced and that students can choose what they want to do. With older students and for those who have experienced Workshop in early grades, you may want to introduce the concept of Workshop and discuss the range of Workshop options from working on fluency to completing their writing.

> *Workshop is the period of time each day in which students work independently or collaboratively to practice and review material taught in the lessons.*

Establish and discuss rules for Workshop with students. Keep them simple and straightforward. You may want to write the finalized rules on the board or on a poster. You may want to review these rules each day at the beginning of Workshop for the first few lessons or so. You may also wish to revisit and revise the rules from time to time. Suggested rules include the following:

- Share.
- Use a quiet voice.
- Take only the materials you need.
- Return materials.
- Always be working.
- When the teacher is working with a student or small group, do not interrupt.

Early in the process, review rules routinely, and discuss how Workshop is going. Is the class quiet enough for everyone to work on his or her own? Are there any rules that need changing? What problems are students having with materials?

For young students in the beginning you will assign the Workshop activities to help them learn to work on their own. Point out the shelf or area of the classroom where Workshop materials are stored. Tell students that when they finish working with the materials for one activity, they will choose something else from the Workshop shelf. New activity materials will be added to the shelf from time to time. Make sure students know that they may always look at books during Workshop.

Tell older students that they will have an opportunity each day to work on their unit inquiry activities, their writing, and other projects. Students will be working independently and collaboratively during this time.

Guidelines

- ✦ Make sure each student knows what he or she needs to do during Workshop.

- ✦ Demonstrate for the entire group any activity or game assigned for Workshop, for example, teaching students a new game, introducing new materials or projects, or explaining different areas.

- ✦ For young students, it is essential to introduce and demonstrate different activities and games before students do them on their own. With games, you may want to have several students play while the others watch. Make sure that all students know exactly what is expected of them.

- ✦ In the beginning, plan to circulate among students, providing encouragement and help as necessary.

- ✦ When students are engaged in appropriate activities and can work independently, meet with those students who need your particular attention. This may include individual students or small groups.

- ✦ Let students know that they need to ask questions and to clarify assignments during Workshop introduction so that you are free to work with small groups.

- ✦ Be sure that students know what they are to do when they have finished an activity and where to put their finished work.

Setting Up Your Classroom for Workshop

Carefully setting up your classroom to accommodate various Workshop activities will help assure that the Workshop period progresses smoothly and effectively. While setting up your classroom, keep the primary Workshop activities in mind. During Workshop, students will be doing independent and collaborative activities. In kindergarten and first grade, these activities may include letter recognition and phonemic awareness activities and writing or illustrating stories or projects. In addition, they will be working on individual or small-group projects.

Many classrooms have areas that students visit on a regular or rotating basis. Unlike traditional centers, all students do not rotate through all the areas each day.

The following are suggestions for space and materials for use during Workshop:

1. Reading Area supplied with books and magazines. The materials in the Reading Area should be dynamic—changing with students' abilities and reflecting unit themes they are reading. You may wish to add books to your classroom library.

2. Writing Area stocked with various types and sizes of lined and unlined paper, pencils, erasers, markers, crayons, small slates, and chalk. The area should also have various **Letter Cards** and other handwriting models for those students who want to practice letter formation or handwriting. Students should know that this is where they come for writing supplies. In addition to the supplies described above, the Writing Area can also have supplies to encourage students to create and write on their own:

   - Magazines and catalogs to cut up for pictures; stickers, paint, glue, glitter, and so on to decorate books and book covers; precut and stapled blank books for students to write in (Some can be plain and some cut in special shapes.)
   - Cardboard, tag board, construction paper, and so on for making book covers (Provide some samples.)
   - Tape, scissors, yarn, hole punches for binding books
   - Picture dictionaries, dictionaries, thesauruses, word lists, and other materials that may encourage independence

3. Listening Area supplied with tape recorder, CD player, optional headphones, and CDs of stories, poems, and songs for students to listen to and react to. You might also want to provide blank tapes and encourage students to retell and record their favorite stories or to make up and tell stories for their classmates to listen to on tape. You may also want to make available the Listening Library CDs that are available with the program.

4. Phonics Activities supplied with **Alphabet Flash Cards,** individual **Alphabet Sound Card** sets (Kindergarten), individual **Sound/Spelling Cards** and **High-Frequency Flash Cards** (Grades K, 1, 2, and 3), and other materials that enhance what students are learning. Other commonly used classroom materials that enhance reading can be included, for example, plastic letters, puzzles, and games.

5. Fluency Area supplied with **Pre-Decodables and Decodables, Leveled Readers, Leveled Science Readers** and **Leveled Social Studies Readers,** and other resources for practicing fluency. Some teachers have folders for each student with materials to practice during the week. In addition, some Fluency areas have timers and tape recorders as well.

Because students will be working on their inquiry/investigations during Workshop, make sure there are adequate supplies to help them with their research. These might include dictionaries, encyclopedias, magazines, newspapers, and computers—preferably with Internet capability.

Students thrive in an environment that provides structure, repetition, and routine. Within a sound structure, students will gain confidence and independence. This setting allows you to differentiate instruction to provide opportunities for flexibility and individual choice. This will allow students to develop their strengths, abilities, and talents to the fullest.

Suggestions for English Learners

Workshop affords students who are English Learners a wealth of opportunities for gaining proficiency in English. It also encourages them to share their backgrounds with peers. Since you will be working with all students individually and in small groups regardless of their reading ability, students who need special help with language will not feel self-conscious about working with you.

In addition, working in small groups made of students with the same interests rather than the same abilities will provide them with the opportunity to learn about language from their peers during the regular course of Workshop activities.

Some suggestions for meeting the special needs of students with diverse backgrounds are as follows:

- ✦ Preread a selection with English Learners to help them identify words and ideas they wish to talk about. This will prepare them for discussions with the whole group.
- ✦ Preteach vocabulary and develop selection concepts that may be a challenge for students.
- ✦ Negotiate the meaning of selections by asking questions, checking for comprehension, and speaking with English Learners as much as possible.
- ✦ Draw English Learners into small-group discussions to give them a sense that their ideas are valid and worth attention.
- ✦ Pair English Learners with native English speakers to share their experiences and to provide new knowledge to other students.
- ✦ Have English Learners draw or dictate to you or another student a description of a new idea they may have during Workshop activities.

Book Review

Sessions can be small or large. Workshop is a good time for students to share the reading they do on their own. They can discuss a book they have all read, or one person can review a book for the others and answer questions from the group.

During Workshop, students can discuss and review a variety of books:

- ✦ Full-length versions of **Student Reader** selections
- ✦ Books that students learn about when discussing authors and illustrators
- ✦ Books related to the investigations of unit concepts that can be shared with others who might want to read them
- ✦ Interesting articles from magazines, newspapers, and other sources

When a student reviews a book others have not read, he or she can use some of the sentence starters to tell about the book. These may include "This book is about . . . ," "I chose this book because . . . ," "What I really like/don't like about this book is . . . , " and so on.

- When several students read the same book and discuss it during Workshop, they can use discussion starters.

Encouraging Reading

- Read aloud to your students regularly. You can read from your classroom library or full-length versions of **Student Reader** selections.

- Provide a time each day for students to read silently. This time can be as short as 10–15 minutes but should be strictly observed. You should stop what you are doing and read. Students should be allowed to choose their own reading materials during this time and record their reactions in the response journal section of their Writer's Notebooks.

- Establish a classroom library and reading center with books from the school or local library, or ask for donations of books from students, parents, and community members.

- Take your students to the school library or to the public library.

Workshop Management Tips

Use the following Workshop management tips to ensure that Workshop runs smoothly.

Note that these suggestions for a weekly unit/lesson may not exactly correspond to a particular unit/lesson in a given grade level but will give you a sense of how Workshop should progress. All of the time suggestions depend upon the needs of the class and their readiness to work independently.

Kindergarten through Grade 1

Unit 1, Week 1 Introduce Workshop as whole-class workshop. Explain Workshop and its rules. Give the class an activity to do, for example, putting letters in alphabetical order (Grade 1) or copying their names (kindergarten). Tell the class that they will be doing Workshop today. As they do their activity, you will walk around, observing students and noting how well Workshop is going. The class is working quietly and independently. Workshop may last only a few minutes in kindergarten and about ten minutes in first grade.

Unit 1, Weeks 2 and 3 Depending upon your class, you can move to whole-group Workshop with two activities. Give half the class one activity and the other half the other. Explain to the class that for the next few Workshop sessions, there will be two different activities but that the class is supposed to work quietly and independently. Switch activities for the next day, and repeat this format for the next few days or so. Introduce the concept of "debriefing." Take a few minutes at the end, have several students share what they did or learned during Workshop. You may want to have students tell what they like about Workshop and if any changes need to be made.

Unit 2, Week 1 Begin introducing Workshop Areas, explaining the materials and how they can be used. Explain to students that the materials in these areas will be changing regularly so students will be able to practice and use their new reading and writing skills. Workshop activities should change routinely and reflect the changing nature of the curriculum. Often, during the early weeks of Workshop, teachers assign students to different activities and, as students become ready, turn over to students the responsibility for choosing activities.

Unit 3 Add new activities for students. Encourage them to do a couple of Workshop activities each day, perhaps working on their writing in progress and fluency practice (reading a Pre-Decodable or Decodable). Other options might include on-line phonemic awareness and phonics activities, phonics activities such as word sorts, using blended words in written sentences, practicing high-frequency sight words, and so on.

Unit 4 By this time, students should be making choices and working independently. Each Workshop session may be fifteen minutes long with the teacher working with small groups. Take time to review Workshop activities to be sure they are being used and that students are learning from the activities. If activities become stale, vary them, or change them altogether.

Grades 2–6

Unit 1, Lesson 1 Introduce Workshop to students. Make sure they know where materials are located. Post the rules on the board or other prominent place in the classroom. Keep Workshop time short (less than thirty minutes) and very directed during the first few weeks until students can work independently.

Unit 1, Lesson 2 Discuss using small groups for pre-/reteaching purposes and how you will indicate who will be in the groups. Start by forming one small group randomly and having other students do something specific such as a writing assignment. When you have finished with the small group, send them to do independent work. Call another small group of students to work with you. Continue this each day until students are accustomed to forming groups and working independently.

Unit 1, Lesson 3 Reading Roundtable is a student-formed and student-run book discussion. Encourage students participating in Reading Roundtable to choose a book that they all will read and discuss. Several different Reading Roundtable groups may form on the basis of the books students choose.

Unit 1, Lesson 4 For the first few weeks of the school year, make sure each student has a plan for using Workshop time.

Unit 1, Lesson 5 (Days 1–5) Allow time for presentation and discussion of research activities. Use an entire Workshop day, and have all groups present their findings, or split the presentations over several days, depending on the small-group needs of your class.

Unit 1, Lesson 5 (Days 6–10) Review how students have used Workshop during this unit. Have they used their time well? Do they have the materials they need? Discuss suggestions for improving their use of this time. Take a few minutes at the beginning of each Workshop to make sure students know what they will be doing.

Unit 2, Lesson 1 Form small extra-practice groups with the more advanced students from time to time, as they also need special attention.

Unit 2, Lesson 2 To keep the entire class informed about the independent research being done, every other day or so invite a research group to explain what it is doing, how the research is going, and any problems they are encountering.

Unit 2, Lesson 3 Discuss the use of Workshop time for doing Inquiry and research projects, and share **eInquiry** with different research activities.

Unit 2, Lesson 4 Make sure small extra-practice groups are formed based on your observations of students' work on the different daily lessons. Small groups should be fluid and based on demonstrated need rather than become static and unchanging.

Unit 2, Lesson 5 (Days 1–5) One purpose of Workshop is to help students learn independence and responsibility. Assign students to monitor Workshop materials. They should alert you whenever materials are running low or missing, and they can be responsible for checking on return dates of library books and making sure the books are either returned or renewed.

Unit 2, Lesson 5 (Days 6–10) Students sometimes have difficulty starting discussions in Reading Roundtable. Try some of these discussion starters with students, and print them on a poster for student use.

> I didn't know that . . .
> I liked the part where . . .
> Does anyone know . . .
> I'm still confused by . . .
> I figured out that . . .
> This made me think . . .
> I agree/disagree with because . . .

Unit 3, Lesson 1 By this time students should be accustomed to the routines, rules, expectations, and usage of Workshop time and be moving smoothly from small teacher-led groups to independent work. Monitor small groups occasionally to see that they are on task and making progress on their activities.

Unit 3, Lesson 2 Make a practice of reading aloud to students. All students enjoy being read to, no matter their age or grade. Encourage them to discuss the shared reading in groups and to bring books and read them aloud to their classmates.

Unit 3, Lesson 3 Encourage cooperation and collaboration by providing students with opportunities to engage in small groups.

Unit 3, Lesson 4 Spend a few minutes each day circulating around the room and monitoring what students are doing independently or in small groups. Students can then share with you on a timely basis any questions or problems they are having.

Unit 3, Lesson 5 (Days 1–5) Take note of various small groups. Make sure that quieter students are able to participate in the discussions. Often the stronger, more confident students dominate such discussions. Encourage them to give all participants an opportunity to share their ideas.

Unit 3, Lesson 5 (Days 6–10) If students are not productive during Workshop, keep them in the small group you are working with until they can successfully benefit from independent work. Discuss strategies they could use to become more independent.

Unit 4, Lesson 1 Individual students can monitor Workshop materials and alert you when materials or supplies are running low or missing and can check that library books are either returned or renewed.

Unit 4, Lesson 2 From time to time, join a Reading Roundtable group, and take part in their discussion. Make sure students lead the discussion.

Unit 4, Lesson 3 Encourage responsibility and independence by reminding students to show respect for each other and the materials provided.

Unit 4, Lesson 4 Be sure students discuss during Reading Roundtable what they like or dislike about a book, why they wanted to read it, and how the book either lived up to their expectations or disappointed them. Discussions should not be about basic comprehension but should help students think more deeply about the ideas presented in the book.

Unit 4, Lesson 5 (Days 1–5) Make sure students continue to use the activities provided for use with this unit at **SRAonline. com.**

Unit 4, Lesson 5 (Days 6–10) If students are not productive in Workshop, keep them in the small group you are working with until they can successfully benefit from independent work. Discuss strategies they could use to become more independent.

Unit 5, Lesson 1 Students often make great tutors for other students. They are uniquely qualified to understand problems that others might be having. Encourage students to pair up during Workshop to help each other with their daily lessons.

Unit 5, Lesson 2 Form small extra-practice groups with the more advanced students from time to time, as they also need special attention.

Unit 5, Lesson 3 To keep the entire class informed about the independent research being done, every other day or so, invite a research/investigation group to explain what it is doing, how the research is going, and any problems they are encountering.

Unit 5, Lesson 4 Most of the authors of the **Student Reader** selections are well known and have written many, many pieces of fine literature. Encourage students who enjoy the selections to find other books by the same author. Encourage them to think about and discuss what about that particular author's work attracts them.

Unit 5, Lesson 5 (Days 1–5) Share your impressions of books from your classroom library or other readings during Reading Roundtable. Note which students initiate sharing and which are reluctant to share.

Unit 5, Lesson 5 (Days 6–10) Review with students the time they have used in Workshop. Have they used their time well? Do they have the materials they need? Discuss suggestions for improving the use of this time.

Unit 6, Lesson 1 Spend a few minutes each day circulating and monitoring what students are doing independently or in small groups. Students can share with you on a timely basis any questions or problems they are having.

Unit 6, Lesson 2 Students should be accustomed to the routines, rules, expectations, and usage of Workshop time and be moving smoothly from small teacher-led groups to independent work. Make sure to monitor small groups occasionally to see that they are on task and making progress with their activities.

Unit 6, Lesson 3 Make sure students continue to use the activities provided for use with this unit at **SRAonline.com.**

Unit 6, Lesson 4 If the reading selection is an excerpt from a longer piece, encourage students to read the book from which the excerpt is taken and to discuss how the excerpt fits into the larger work.

Unit 6, Lesson 5 (Days 1–5) Students often make great tutors for other students. The fact that they, too, are just learning the materials makes them uniquely qualified to understand problems that others might be having. Encourage students to pair up during Workshop to help each other on their daily lessons.

Unit 6, Lesson 5 (Days 6–10) Allot time for presentation and discussion of research activities. You may want to use a whole Workshop day and have all groups present their findings or split the presentations over several days, depending on the urgency of the small-group instruction your class needs.

Scope and Sequence

Reading

	K	1	2	3	4	5	6
Print/Book Awareness (Recognize and understand the conventions of print and books)							
Capitalization	X	X					
Constancy of Words		X					
Differentiate between Letter and Word	X						
Differentiate between Word and Sentence	X						
End Punctuation	X	X					
Follow Left-to-Right, Top-to-Bottom	X	X					
Letter Recognition and Formation	X	X					
Page Numbering	X	X					
Parts of a Book	X	X					
Picture/Text Relationship	X	X					
Punctuation	X	X					
Quotation Marks	X	X					
Relationship Between Spoken and Printed Language	X	X					
Sentence Recognition	X	X					
Spacing Between Sentences	X	X					
Spacing Between Words	X	X					
Table of Contents	X	X					
Text Features		X					
Text Relationships		X					
Word Length	X	X					
Word Boundaries		X					
Write Left-to-Right, Top-to-Bottom	X	X					
Phonemic Awareness (Recognize Discrete Sounds in Words)							
Oral Blending: Words/Word Parts	X	X					
Oral Blending: Onset and Rime	X	X					
Oral Blending: Syllables	X	X					
Oral (Phoneme) Blending: Initial Sounds	X	X					
Oral (Phoneme) Blending: Final Sounds	X	X					
Oral Blending: Initial Vowels		X					
Oral Blending: Vowel Replacement		X					
Rhyming	X	X					
Phoneme Matching: Initial Sounds	X	X					
Phoneme Matching: Final Sounds	X	X					
Phoneme Matching: Medial Sounds	X	X					
Phoneme Manipulation: Initial Sounds	X	X					
Phoneme Manipulation: Final Sounds	X	X					
Phoneme Manipulation: Medial Sounds	X	X					
Segmentation: Final Consonants	X	X					
Segmentation: Initial Consonants/Blends		X					
Segmentation: Words/Word Parts	X	X					
Segmentation: Syllables	X	X					
Segmentation: Identifying the Number and Order of Sounds in Words	X	X					

Reading (continued)

	K	1	2	3	4	5	6
How the Alphabet Works							
Letter Knowledge (Alphabetic Knowledge)	X	X					
Letter Order (Alphabetic Order)	X	X					
Letter Sounds	X	X					
Sounds in Words	X	X					
Phonics (Associate Sounds and Spellings to Read Words)							
Blending Sounds into Words	X	X	X	X			
Consonant Clusters		X	X	X			
Consonant Digraphs		X	X	X			
Phonograms		X	X	X			
Schwa			X	X			
Silent Consonants			X	X			
Syllables		X	X	X			
Vowel Diphthongs		X	X	X			
Vowels: Long Sounds and Spellings	X	X	X	X			
Vowels: r-controlled		X	X	X			
Vowels: Short Sounds and Spellings	X	X	X	X			
Comprehension Strategies							
Adjusting Reading Speed			X	X	X	X	X
Asking Questions/Answering Questions	X	X	X	X	X	X	X
Clarifying	X	X	X	X	X	X	X
Making Connections	X	X	X	X	X	X	X
Predicting/Confirming Predictions	X	X	X	X	X	X	X
Summarizing		X	X	X	X	X	X
Visualizing	X	X	X	X	X	X	X
Comprehension Skills							
Author's Point of View			X	X	X	X	X
Author's Purpose			X	X	X	X	X
Cause and Effect	X	X	X	X	X	X	X
Classify and Categorize	X	X	X	X	X	X	X
Compare and Contrast	X	X	X	X	X	X	X
Drawing Conclusions	X	X	X	X	X	X	X
Fact and Opinion			X	X	X	X	X
Main Idea and Details	X	X	X	X	X	X	X
Making Inferences		X	X	X	X	X	X
Reality and Fantasy	X	X	X	X			
Sequence	X	X	X	X	X	X	X
Vocabulary							
Apposition		X	X	X	X	X	X
Concept Words		X	X	X	X	X	X
Context Clues		X	X	X	X	X	X
Expanding Vocabulary		X	X	X	X	X	X
High-Frequency Words	X	X	X	X			
Idioms					X	X	X
Multiple-Meaning Words		X	X	X	X	X	X
Selection Vocabulary	X	X	X	X	X	X	X
Time and Order Words (Creating Sequence)	X	X	X	X	X	X	X
Utility Words (Colors, Classroom Objects, etc.)	X	X					

Reading (continued)

Reading with a Writer's Eye	K	1	2	3	4	5	6
Author's Purpose	X		X	X	X	X	
Alliteration			X		X		X
Captions and Headings			X	X		X	X
Characterization	X	X	X	X	X	X	X
Choosing Good Examples				X	X		
Description		X	X	X	X	X	X
Diagrams							X
Dialect						X	
Dialogue		X	X	X	X	X	X
Effective Beginnings					X	X	
Effective Endings					X		
Event Sequence	X	X	X	X		X	
Expository Writing Techniques					X	X	
Fable Characteristics					X		
Figurative Language		X	X	X	X	X	X
Flashback							X
Genre Knowledge	X		X	X	X	X	X
Idiom						X	X
Irony					X		
Language Use	X		X	X	X	X	X
Mood and Tone		X	X	X			X
Onomatopoeia			X	X	X		X
Personification			X	X		X	X
Persuasive Techniques					X	X	
Plot (Problem/Solution)	X	X	X	X	X	X	X
Point of View					X	X	
Punctuation					X	X	
Quoting Sources					X		
Rhyme	X		X			X	X
Sensory Details		X		X		X	
Sentence Variety						X	
Setting	X	X	X	X	X	X	X
Sidebars							X
Similes and Metaphors					X	X	X
Stage Directions					X		
Style							X
Suspense and Surprise					X	X	
Text Structure	X		X	X	X	X	X
Theme	X		X	X	X	X	X
Transitions					X		X
Using Comparisons		X	X	X		X	
Voice					X	X	X
Word Choice				X			X

Word Structure	K	1	2	3	4	5	6
Antonyms			X	X	X	X	X
Comparatives/Superlatives			X	X	X	X	
Compound Words	X	X	X	X	X	X	X
Contractions			X	X	X	X	
Connotation and Denotation							X
Content/Concept Words							X

Reading (continued)

	K	1	2	3	4	5	6
Foreign Words and Phrases						X	X
Gerunds							X
Greek and Latin Roots				X	X	X	X
Homographs			X	X	X	X	X
Homonyms/Homophones			X	X	X	X	X
Inflectional Endings			X	X	X	X	X
Irregular Plurals			X	X	X	X	
Multiple-Meaning Words					X	X	X
Multisyllabic Words			X	X	X	X	
Plurals			X	X	X	X	
Position Words	X	X					
Prefixes			X	X	X	X	X
Root or Base Words			X	X	X	X	X
Shades of Meaning/Levels of Specificity						X	X
Suffixes			X	X	X	X	X
Synonyms			X	X	X	X	X
Word Families			X	X	X	X	X
Word Origins					X	X	X

Inquiry and Study Skills

	K	1	2	3	4	5	6
Study Skills							
Comparing Information across Sources		X		X		X	
Charts, Graphs, and Diagrams/Visual Aids	X	X	X	X	X	X	X
Collaborative Inquiry	X	X	X	X	X	X	X
Communicating Research Progress Results		X	X	X	X	X	X
Compile Notes		X			X	X	X
Conducting an Interview		X	X	X	X	X	X
Finding Needed Information	X	X	X	X	X	X	X
Follow Directions	X		X	X	X		X
Formulate Questions for Inquiry and Research	X	X	X	X	X	X	X
Give Reports	X		X	X	X	X	X
Make Outlines			X	X	X	X	X
Making Conjectures	X	X	X	X	X	X	X
Maps	X	X	X	X	X	X	
Note Taking		X	X	X	X	X	X
Parts of a Book	X	X	X	X	X		
Planning Inquiry		X	X	X	X	X	X
Recognizing Information Needs		X	X	X	X	X	X
Revising Questions and Conjectures	X	X	X	X	X	X	X
Summarize and Organize Information		X	X	X	X	X	X
Time Lines		X	X	X	X		
Use Appropriate Resources (Media Sources, Reference Books, Experts, Internet)		X	X	X	X	X	X
Using a Dictionary/Glossary		X	X	X	X		
Using a Media Center/Library		X	X	X	X		
Using a Thesaurus			X	X	X	X	
Using an Encyclopedia		X	X	X	X		
Using Newspapers and Magazines		X	X		X		X
Using Technology	X	X	X	X	X	X	X

Language Arts
Writing/Composition

	K	1	2	3	4	5	6
Approaches							
Collaborative Writing	X	X	X	X	X	X	X
Individual Writing	X	X	X	X	X	X	X
Writing Process							
Brainstorming/Prewriting	X	X	X	X	X	X	X
Drafting	X	X	X	X	X	X	X
Revising	X	X	X	X	X	X	X
Editing	X	X	X	X	X	X	X
Proofreading	X	X	X	X	X	X	X
Publishing	X	X	X	X	X	X	X
Writing Genres							
Action Tale			X				
Autobiography/Biography	X	X	X	X	X	X	X
Book Review		X	X	X	X	X	
Business Letter			X	X		X	X
Describe a Process		X	X	X	X	X	X
Descriptive Writing	X	X	X	X	X	X	X
Expository/Informational Text	X	X	X	X	X	X	X
Fantasy		X	X	X			
Folklore (Folktales, Fairy Tales, Tall Tales, Legends, Myths)		X	X	X	X	X	
Friendly Letter	X	X	X	X	X	X	X
Historical Fiction					X		X
Invitation		X		X		X	
Journal Writing			X	X	X		
Magazine Article						X	X
Making a List	X	X	X	X	X	X	X
Mystery				X			
Narrative	X	X	X	X	X	X	X
News Story		X	X	X	X		
Personal Writing	X	X	X	X	X	X	X
Persuasive Writing	X	X	X	X	X	X	X
Play/Dramatization			X	X	X	X	X
Poetry	X	X	X	X	X	X	X
Realistic Fiction		X	X	X	X	X	X
Summary		X	X	X	X	X	X
Timed Writing		X	X	X	X	X	X
Writing Traits							
Audience		X	X	X	X	X	X
Conventions	X	X	X	X	X	X	X
Elaboration		X	X	X	X	X	X
Focus		X	X	X	X	X	X
Ideas/Content	X	X	X	X	X	X	X
Organization		X	X	X	X	X	X
Presentation	X	X	X	X	X	X	X
Purpose		X	X	X	X	X	X
Sentence Fluency	X	X	X	X	X	X	X
Sentence Variety		X			X	X	X
Vocabulary		X	X	X	X	X	X
Voice	X	X	X	X	X	X	X
Word Choice	X	X	X	X	X	X	X

Language Arts
Writing/Composition (continued)

Writing Strategies	K	1	2	3	4	5	6
Action and Describing Words	X	X	X	X			
Adding Details	X	X	X	X	X	X	X
Addressing Audience Needs		X	X	X	X	X	X
Brainstorming	X	X	X	X	X	X	X
Categorizing Ideas						X	
Cause and Effect					X	X	X
Character Sketch					X	X	
Choosing a Topic	X	X	X	X	X	X	X
Compare and Contrast			X			X	X
Conveying a General Mood				X	X	X	
Creating Suspense				X			X
Creating Vivid Images		X		X	X	X	
Dialogue	X	X	X	X	X	X	X
Effective Beginnings					X	X	X
Elements of a Letter		X	X	X	X	X	X
Elements of Persuasion			X	X	X	X	
Eliminating Irrelevant Information		X	X	X	X	X	X
Eliminating Wordiness			X	X	X	X	X
Evaluate Personal Growth as a Writer			X	X	X	X	
Explanatory Paragraphs		X					
Figurative Language			X	X	X	X	X
Formality of Language		X	X	X	X	X	
Format		X			X	X	X
Generate Additional Ideas		X	X	X	X		
Highlight a Memorable Event		X			X		
Identifying Best Feature of Something Written			X	X			
Illustrations and Drawings	X	X	X	X			
Information from Multiple Sources					X	X	X
Main Idea and Details					X	X	
Making Connections							X
Organizing a Multi-Paragraph Composition					X	X	X
Planning		X			X	X	X
Plot Structure—Beginning, Middle, Climax, and End		X		X	X	X	X
Point of View						X	X
Presenting Facts and Examples Objectively					X	X	X
Proofreading	X	X	X	X	X	X	X
Purpose		X	X	X	X	X	X
Realism					X	X	X
Referencing a Source					X	X	
Revising	X	X	X	X	X	X	X
Rhythm and Rhyme		X	X			X	
Sensory Details				X	X	X	X
Sentence Combining			X	X	X	X	X
Sequence	X	X	X	X		X	
Setting		X	X	X	X	X	X
Story Elements		X	X	X	X	X	
Style							X
Summary			X	X	X	X	X
Taking Notes		X	X	X	X	X	X

Language Arts

Writing/Composition (continued)

	K	1	2	3	4	5	6
Timed Writing		X	X	X	X	X	X
Time Line			X	X		X	
Transition Words/Devices			X	X	X	X	X
Using a Checklist		X	X	X	X	X	
Using a Graphic Organizer		X	X	X	X	X	X
Using a Model as a Guide to Writing			X	X		X	
Using Outlines to Organize Information				X	X	X	X
Using Multimedia Sources			X	X	X	X	X
Vary Sentence Beginnings			X	X	X	X	
Vary Sentence Length		X	X			X	
Vary Sentence Types	X	X	X	X	X	X	
Voice				X		X	
Voicing an Opinion		X				X	X
Word Choice		X	X	X	X	X	X
Working Collaboratively						X	X
Writing Coherent Paragraphs		X	X	X	X	X	X

Language Arts

Grammar

	K	1	2	3	4	5	6
Parts of Speech							
Adjectives (Describing Words)	X	X	X	X	X	X	X
Adverbs			X	X	X	X	X
Conjunctions			X	X	X	X	X
Nouns	X	X	X	X	X	X	X
Prepositions				X	X	X	X
Pronouns	X	X	X	X	X	X	X
Verbs	X	X	X	X	X	X	X
Sentences							
Complete and Incomplete Sentences		X	X	X	X	X	X
Fragments			X	X	X	X	X
Independent and Dependent Clauses							X
Parts (Subjects and Predicates)			X	X	X	X	X
Run-on Sentences					X		X
Sentence Combining			X	X	X	X	X
Structure (Simple, Compound, Complex, Compound-Complex)			X	X	X	X	X
Subject/Verb Agreement		X	X	X	X	X	X
Types (Declarative, Interrogative, Exclamatory, Imperative)	X	X	X	X	X	X	X
Usage							
Adjectives		X	X	X	X	X	X
Adverbs			X	X	X	X	X
Antonyms		X	X				
Articles			X	X		X	X
Contractions			X	X	X		
Nouns		X	X	X	X	X	X
Pronouns		X	X	X	X	X	X
Regular and Irregular Plurals					X	X	X
Synonyms		X	X				
Verb Tenses		X	X	X	X	X	X
Verbs (Action, Helping, Linking, Regular/Irregular)		X	X	X	X	X	X

Language Arts
Grammar (continued)

	K	1	2	3	4	5	6
Mechanics							
Capitalization (Sentence, Proper Nouns, Titles, Direct Address, Pronoun "I")	X	X	X	X	X	X	X
Punctuation (End Punctuation, Comma Use, Quotation Marks, Apostrophe, Colon, Semicolon, Hyphen, Parentheses)	X	X	X	X	X	X	X
Spelling							
Antonyms					X	X	X
Base or Root Words					X	X	
Comparatives/Superlatives				X	X	X	X
Compound Words				X	X	X	
Connotation and Denotation							X
Content/Concept Words							X
Contractions				X	X		X
Foreign Words and Phrases							X
Gerunds							X
Greek and Latin Roots				X	X	X	X
Homographs				X	X	X	X
Homonyms/Homophones				X	X	X	X
Inflectional Endings		X		X	X	X	X
Irregular Plurals		X		X	X	X	
Irregular Verbs						X	
Long Vowel Patterns		X	X	X	X		
Multiple-Meaning Words					X	X	X
Multisyllabic Words		X	X	X	X		X
Phonograms		X					
Prefixes				X	X	X	X
r-Controlled Vowel Spellings		X	X				
Shades of Meaning					X		X
Short Vowel Spellings		X	X	X	X		
Silent Letters			X	X	X		
Sound/Letter Relationships	X	X	X				
Special Spellings Patterns/Rules		X	X	X	X	X	
Special Vowel Spellings		X	X	X			
Suffixes		X		X	X	X	X
Synonyms					X	X	X
Word Families		X		X		X	X

Listening/Speaking/Viewing

	K	1	2	3	4	5	6
Listening							
Analyze/Evaluate Intent and Content of Speaker's Message		X	X	X		X	X
Ask Questions		X	X	X	X	X	X
Determine Purposes for Listening		X	X	X	X	X	X
Drawing Conclusions and Making Inferences						X	
Follow Directions	X	X		X	X	X	X
Learn about Different Cultures through Discussion				X	X		
Listen for Poetic Language (Rhythm/Rhyme)	X	X				X	X
Listening for Details			X	X	X		
Listening for Information				X	X		
Participate in Group Discussions	X	X	X	X	X	X	X
Recalling What Was Heard				X			
Recognizing Fact and Opinion				X			
Respond to Speaker	X	X	X	X	X	X	X
Use Nonverbal Communication Techniques		X		X	X	X	X
Speaking							
Answer Questions	X	X	X	X	X	X	X
Asking Questions		X		X	X		
Describe Ideas and Feelings	X	X	X				X
Effective Word Choice/Voice			X	X	X	X	
Engaging the Audience					X	X	
Give Directions		X			X	X	X
Learn About Different Cultures through Discussion		X		X			X
Listen and Respond		X		X	X		
Making Announcements and Introductions		X					
Organizing Presentations				X	X	X	X
Paraphrasing			X	X			
Participate in Group Discussion	X	X	X	X	X	X	X
Present Oral Reports		X	X	X	X	X	X
Purposes of Speech		X					
Read Fluently with Expression, Phrasing, and Intonation		X	X	X	X	X	X
Read Orally	X	X	X	X	X	X	X
Share Information		X	X	X	X	X	X
Small Group Discussion			X	X	X	X	X
Speak Clearly at Appropriate Volume		X	X	X	X	X	X
Speaking Strategies				X	X		
Staying on Topic		X					
Summarize/Retell Stories	X	X	X	X	X	X	X
Understand Formal and Informal Language		X		X	X	X	X
Use Appropriate Language for Audience		X		X	X	X	X
Use Nonverbal Communication Techniques		X	X	X	X	X	X

Listening/Speaking/Viewing (continued)

	K	1	2	3	4	5	6
Viewing							
Analyze Purposes and Techniques of the Media			X	X	X	X	X
Appreciate/Interpret Artist's Techniques		X					
Compare Visual and Written Material on the Same Subject		X					X
Culture in Media		X			X	X	
Describe Pictures			X				
Gather Information from Visual Images		X	X	X	X	X	X
Interpreting Media				X	X		
Language Development							X
Literary Devices				X			X
Relating to Content				X	X		
Understanding Gestures				X	X		
Using Multimedia				X	X	X	
View Critically		X		X	X	X	X
Penmanship							
Cursive Letters			X	X			
Manuscript Letters	X	X					
Numbers	X	X					

Unit Themes

	Level K	Level 1	Level 2
Unit 1	Off to School	Back to School	Kindness
Unit 2	Patterns	Where Animals Live	Let's Explore
Unit 3	Finding Friends	I Am Responsible!	Around the Town
Unit 4	By the Sea	Our Neighborhood at Work	Look Again
Unit 5	Stick to It	What's the Weather?	Courage
Unit 6	My Shadow	North, South, East, West	America's People
Unit 7	Teamwork	I Think I Can	
Unit 8	Ready, Set, Grow!	Away We Grow!	
Unit 9	Red, White, and Blue	Home, Sweet Home	
Unit 10	Windy Days	I Am Brave	

Level 3	Level 4	Level 5	Level 6
Friendship	Risks and Consequences	Heritage	Taking a Stand
Animals and Their Habitats	Nature's Delicate Balance	Energy at Work	Ancient Civilizations
Money	A Changing America	Making a New Nation	Ecology
Earth, Moon, and Sun	Science Fair	Our Corner of the Universe	Great Expectations
Communities across Time	America on the Move	Going West	Earth in Action
Storytelling	Dollars and Sense	Call of Duty	Art and Impact

Glossary of Reading Terms

This glossary includes linguistic, grammatical, comprehension, and literary terms that may be helpful in understanding reading instruction.

acronym a word formed from the initial letter of words in a phrase, **scuba (self-contained underwater breathing apparatus).**

acrostic a kind of puzzle in which lines of a poem are arranged so that words or phrases are formed when certain letters from each line are used in a sequence.

adjective a word or group of words that modifies or describes a noun.

adventure story a narrative that features the unknown or unexpected with elements of excitement, danger, and risk.

adverb a word or group of words that modifies a verb, adjective, or other adverb. An adverb answers questions such as **how, when, where,** and **how much.**

affective domain the psychological field of emotional activities such as interests, attitudes, opinions, appreciations, values, and emotional sets

affix a word part, either a prefix or a suffix, that changes the meaning or function of a word root or stem.

affricate a speech sound that starts as a stop but ends as a fricative, the /ch/ in **catch.**

agreement the correspondence of syntactically related words; subjects and predicates are in agreement when both are singular or plural.

alliteration the repetition of the initial sounds in neighboring words or stressed syllables.

alphabet the complete set of letters representing speech sounds used in writing a language. In English there are twenty-six letters.

alphabet book a book for helping young children learn the alphabet by pairing letters with pictures whose sounds they represent.

alphabetic principle the association between sounds and the letters that represent them in alphabetic writing systems.

alveolar a consonant speech sound made when the tongue and the ridge of the upper and lower jaw stop to constrict the air flow, as /t/.

anagram a word or phrase whose letters form other words or phrases when rearranged, for example, **add** and **dad.**

analogy a likeness or similarity.

analytic phonics also deductive phonics, a whole-to-part approach to phonics in which a student is taught a number of sight words and then phonetic generalizations that can be applied to other words.

antonym a word that is opposite in meaning to another word.

appositive a word that restates or modifies a preceding noun, for example, **my daughter, Charlotte.** Appositives are also definitions of words usually set off by commas.

aspirate an unvoiced speech sound produced by a puff of air, as /h/ in **heart.**

aspirated stop a stop consonant sound released with a puff of air, as /k/, /p/, and /t/.

auditory discrimination the ability to hear phonetic likenesses and differences in phonemes and words.

author's purpose the motive or reason for which an author writes; includes to entertain, inform, persuade, and explain how.

automaticity fluent processing of information, requiring little effort or attention.

auxiliary verb a verb that precedes another verb to express time, mood, or voice; includes verbs such as **has, is,** and **will.**

ballad a narrative poem, composed of short verses to be sung or recited, usually containing elements of drama and often tragic in tone.

base word a word to which affixes may be added to create related words.

blank verse unrhymed verse, especially unrhymed iambic pentameter.

blend the joining of the sounds of two or more letters with little change in those sounds, for example, /spr/ in **spring;** also **consonant blend** or **consonant cluster.**

blending combining the sounds represented by letters or spellings to sound out or pronounce a word; contrast with **oral blending.**

breve the symbol placed above a vowel to indicate that it is a short vowel.

browse to skim through or look over in search of something of interest.

canon in literature, the body of major works that a culture considers important at a given time.

case a grammatical category that indicates the syntactic/semantic role of a noun phrase in a sentence.

cause-effect relationship a stated or implied association between an outcome and the conditions that brought it about; also the comprehension skill associated with recognizing this type of relationship as an organizing principle in text.

chapter book a book long enough to be divided into chapters, but not long or complex enough to be considered a novel.

characterization the way in which an author presents a character in a story, including describing words, actions, thoughts, and impressions of that character.

choral reading oral group reading to develop oral fluency by modeling.

cinquain a stanza of five lines, specifically one that has successive lines of two, four, six, eight, and two syllables.

cipher a system for writing in code.

clarifying a comprehension strategy in which the reader rereads text, uses a dictionary, uses decoding skills, or uses context clues to comprehend something that is unclear.

clause a group of words with a subject and a predicate used to form a part of or a whole sentence, a dependent clause modifies an independent clause, which can stand alone as a complete sentence.

collaborative learning learning by working together in small groups.

command a sentence that asks for action and usually ends with a period.

common noun in contrast to **proper noun,** a noun that denotes a class rather than a unique or specific thing such as **girl** versus **Susan.**

comprehension the understanding of what is written or said.

comprehension skill a skill that aids in understanding text, including identifying **author's purpose, author's point of view,** comprehending **cause-and-effect** relationships, **clarifying, comparing and contrasting** items and events, **drawing conclusions,** distinguishing **fact from opinion,** identifying **main ideas, making inferences,** distinguishing **reality from fantasy,** and understanding **sequence.**

comprehension strategy a sequence of steps for monitoring and understanding text, includes adjusting reading speed, asking questions, clarifying, making connections, predicting, summarizing, and visualizing.

conjugation the complete set of all possible inflected forms of a verb.

conjunction a part of speech used to connect words, phrases, clauses, or sentences, including the words **and, but,** and **or.**

consonant a speech sound, and the alphabet letter that represents that sound, made by partial or complete closure of part of the vocal tract, which obstructs air flow and causes audible friction.

context clue information from the immediate and surrounding text that helps identify a word.

contraction a short version of a written or spoken expression in which letters are omitted, for example, **can't.**

convention an accepted practice in spoken or written language, usually referring to spelling, mechanics, or grammar rules.

cooperative learning a classroom organization that allows students to work together to achieve their individual goals. Related term is **collaboration.**

creative writing prose and poetic forms of writing that express the writer's thoughts and feelings imaginatively.

cueing system any of the various sources of information that help identify an unrecognizable word in reading, including phonetic, semantic, and syntactical information.

cumulative tale a story, such as "The Gingerbread Man," in which details are repeated until the climax.

dangling modifier usually a participle that because of its placement in a sentence modifies the wrong object.

decodable text text materials controlled to include a majority of words whose sound/spelling relationships are known by the reader.

decode to analyze spoken or graphic symbols for meaning.

diacritical mark a mark, such as a breve or macron, added to a letter or graphic character to indicate a specific pronunciation.

dialect a regional variety of a particular language with phonological, grammatical, and lexical patterns that distinguishes it from other varieties.

dialogue a piece of writing written as conversation, usually punctuated by quotation marks.

digraph two letters that represent one speech sound, for example, /sh/ or /ch/.

diphthong a vowel sound produced when the tongue glides from one vowel sound toward another in the same syllable, for example, /oi/ or /ou/.

direct object the person or thing that receives the action of a verb in a sentence, for example, the word **cake** in this sentence: **Madeline baked a cake.**

drafting the process of writing ideas in rough form to record them.

drama a story in the form of a play, written to be performed.

edit in the writing process, to revise or correct a manuscript. Often this is part of the final step in the process with a focus on correcting grammar, spelling, and mechanics rather than content, structure, and organization.

emergent literacy the development of the association of meaning and print that continues until a child reaches the stage of conventional reading and writing.

emergent reading a child's early interaction with books and print before the ability to decode text.

encode to change a message into symbols, for example, to change speech into writing.

epic a long narrative poem, usually about a hero.

exclamatory sentence a sentence that shows strong emotion and ends with an exclamation point.

expository writing or **exposition** a composition in writing that explains an event or process.

fable a short tale that teaches a moral.

fantasy a highly imaginative story about characters, places, and events that cannot exist.

fiction imaginative narrative designed to entertain rather than to explain, persuade, or describe.

figure of speech the expressive, nonliteral use of language usually through metaphor, simile, or personification.

fluency freedom from word-identification problems that hinder comprehension in reading. Fluency involves rate, accuracy, and expression.

folktale a narrative form of genre such as an epic, myth, or fable that is well-known through repeated storytellings.

foreshadowing giving clues to upcoming events in a story.

free verse verse with irregular metrical pattern.

freewriting writing that is not limited in form, style, content, or purpose; designed to encourage students to write.

genre a classification of literary works, including tragedy, comedy, novel, essay, short story, mystery, realistic fiction, and poetry.

grammar the study of the classes of words, their inflections, and their functions and relations in sentences; includes phonological, morphological, syntactic, and semantic descriptions of a language.

grapheme a written or printed representation of a phoneme, such as **c** for /k/.

guided reading reading instruction in which the teacher provides the structure and purpose for reading and responding to the material read.

handing off a method of turning over to students the primary responsibility for controlling discussion.

indirect object in a sentence, the person or thing to or for whom an action is done, for example, the word **dog** in this sentence: **Madeline gave the dog a treat.**

inference a conclusion based on facts, data, or evidence.

infinitive the base form of a verb, usually with the infinitive marker, for example, **to go.**

inflectional ending an ending that expresses a plural or possessive form of a noun, the tense of a verb, or the comparative or superlative form of an adjective or adverb.

interrogative word a word that marks a clause or sentence as a question, including **interrogative pronouns who, what, which, where.**

intervention a strategy or program designed to supplement or substitute instruction, especially for those students who fall behind.

invented spelling the result of an attempt to spell a word based on using the sounds in the letter names to determine the sound the letter names. Gradually sounds are connected to letters, which leads to conventional spelling..

irony a figure of speech in which the literal meanings of the words is the opposite of their intended meanings.

journal a written record of daily events or responses.

juvenile book a book written for children or adolescents.

legend a traditional tale handed down from generation to generation.

leitmotif a repeated expression, event, or idea used to unify a work of art such as writing.

letter one of a set of graphic symbols that forms an alphabet and is used alone or in combination to represent a phoneme, also **grapheme.**

linguistics the study of the nature and structure of language and communication.

literary elements the elements of a story such as **setting, plot,** and **characterization** that create the structure of a narrative.

macron a diacritical mark placed above a vowel to indicate a long vowel sound.

main idea the central thought or chief topic of a passage.

making connections a reading strategy used to connect information being read to one's own experiences to other reading materials or to one's knowledge of the world. Making connections fosters engagement, while reading helps the reader make sense of the text and connect information.

mechanics the conventions of capitalization and punctuation.

metacognition awareness and knowledge of one's mental processes or thinking about what one is thinking about.

metaphor a figure of speech in which a comparison is implied but not stated; for example, **She is a jewel.**

miscue a deviation from text during oral reading in an attempt to make sense of the text.

modeling an instructional technique in which the teacher makes public the thinking needed to use critical reading and writing behaviors.

mood the literary element that conveys the emotional atmosphere of a story.

morpheme a meaningful linguistic unit that cannot be divided into smaller units, for example, **word; a bound morpheme** is a morpheme that cannot stand alone as an independent word, for example, the prefix **re-**; a **free morpheme** can stand alone, for example, **dog.**

myth a story designed to explain the mysteries of life.

narrative writing or **narration** a composition in writing that tells a story or gives an account of an event.

nonfiction prose designed to explain, argue, or describe rather than to entertain with a factual emphasis; includes biography and autobiography.

noun a part of speech that denotes persons, places, things, qualities, or acts.

novel an extended fictional prose narration.

onomatopoeia the use of a word whose sound suggests its meaning, for example, **purr.**

oral blending the ability to fuse discrete phonemes into recognizable words; oral blending puts sounds together to make a word, **see also segmentation.**

orthography correct or standardized spelling according to established usage in a language.

oxymoron a figure of speech in which contrasting or contradictory words are brought together for emphasis.

paragraph a subdivision of a written composition that consists of one or more sentences, deals with one point, or gives the words of one speaker, usually beginning with an indented line.

participle a verb form used as an adjective, for example, **the skating party.**

personification a figure of speech in which animals, ideas, or things take on human characteristics.

persuasive writing a composition intended to persuade the reader to adopt the writer's point of view.

phoneme the smallest sound unit of speech, for example, the /k/ in **book.**

phonemic awareness the ability to recognize that spoken words are made of discrete sounds and that those sounds can be manipulated.

phonetic spelling the respelling of entry words in a dictionary according to a pronunciation key.

phonetics the study of speech sounds.

phonics a way of teaching reading that addresses sound/symbol relationships, especially in beginning instruction.

phonogram a letter or symbol that represents a phonetic sound.

phonological awareness the ability to attend to the sound structure of language; includes sentence, word, syllable rhyme and phonological awareness.

plot the literary element that provides the structure of the action of a story, which may include rising action, climax, and falling action leading to a resolution or denouement.

plural a grammatical form of a word that refers to more than one in number; an irregular plural is one that does not follow normal patterns for inflectional endings.

poetic license the liberty taken by writers to ignore conventions.

poetry a metrical form of composition in which language is chosen and arranged to create a powerful response through meaning, sound, or rhythm.

possessive showing ownership either through the use of an adjective, an adjectival pronoun, or the possessive form of a noun.

predicate the part of the sentence that expresses something about the subject and includes the verb phrase; a **complete predicate** includes the principal verb in a sentence and all its modifiers or subordinate parts.

predicting a comprehension strategy in which the reader attempts to anticpate what will happen, using clues from the text and prior knowledge, and then confirms predictions as the text is read.

prefix an affix attached before a base word that changes the meaning of the word.

preposition a part of speech in the class of function words such as **of, on,** and **at** that precede noun phrases to create prepositional phrases.

prewriting the planning stage of the writing process in which the writer formulates ideas, gathers information, and considers ways to organize them.

print awareness in emergent literacy, a child's growing recognition of conventions and characteristics of written language, including reading from left to right and from top to bottom in English and that words are separated by spaces.

pronoun a part of speech used as a substitute for a noun or noun phrase.

proofreading the act of reading with the intent to correct, clarify, or improve text.

pseudonym an assumed name used by an author; a pen name or nom de plume.

publishing the process of preparing written material for presentation.

punctuation graphic marks such as commas, periods, quotation marks, and brackets used to clarify meaning and to give speech characteristics to written language.

question an interrogative sentence that asks a question and ends with a question mark.

realistic fiction a story that attempts to portray characters and events as they actually are.

rebus a picture or symbol that suggests a word or syllable.

revise in the writing process, to change or correct a manuscript to make its message more clear.

rhyme identical or very similar recurring final sounds in words, often at the ends of lines of poetry.

rime a vowel and any following consonants of a syllable.

segmentation the ability to break words into individual sounds; **see also oral blending.**

semantic mapping a graphic display of a group of words that are meaningfully related to support vocabulary instruction.

semantics the study of meaning in language, including the meanings of words, phrases, sentences, and texts.

sentence a grammatical unit that expresses a statement, question, or command; a **simple sentence** is a sentence with one subject and one predicate; a **compound sentence** is a sentence with two or more independent clauses usually separated by a comma and conjunction, but no dependent clause; a **complex sentence** is a sentence with one independent and one or more dependent clauses.

sentence combining a teaching technique in which complex sentence chunks and paragraphs are built from basic sentences.

sentence lifting the process of using sentences from children's writing to illustrate what is wrong or right to develop children's editing and proofreading skills.

sequence the order of elements or events.

setting the literary element that includes the time, place, and physical and psychological background in which a story takes place.

sight word a word that is taught to be read as a whole word, usually words that are phonetically irregular.

simile a figure of speech in which a comparison of two things that are unlike is directly stated, usually with the words **like** or **as**; for example, **She is like a jewel.**

spelling the process of representing language by means of a writing system.

statement a sentence that tells something and ends with a period.

study skills a general term for the techniques and strategies that help readers comprehend text with the intent to remember; includes following directions, organizing, locating, and using graphic aids.

style the characteristics of a work that reflect the author's particular way of writing.

subject the main topic of a sentence to which a predicate refers, including the principal noun; a **complete subject** includes the principal noun in a sentence and all its modifiers.

suffix an affix attached at the end of a base word that changes the meaning and the function of the word.

summarizing a comprehension strategy in which the reader constructs a brief statement that contains the essential ideas of a passage.

syllable a minimal unit of sequential speech sounds comprised of a vowel sound or a vowel-sound combination.

symbolism the use of one thing to represent something else to represent an idea in a concrete way.

synonym a word that means the same as another word.

syntax the grammatical pattern or structure of word order in sentences, clauses, and phrases.

tense the way in which verbs indicate past, present, and future time of action.

text structure the various patterns of ideas that are built into the organization of a written work.

theme a major idea or proposition that provides an organizing concept through which, by study, students gain depth of understanding.

topic sentence a sentence intended to express the main idea of a paragraph or passage.

tragedy a literary work, often a play, in which the main character suffers conflicts and which presents a serious theme and has an unfortunate ending.

usage the way in which a native language or dialect is used by the members of the community.

verb a word that expresses an action or state that occurs in a predicate of a sentence; an irregular verb is a verb that does not follow normal patterns of inflectional endings that reflect past, present, or future verb tense.

visualizing a comprehension strategy in which the reader constructs a mental picture of a character, setting, or process.

vowel a voiced speech sound and the alphabet letter that represents that sound, made without stoppage or friction of the air flow as it passes through the vocal tract.

vowel digraph a spelling pattern in which two or more letters represent a single vowel sound.

word calling proficiency in decoding with little or no attention to word meaning.

writing also **composition** the process or result of organizing ideas in writing to form a clear message; includes persuasive, expository, narrative, and descriptive forms.

writing process the many aspects of the complex act of producing a piece of writing, including prewriting, drafting, revising, editing/proofreading, and publishing.

Songs and Games

Alphabet Song

A, B, C, D, E, F, G,   H, I, J, K,

L, M, N,   O, P, Q,   R, S, T,

U, V, W.____   X, Y, Z.   Now I nev - er
(dou-ble u)

will for - get,   How to say the al - pha-bet.

a b c d e f g
h i j k l m n
o p q
r s t
u v w
x y z

Alphabet Rap

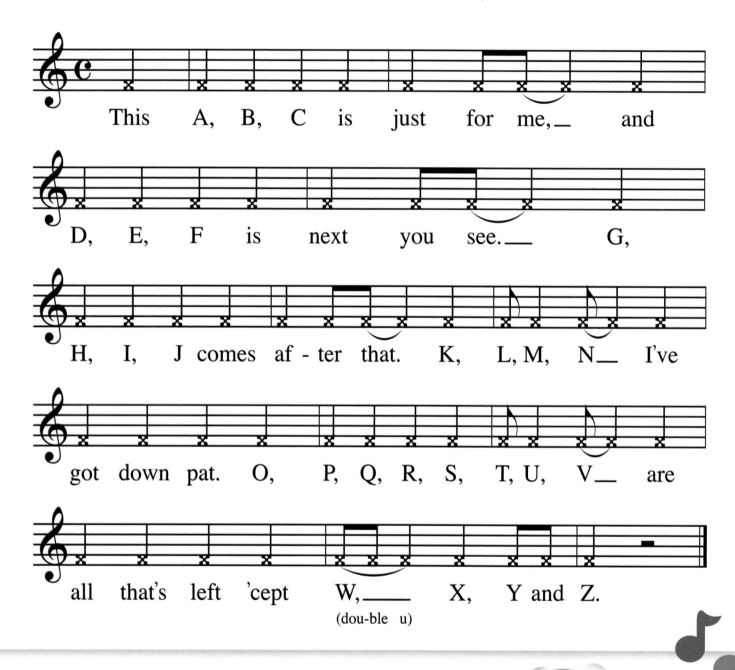

This   A,   B,   C   is   just   for   me,__   and

D,   E,   F   is   next   you   see.__   G,

H,   I,   J   comes   af - ter   that.   K,   L, M,   N__   I've

got   down   pat.   O,   P, Q,   R,   S,   T, U,   V__   are

all   that's   left   'cept   W,____   X,   Y and   Z.
(dou-ble u)

Alphabet Cheer

We're So Glad You're Here

We're so glad you're here.   We're so glad you're here.   We're so glad that Jor - dan's here.   We're so glad he's here.

We're so glad you're here
We're so glad you're here
We're so glad that <u>Katie</u>'s here
We're so glad <u>she</u>'s here

We're so glad you're here
We're so glad you're here
We're so glad that _____'s here
We're so glad ___'s here

If You're Happy and You Know It

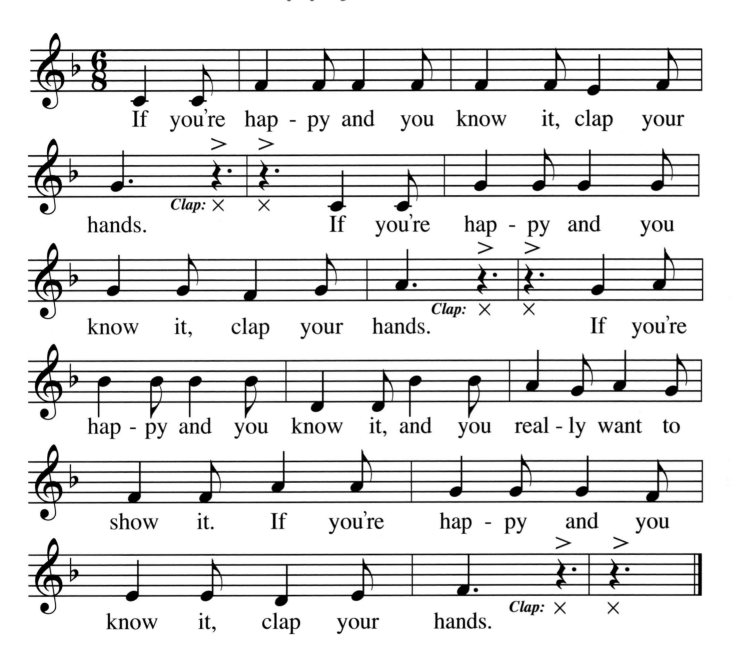

This is the Way We Come to Circle

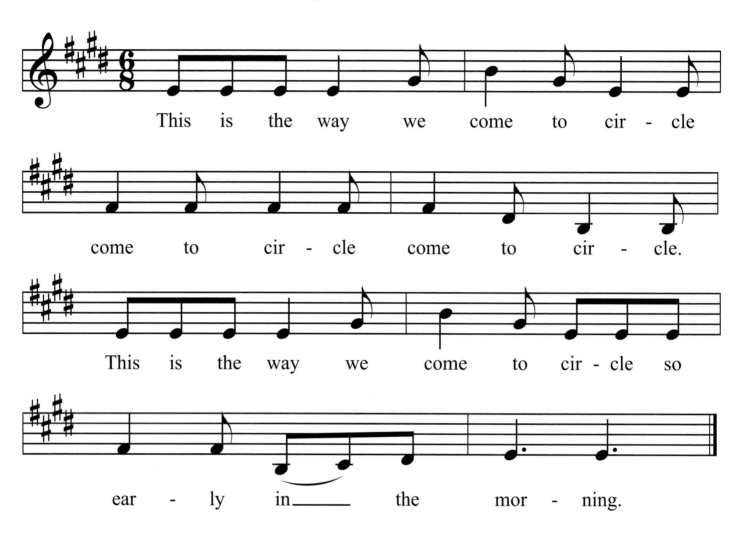

This is the way we come to cir - cle come to cir - cle come to cir - cle. This is the way we come to cir - cle so ear - ly in the mor - ning.

This is the way we sit right down,
Sit right down, sit right down.
This is the way we sit right down,
So early in the morning.

This is the way we fold our hands,
Fold our hands, fold our hands.
This is the way we fold our hands,
So early in the morning.

Hello

Hel - lo   Lu - cy.   Hel - lo   Lu - cy.

Hel - lo   Lu - cy   please   stand   and   take   a   bow.

Hello Jose, hello Jose,
Hello Jose, please stand, and take a bow.

Hello _____, hello _____,
Hello _____, please stand, and take a bow.

I'm a Little Teapot

Are You Sleeping?

Where is <u>Charlotte</u>? Where is <u>Charlotte</u>?
Here I am! Here I am!
Hello to you <u>Charlotte</u>. We are glad to see you.
Take a bow. Take a bow.

Where is _____? Where is _____?
Here I am! Here I am!
Hello to you _____. We are glad to see you.
Take a bow. Take a bow.

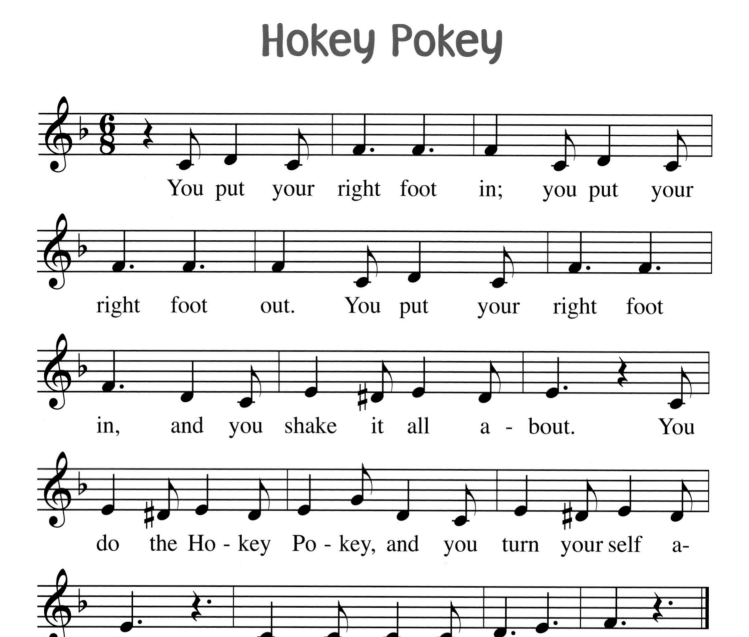

Hokey Pokey

You put your right foot in; you put your right foot out. You put your right foot in, and you shake it all a - bout. You do the Ho - key Po - key, and you turn your self a - round. That's what ___ it's all a - bout!

You put your right hand in; you take your right hand out.
You put your right hand in, and you shake it all about.
You do the hokey pokey, and you turn yourself around.
That's what it's all about!

You put your left foot in; you take your left foot out.
You put your left foot in, and you shake it all about.
You do the hokey pokey, and you turn yourself around.
That's what it's all about!

You put your left hand in; you take your left hand out.
You put your left hand in, and you shake it all about.
You do the hokey pokey, and you turn yourself around.
That's what it's all about!

Teddy Bear, Teddy Bear

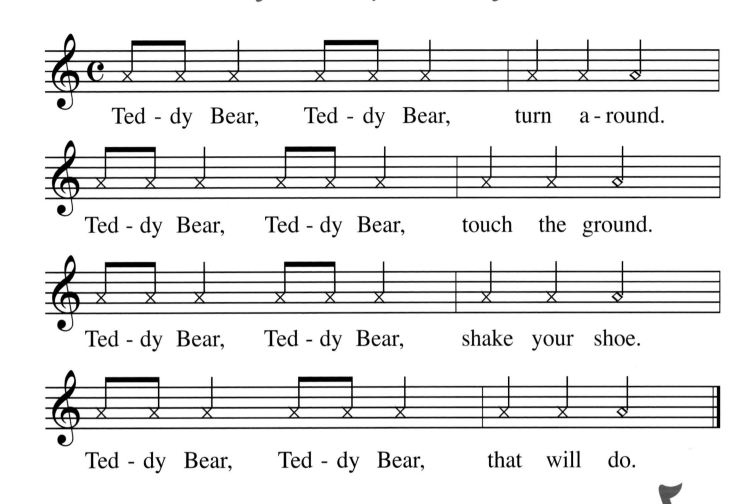

Ted - dy Bear,   Ted - dy Bear,   turn   a - round.

Ted - dy Bear,   Ted - dy Bear,   touch   the   ground.

Ted - dy Bear,   Ted - dy Bear,   shake   your   shoe.

Ted - dy Bear,   Ted - dy Bear,   that   will   do.

Down By the Bay

Down by the bay. Where the wa-ter mel-lons grow. Back to my home. I dare not go. For if I do, My mo ther will say, "Did you ev-er see a fly wear-ing a tie?" Down by the bay.

Down by the bay	Down by the bay	Down by the bay
Where the watermelons grow	Where the watermelons grow	Where the watermelons grow
Back to my home	Back to my home	Back to my home
I dare not go	I dare not go	I dare not go
For if I do	For if I do	For if I do
My mother will say	My mother will say	My mother will say
"Did you ever see a bear	"Did you ever see a moose	"Did you ever see a whale
Combing his hair?"	Kissing a goose?"	With a polka dot tail?"
Down by the bay	Down by the bay	Down by the bay

Apples and Bananas

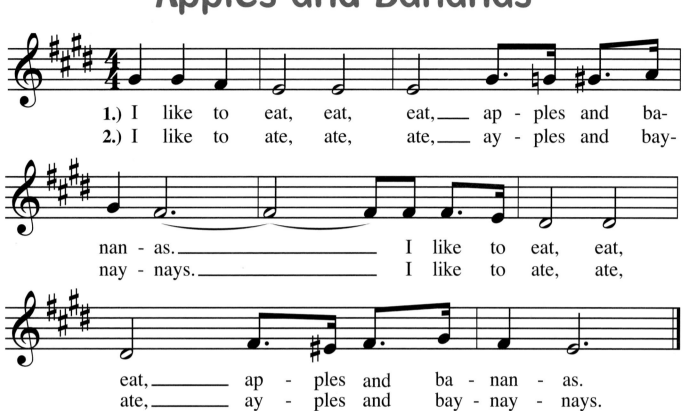

1.) I like to eat, eat, eat,____ ap - ples and ba-
2.) I like to ate, ate, ate,____ ay - ples and bay-

nan - as._____ I like to eat, eat,
nay - nays._____ I like to ate, ate,

eat,_____ ap - ples and ba - nan - as.
ate,_____ ay - ples and bay - nay - nays.

Vowel Song

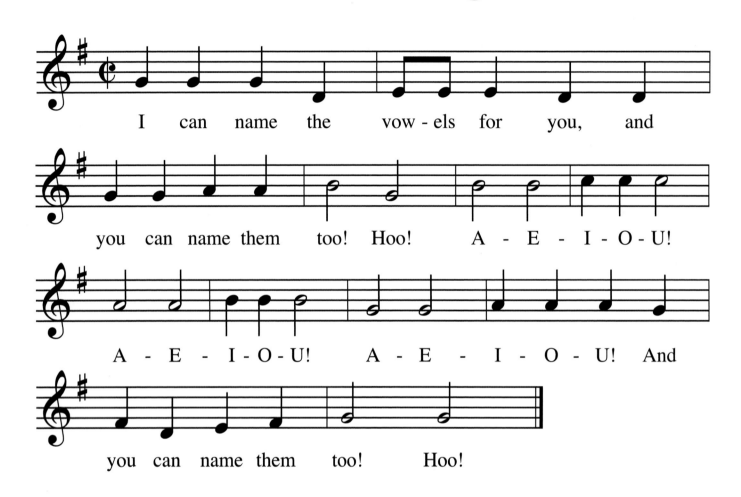

I can name the vow - els for you, and

you can name them too! Hoo! A - E - I - O - U!

A - E - I - O - U! A - E - I - O - U! And

you can name them too! Hoo!

The Ship Is Loaded With _____

Purpose

To provide students with a movement activity that will reinforce rhyming words and initial consonant sounds

Instruction

Have students sit in a circle. Explain that you are loading a ship with items that sound alike. Each student will have a chance to say a rhyming word. Use a ball or anything that can be rolled from student to student. Ask for a volunteer, and have that student say *The ship is loaded with cheese.* The student then rolls the ball to someone else who must repeat the line, substituting a rhyming word for cheese (for example, *peas, bees, keys, breeze, fleas,* or *trees).*

At this point, you might have the student roll the ball back to the first student, who will repeat *The ship is loaded with* cheese. Or have the student roll the ball to someone else for a new rhyming word.

Play the game using the following words:

The ship is loaded with *cats (mats, rats, bats, hats).*

The ship is loaded with *logs (frogs, hogs, dogs, bogs).*

The ship is loaded with *cans (fans, bans, Dans, pans).*

Play The Ship Is Loaded with _____ game, and have students choose words with the same initial sound. For example, if they choose /b/, students can say *The ship is loaded with* basketballs, begonias, baseballs, balls, *and* blankets.

Ordering Letters Game

Give each student a set of **Alphabet Letter Cards** *Aa–Nn.* (You may add letters as the student's knowledge of new letters increases). The cards in each set should be shuffled out of order and should face different ways.

Tell students they should do two things with these cards. First they should turn all the cards so they are showing either all capitals or all small letters. Then students should each show the set to a partner to check.

Next have each student work with a partner and match each capital letter with a small letter.

Simon Says

Purpose

To reinforce word concepts using a game format

Instruction

Tell students you are going to play Simon says. For those unfamiliar with the game, explain that when Simon says to do something, they must follow the instructions. Also, tell them they should not follow any directions that do not start with the words *Simon says*. Give the following instructions:

> **Simon says pat your head.**
> **(Students pat their heads.)**
>
> **Simon says rub your tummy.**
> **(Students rub their tummies.)**
>
> **Simon says hop on one foot.**
> **(Students hop on one foot.)**
>
> **Simon says hop on your left foot.**
> **(Students hop on their left feet.)**

After giving several different instructions, give another one, omitting *Simon says:*

> Jump in place.
>
> (Students should stand still.)

Students are "out" when they

- do something Simon does not say to do.
- do something other than what Simon says.
- do not do what Simon says.

When a student is "out," you can have him or her sit down. Continue the game until one student is left standing. Another alternative is to give each student an ***Alphabet Letter Card*** to identify if they miss an instruction. If the student correctly identifies the letter, he or she can stay in the game.

To reinforce language skills, try different and gradually more challenging instructions, such as the following:

- Students can touch their noses and then turn around.

- Add numbers *(jump three times; clap four times; pat tummy once).*

- Add prepositions and prepositional phrases designating location *(over, under, in front of, behind).*

- Add conjunctions (hop *and* skip).

- Use adjectives (take *big* steps).

- Use adjectival strings (*take three big* steps).

- Use adverbs *(clap softly).*

- Add negatives *(don't clap your hands).*

- Add conditionals *if, when, unless, until, while (rub your tummy while you pat your head).*

Mat Games

Purpose

To help students match sounds to letters

Instruction

Play each of these games on a *Game Mat,* using game markers to move around the squares. Place the mat on a table or on the floor. Have students gather around the mat, and explain to them that as they move around the squares, they will be naming letters and sounds.

Each of the *Game Mats* is generic and can be used for not only the games described here, but also for games you create with students. You and your class might enjoy creating variations of the games described here or creating entirely new games to play on the mats.

Create new rules and difficulty levels as your class needs or wants them. Challenge students to think of new games to play on the mats.

Difficulty Levels

The levels of difficulty described here are simply suggestions. Your students may need to begin with much easier tasks, or they may not be challenged enough by them. Always suit the games to the activities and levels of difficulty where you know your class will be most comfortable. The games should be difficult enough to challenge students yet easy enough for them to experience success and have fun.

Hop Along Game

The object of this game is to move the game marker from the bunny to the carrot at the end of the trail. Use a number cube to determine how many spaces a student may move the marker along the trail. If the student lands on a letter, he or she must do one of the following, depending on the level of difficulty you have chosen:

Name the letter	(Level 1)
Name the sound of the letter	(Level 2)

If the student does not name the correct letter or sound, he or she must do one of the following:

Lose a turn	(Level 1)
Go back a space until he or she is able to name the correct letter or sound	(Level 2)

If the student lands on a happy face, he or she may take an extra turn.

Ball Diamond, School Yard, A Day at the Beach, My Neighborhood, Race Track

Play all these games with the same rules. Each student rolls the number cube and moves the game marker the correct number of spaces. Use the **Alphabet Letter Cards** for Level 1 and the **Alphabet Sound Cards** for the card pack on Levels 2, 3, and 4. Have each student draw a card. Depending on the level, students will do the following:

State the name of the letter	(Level 1)
State the sound the letter makes	(Level 2)
Name a word that begins with the sound	(Level 3)
Name the letter, the sound, and a word that begins with the sound	(Level 4)

If students do not guess correctly, they lose the next turn.

Winning the Games

These games can be played quickly, or you can have students extend them. For a quick game, have them play until the first student reaches the goal at the end of the trail. If a student has not reached the goal when the cards run out, the student closest to the goal wins.

To extend the games, tell students to shuffle the cards when the last card has been chosen and to keep playing. The number of times the cards are shuffled will determine the length of the game. Again, the student who reaches the goal or is closest to the goal when the cards run out for the last time wins the game.

Challenges

These games are designed to be played independently by students. This means students must determine whether each given answer is correct. Encourage them to discuss any differences of opinion they may have. If they are not able to decide whether the answer is correct, tell them to raise their hands so you can help them.

Penmanship

SRA !magine It! develops handwriting skills through Penmanship lessons three days each week. The instruction for these lessons appears in the Sounds and Letters part in this grade level. The purpose of these lessons is to develop important handwriting skills necessary for producing legible, properly spaced documents. In kindergarten, penmanship practice reinforces the sound-letter correspondence in the lesson.

The overhead projector, in addition to the board, can be an effective device for teaching penmanship. Students can move their pencils at the same time you form letters on the transparency. To further help students, you should also recite the descriptions or chants that go with each letter.

Penmanship in Grades K–1

Beginning in kindergarten, the Penmanship lessons expand on the sound/letter instruction by introducing letters students study in Sounds and Letters. Students learn that those letters are made of four basic lines: curved lines, horizontal lines, vertical lines, and slanted lines.

Next students learn letter and number formation. Students practice letter formation by writing the letter being studied and then words that contain the particular letter. This instruction continues in Level 1 and is tied to the letter formation instruction in Language Arts.

Manuscript Penmanship Models

The lessons present ball-and-stick models of manuscript handwriting, while this appendix offers an alternative method with continuous stroke models.

Hand and Paper Positioning

The **hand and paper positioning** models are for your reference and enhance the written instruction of positioning lessons. The diagrams give you a visual aid so you may better understand and demonstrate an effective technique of positioning.

A right-handed student should hold the pencil loosely about one inch above the point, between the thumb and middle finger. A left-handed student should hold the pencil the same way, but up to one half inch farther away from the point. The index fingers of both writers should rest lightly on the top of the pencil. The wrist should be level and slightly raised from the desk.

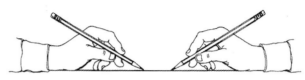

Left-handed writers Right-handed Writers

For both kinds of writers, the paper should lie straight in front of the student with the edges parallel to the edges of the desk. A left-handed writer may find it easier to slant the paper slightly to the right and parallel to the left forearm. A right-handed writer's writing hand should be kept well below the writing. The left hand should hold down the paper.

Left-handed writers   Right-handed Writers

Ball and Stick Penmanship Models

The **ball-and-stick** models of manuscript handwriting provide you with a systematic method for teaching students to form uppercase and lowercase letters of the alphabet. The dots on the letters indicate starting points for students. The numbered arrows show students in which order and direction the line they are drawing should go to form the particular letter. You may use the chants to describe the letter step by step as students model the formation on the board. Students may also recite the chants in unison as they practice the formation, whether they are writing the letter or tracing it on the board.

Ball-and-Stick Penmanship Models

capital *A*

a   Starting point, around left all
the way
Starting point, straight down,
touching the circle: small *a*

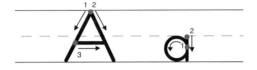

A   Starting point, slanting down left
Starting point, slanting down right
Starting point, across the middle:

B   Starting point, straight down
Starting point, around right and in
at the middle, around right and in at

d   Starting point, around left all
the way
Starting point, straight down,
touching the circle: small *d*

D   Starting point, straight down
Starting point, around right and in
at the bottom: capital *D*

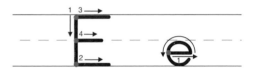

E   Starting point, straight down
Starting point, straight out
Starting point, straight out

g   Starting point, around left all
the way
Starting point, straight down,
touching the circle, around left to
stopping place: small *g*

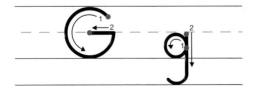

G   Starting point, around left, curving
up and around
Straight in: capital *G*

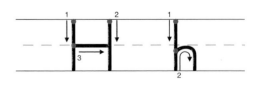

H   Starting point, straight down
Starting point, straight down
Starting point, across the middle:

Ball-and-Stick Penmanship Models

j   Starting point, straight down, around left to stopping place Dot exactly above: small *j*

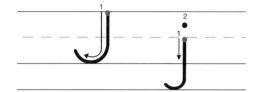

J   Starting point, straight down, around left to stopping place: capital *J*

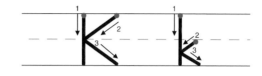

K   Starting point, straight down Starting point, slanting down left, touching the line, slanting down

right, straight down: capital *M*

m   Starting point, straight down, back up, around right, straight down, back up, around right, straight down: small *m*

n   Starting point, straight down, back up, around right, straight down: small *n*

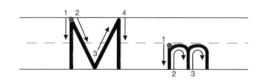

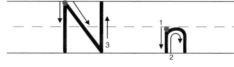

M   Starting point, straight down Starting point, slanting down right to the point, slanting back up to the

N   Starting point, straight down Starting point, slanting down right, straight back up: capital *N*

p   Starting point, straight down Starting point, around right all the way, touching the line: small *p*

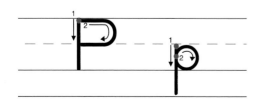

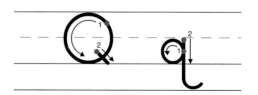

P   Starting point, straight down Starting point, around right and in at the middle: capital *P*

Q   Starting point, around left all the way Starting point, slanting down right:

Ball-and-Stick Penmanship Models

s Starting point, around left, curving right and down around right,

curving left and up to stopping place: small *s*

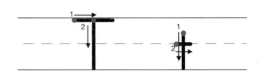

S Starting point, around left, curving right and down around right, curving left and up: capital *S*

T Starting point, straight across
Starting point, straight down: capital *T*

v Starting point, slanting down right, slanting up right: small *v*

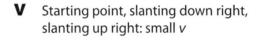

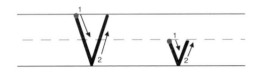

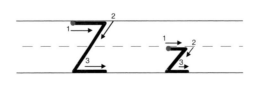

V Starting point, slanting down right, slanting up right: capital *V*

W Starting point, slanting down right, slanting up right, slanting down right, slanting up right: capital *W*

z Starting point, straight across, slanting down left, straight across: small *z*

Y Starting point, slanting down right, stop
Starting point, slanting down left, stop
Starting point, straight down: capital *Y*

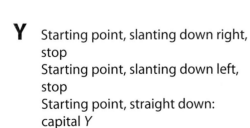

y Starting point, slanting down right
Starting point, slanting down left, connecting the lines: small *y*

Z Starting point, straight across, slanting down left, straight across: capital *Z*

Continuous Stroke Penmanship Models

Continuous stroke models of manuscript handwriting provide you with an alternative to the ball-and-stick method. The purpose of these models is geared toward teaching students to write letters without lifting their pencils.

Aa Bb Cc Dd Ee

Ff Gg Hh Ii Jj

Kk Ll Mm Nn Oo

Pp Qq Rr Ss Tt

Uu Vv Ww Xx

Yy Zz

Numbers

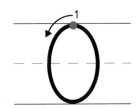

0 Starting point, curving left all the way around to starting point: *0*

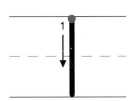

1 Starting point, straight down: *1*

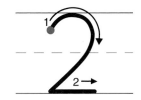

2 Starting point, around right, slanting left and straight across right: *2*

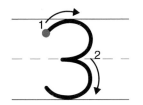

3 Starting point, around right, in at the middle, around right: *3*

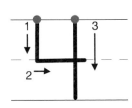

4 Starting point, straight down
Straight across right
Starting point, straight down, crossing line: *4*

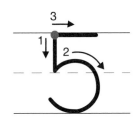

5 Starting point, straight down, curving around right and up
Starting point, straight across right: *5*

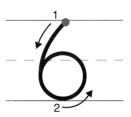

6 Starting point, slanting left, around the bottom curving up, around right and into the curve: *6*

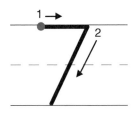

7 Starting point, straight across right, slanting down left: *7*

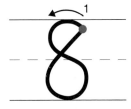

8 Starting point, curving left, curving down and around right, slanting up right to starting point: *8*

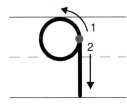

9 Starting point, curving around left all the way, straight down: *9*

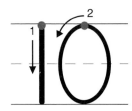

10 Starting point, straight down
Starting point, curving left all the way around to starting point: *10*

Alphabet Activities

Purpose

To provide students with activities for reinforcement of letter shapes

About the Activities

During Workshop of lessons in which you introduce letters, include activities in which students can make letters. Activities like these are included in the lessons already, while some letter-making activities you can establish in your classroom are listed below.

Most students will probably need a visual model to help them get started. Use red, blue, or green markers to print the letters on sturdy cardboard or poster board cards. Students will make yarn letters, glue letters, or other types by tracing the model.

All these activities, in addition to reinforcing letter formation, will help students' visual, perceptual, and fine-motor development.

Yarn Letters

Give each student four 4-inch pieces, four 8-inch pieces, and four 12-inch pieces of heavy yarn (such as rug yarn) to form letters. Each different length of yarn can be a different color (for example, 4-inch—red, 8-inch—blue, and 12-inch—green). When you work with students to form a particular letter, you can help them by using colors. For example, if students are making a capital *A,* they can use one blue piece and one red. Keep the yarn pieces in small plastic bags for reuse each time you introduce a new letter.

Clay Letters

Have students roll modeling clay into sticks that can be broken into different lengths and curved as necessary to form letters. When they are finished, have students roll their letters back into balls of clay. Keep these in sealed plastic bags for reuse.

Sand Letters

Provide each student with a small Styrofoam grocery tray filled halfway with sand. Have students trace with their fingers the letters they are practicing. In later lessons, have students trace words.

Pipe Cleaner Letters

Cut 12-inch pipe cleaners into 4-inch and 8-inch pieces, leaving some 12-inch pieces. Instruct students to form letters with the different lengths of pipe cleaners.

Glue Letters

Provide each student with large printed models of the letters. Tell students to trace the letters with glue and then sprinkle the glue with glitter, colored sand, confetti, salt, oatmeal, rice, or any other material that is not too bulky to stick to the glue. After the glue has begun to dry, have students shake off any excess material.

Drinking Straw Letters

Cut 8-inch drinking straws in half to make 4-inch pieces. Then cut them in fourths to make 2-inch pieces. Leave some the 8-inch length. Have students form letters using the pieces. Drinking straws are not suitable for letters that have curved lines but work well for those with straight and slanted lines.

Floor Letters

Have students form letters from various classroom materials, such as jump ropes, building blocks, beads, string, and so on.

Finger-Paint Letters

Using finger paints and finger-paint paper, have students trace letters with their fingers.

Board Letters

Encourage students to use the board or chart paper to practice their letters.

The Pocket Chart

Purpose

To provide a device that will allow students to practice word substitutions and to play with words

Developing Concepts Using the *Pocket Chart*

The *Pocket Chart* will help students understand written language. They will begin to understand the concept of words, phrases, and sentences. It is easy to substitute and play with words in the ten-line *Pocket Chart.*

Introducing Print At the beginning of the year, use the *Pocket Chart* to introduce print in another way to students. Seeing the words in the *Pickled Peppers Big Book* on the board, on chart paper, or in the *Pocket Chart* gives students several opportunities to understand print.

Words Take the *Pocket Chart Word Cards* out of the *Pocket Chart,* and allow students to handle the individual cards. Students will begin to comprehend the concept of words and learn that words vary in length.

Sequence Arrange the *Pocket Chart Word Cards* and *Pocket Chart Picture Cards* out of sequence and "read" them. Have students help you rearrange the cards in order, reinforcing their understanding of word order in phrases and sentences.

Matching Words to Pictures Show students a *Pocket Chart Picture Card.* Have them say the name of the picture, and ask them for the beginning and ending sounds of the picture name. Allow them to choose the matching *Pocket Chart Word Card* based on their answers to your questions. After students have had many experiences with written words and the *Pocket Chart,* place the *Word Cards* in the *Pocket Chart,* and have students match the *Picture Cards* with the *Word Cards.*

Matching Words to Words Use *Pickled Peppers* selections that repeat words or entire lines several times. Place portions of a selection in the *Pocket Chart,* leaving space for students to complete the excerpt by placing the appropriate repeated *Pocket Chart Word Cards* in the *Pocket Chart.*

Rhyme and Substituting Words After students have learned a *Pickled Peppers* selection, place a portion of it in the *Pocket Chart,* then substitute rhyming *Pocket Chart Word Cards* or *Picture Cards* for various words. Although the result may be a change in meaning, students will hear a new rhyme. You may want to place *Alphabet Letter Cards* over the letters that make the initial sound of key words to create rhyming words with different initial sounds. For example, you may want to place the *Mm* card over the initial consonants in "Peter Piper picked" to make "Meter Miper micked."

Position Words and Prepositional Phrases Place in the *Pocket Chart* a phrase such as "under the [picture of a bed]" and substitute the *Pocket Chart Word Cards* to make other phrases. Ask students to change the phrase by changing the position word or the *Pocket Chart Picture Card.* Position words include *after, against, at, behind, down, here, in, on, out, over, right, underneath,* and *up.*

Framing Sentences Place only the beginning of a sentence in the *Pocket Chart Pocket Chart,* such as "I hear a _____ ."

Ask students to finish the sentence by placing a *Pocket Chart Word Card* or *Picture Card* at the end. You may also choose to set incomplete lines from "Keep a Poem in Your Pocket" in the *Pocket Chart,* asking students to complete the line with an appropriate card.

Pocket Chart Card Lists

The following lists are intended to save time in gathering *Pocket Chart Word Cards* and *Picture Cards* for *Pickled Peppers* selections and other activities. *Picture Cards* are in **boldfaced type.**

Numbers

0/zero, **1**/one, **2**/two, **3**/three, **4**/four, **5**/five, **6**/six, **7**/seven, **8**/eight, **9**/nine, **10**/ten

Colors

black/black, **blue**/blue/azul, **brown**/brown, **gray, green**/green/ verde, **orange**/orange/anaranjada, **pink**/pink, **purple**/purple, **red**/red, **white**/white, **yellow**/yellow/amarilla

Foods

apple, apple juice, berry/berry, **bowls of spaghetti, cherry**/ cherry, **corn**/corn, **eggplants, ice, jam, juice, loaf, bread, loaves of bread, meat, noodle,** orange, **peanut butter, peppers**/peppers, **pickled pears, pie, pizza pies, potatoes, pumpkins, rice, roasted turkeys, tomatoes, vegetables, water**/water, **watermelons, yam**

Opposites

big, little; **black**/black, **white**/white; **day, night**/night; for, against; in, out; short, tall; up, down

Pickled Peppers Big Book **Selections**

I'm a Little Teapot* a, all, and, and, get, handle, hear, here, Here, I, I'm, is, is, little, me, me, me, my, my, out, over, pour, short, shout, spout, stout, **teapot/**teapot, Tip, up, When

One, Two, Buckle My Shoe* **1/**One, **2/**two, **3/**Three, **4/**four, **5/**Five, **6/**six, **7/**Seven, **8/**eight, **9/**Nine, **10/**ten, A, big, Buckle, **door/**door, fat, **hen/**hen, Lay, my, Pick, **shoe/**shoe, Shut, **sticks/**sticks, straight, the, them, up

Little Boy Blue**** after, blow, **boy/**boy, **Boy Blue/**Boy Blue, Come, **corn/**corn, cow's, **horn/**horn, in, in, is, looks, meadow, **sheep/**sheep, sheep's, the, the, the, the, The, The, Where, Who, your

Jack and Jill* a, after, and, And, And, broke, came, **crown/**crown, down, fell, fetch, **hill,** hill, his, **Jack/**Jack, Jack, **Jill/**Jill, Jill, of, **pail/**pail, the, To, tumbling, up, **water/**water, Went

Humpty Dumpty* a, a, again, all, All, and, Couldn't, fall, great, had, **horses/**horses, Humpty, **Humpty Dumpty/**Humpty Dumpty, Humpty Dumpty, King's, King's, **men/**men, on, put, sat, the, the, together, **wall/**wall

Little Bo Peep* alone, and, And, behind, **Bo Peep/**Bo Peep, come, doesn't, find, has, her, know, Leave, Little, lost, **sheep/**sheep, **tails/**tails, them, them, their, them, they'll, to, Wagging, where

Peter Piper** a, A, of, of, **peck/**peck, peck, **peppers/**peppers, peppers, **Peter Piper/**Peter Piper, Peter Piper, picked, picked, pickled, pickled

One Hungry Monster** **1/**One, **2/**two, **3/**Three, **4/**four, **5/**Five, **6/**six, **7/**Seven, **8/**eight, **9/**Nine, **10/**ten, and, **apple juice,** be, **bed/**bed, begging, **bowls of spaghetti, clam, eggplants,** fed, groaning, hungry, **jam, loaves of bread,** moaning, **monster/**monster, **monsters,** my, **orange/**orange, **peanut butter, pickled pears, pizza pies, pumpkins, purple/**purple, **roasted turkeys,** to, underneath, **watermelons**

Rope Rhyme** and, and, and, Bounce, clappedy-slappedy, Get, giggle, **ground/**ground, hits, in, it, jump, kick, Listen, Listen, now, ready, right, **rope/**rope, set, sound, spin, that, the, the, to, to, when

Who Said Red?** A, A, A, **berry/**berry, **cherry/**cherry, Did, **red/**red, red, red, red, red, red, Santa, say, sign, stop, **stop sign,** very, Who, you

Rhyme*** a, A, A, and, **black/**black, blunder, Come, down, dunder, **hills/**hills, I, I, it, like, like, see, see, slow, **storm/**storm, storm, storm, stumbling, the, thunder, to, to

Tent***** A, **bone/**bone, bone, canvas, cut, for, from, I, is, It's, It's, Just, like, me, measure, My, sewn, **skin/**skin, stretched, **tent/**tent, That's, to, to, where, wonder

Little Pine* a, a, against, But, doesn't, even, feet, few, grows, have, I, I, is, it, it, it, It, just, keep, little, measuring, more, My, myself, **pine/**pine, slower, tall, the, the, **tree/**tree, trunk, watch, yet

Houses/Casitas (English)* **1/**one, A, a, a, a, an, **blue/**blue, bouquet, **bouquet of flowers,** down, **flowers/**flowers, **green/**green, **house/**house, house, house, house, is, Just, Like, look, of, **orange/**orange, ours, **street/**street, the, The, **yellow/**yellow

Houses/Casitas (Spanish)*** a, **amarilla/**amarilla, **anaranjada/**anaranjada, Asómate, **azul/**azul, **calle/**calle, **casita/**casita, casita, casita, casita, la, mira, Una, una, una, una, **verde/**verde, y

Keep a Poem in Your Pocket** a, a, and, and, at, **bed/**bed, feel, **head/**head, in, in, in, Keep, lonely, never, night, picture, **pocket/**pocket, poem, when, you'll, your, your, you're

* There are *Pocket Chart Word* or *Picture Cards* for the entire selection.

**There are *Pocket Chart Word* or *Picture Cards* for the first four lines of the selection.

***There are *Pocket Chart Word* or *Picture Cards* for the first five lines of the selection.

****There are *Pocket Chart Word* or *Picture Cards* for the first six lines of the selection.

*****There are *Pocket Chart Word* or *Picture Cards* for the first eight lines of the selection.

Introduction of Letters and Sounds

Lesson	Letters and Sounds	Pre-Decodables/Decodables	High-Frequency Words
Unit 1			
Lesson 1	A		
Lesson 2	B	*Pre-Decodable* 1: The First Day of Kindergarten	
Lesson 3	C		
Lesson 4	D	*Pre-Decodable* 2: Apple Pie	
Lesson 5	E		
Lesson 6	F		
Lesson 7	A-F	*Pre-Decodable* 3: A Farm	a
Lesson 8	G		
Lesson 9	H	*Pre-Decodable* 4: The Lunch	the
Lesson 10	I		
Lesson 11	J		
Lesson 12	K	*Pre-Decodable* 5: School	and
Lesson 13	L		
Lesson 14	M	*Pre-Decodable* 6: Go Play!	go
Lesson 15	G-M		
Unit 2			
Lesson 1	N		
Lesson 2	O	*Pre-Decodable* 7: The Zoo	had
Lesson 3	P		
Lesson 4	Q	*Pre-Decodable* 8: Colors	he
Lesson 5	R		
Lesson 6	S		
Lesson 7	N-S	*Pre-Decodable* 9: Shapes	I
Lesson 8	T		
Lesson 9	U	*Pre-Decodable* 10: Animal Tracks	see
Lesson 10	V		
Lesson 11	W		
Lesson 12	X	*Pre-Decodable* 11: The Tree	has
Lesson 13	Y		
Lesson 14	Z	*Pre-Decodable* 12: Flowers	you
Lesson 15	T-Z		

Lesson	Letters and Sounds	Pre-Decodables/Decodables	High-Frequency Words
Unit 3			
Lesson 1	initial /s/		
Lesson 2	final /s/		
Lesson 3	initial /m/		
Lesson 4	final /m/		
Lesson 5	review /s/ and /m/	*Pre-Decodable* 13: We Go	we
Lesson 6	initial /d/		
Lesson 7	final /d/		
Lesson 8	initial /p/		
Lesson 9	final /p/		
Lesson 10	review /d/ and /p/	*Pre-Decodable* 14: We Carry	of
Lesson 11	/a/		
Lesson 12	/a/		
Lesson 13	review /s/, /m/, and /a/	*Pre-Decodable* 15: In the Park	in
Lesson 14	blending		
Lesson 15	/s/, /m/, /a/, /d/ and /p/	*Decodable* 1: Sam and Pam	am
Unit 4			
Lesson 1	initial /h/		
Lesson 2	initial /h/		
Lesson 3	initial /t/		
Lesson 4	final /t/		
Lesson 5	review /h/ and /t/	*Decodable* 2: A Hat!	at, to
Lesson 6	initial /n/		
Lesson 7	final /n/		
Lesson 8	initial /l/		
Lesson 9	final /l/		
Lesson 10	review /n/ and /l/	*Decodable* 3: Nan and Lad	as, have
Lesson 11	/i/		
Lesson 12	/i/		
Lesson 13	review /h/, /t/, and /i/		
Lesson 14	review /n/, /l/, and /i/		
Lesson 15	/h/, /t/, /i/, /n/, and /l/	*Decodable* 4: Tim in Sand	is, it

Lesson	Letters and Sounds	Pre-Decodables/Decodables	High-Frequency Words
Unit 5			
Lesson 1	initial /b/		
Lesson 2	final /b/		
Lesson 3	/k/ spelled *Cc*		
Lesson 4	/k/ spelled *Cc*		
Lesson 5	/b/ and /k/	*Decodable* 5: Cal Can Bat	can, his
Lesson 6	/o/		
Lesson 7	/o/		
Lesson 8	initial /r/		
Lesson 9	final /r/		
Lesson 10	initial /g/	*Decodable* 6: Ron Hops	him, on
Lesson 11	final /g/		
Lesson 12	review /r/ and /g/		
Lesson 13	review /b/, /k/, and /o/		
Lesson 14	review /r/, /g/, and /o/		
Lesson 15	/b/, /k/, /o/, /r/, and /g/	*Decodable* 7: Glad Pam	did, girl
Unit 6			
Lesson 1	initial /j/		
Lesson 2	initial /j/		
Lesson 3	initial /f/		
Lesson 4	final /f/		
Lesson 5	review /j/ and /f/	*Decodable* 8: Jam Pot	for
Lesson 6	/u/		
Lesson 7	/u/		
Lesson 8	/ks/ (*Xx*)		
Lesson 9	/ks/ (*Xx*)		
Lesson 10	/z/	*Decodable* 9: Bud and Max	but, up
Lesson 11	/z/ spelled Ss		
Lesson 12	review /ks/ and /z/		
Lesson 13	review /j/, /f/, and /u/		
Lesson 14	review /ks/, /z/, and /u/		
Lesson 15	/j/, /f/, /u/, /ks/, and /z/	*Decodable* 10: Liz and Tad	all

Lesson	Letters and Sounds	Pre-Decodables/Decodables	High-Frequency Words
Unit 7			
Lesson 1	initial /w/		
Lesson 2	final /w/		
Lesson 3	/k/ spelled Kk		
Lesson 4	/k/ spelled Kk		
Lesson 5	review /w/ and /k/	*Decodable* 11: Kim and Sam	look, with
Lesson 6	/e/		
Lesson 7	/e/		
Lesson 8	initial /kw/ (*Qu*)		
Lesson 9	initial /kw/ (*Qu*)		
Lesson 10	initial /y/	*Decodable* 12: Quin and the Jets	her, what
Lesson 11	initial /v/		
Lesson 12	review /y/ and /v/		
Lesson 13	review /w/, /k/, and /e/		
Lesson 14	review /kw/, /y/, /v/, and /e/		
Lesson 15	/w/, /k/, /e/, /kw/, /y/, and /v/	*Decodable* 13: Vic Yelps	was, were
Unit 8			
Lesson 1	initial /ā/		
Lesson 2	initial and medial /ā/		
Lesson 3	medial /ā/		
Lesson 4	medial /ā/ and a_e		
Lesson 5	blending with /ā/	*Decodable* 14: Jake Plants Grapes	said, that
Lesson 6	initial /ī/		
Lesson 7	initial and medial /ī/		
Lesson 8	medial /ī/		
Lesson 9	medial /ī/ and i_e		
Lesson 10	blending with /ī/	*Decodable* 15: Mike and Spike	down, they
Lesson 11	review /ā/ and /ī/		
Lesson 12	review /ā/ and /ī/		
Lesson 13	review /ā/ and /ī/		
Lesson 14	review /ā/ and /ī/		
Lesson 15	blending with /ā/ and /ī/	*Decodable* 16: A Nut Pile	some, there

Lesson	Sound and Letters	Pre-Decodables/Decodables	High-Frequency Words
Unit 9			
Lesson 1	initial /ō/		
Lesson 2	initial and medial /ō/		
Lesson 3	medial /ō/		
Lesson 4	medial /ō/ and o_e		
Lesson 5	blending with /ō/	*Decodable* 17: An Old Flag	boy, out
Lesson 6	initial /ū/		
Lesson 7	initial and medial /ū/		
Lesson 8	medial /ū/		
Lesson 9	medial /ū/ and u_e		
Lesson 10	blending with /ū/	*Decodable* 18: Cute Little Mule	do, little
Lesson 11	review /ō/ and /ū/		
Lesson 12	review /ō/ and /ū/		
Lesson 13	review /ō/ and /ū/		
Lesson 14	review /ō/ and /ū/		
Lesson 15	blending with /ō/ and /ū/	*Decodable* 19: The Cutest Pet	when, then
Unit 10			
Lesson 1	initial /ē/		
Lesson 2	initial and medial /ē/		
Lesson 3	medial /ē/		
Lesson 4	medial /ē/		
Lesson 5	blending with /ē/	*Decodable* 20: We Did It!	be, she
Lesson 6	review /ā/ and /ă/		
Lesson 7	review /ī/ and /ĭ/		
Lesson 8	review /ā/, /ă/, /ī/, and /ĭ/		
Lesson 9	review /ō/ and /ŏ/		
Lesson 10	review /ū/ and /ŭ/		
Lesson 11	review /ō/, /ŏ/, /ū/, and /ŭ/		
Lesson 12	review /ē/ and /ĕ/		
Lesson 13	/ā/, /ī/, /ō/, /ă/, /ŏ/, /ĭ/		
Lesson 14	/ū/, /ē/, /ŭ/, /ĕ/		
Lesson 15	review		

Alphabet Sound Card Stories

Card 2: /b/ Ball

Bobby loves his basketball.

He bounces it all day.

The ball goes /b/ /b/ /b/ /b/ /b/

As it bounces on its way.

Card 4: /d/ Dinosaur

Dinah, the dancing dinosaur,

Had huge and clumsy feet.

They went /d/ /d/ /d/ /d/ /d/

As Dinah kept the beat.

Card 3: /c/ Camera

Carlos clicks his camera

/k/ /k/ /k/ /k/ /k/ /k/ it goes.

The pictures come out crisp and clear.

So give a smile, /k/ /k/ /k/ Carlos is here.

Card 6: /f/ Fan

Franny the fan spins, oh, so fast.

Spreading fresh air with a regular blast.

When Franny the fan goes round and round

/f/ /f/ /f/ /f/ /f/ /f/ is her fast fan sound.

Card 7: /g/ Gopher

Gary is a gopher

Who gulps green grapes all day.

When he gulps and giggles,

/g/ /g/ /g/ /g/ /g/ /g/ is what he'll say.

Card 10: /j/ Jump

Jenny and Jackson like to have fun.

They play jacks, jump rope, and juggle in the sun.

Each time they jump, their feet hit the ground.

/j/ /j/ /j/ /j/ /j/ is the jumping-rope sound.

Card 8: /h/ Hound

Harry the hound dog

Hurries around.

/h/ /h/ /h/ /h/ /h/ /h/

Is his hurrying sound.

Card 11: /k/ Camera

Carlos clicks his camera

/k/ /k/ /k/ /k/ /k/ /k/ it goes.

The pictures come out crisp and clear.

So give a smile, /k/ /k/ /k/ Carlos is here.

Card 12: /l/ Lion

Look! It's Leon the Lion.

Leon loves to lap water from lakes.

This is the lapping sound Leon makes:

/l/ /l/ /l/ /l/ /l/ /l/.

Card 14: /n/ Nest

n/ /n/ /n/ /n/

What is in that noisy nest?

A nervous night owl crying?

A nosy nuthatch chatting?

A nightingale that's sighing?

No! It's a bluebird napping!

/n/ /n/ /n/ /n/

Card 13: /m/ Monkey

For Muzzy, the Monkey,

Bananas are yummy.

She munches so many,

They fill up her tummy.

She says /m/ /m/ /m/ /m/ /m/!

Card 16: /p/ Popcorn

Popcorn! Popcorn! Ping and Pong shouted,

Let's pop some in a pot, because we like it hot!

/p/ /p/ /p/ /p/ /p/ was the sound it made.

Card 17: /kw/ Quacking ducks

Quincy the duck couldn't quite quack.

He said /kw/ /kw/ /kw/.

Quincy kept trying, but all he could say was:

/kw/ /kw/ /kw/ /kw/ /kw/.

Card 19: /s/ Sausages

Sue buys sausages on Saturday.

Sam cooks sausages on Sunday.

The sausages sizzle /s/ /s/ /s/ /s/ /s/ /s/ when hot.

Sam eats sausages, but Sue does not.

Card 18: /r/ Robot

Rosie the Robot just runs and runs: /r/ /r/ /r/,

Racing around to get her chores done /r/ /r/ /r/.

Running here, running there,

Running almost everywhere: /r/ /r/ /r/.

Card 20: /t/ Timer

Tom Tuttle's timer ticks like this:

/t/ /t/ /t/ /t/ /t/.

Tonight Tom Tuttle wants tomatoes on toast.

He sets his timer. Listen carefully:

/t/ /t/ /t/ /t/ /t/.

What sound would the timer make if you set it?

/t/ /t/ /t/ /t/ /t/.

Card 22: /v/ Vacuum

Vinny the Vacuum is cleaning again.

Before visitors visit, he always begins.

This is the sound of his very loud voice:

/v/ /v/ /v/ /v/ /v/ /v/

As he vacuums and vacuums all over the place:

/v/ /v/ /v/ /v/ /v/ /v/.

Card 24: /ks/ Exit

Rex is called the Exiting X.

He runs to guard the door.

To get past Rex,

Make the sound of the x:

/ks/ /ks/ /ks/ /ks/ /ks/.

Card 23: /w/ Washer

Willie the Washer washed white clothes all week.

When he washed he went
/w/ /w/ /w/ /w/ /w/ /w/.

Willie the Washer was tired; he sprang a leak.

He washed and washed and he went:
/w/ /w/ /w/ /w/.

Card 25: /y/ Yaks

Yolanda and Yoshiko are yaks.

They don't yell.

They just yak: /y/ /y/ /y/ /y/ /y/.

Yakety-yak! Yakety-yak!

What is the sound of the curious yaks?

/y/ /y/ /y/ /y/ /y/.

Card 26: /z/ Zipper

Zack's jacket has a zipper.

Zack zips it up and it makes this sound:

/z/ /z/ /z/ /z/ /z/ /z/.

Zack zips it down and it makes this sound:

/z/ /z/ /z/ /z/ /z/ /z/.

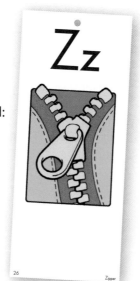

Card 28: /e/ Hen

Jen's pet hen likes to peck, peck, peck: /e/ /e/ /e/.

She pecks at a speck on the new red deck: /e/ /e/ /e/.

This is how her pecking sounds:

/e/ /e/ /e/ /e/ /e/ /e/

When she pecks at a speck on the hen house deck.

Card 27: /a/ Lamb

I'm Pam the lamb, I am.

This is how I tell the farmer where I am:

/a/ /a/ /a/ /a/ /a/.

I'm Pam the lamb, I am.

This is how I tell my friends where I am:

/a/ /a/ /a/ /a/ /a/.

Card 29: /i/ Pig

Here sits Pickles the Pig.

Tickle Pickles, and she'll get the giggles.

This is the sound of Pickles' giggles:

/i/ /i/ /i/ /i/ /i/ /i/.

Card 30: /o/ Fox

Bob the fox did not feel well at all.

He jogged to the doctor's office.

"Say /o/, Mr. Fox. /o/ /o/ /o/."

"My head is hot, and my throat hurts a lot."

"Say /o/, Mr. Fox, /o/ /o/ /o/."

Card 31: /u/ Tug

Tubby the Tugboat can huff and puff

And push and pull to move big stuff.

/u/ /u/ /u/ /u/ /u/

That's the sound of Tubby the Tug.

He works all day from dawn till dusk.

/u/ /u/ / u/ /u/ /u/.

High-Frequency Word List

Level Pre-K High-Frequency Words

a	go	in	the
and	had	is	up
at	have	on	was
can	he	see	with
down	I	she	you

Level K High-Frequency Words

all	for	look	there
am	girl	of	they
as	has	out	to
be	her	said	we
boy	him	some	were
but	his	that	what
did	it	then	when
do	little		

Supplemental Word List

You can use the following word list in a number of ways to extend the lessons. Words are listed by beginning sounds, ending sounds, and medial vowel sounds.

Beginning Sounds

Beginning /ā/
acorn
ape
apron

Beginning /a/
acrobat
alligator
apple
apple juice
astronaut

Beginning /b/
bag
bait
ball
balloon
banana
baseball
basketball
bat
beans
bed
bee
bell
bird
boat
book
bow
bowl
bowling ball
box
bread

broom
bug
bus

Beginning /k/
cake
can
cane
cap
cat
clam
coat
cook
core
cup
cut

Beginning /d/
dad
deer
dice
dime
dish
dog
doll
dollar
donkey
door
dress
drum
duck

Beginning /ē/
eagle
ear
earphones
easel
eel

Beginning /e/
Eggplant
elephant
elk

envelope

Beginning /f/
falcon
fan
feet
fern
fir
fish
five
fly
food
football
fork
four
fox
Frisbee
frog

Beginning /g/
game
gate
glue
goat
goose
grass
green
guitar

Beginning /h/
ham
hand
hat
hawk
heaven
hen
hive
hog
hole
hook
horse
hot

house
hug

Beginning /ī/
ice
ice cream
icicles
iron
island
ivy

Beginning /i/
igloo
ill
inch
infant
insect

Beginning /j/
jam
jar
jeans
jellybean
jellyfish
judge
juice

Beginning /k/
kangaroo
kettle
keys
kitchen
kittens
koala

Beginning /l/
ladybug
lake
lamp
lion
lock
lockers

Beginning /m/
magnet

mailbox
man
map
mask
mat
meal
meat
milk
mittens
monkey
moon
moose
mop
mouse
mug

Beginning /n/
nails
necklace
needle
nest
newspaper
nickle
nine
noodle
nurse

Beginning /ō/
oak tree
oasis
oatmeal
oboe
ocean
overalls

Beginning /o/
octopus
olive
ostrich
otter
ox

Beginning /p/
pail
pan
panda
pants
pear
peas
pen
penny
pickle
pickled pears
pie
pig
pineapple
pink
pizza pies
plum bun
popcorn
post
pot
potatoes
pumpkins
purple
Beginning /kw/
quail
quart
queen
quill
quilt
Beginning /r/
raccoon
racer
radio
rake
rat
red
rice
road
robot
rock

rocket
rug
ruler
Beginning /s/
sack
sad
sail
Sam
sand
sandals
seal
seven
silk
six
skate
soccer ball
sock
spoon
star
stew
sticks
stir
store
storm
sun
Beginning /t/
table
tail
tap
tape
target
tear
telephone
television
ten
tie
toad
toast
toe
tomatoes

top
tree
turkey
turtle
two
Beginning /ū/
ukulele
unicorn
uniform
United States
utensil
Beginning /u/
umbrella
umpire
uncle
under
usher
Beginning /v/
van
vase
vegetables
veil
vine
violin
volcano
Beginning /w/
wagon
wallet
walrus
watch
well
wig
wing
Beginning /y/
yam
yard
yarn
yell
yellow

yo-yo
yolk
Beginning /z/
zebra
zero
zinnia
zither
zoo

Ending Sounds
Ending /ā/
away
bay
day
gray
hay
Jay
may
Monday
play
ray
say
today
Ending /b/
Bob
cab
cob
cub
cube
jab
job
mob
rob
robe
rub
scrub
tab
tub
web

Ending /d/
bad
bed
bread
did
feed
had
lid
mad
mud
red
rid
sad
seed
weed
yard
Ending /ē/
bee
Frisbee
he
key
knee
me
monkey
see
she
three
tree
turkey
we
Ending /f/
calf
cough
cuff
deaf
elf
half
laugh
off
rough

stiff
stuff
tough

Ending /g/
bag
big
dog
egg
hog
hug
jog
ladybug
leg
log
pig
rag
rug
tag
twig
wig

Ending /ī/
by
cry
die
dry
fly
high
my
pie
sigh
tie
why

Ending /k/
bike
black
clock
cook
dock
duck

elk
fork
hook
lake
like
lock
milk
pack
pink
poke
rack
rake
rock
sock
take

Ending /l/
basketball
bell
bill
eel
feel
football
oatmeal
pail
quail
rail
seal
snail
tail

Ending /m/
broom
dime
drum
game
hum
jam
room
seem
uniform
yam

Ending /n/
can
fern
green
hen
kitchen
lion
moon
ocean
queen
raccoon
spoon
sun
ten
unicorn
van
vine
violin
wagon
yarn

Ending /ō/
blow
bow
doe
flow
go
low
mow
no
radio
row
slow
so
toe
volcano
yellow
yo-yo
zero

Ending /p/
cap
cape
cup
deep
hip
hop
keep
lip
map
pup
skip
sleep
tap
tip
top
trap

Ending /r/
alligator
bar
car
core
deer
door
fur
four
guitar
jar
more
newspaper
otter
pour
roar
ruler
stir
usher

Ending /s/
bus
class
dress

goose
grass
horse
house
miss
moss
mouse
octopus
pass
toss
walrus
yes

Ending /t/
astronaut
bat
cat
coat
feet
gate
goat
hat
hot
infant
kite
knot
meat
pot
quilt
wallet
white

Ending /ū/
cue
few
hue
menu
nephew
preview
rescue
review
view

Ending /v/
brave
cave
dive
dove
eve
five
gave
give
glove
have
hive
live
love
save
shave
stove

Ending /ks/
ax
box
fix
flax
fox
mix
ox
relax
six
wax

Ending /z/
breeze
buzz
daze
fizz
freeze
fuzz
haze
jazz
maze
peas
quiz

size
sneeze
squeeze
trees

Medial Sounds

Medial /ā/
date
face
fade
game
gate
gave
lake
lane
late
made
make
mate
race
rake
table
wave

Medial /a/
bat
black
can
cap
hat
jam
ham
lamp
pants
sad
van
yam

Medial /ē/
beam
bean
feet

heap
keep
mean
meat
neat
seal
seed
seen
sneeze
team
weed

Medial /e/
bed
bet
head
hen
let
men
met
nest
net
pen
pet
red
set
ten

Medial /ī/
five
hide
hive
kite
life
line
mine
nice
nine
rice
ride
right

side
sight
time
vine

Medial /i/
bib
dish
fib
fin
fish
him
kittens
lip
milk
mittens
pig
pin
pink
rip
tin
tip
wig
win

Medial /ō/
boat
bowl
coal
coat
goat
hole
home
joke
mole
nose
poem
poke
post
roll
rose
toes

Medial /o/
dot
hot
knot
lock
lot
mop
not
pot
rock
sock
top

Medial /ū/
cube
cute
feud
fuel
fuse
huge
mule

Medial /u/
bug
bun
cup
cut
duck
dust
fun
hug
hug
must
nut
rub
rug
run
sun
tub
tug

Index

Science Lap Book

Selections

Index

Notes

Use this page to record lessons or elements that work well or need to be adjusted for future reference.

Lessons that work well.

Lessons that need adjustments.

Notes

Use this page to record lessons or elements that work well or need to be adjusted for future reference.

Lessons that work well.

Lessons that need adjustments.

Notes

Use this page to record lessons or elements that work well or need to be adjusted for future reference.

Lessons that work well.

Lessons that need adjustments.

Notes

Use this page to record lessons or elements that work well or need to be adjusted for future reference.

Lessons that work well.

Lessons that need adjustments.

Notes

Use this page to record lessons or elements that work well or need to be adjusted for future reference.

Lessons that work well.

Lessons that need adjustments.

Notes

Use this page to record lessons or elements that work well or need to be adjusted for future reference.

Lessons that work well.

Lessons that need adjustments.

Notes

Use this page to record lessons or elements that work well or need to be adjusted for future reference.

Lessons that work well.

Lessons that need adjustments.

Notes

Use this page to record lessons or elements that work well or need to be adjusted for future reference.

Lessons that work well.

Lessons that need adjustments.

Notes

Use this page to record lessons or elements that work well or need to be adjusted for future reference.

Lessons that work well.

Lessons that need adjustments.

Notes

Use this page to record lessons or elements that work well or need to be adjusted for future reference.

Lessons that work well.

Lessons that need adjustments.